Lauren Squires (Ed.)
**English in Computer-Mediated Communication**

# Topics in English Linguistics

Editors
Elizabeth Closs Traugott
Bernd Kortmann

## Volume 93

# English in Computer-Mediated Communication

Variation, Representation, and Change

Edited by
Lauren Squires

DE GRUYTER
MOUTON

ISBN 978-3-11-061072-7
e-ISBN (PDF) 978-3-11-049081-7
e-ISBN (EPUB) 978-3-11-048843-2
ISSN 1434-3452

**Library of Congress Cataloging-in-Publication Data**
A CIP catalog record for this book has been applied for at the Library of Congress.

**Bibliographic information published by the Deutsche Nationalbibliothek**
The Deutsche Nationalbibliothek lists this publication in the Deutsche Nationalbibliografie; detailed bibliographic data are available on the Internet at http://dnb.dnb.de.

© 2018 Walter de Gruyter GmbH, Berlin/Boston
This volume is text- and page-identical with the hardback published in 2016.
Cover image: Brian Stablyk/Photographer's Choice RF/Getty Images
Typesetting: RoyalStandard, Hong Kong
Printing and binding: CPI books GmbH, Leck

♾ Printed on acid-free paper
Printed in Germany

www.degruyter.com

# Table of contents

Lauren Squires
Introduction: Variation, representation, and change in English in CMC —— 1

## I  Code and Variety

Lars Hinrichs
Modular repertoires in English-using social networks: A study of language choice in the networks of adult Facebook users —— 17

Taylor Jones
Tweets as graffiti: What the reconstruction of Vulgar Latin can tell us about Black Twitter —— 43

Cecilia Cutler
"Ets jast ma booooooooooooo": Social meanings of Scottish accents on YouTube —— 69

## II  Contact, Spread, and Innovation

Theresa Heyd
Global varieties of English gone digital: Orthographic and semantic variation in digital Nigerian Pidgin —— 101

Matt Garley and Benjamin Slade
Virtual meatspace: Word formation and deformation in cyberpunk discussions —— 123

Axel Bohmann
Language change because Twitter? Factors motivating innovative uses of *because* across the English-speaking Twittersphere —— 149

Steven Coats
Grammatical feature frequencies of English on Twitter in Finland —— 179

## III Style and Identity

Lauren Squires
**Stylistic uniformity and variation online and on-screen: A case study of *The Real Housewives* —— 213**

Patrick Callier
**Exploring stylistic co-variation on Twitter: The case of DH —— 241**

Rebecca Childs
**Who I am and who I want to be: Variation and representation in a messaging platform —— 261**

## IV Mode and Medium

Markus Bieswanger
**Electronically-mediated Englishes: Synchronicity revisited —— 281**

Nathan LaFave
**Social factors and lexical frequency influencing English adjective gradation in speech and CMC —— 301**

Josh Iorio
**Implications of attitudes about non-standard English on interactional structure in the computer-mediated workplace: A story of two modes —— 327**

Lauren Collister
**"At least I'm not Chinese, gay, or female": Marginalized voices in *World of Warcraft* —— 351**

**Index —— 377**

# Contributors

**Axel Bohmann**
The University of Texas at Austin
204 W 21st Street B5000, Calhoun Hall
Austin, TX 78712-1164, USA
axel@bohmann.de

**Markus Bieswanger**
University of Bayreuth
95440 Bayreuth
Germany
markus.bieswanger@uni-bayreuth.de

**Patrick Callier**
Lab41
Menlo Park, CA, USA
pcallier@lab41.org

**Becky Childs**
Department of English
Coastal Carolina University
P.O. Bo 261954
Conway, SC 29528-6054
USA
rchilds@coastal.edu

**Steven Coats**
University of Oulu
English Philology
Faculty of Humanities, P.O. Box 1000,
FIN-90014
University of Oulu
Finland
steven.coats@oulu.fi

**Lauren B. Collister**
University of Pittsburgh
3960 Forbes Avenue
Pittsburgh, PA 15260, USA
lbcollister@pitt.edu

**Cecelia Cutler**
City University of New York, Lehman College
250 Bedford Park Blvd.
West Bronx, NY 10468, USA
Cecelia.Cutler@lehman.cuny.edu

**Matt Garley**
York College, City University of New York
94-20 Guy R Brewer Blvd.
Jamaica, NY 11451, USA
mgarley@york.cuny.edu

**Theresa Heyd**
Freie Universität Berlin
Institut für Englische Philologie
Habelschwerdter Allee 45
14195 Berlin
Germany
theresa.heyd@fu-berlin.de

**Lars Hinrichs**
The University of Texas at Austin
English Department
204 W 21st Street, B5000
Austin, TX 78712, USA
larshinrichs@utexas.edu

**Josh Iorio**
Virginia Tech
1342 Perry Street
Blacksburg, VA 24061, USA
iorio@vt.edu

**Taylor Jones**
University of Pennsylvania
Department of Linguistics
619 Williams Hall
255 S. 36th Street
Philadelphia, PA 19104-6305, USA
tayjones@sas.upenn.edu

**Nathan LaFave**
New York University
Department of Linguistics
10 Washington Place
New York, NY 10003, USA
nathan.lafave@nyu.edu

**Benjamin Slade**
University of Utah, Languages and
Communication Building
255 South Central Campus Drive, Room 2300
Salt Lake City, UT 84112, USA
b.slade@utah.edu

**Lauren Squires**
The Ohio State University
Department of English
421 Denney Hall,
164 Annie & John Glenn Ave.
Columbus, OH 43210, USA
squires.41@osu.edu

Lauren Squires
# Introduction: Variation, representation, and change in English in CMC

## 1 Introduction

Computer-mediated communication (CMC), once a domain of interaction exciting for its novelty, is now squarely mundane in the business of daily life for much of Anglophone culture. This is at least true in heavily mediatized, networked societies, and it is also true in places where personal computer access is rare but mobile phones afford a widely accessible form of screen-based communication. At the same time as the presence of computing devices has come to seem ubiquitous, the capabilities of those devices have become ever more sophisticated and, in some cases, genuinely surprising.

This fast-paced trajectory of innovation has been accompanied by a steady churn of scholarship devoted to understanding human social behavior with, through, and because of digital media. Centrally in internet studies, communication studies, and sociology, scholars have endeavored to locate the line between the extraordinary and the ordinary. What are people doing with, through, and because of new technology that they were not doing before? What are they doing differently than before? And what are they doing in the same ways, but for different reasons, or with different outcomes? In terms of linguistic behavior, Herring (2013) summarizes these possibilities as discourse *familiar, reconfigured*, or *emergent*. But already nearly a decade earlier, Herring (2004) aptly considered the issue in a paper suggesting that CMC may have been "slouching toward the ordinary." Specifically, Herring (2004: 34) put forth a prediction that the internet would, five years hence, be "a simpler, safer, and – for better or for worse – less fascinating communication environment," and continue to evolve in that direction.

More than a decade later, it is certainly true that some of the communication happening in CMC has lost its "edge." But it is also true that in other ways, things have gotten more complex – there are more media available, more configurations of the media that exist, more platforms, more economic complications, more millions of interlocutors, more layers of intertextuality – and there remain risks, both physical and symbolic. Language, of course, continues to be central to our use, negotiation, and understanding of digital spaces.

It is perhaps the ostensible ordinariness of CMC now that has motivated the chapters in this volume to take the approaches they do, in various ways. In much previous research on language in CMC, more so in the earlier days but continuing up to now, the focus was on how CMC was changing linguistic practice, how CMC created spaces for "new" kinds of language. We have come to a point of acknowledging that in many of the most important ways, language used through CMC is just like language used outside of it. It is thus "ordinary" in the sense not only of being "everyday," but also in the sense of being typical in the way that it participates in linguistic and social processes. English within CMC, as with English in non-mediated environments, is best characterized by diversity and variety, rather than homogeneity.

As the terms in the subtitle of this book preview, the authors here examine English in CMC as it relates to these ordinary processes of *variation, representation,* and *change*, all broadly construed. We take for granted that language in CMC varies; language in CMC is represented and represents; language in CMC changes and is changed. These premises position us to ask the much more interesting *how* questions, approached from a range of analytical perspectives including quantitative language variation, diachronic change, language contact, language ideology, sociolinguistic identity, social networks, and style.

"Computer-mediated communication" is a broad designator that encompasses multiple semiotic/linguistic modes (including voice, text, and image) as well as technological interfaces and platforms (mobile phones, tablets, social media, immersive online games, virtual workplace environments, and more). The term circumscribes communication that is carried out via a mediating interface, and these mediating interfaces produce layers of structure that require linguistic and social negotiation. No matter the environment – whether face-to-face, in a chat room through a computer, or messaging via a phone – where there is human interaction, there is language. As a functional and symbolic system, language is perhaps the ultimate carrier of humanness into the disembodied (though not entirely so) realms of the digital. As we send linguistic material through them, computers become vehicles of interpersonal interaction and all that it entails: social change, identity formation, teamwork, and community creation, along with the very human tendencies toward exclusion, harassment, and misunderstanding. It is language that gives these media their social purposes. And language takes with it to these digital spheres all of its history and possibility, its politics, its social stratification, its structural ambiguities, its mutability. Through the use of language in CMC, cultures are formed, social goals are accomplished, ideologies are shaped, power is contested, and sociolinguistic boundaries are crossed and blurred.

This volume examines the English language in CMC – what it looks like, what it accomplishes, and what it means to speakers. Much of English users' daily experiences and interactions with the language now occur through some form of CMC. Therefore, to understand fully the linguistic and social properties of contemporary English and its speakers, we must consider the multiple contexts in which it is found, and how mediating technologies shape or reshape the forms, functions, and meanings of the language. The term *enregisterment* (Agha 2003) is typically used to discuss the metalinguistic construction of language varieties – as in dialects, registers, or styles. Yet "the English language" itself is also constantly being enregistered, figured and refigured as an object of reference, of inquiry, of use, and of contestation. Put simply, the authors here position CMC as relevant to understanding what English *is*, and what it will become.

The English language has enjoyed a privileged status within CMC, particularly vis-à-vis networked computing and the internet. Networking protocols were designed to transmit symbols specific to the English writing system, and in this way, the language has been graphemically transferred from paper to screen rather unremarkably (Squires 2016). English has also been centered in both public and academic debates about the internet. Some have wondered whether the internet will lead to even more increased worldwide dominance of English (Crystal 2001) while others have stressed that the internet is indeed a multilingual, heteroglossic site of practice (Danet and Herring 2007; Androutsopoulos 2011). Yet empirical research that directly investigates how *English in CMC* is to be characterized – as a point of departure, and as a question in and of itself – remains scarce.

Thus, the chapters in this volume take a step back from the novelty (real or imagined) of the technologies themselves and consider connections between how "the English language" is conceived and its modes and media of conveyance. Who is an English speaker (or writer)? What kinds of Englishes are there? How does English change across setting, mode, genre, etc.? How do new(ish) settings, modes, and genres change written English and interact with the spoken language? The search for answers to these questions, necessary for any full definition of the language, must now account for linguistic practice in CMC as a contributing factor.

The goal of this volume is not to provide a comprehensive overview of (socio)linguistic research on CMC generally speaking; several excellent existing volumes contribute to that project (Herring, Stein, and Virtanen 2013; Georgakopoulou and Spilioti 2016; Tannen and Trester 2013; Thurlow and Mroczek 2011). Nor is it to provide a compendium of all varieties or communities of English users, or all CMC settings. Rather, in their focus on English in CMC contexts, these 14 chapters represent a current set of issues at stake in the intersection of English and CMC research. Namely, they highlight how the diversity of form present in English offline ("in real life," "F2F," in "unmediated" contexts) is transferred to the English found in CMC, as well as how communicative practices that are "indigenous" to online spaces might reconfigure the dimensions of structured and meaningful variation within the language.

Several chapters offer new perspectives on well-worn questions from CMC research, applying these specifically to English in its contemporary linguistic ecology: What is the connection between written and spoken modalities of the language (Childs; Collister; Iorio; Jones; LaFave)? What role does English, among other languages, play in carrying out social action in digital spaces (Cutler; Heyd; Hinrichs)? How are the linguistic structures of English marshaled in the creation of online communities and online identities (Garley and Slade; Squires)? How are we best to characterize the relationship of technological factors to language form (Bieswanger; Bohmann)?

Other chapters treat CMC as a "new" site in which to explore "old" questions: What is the social significance of the choice of English – and written or spoken English – as one code among several possibilities (Collister; Hinrichs)? How do varieties of English manifest in digital written spheres – with or without spoken analogues (Coats; Heyd; Jones)? How does personal style develop using the linguistic resources available in CMC (Callier; Childs; Squires)? How does CMC facilitate processes of linguistic change at both small and large scales (Bohmann; Garley and Slade)? What is the role of digital interaction in shaping language attitudes towards English and varieties of English (Collister; Cutler; Iorio)? And when we are dealing with CMC data, what kinds of evidence for claims about English are we dealing with (Bieswanger; Jones)?

The volume is organized into four sections. *Code and Variety* deals with English as a code to be chosen among others, and English varieties as they manifest and are configured through online discourse. *Contact, Spread, and Innovation* explores some sociolinguistic outcomes of the global spread of English and CMC in tandem, as well as the role of CMC in linguistic innovation, whether through language contact or another actuating force. In *Style and Identity*, specific features of English in CMC are investigated for the work they do in constructing sociolinguistic personae. Finally, *Mode and Medium* reconsiders the relationship between language, social factors, and technological or mediating factors, including how language attitudes shape the use of media. Throughout these four sections, *variation, representation*, and *change* run as underlying themes fundamental to our holistic understanding of the English language. In what follows, I sketch the contributions of the volume to these three motifs so central to the field of English linguistics.

## 2 Variation

If there is one shared goal of all 14 chapters, it is to present the analysis of the English language in CMC as grounded in the inevitability of linguistic heterogeneity. Variation is dealt with broadly, across a range of settings and variables. When prior research has focused on linguistic variation in CMC, a quantitative approach has tended to examine sets of alternating sociolinguistic variables. These variables are usually on the level of orthographic (spelling) features, some of which correspond to phonological features or processes (such as phonetic spellings like <u> for <you>; e.g., Paolillo 2001; Squires 2012). The chapters here broaden the array of English features considered in CMC, the dimensions of their variability, and their relationship to each other. Graphemic and lexical variables are still present in several chapters, including Callier, Coats, Heyd, Iorio, and Squires. But widening the scope are Garley and Slade investigating morphological processes in subcultural word formation; LaFave discussing morphosyntactic alternation across written and spoken modes; Bieswanger using syntactic reduction as a variable to explore effects of medium versus situation; and Bohmann investigating syntactic change via Twitter. Methodologically, Squires takes advantage of the scale of CMC textual data to robustly show that what is socially meaningful about linguistic variation is often the interrelation of multiple variables, a focus shared by Callier.

Another important contribution the volume makes to variation study is the range of social factors in focus. "Traditional" sociolinguistic factors such as gender, race/ethnicity, and social class are included almost by default in most quantitative variationist studies of English. At the same time, this type of quantitative-demographic approach has been recently critiqued for being inadequate in its oversimplification of the social world and social identity (see some discussion in Buchotz 2015; Meyerhoff 2015). Somewhat ironically, these social factors have often been neglected in prior literature on CMC, partly due to the fact that CMC settings are often what Iorio (2009) calls "demographically lean." While gender has been frequently considered in CMC research (though mostly within discourse-analytic or pragmatic frameworks; for a review, see, Herring and Stoerger 2014), other social factors like race and ethnicity have received less attention. Indeed, there remains a notable paucity of work on language and ethnoracial identity online – something the present volume addresses with chapters by Jones, Childs, Callier, Collister, and Squires, but leaving so much more to be done (and with much to gain from engagement with work from outside of linguistics, e.g., Nakamura 2002).

Importantly, the relationship between social and technological factors in variation is also at issue: while sometimes social factors condition language variation regardless of the medium or mode, they may not always have the same relevance in different media/modes. For instance, LaFave incorporates education, gender, age, and dialect region into his analysis of adjective gradation and finds no difference in the effect of social factors between instant messaging, speech, and formal writing. But Iorio's study of virtual workplace interactions shows that language attitudes toward ethnically-marked variants are more pertinent to written interactions than spoken ones. Relatedly, Collister discusses both the linguistic profiling and linguistic adoration that occur among *World of Warcraft* players who are perceived to inhabit differing identity positions pertaining to race, sex, and language. While these identities are somewhat concealable in the textual mode, they are revealed via voice interactions, thus social factors directly impact one's choice of how to play the game. In sum, the chapters take us beyond dichotomous linguistic variables with clear-cut indexical associations, providing more nuanced understanding of the scope and structure of variation within CMC English and, so importantly, its social parameters.

Leveling up, so to speak, several chapters ask how (non-standard) varieties of English transfer to computer-mediated spaces. Included here are African American (Vernacular) English (Jones; Callier; Childs), Nigerian Pidgin (Heyd), Finland English (Coats), Indian English (Iorio), and Scottish English (Cutler). While obviously not comprehensive in scope, the range of varieties discussed should be beneficial to others interested in understanding how English varieties move across mediated spaces. In particular, this interest departs from an assumption implicit in much earlier work, that when Standard Written English is deviated from, the deviations are markers primarily of the technology itself (see Squires 2010). Rather, nonstandard manifestations of the language online are often grounded in the varieties in use offline, though with additional social meanings potentially accruing because of the mediated environment. For instance, Heyd shows that "little words" in Nigerian Pidgin are used in an online forum to index authentic local speaker status, but simultaneously can be used to index a more global "nonstandardness" which carries international prestige (and which has developed in part through CMC). Similarly, Coats shows that the English in use on Twitter by users in Finland has distinct characteristics, including preferences for which vowels to prosodically lengthen by orthographic means, which are different from the tendencies in Twitter English originating in other locations. To the extent that there is a digital English "supervernacular" (Blommaert 2012), it is clear that the features which mark it often mark more localized meanings as well.

## 3 Representation

Essential to understanding the use and/or emergence of varieties in CMC come questions of *representation*. These questions are both material and symbolic. Materially, how are spoken varieties to be represented in text-based spaces? The other way around, what do the representations we see in text-based spaces tell us about spoken varieties? Part of Heyd's contribution is to show that through internet communication, spellings of the vernacular become *de facto* standards with little apparent contestation (compare to cases of overt projects for spelling vernacular varieties, e.g., Schieffelin and Doucet 1994). Jones' chapter – one of the few extant pieces of scholarship to examine the phenomenon of "Black Twitter" from a linguistic perspective, despite the sphere's strong cultural relevance – takes language on Twitter as a window onto phonological patterns in African American English (and potentially, by extension, other dialects). Jones argues that orthographic nonstandardisms are often intentional, rooted in phonological correspondence; and, just as philologists had to triangulate between forms of written evidence to reconstruct Vulgar Latin, sociolinguists may find Twitter data useful not only for its own sake, but for what it indicates about spoken variation.

Orthographic representation of spoken features is also central to the chapter by Callier, who shows that a feature strongly associated with African American English, DH-stopping, is itself "packaged" with another variety feature – postvocalic /r/-lessness – as well as with a feature more associated with the internet itself, initialisms like OMG. These two packagings appear to be done by different sets of speakers, to effect different stylistic personae. Childs also discusses the representation of /r/-lessness, showing that speakers whose spoken variety does not tend to be /r/-less can use /r/-lessness orthographically in order to identify stylistically with speakers of an /r/-less variety, in this case African American English. Representing linguistic features is thus not a matter just of directly rendering speech in text, but also of representing *oneself* through features that signal desired indexical associations. The representation of desired social personae in CMC is also the focus of Squires' investigation of differing femininities being performed through clusters of textual features.

In addition to individuals' use of language to represent themselves, representation is fundamental to language ideological processes that configure attitudes about English in a mediated world. What/who does English represent when it is used in CMC? The status of English is not always straightforward. For instance, in Hinrichs' work, we see that in multilingual contexts, dominant symbolic status is not always at the fore of the choice to use English; sometimes code choice is merely functional. As Facebook users seek to represent themselves as certain types of people, the use of English is a way to achieve maximal understanding across audience members, and to achieve faithfulness in intertextuality when relevant; the positive associations of English as a prestige language are less relevant. The status of English is important, however, in the community studied by Collister: English enjoys a privileged position within language ideologies about players in *World of Warcraft*, with non-English speakers being stigmatized. As mentioned above, the social meanings of particular kinds of English motivate players to use one mode of play over another.

In the realm of language attitudes, Iorio shows that an international virtual workplace is an environment in which there is contact between speakers of different English varieties. Some represent their spoken variety in text, and others do not; language attitudes surface in this multimodal setting in ways that influence the efficacy of teamwork. And Cutler shows that the multimodality of YouTube makes it a rich setting in which language attitudes about varieties of English are forged through representational play. Videos portraying Scottish English are circulated and commented on, and the spoken is re-represented in the written, with orthographic resources deployed to codify and exaggerate what are perceived to be variety-specific features, in layered intertextual processes. Cutler's work also provides a good example of how the representation that happens in CMC can have implications for speakers offline: the ideologies about Scottish accents being negotiated on YouTube presumably hold for people whether or not they are interacting on YouTube. This shows us one reason that CMC interactions must be viewed as a part of the total ecology of English in the 21st century.

# 4 Change

The final macro-level theme of the volume is *change*, which has had something of a fraught relationship to both research and public discourse about English-language CMC. Earlier work hypothesized that CMC might lead to dramatic changes in linguistic practice and the language itself (Baron 1984; Crystal 2001), and public discourse about language online has frequently served to heighten anxiety about the long-term consequences of supposedly new trends (Thurlow 2006; Squires 2010). These sentiments seem to suggest that we should be expecting wholesale differences in the language itself several decades post-CMC as compared to before it. Yet we are still likely not in a position to do such analysis; any structural changes to "the English language" due in part or whole to CMC will take yet more decades to be realized. Rather, what this volume deals with is better conceived of as *sociolinguistic change* (Androutsopoulous 2014; Coupland 2014), a notion that encompasses many types of change in many types of elements, both linguistic and social.

Coupland (2014: 67) defines *sociolinguistic change* as "a broad set of language-implicating changes that are socially consequential, even though particular forms or 'states' of a language may not themselves change as part of the process." Here, we treat change in the language, but also change in how language works within specific communities of practice, and change in language attitudes and ideologies. The chapter most directly concerned with a "traditional" kind of language change is that of Bohmann, who brings empirical treatment to a phenomenon framed in public discourse as both "new" and internet-specific: non-clausal complementation of *because*. This is perceived among many speakers to be a change in progress, and Bohmann takes a novel approach to investigating the plausibility of the feature as such. He incorporates other factors associated with change in written English in the Late Modern period, finding that density is a good predictor of the *because* structure, and hence the innovation follows a more general densification trend in current English. This historicization is an important check on our assumption of novelty, and positions perceived change in CMC as being part of processes of change already going on in the language – in CMC and out of it. LaFave likewise hypothesizes that his finding of a gender-based pattern in adjective gradation may be related to a change in adjective choice in progress in English, unrelated to the use of language in different media.

Another study of innovation comes from Garley and Slade, who outline the morphological processes underlying word formation in a diffuse, "digitally native" subculture that is emblematic of some of the social meanings of technology: cyberpunk. Garley and Slade show that the use of a marked lexis is a symbol of engagement with the media of cyberpunk, and they demonstrate that CMC settings are fertile ground for the innovation and diffusion of neologisms. Looking back over a long history of online data among cyberpunk fans, Garley and Slade are able to show the role of lexical innovations in the diachronic continuity of this diverse community. Linguistic change and continuity work hand in hand to forge and maintain community identity. Relatedly, Coats positions CMC as a factor in the emergence of a distinctive English register among users of Twitter on Finland; here, the change-related concept of *spread* is pertinent to thinking about both English as a global language and Twitter as a global technology. Heyd also investigates the registers and varieties that emerge from processes of linguistic and technological spread. Characteristically, some of these emergent varieties are heavy in features recognizable from the spoken variety (as in the Nigerian Pidgin case); others are not (as in the Finland English case).

Two final notions of change are worth highlighting here, both metalinguistic in scope. First are changing language ideologies and attitudes about English. Cutler's chapter shows clearly how multimodal CMC practice affords metalinguistic interaction in which ideas about varieties are put forth and negotiated. Squires' data show that plenty of features often ideologized as "youthful" (Thurlow 2003; Squires 2010) are in practice among middle-aged women on Twitter, suggesting that the place of features like "OMG" or "LOL" within regimes of linguistic evaluation are changing, at least among a segment of English speakers. And Hinrichs' findings about English as a functional rather than status-driven code choice raises questions about the role of multilingual technology users in altering global social meanings of English.

Second are changing analytical constructs for investigating language in CMC. In an important intervention, Bieswanger calls for a reconfiguration of how "synchronicity" – a property commonly used to categorize different CMC technologies throughout the history of the field – is taken as relevant to linguistic practice. Rather than synchronicity of the technology itself, Bieswanger suggests understanding synchronicity of one's *use* of the technology as more pertinent to linguistic patterns. Bieswanger is joined in making methodological advancement by Callier and Squires, who advocate investigating clusters of linguistic variables rather than singletons, and Iorio, who triangulates multiple sources of data to understand what is going on in each. Indeed, the volume offers an array of methodological models for doing research on English in CMC. Some authors investigate English directly, using CMC to enrich our understanding of the language at large; others explore English-based practice in CMC as a way to make claims about how these technologies may shape linguistic practice more generally. Many of the chapters carefully circumscribe particular communities of interest, which makes the work in this volume different from much current work investigating large-scale corpora of CMC texts from computational perspectives (e.g., Bamman, Eisenstein, and Schnoebelen 2014). The volume covers a wide range of sites of English-based practice in CMC, including instant messaging, Twitter, online web forums, role-playing games, YouTube, and virtual workplaces. Different sites call for different methodologies.

The current of *change*, of course, unavoidably undergirds this entire volume: without the ever-changing linguascapes created by CMC, there would be no call for investigation into English in CMC. It is clear that these two objects of study are not leaving us anytime soon – both English and CMC will continue their spread, in ways both mundane and surprising. Our hope with this volume is to strike a balance between assuming that what the technology does to language must be drastic, and assuming the technology does nothing at all; between figuring language as independent of its means of conveyance and figuring it as predetermined by its means of conveyance; between treating English and CMC as global sociolinguistic phenomena and considering their local manifestations and meanings. We hope to have raised important questions for a future in which English and its speakers will continue to be shaped (obviously; subtly) by the presence and use of computer-mediated communication.

## 5 Acknowledgements

I owe a great many thanks to others who made the production of this book possible. First, of course, I thank the chapter authors for their commitment to making this happen: for doing interesting and exciting work, for providing valuable feedback to each other and to me, and for being both patient and encouraging as I worked through the editorial process. I owe special thanks to Matt Garley for organizing the ICLCE 5 panel on CMC, and to Lars Hinrichs and Markus Bieswanger for suggesting the volume into existence. Thanks, Axel Bohmann and Josh Iorio, for the extra reviews. Regarding this Introduction, I am grateful to Lars for a thorough read and helpful comments just when I needed them; and to Markus and Steven Coats for other thoughtful notes.

Thank you to Bernd Kortmann, from all of us, for your enthusiasm, your editorial sensibility, and your equally sharp and encouraging evaluative eye; and to Julie Miess and Birgit Sievert for your logistical assistance. And thanks to you all for your patience. Finally, I am grateful to all of the scholars who took time out of their busy schedules to provide insightful peer reviews of the chapters in this volume: Michael Adams, Douglas S. Bigham, Alexandra D'Arcy, Maeve Eberhardt, Astrid Ensslin, Kathryn Campbell-Kibler, Anu Harju, Jane Hodson, Graham Jones, Ewa Jonsson, Qiuana Lopez, Christian Mair, Cornelius Puschmann, Philip Seargeant, and Caroline Tagg.

## 6 References

Agha, Asif. 2003. The social life of cultural value. *Language & Communication* 23(3). 231–273.
Androutsopoulos, Jannis. 2011. From variation to heteroglossia in the study of computer-mediated discourse. In Crispin Thurlow & Kristine Mroczek (eds.), *Digital discourse: Language in the new media*, 277–298. Oxford: Oxford University Press.

Androutsopoulos, Jannis. 2014. Mediatization and sociolinguistic change. Key concepts, research traditions, open issues. In Jannis Androutsopoulos (ed.), *Mediatization and sociolinguistic change*, 3–48. Berlin: De Gruyter.
Bamman, David, Jacob Eisenstein & Tyler Schnoebelen. 2014. Gender identity and lexical variation in social media. *Journal of Sociolinguistics* 18(2). 135–160.
Baron, Naomi S. 1984. Computer-mediated communication as a force in language change. *Visible Language* XVIII(2). 118–141.
Blommaert, Jan. 2012. Supervernaculars and their dialects. *Dutch Journal of Applied Linguistics* 1(1). 1–14.
Bucholtz, Mary. 2015. The elements of style. In Ahmar Mahboob, Dwi Noverini Djenar & Ken Cruickshank (eds.), *Language and identity across modes of communication*, 27–60. Berlin: De Gruyter Mouton.
Coupland, Nikolas. 2014. Sociolinguistic change, vernacularization and broadcast British media. In Jannis Androutsopoulos (ed.), *Mediatization and sociolinguistic change*, 67–96. Berlin: De Gruyter.
Crystal, David. 2001. *Language and the Internet*. Cambridge: Cambridge University Press.
Danet, Brenda & Susan C. Herring (eds.). 2007. *The multilingual Internet: Language, culture, and communication online*. Oxford: Oxford University Press.
Georgakopoulou, Alexandra & Tereza Spilioti (eds.). 2016. *Routledge handbook of language and digital communication*. London/New York: Routledge.
Herring, Susan C. 2004. Slouching toward the ordinary: Current trends in computer-mediated communication. *New Media & Society* 6(1). 26–36.
Herring, Susan C. 2013. Discourse in Web 2.0: Familiar, reconfigured, and emergent. In Deborah Tannen & Anna Marie Trester (eds.), *Discourse 2.0: Language and new media*, 1–25. Washington, DC: Georgetown University Press.
Herring, Susan, Dieter Stein & Tuija Virtanen (eds.). 2013. *Pragmatics of computer-mediated communication*. Berlin/Boston: Walter de Gruyter.
Iorio, Josh. 2009. Effects of audience on orthographic variation. *Studies in the Linguistic Sciences: Illinois Working Papers* 2(1). 127–140.
Meyerhoff, Miriam. 2015. All these years and still counting: why quantitative methods still appeal. In Ahmar Mahboob, Dwi Noverini Djenar & Ken Cruickshank (eds.), *Language and identity across modes of communication*, 61–82. Berlin: De Gruyter Mouton.
Nakamura, L. 2002. *Cybertypes: Race, ethnicity, and identity on the Internet*. New York: Routledge.
Paolillo, John C. 2001. Language variation on Internet Relay Chat: A social network approach. *Journal of Sociolinguistics* 5(2). 180–213.
Schieffelin, Bambi B. & Rachelle Charlier Doucet. 1994. The "real" Haitian Creole: Ideology, metalinguistics, and orthographic choice. *American Ethnologist* 21(1). 176–200.
Squires, Lauren. 2010. Enregistering internet language. *Language in Society* 39(4). 457–492.
Squires, Lauren. 2012. Whos punctuating what? Sociolinguistic variation in instant messaging. In Alexandra Jaffe, Jannis Androutsopoulos, Mark Sebba, & Sally Johnson (eds.), *Orthography as social action: Scripts, spelling, identity and power* (Language and Social Processes), 289–324. Berlin: Walter de Gruyter.
Squires, Lauren. 2016. Computer-mediated communication and the English writing system. In Vivian Cook & Des Ryan (eds.), *Routledge handbook of the English writing system*, 471–486. New York and London: Routledge.
Tannen, Deborah & Anna Marie Trester (eds.). 2013. *Discourse 2.0: Language and new media*. Washington, DC: Georgetown University Press.

Thurlow, Crispin. 2003. Generation Txt? The sociolinguistics of young people's text-messaging. *Discourse Analysis Online* 1(1). Article 3.

Thurlow, Crispin. 2006. From statistical panic to moral panic: The metadiscursive construction and popular exaggeration of new media language in the print media. *Journal of Computer-Mediated Communication* 11(3). 667–701.

Thurlow, Crispin & Kristine Mozcrek (eds.). 2011. *Digital discourse: Language in the new media* (Oxford Studies in Sociolinguistics). Oxford: Oxford University Press.

# I Code and Variety

Lars Hinrichs
# Modular repertoires in English-using social networks: A study of language choice in the networks of adult Facebook users

## 1 Introduction

Research on the use of English in locales where it has no official status (i.e., where "expanding circle" varieties of English are used, cf. Kachru 1985) has by and large used public texts or student writing as data. In general, such work has stressed the dominance of English discourse integrated into local-language writing in terms of the textual positions of English ("English on top," Androutsopoulos 2012) and its symbolic appeal (Gerritsen et al. 2007; Martin 2002; Piller 2001; Stanlaw 1992; Takashi 1990). By studying semi-public text types, such as writing on social networking sites, I argue that our understanding of the dynamics and motivations underlying the inclusion of English in written discourse can significantly improve. To that end, this chapter presents an analysis of language choice and language negotiation in initial posts and follow-up message threads by German Facebook users. My methodological approach is a form of sociolinguistic online ethnography (Kytölä 2012; Jonsson and Muhonen 2014).

This work informs our understanding of the place that English holds in the new kinds of linguistic repertoires that are emerging around the world, as globalization – and communication on the internet as one facet of it – drastically changes local and global linguascapes (Coupland 2003), and of those repertoires themselves (Tagg and Seargeant 2014; see also Heyd's chapter in this volume). Specifically, communication on social networks such as Facebook allows for the observation of the language selection strategies that users develop under the technical-communicative affordances of the site's software (Androutsopoulos 2014; Marwick and boyd 2011; Seargeant, Tagg, and Ngampramuan 2012).

### 1.1 Background

This study touches upon three strands of current scholarly discourse in linguistics: research on computer-mediated discourse (CMD), the study of language and globalization, and World Englishes studies.

---

**Lars Hinrichs,** The University of Texas at Austin

First, the study of language choice in CMD falls into the broader area of research on online multilingualism (Danet and Herring 2007; Kytölä 2012; Leppänen et al. 2009). Much linguistic work in this area has studied both language choice and code-switching with an interest in the discourse functions of selections and switches among languages and codes, in other words: in the functions of what I propose to call *digital language contrasting*. Both the choice of a language[1] from a repertoire of several available languages and the switch from one language to another within discourse are possible patterns for languages to co-occur at the discourse level, with interpretable meanings emerging from the contrast between them. As part of the study of digital language contrasting, then, this paper first pursues a descriptive interest in the observable strategies according to which languages co-occur in the data.

Second, digital language contrasting is implicated in innovations and reconfigurations in the language practices in urban and online contexts that have been described in recent sociolinguistic work. Broadly, sociolinguists and online ethnographers are seeing new linguistic practices and new kinds of repertoires emerging as a result of globalization. In urban contexts, globalization has led to highly diverse inner-city language contact which is producing – for example, in many large cities in Europe – multiethnolects that are characterized partly by new combinations of structural features, and partly by the emergence of new linguistic practices and conventions (see e.g., Cheshire et al. 2011 for Multiethnic London English; or Wiese 2009 for Kiezdeutsch, spoken in Berlin). Such contact-induced mixing under extreme diversity has prompted researchers of urban and digital language practices to question the validity of the "language" and the "variety" as abstractions in the description of language use (Blommaert 2012; Pennycook 2007; Seargeant and Tagg 2011). I point out problems with this seemingly rebellious call elsewhere (Hinrichs 2015); at this point it is worth noting that linguists proclaiming the end of the "language" have so far failed to find ways of discussing practices *without* recourse to traditional language labels such as "Thai," "English," "French," etc. For this and other reasons, I expect that we will have to use the terms "language" and "variety" for a little while longer, and continue to improve our ways of describing hybridity within socio- and ideolectal practices in other ways.

In online environments, superdiverse (Vertovec 2007) cultural and linguistic participant mixes meet with low formality regiments to create new, dynamic conventions at every level of the (written) linguistic system (Herring 2012).

---

[1] The terms *language* and *code* will for the most part be equally applicable throughout this section, but I will refrain from making double mentions at each occurrence.

Blommaert (2012) makes explicit the parallel between such globalization-induced linguistic innovations in urban and online contexts when he refers to both as "supervernaculars" (with "super-" in the sense of 'trans-', not 'great'). While this conceptual simplification is problematic for more than one reason – a close examination should reveal more differences than similarities between the new linguistic practices in urban and in online contexts – Blommaert is justified in pointing out that both of these types of new linguistic practices do indeed emerge out of linguistic ecologies that are characteristic of globalization, superdiversity, and late modernity. Androutsopoulos (2015) appears to agree when he writes:

> Their differences put aside, concepts such as polylingualism, metrolingualism and translanguaging signal a shift of focus from linguistic systems to multilingual speakers and practices; a critical view of 'language' as an ideological construct; and a move towards theorising 'fluid' and 'flexible' relations between language, ethnicity and place as well as between linguistic practice and the ownership of language. (185)

The theoretical terms cited here – "polylingualism, metrolingualism and translanguaging" – have all been proposed as labels for new, multiethnic linguistic practices emerging in urban centers in Europe.[2] Androutsopoulos proceeds in his paper to demonstrate the validity of these labels for processes he finds in multilingual CMD.

Characterization of the new kinds of linguistic repertoires plays a central role in work on these emerging linguistic phenomena. Despite a striking emphasis on the increasing fluidity of analytical categories and an insistence among some critics on the inadequacy of "language"/"variety" as ideological constructs, when these new types of linguistic repertoires are described, hierarchical ordering – the stratification of constituent resources – plays a surprisingly large role. For example, Androutsopoulos (2015: 185, emphasis added) writes that "networked multilingualism is [...] based on a wide and *stratified* repertoire." Blommaert (2010: chapter 4) devotes a chapter of his influential programmatic book on necessary new departures in sociolinguistics on "truncated" linguistic repertoires in globalization. Such stratified models inevitably see English "on

---

[2] An anonymous reviewer points out that my brief presentation of the issue of urban linguistic contact phenomena, and specifically the labels of polylingualism, metrolingualism and translanguaging, may suggest a hesitancy on my part. To clarify: I think that each of these terms describes the linguistic practices encountered in metropolitan centers of present-day Europe in slightly different, largely fitting ways; my only hesitancy, perhaps, is with regard to the unnecessarily disorderly array of theoretical terms that I fear we might be creating.

top"[3] (as in the title of Androutsopoulos 2012) of mixed repertoires. At the level of the geopolitical hierarchy of languages, the view of "English on top" harkens back to de Swaan's "world system" of languages (de Swaan 2010; note that Androutsopoulos 2012 does not acknowledge any influence from de Swaan).[4]

The symbolic meanings of language choice can be discussed in terms of indexicality: according to the indexicality framework (Silverstein 2003, 2006), linguistic forms add metapragmatic meaning to discourse by virtue of their own history in social context. As the notion of indexical orders makes clear, a linguistic form has a "first order" indexical meaning which arises from basic, demographic characteristics of the group who is generally known to use it (e.g., pronominal *y'all* has a first-order indexical meaning of "Southern U.S."). Over time, forms can ascend to higher indexical orders and begin to accrue stronger stereotypification, with indexed meanings that relate to specific (stereotypical) qualities of typical users of the form (e.g., *y'all* can index the ideological mindset of "rednecks" from the Southern U.S.).

While there is much evidence to support the validity of the vertical metaphor, I also argue here that it erases some important features of the new linguistic repertoires. Specifically, I propose *modularizing repertoires* as an alternative referent. It stands in explicit contrast to the monosystemic repertoires that are described in variationist work on pre-globalized settings featuring monolingual dialect-standard continua (Blommaert 2010 argues that under globalization, sociolinguistics has to abandon its focus on monolingual continua and develop ways of describing the linguistic results of mass migration and superdiversity).

The task of theoretically characterizing online multilingualism is focalized in the somewhat simpler task of accurately describing the role of English in the linguistic repertoires of expanding-circle Facebook users. Androutsopoulos (2012: 234) proposes the notion of "English on top" as a descriptor for language relations that can be encountered "across media types and genres." His data is taken from Germany, i.e., a social context in which the primary code of written communication is, traditionally, the German language. He presents his approach explicitly as a departure from "Anglicisms research," i.e., the tradition of study that considers the integration of English material into written German at a micro, lexical level. Androutsopoulos encourages readers to "theorise 'English

---

**3** "English on top" is in fact the label Androutsopoulos chooses for an "approach" toward the study of online multilingualism. As the name suggests, the primacy of English is assumed a priori. Its different facets that Androutsopoulos presents by way of a discourse-analytical framework can aid in the description of the particular ways in which the primacy of English is manifested in a given dataset.

**4** Clearly, individual languages are still very much part of the picture even for Blommaert when it comes to analyses such as this.

on top' as a framing device that establishes, symbolically or indexically, frames of interpretations for the adjacent national-language content" (234). The focal question pursued in the present paper, therefore, is whether "English on top" is the most suitable descriptor for the relationship among languages observed in the data.

## 1.2 Facebook

Facebook is currently the most widely used electronic social network platform (Davenport et al. 2014; Lang 2015). Likely readers of the present paper will be familiar with its functionality; useful introductions to this mode of CMD are available in extant literature (Androutsopoulos 2014: 62–63 gives a concise introduction; for a general introduction see Ellison, Steinfield, and Lampe 2007; also Joinson 2008; West and Trester 2013). This section will therefore be restricted to an introduction of terms that will be used throughout the paper.

The *Facebook wall* is the place where each Facebook user's (semi-)public interactions are collected, retrievable for all members of his or her network (or, if users so choose, to even larger groups of internet users). The contrasting type of textual interactions, the one that is not published on the wall, is constituted by private interactions: users have the option of writing messages to one another that only sender and recipient can see.

Users can participate in interactions that appear on their wall in one of two roles: they can either make the *initial* post, or they can contribute a *responding* post to another user's initial post. (It is also possible to contribute responding posts to initial posts of one's own.[5]) Initial posts fall into either one of two broad categories: they can be either *text-only*, i.e., consist of a verbal composition by the user making the initial post, or they can be a *content post*, in other words they consist of a visual link to another website, a video, an audio file, or an image that the user posts, i.e., makes visible in the context of their Facebook wall. Such content can be either *original content* – material that the user has made and is posting to the internet for the first time – or *re-posted third-party content*, such as a video that "lives" on YouTube, an article on a newspaper website, etc. Users can choose to either verbally comment on content they post,

---

5 During the final revision stages of this volume, Facebook also made it possible to post direct responses *to a response*, which has important consequences for the audience effects that may factor into language choice. However, during the period of data collection, this technical option did not exist yet.

or not to comment. Given this paper's interest in the language choices users make, I only consider here text-only posts and content posts with comments.

At the time of this writing, Facebook was still the most widely used social network platform by far, but it was also commonly perceived to be the most mainstream of social networks, with many young people migrating to alternative services such as Twitter, Instagram, and others (Lang 2015).

### 1.3 Audience design theory

Sociolinguistic studies that have engaged the issue of language choice in social media (Androutsopoulos 2014; Seargeant, Tagg, and Ngampramuan 2012) have generally gravitated toward the well-known "audience design" framework. At its core, the model postulates (Bell 1984) that, as a general principle, speakers design their own speech to be more like the speech of their audience. This prediction holds for all levels of linguistic analysis, including frequency of morphosyntactic and phonetic variants, lexical register, as well as code and language choice. Depending on a person's role in the audience, the extent of their influence upon a speaker's style varies, in other words: speakers converge with audience members to different degrees depending on whether a person is (i) their direct addressee, (ii) an auditor to the communicative act (ratified bystander), (iii) an unratified overhearer, or (iv) an eavesdropper. For the purposes of the present paper, the role of audience as a strong influence on the speaker's/writer's stylistic choices will be remembered (for further discussion of the applicability of audience design to Facebook data, see Androutsopoulos 2014; Tagg and Seargeant 2014).

## 2 Study design

The method used in this project is sociolinguistic online ethnography (Jonsson and Muhonen 2014; Kytölä 2012), a discourse-centered technique of participant observation with a focus on qualitative, interpretive analytical approaches. Participants were enlisted from among my network of Facebook friends. All participants met these selection criteria:

- They are native speakers of German,
- They are *not* native speakers of English, but use English competently in speech and writing,
- They received most of their primary and secondary education in Germany,

- They lived in Germany throughout the period of study (November 2013 to November 2014),
- They are adults in the sense defined by Arnett (2004): they have completed degrees in higher education, are employed in a chosen career path, and have life partners as well as, in some cases, children.[6]

The fact that all participants are adults is significant, since research on computer-mediated interactions is very often conducted using data from adolescents and emerging adults. Compared to younger people, the informants in the present study have fairly stable and established identities, a factor that we can expect to have an impact on practices of linguistic repertoire deployment to the extent that play with different identities, represented in language through voices, is concerned (see also Collister's chapter in this volume on socially marginalized voices).

The participants, listed in Table 1 by their pseudonyms, are highly competent users of an "expanding circle" English (Kachru 1985). Three of the participants (Andreas, Rolf, Ann-Marie) also use additional languages on Facebook on more than one occasion.

**Table 1:** Participant characteristics

| Pseudonym | Gender | Dominant language choice in initial posts | Additional languages used[*] |
|---|---|---|---|
| Andreas | male | German | Spanish, Italian, French |
| Rolf | male | German | Portuguese |
| Jenny | female | English | – |
| Gisbert | male | German | – |
| Eduard | male | English | – |
| Ann-Marie | female | German | Swedish |

* in addition to English and German

The observation period covered roughly one year. All participants gave explicit written permission for their Facebook walls to be used as research material for this study, with all identifying information removed. The data for

---

[6] Arnett's life stages model is widely employed by social science researchers. Its merit lies in the fact that it introduces a new stage between adolescence and adulthood which Arnett calls "emerging adulthood." By distinguishing adulthood from this precursor phase, Arnett helps sharpen the definition of adulthood to what it needs to be for this study: a period of stable identity.

this study was compiled from all *initial* posts that these participants published on their walls during the study period, including information about any responding posts these elicited from members of the primary participants' networks. All types of posts – text-only posts, original content posts, and third-party content re-posts – were included, so long as they included a textual contribution by the primary participant. In other words, content posts that did not include a verbal comment from the user in the initial post were excluded. When a verbal contribution was present, but consisted of nothing but a direct quote from the posted content, such posts were also excluded.

# 3 Language choice in initial posts

Facebook users in my sample have an identifiable primary, or baseline, language in which they make the majority of their posts. As Table 1 shows, four of the participants post primarily in German and two primarily in English. The choice of a user's baseline language is a reflection of whether they conceive of all members of their audience[7] as being competent in German or not: if their notion of their primary audience includes non-speakers of German, their baseline choice will be English. Andreas, Rolf, Gisbert and Ann-Marie address German speakers with the majority of their initial posts, while Jenny and Eduard usually initiate posts in English. Without exception in my data, all departures from these baseline choices can be explained by either one of two factors: audience specification or use of formulaic language.

## 3.1 Audience specification

Some of the initial posts that do not follow the user's primary code preference can be explained by a practical interest in making the post available to its intended audience. Two sub-types of *audience specification* exist, following Androutsopoulos (2014: 66):

---

[7] Androutsopoulos (2014) offers a critique of the term "imagined audience" when he cites Marwick and boyd's (2011) use of the term and notes, accurately, that in social networking contexts, specifically on Facebook, an audience "consists of a limited number of members and is therefore not imagined in the same way as the large, anonymous audiences of broadcasting" (63). In other words: Facebook users tend to know their network of "friends" sufficiently well to be able to think of it, without imagining, as a concrete group of potential readers.

a. *Audience maximization* through the choice of English, which functions as the lingua franca in all of the participants' networks; and
b. *Audience partitioning* (i.e., subsetting) through the choice of any other language that is neither the participant's baseline code for initial posts nor the lingua franca.

In supplemental interviews, participants by and large explained their own language choices on Facebook as motivated by the desire to make each post understandable to that part of their network which the post was most intended for. For example, Ann-Marie wrote in a Facebook chat with me:

```
ich kann von mir ja sagen, dass ich wie gesagt hauptsächlich
auf deutsch poste und wenn ich denke, dass es für die
Englischsprachigen relevant ist, poste ich auf Englisch.
```
*For myself I can say that, as I said, I post mostly in German, and whenever I think that something might be relevant for the English-speakers [i.e., the English-speaking contingent of her network], I post in English.*

(Ann-Marie, interview, November 2014)

Similarly, Andreas commented on a specific example, his initial post about a political event in Catalonia. I reproduce here first his initial post as it appeared on Facebook and then the relevant excerpt from our Facebook conversation.

(1)
Yesterday some catalans conmemorated the defeat of the Army of Catalonia in its war in favor of Charles of Austria as King of Spain, who in the end let them down...beeing treasoned seems to be worth a party.
Still I'm searching for a dicctionary or cyclopaedia defining "war of independence" this way...
(Andreas, initial/text only, 12 September 2014)

Andreas    z.B. Thema Katalonien. Habe ich oft auf Englisch geschrieben, damit auch die Nichtspanier lesen können

*take for example the topic of Catalonia. I often wrote about it in English so that the non-Spaniards would be able to read it*

Lars    da hättest du ja auch auf spanisch drüber [schreiben] können

*you could have written about that in Spanish*

> Andreas   Aber das Thema wurde auch in Deutschland aktuell, also habe ich zum Englischen gegriffen. So konnten alle es verstehen.
>
> *But the topic became current in German, so I chose English. Thus, everybody was able to understand it.*
>
> (Andreas, interview, November 2014)

Andreas is a native speaker of both German and Spanish; he is additionally competent in Italian and French at levels enabling him to participate in written CMD in those languages. As he writes in our interview, his goal was for "everyone" to understand his opinion post about Catalonia, which motivated his choice of English. He also shows, significantly, that the fact that a topic is clearly tied to one national context, in the way that Catalonian history is to Spain, does *not* command language choice in any binding way.

Along with the choice of English as a lingua franca, Androutsopoulos (2014: 66) mentions two additional strategies that can be used to maximize audiences on Facebook: "replication of a given propositional content in two or more languages; and refraining from linguistic resources altogether." For the first of these, there is exactly one instance in my data. On Christmas Day, Andreas posted:

> (2)
> Liebe Freunde, ich wünsche euch allen frohe Weihnachten!
> Queridos amigos, wie tengais todos muy felices navidades!
> Carissimi amici, buon natale a tutti!
> Dear friends, I wish you all a very happy Christmas!
> Chers amis, très joyeux noël!
>
> (Andreas, initial/text only, 25 December 2013)

I asked Andreas why Christmas was the only occasion when he translated-and-repeated any propositional content on his Facebook wall. He answered:

> zu der Wiederholung auf anderer Sprache: Ich mache das eher aus Höflichkeit. Deswegen bei den Glückwünschen. Aber wenn es nur um Verständnis geht und Englisch es gewährleistet ist es nur doppelte arbeit
>
> *regarding repetitions in another language: I only ever do that out of politeness – hence, for Christmas greetings [lit.: for good wishes]. But when it's just a matter of being understood, and English does the trick, it [i.e., repeating content in another language] would just mean twice the work.*
>
> (Andreas, interview, November 2014)

His answer indicates a conceptual distinction between Facebook speech acts that require facework (West and Trester 2013), i.e., accommodation through language choice to all possible readers of a post, and those speech acts for which language choice only needs to function to create ideal intelligibility. Arguably, these two types could both be seen as performing facework: the choice of English for maximum intelligibility reflects a kind of politeness as well, in the sense that it prevents the greatest possible number of friends from having to translate posts. The first type, of which there is only one instance in the data, can be considered a dispreferred choice of facework strategy and the second, of which there are hundreds of instances, a preferred strategy. The reason for this distribution is economy: clearly, the performance of maximal multilingualism requires the greatest amount of effort in writing.

Androutsopoulos also mentions a third strategy for audience maximization: the complete avoidance of linguistic commentary altogether, in posts of original content (such as photos or videos that the user has made) or in re-posts of outside content. Given the present paper's interest in users' positive linguistic choices, it will not be discussed here.

Turning to audience partitioning, we find illustration in the following initial post that Andreas made in reaction to the June 24, 2014 game of the FIFA World Cup, in which Italy's national team lost 0-1 to Uruguay:

(3)
Cagata di arbitro, cagata di gol, cagata di par[t]ita. Ma andate affanculo!!!!!
*The referee crap, the goal crap, the game crap. Oh for fuck's sake!*
(Andreas, initial/text only, 24 June 2014)

Andreas had been rooting for Italy, and the audience for this post, which invites readers to share in his frustration about the loss, was the subset of his network that understands Italian (by his estimate, about one-fifth of his 352 friends). These are the friends who can most reliably be expected to also be fans of the Italian team.

Audience partitioning usually works through the practical mechanisms of inclusion and exclusion based on the linguistic competence of readers. Only when a user wishes to single out those members of their network who are primary, perhaps even exclusive, speakers of English, is the strategy restricted to a logic of symbolic exclusion: users will address the English speakers among their network in English, but everyone else will understand. Consider, for example, an event type that occurs multiple times in the data, in different users' networks: a Facebook user's journey to England, where he or she visits their English friends. For example, Gisbert – who initiates Facebook conversations mostly in German – posted at various times before, during, and after a trip to England in the Spring of 2014. On that trip he visited old friends whom he knew from his days as an exchange student. Upon his return to Germany, he posted:

> (4)
> Back from England after a most wonderful tour through the North – thank you so much, my open-hearted, always caring, refined and good-natured tour companion [m], to [f], [m] ([m]), [m], [m] and to all the people that instantly made me feel more than at home again.
> There is, however, some disappointment about not having my kidney taken, but hey – you got my heart instead.
> (Gisbert, initial/original photo, 19 April 2014)

The names that I elided in the post are all English names of friends whom Gisbert visited in England. The choice of English here is motivated not by a desire to maximize the audience, but to specify it. It goes along with a specificity of content that narrows the post's addressee group down further: a joke about organ theft in the last sentence of the post is presented in a way to exclude anyone who was not present when the joke was first made among this subset of Gisbert's network.

When English is a participant's baseline choice for initial posts, the choice of German can serve to partition the audience as well. In the following example, Jenny – who prefers English in initial posts – chooses German:

> (5)
> Umzugskartons gesucht: brauchen dieses WE noch ca 20 Kartons. Hat noch jemand welche im Keller stehen?
> *Moving boxes needed: we still need about 20 boxes for this weekend. Does anybody have some in their basement?*
> (Jenny, initial/text only, 12 September 2014)

Jenny prefers English for most of her initial posts, but on a few occasions, when her posts concern specifically local matters, she subsets her audience through the choice of German to only those who speak German. Her search for moving boxes – presumably she is hoping for a donor who lives not too far from her home in Southern Germany – presents one such occasion.

Overall, the strategy of audience maximization accounts for most of the observed unexpected choices of English in initial contributions, and audience partitioning accounts for most unexpected uses of languages that are neither a participant's baseline choice nor English. A fairly small number of selections, however, are commanded by the language of an intertextual model. The next section addresses these.

## 3.2 Formulaic intertextuality

Occasionally, users intertextually mobilize well-known quotes and use them in their posts. In all of the cases I found in my data, these uses of formulaic language occurred alongside other visual (original or re-posted) material, on which they commented. Therefore, examples in this section are presented as screenshots[8] to show linguistic posts next to the visual material on which they comment, where appropriate.

The first example (Figure 1a) shows a text-only initial post with a location tag ("Dortmund Hauptbahnhof," i.e., Dortmund main station), alongside an expression of the user's emotional state ("happy"), which is communicated both through a smiley and verbally. The text string "Driving home for Christmas" is the user's contribution, whereas the information on emotional state and location are formalized notes that users can choose to include in their post: they select the specific information to include from menus provided by Facebook (there is a set menu of different emotional states they can choose from, and a list of possible locations compiled from information about the user's current environment based on geolocation information that their mobile device provides to Facebook). The text string "Driving home for Christmas," in its entirety, is intertextually lifted from the chorus of a pop song that was released in 2000 by the English musician Chris Rea. Confirming that the user was not speaking creatively in her own voice but indeed quoting, one may notice the clash between the mode of transport referenced in the song – *driving* – and the one she actually opted for – the train. She could have adjusted the text to fit the reality of her situation more closely, but the English language (i.e., the language of the intertextual model) holds no readily available monosyllabic word that means 'take the train' and could easily form the disyllabic participle with –*ing* that would be needed to replace *driving* in this quotation while keeping the metric profile of the original. Therefore, Ann-Marie opted to use an identical

---

[8] Participants gave explicit permission for the use of screenshots without identifying information in this paper.

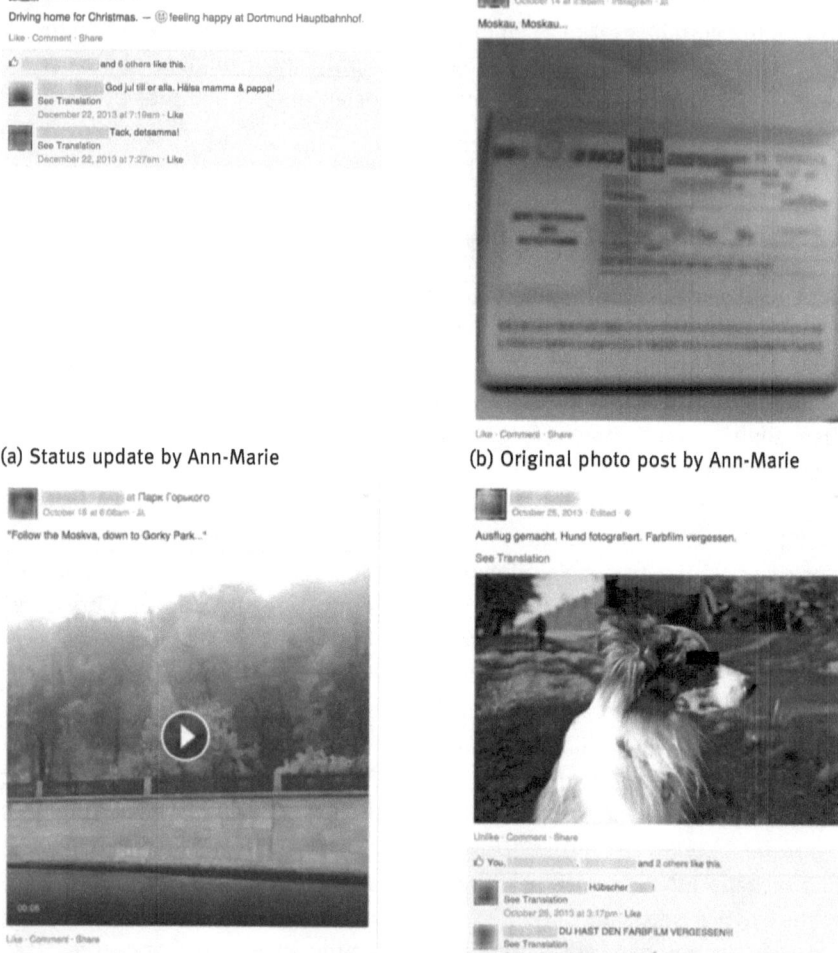

**Figure 1:** Screenshots of four different instances of formulaic intertextuality in initial posts

clone of the source; the slight inaccuracy in its description of her chosen mode of transportation is embraced as a metaphorical reinscription of her reality and heightening of the intertextual reframing of her experience.

In the second example (Figure 1b), Ann-Marie posts a photo of a visa in her passport showing her German name rendered in Cyrillic writing, a symbol of her impending trip to Russia. Her textual contribution is "Moskau, Moskau," the beginning of the chorus lyrics from another pop song that is well known in the German cultural context. Released in 1979 by the Bavarian pop act Dschinghis Khan, the song "Moskau" continues to be a recognized staple in entertainment radio shows, 1970s-themed events, etc. An English-language version of the song, entitled "Moscow" and released by the group in the same year under the Anglicized band name "Genghis Khan," played to some success in Australia, but was and remains irrelevant to the German context. Given the song's pop-cultural history, Ann-Marie's reference to it in her content post is of humorous effect to German readers. The song is known as a kitschy production of a thinly veiled orientalist sentiment that glorifies Moscow, and Russia, as the home of an ancient, mysterious, hard-drinking, dance-prone, soulful people. Quoting the "Moskau, Moskau" line indexes a naïve and simplistic perspective on a foreign culture from which, by invoking it, Ann-Marie distances herself. This sarcastic stance act shapes a broader frame within which she announces to her network that she is soon going to travel to Russia.

The third example (Figure 1c) shows a content post from Ann-Marie's subsequent trip to Moscow. She posts a video that she filmed on the Moskva River. Her linguistic contribution to the post is "I follow the Moskva, down to Gorky Park...," a statement that in this case is as much true to her current situation as it is easily recognizable as lifted from the pop song "Wind of Change," released by the Scorpions in 1990. Unlike in examples (a) and (b), Ann-Marie encloses this quote in quotation marks. This is surprising: in contrast to the first two examples, there is a fairly straightforward relationship between Ann-Marie's actual situation and the propositional content of the quote she inserts here. There is neither a metaphorical break in the truth proposition of the statement she invokes, nor an ironic break in perspective that readers would need to insert in order to fully understand the quote and its relevance to Ann-Marie's current situation in real life. And yet, in this case of a relatively simple relationship between intertextual borrowing and the context of its recontextualization (Squires 2014), the writer resorts to punctuation in order to frame the text as quote. But punctuation is among the first markers of traditional, paper-based written language to be abandoned as writers avail themselves of the freedoms afforded by the relatively more relaxed formality regimes of CMD. In that light, the degree of complexity of this intertextual act, as it emerges from the fairly straightforward semiotic relationships among text, quote, and source, and its conservative embrace of punctuation conventions reinforce each other.

In the last example (Figure 1d), we find another line from the chorus of a pop-song that is deeply set in the collective memory of German culture: "Farbfilm" was a single released by Nina Hagen in 1974 in the Eastern, communist part of Germany. The most recognizable line from the chorus is "Du hast den Farbfilm vergessen" ('you forgot the color film'). The song's speaker is a young woman who is chastising her boyfriend for having left the color film for their camera at home when they are on a beach holiday together, one which holds an abundance of photo opportunities. Eduard posts a black-and-white photo of his dog and writes in the accompanying text:

```
Ausflug gemacht. Hund fotografiert. Farbfilm vergessen.
Went on a day trip. Took picture of the dog. Left the color film.
(Eduard, initial post/original content, 25 October 2013)
```

The quotation of the first line of a pop song's chorus is here only partial, and – in contrast to the other examples – the quote is preceded by two short phrases that are structurally parallel (a head-only object noun phrase followed by a past participle verb form) to the quoted material, and which provide the real-life context to which the initial post relates. The relationship between the facts of Eduard's situation and the textual post into which the quote is embedded is complex: we know that Eduard did not forget the color film, as the picture we are seeing was clearly taken with a digital camera. We can be sure that the reason the photo is in black and white is because of an aesthetic choice the author made. By shifting into the intertextual mode and by giving readers an explanation of observable facts (namely, that the photo is in black and white) that can nonetheless be identified as facetiously counterfactual, the textual part of this post becomes a rhetorical guessing game.

The examples discussed in this section provide grounds for two observations. As manifestations of linguistic playfulness (Bell 2012; Jaworska 2014), they are, first and foremost, extremely rare in the data. In fact, these are the *only* cases of formulaic intertextuality that occur in initial posts in the data. Second, the examples happen to be evenly divided between quotes of English and of German-language source material. Other than the fact that of all the world's languages, English is certainly the language in which the greatest number of pop songs are produced, which results in a predominance of English-language source material for potential quotations, there is no evidence of an elevated symbolic status of English among this group of users based on their use of intertextuality.

# 4 Language choice in response posts

Language choice in responding posts merits consideration as an area of further negotiation of language. A subset of the posts produced by the participants in this study elicits responses. The analysis of language choices shown in Table 2 reflects only the subset of data samples that consist of just an initial post, i.e., which did not receive any responses. It should be noted that the percentages reported here are intended primarily to help orient the reader as to the makeup of this particular dataset. Due to its limited size, the idea of the dataset's representativeness, or that of any statistical distributions in it, should be approached with care.

Among the posts that were initiated in English, 25% of responding posts accommodate by reproducing the initial author's language choice and staying with English. Meanwhile, a much greater portion sees complete divergence, with German-only responses (40.7%, see e.g., Figure 2), or partial divergence in the form of a mix of English and German responses (25.9%).

Moving on to the posts that were initiated in German, we find that only 2.9% of posts are met with a divergent switch to English and 17.6% with response threads in which some posts use German and others English. Meanwhile, the majority of initial posts in German (67.7%) are met with full accommodation, i.e., German-only response threads.

**Table 2:** Combinations of initial and responding post language choices

| Initial post | Subsequent thread | Frequency of combination |
|---|---|---|
| English | English | 25.0% |
| English | German | 40.7% |
| English | Mix of English, German | 25.9% |
| English | Other | 8.4% |
| German | German | 67.7% |
| German | English | 2.9% |
| German | Mix of English, German | 17.6% |
| German | Other | 11.8% |

As this brief analysis has shown, users' preferred language choices differ sharply between initial and responding posts. In initial posts, participants choose English fairly frequently as an audience maximization strategy. By comparison, English is not nearly as strongly preferred in responding posts. Within the networks of this group of participants, responding posts are rarely designed for audience maximization and inclusiveness. Instead, responders like to directly address the initial poster (addressee) in their native language, without designing their contributions for those members of the initial poster's network who may not understand German (auditors). In other words, auditors have a notable effect upon language choice in initial posts, but not on responding posts.

**Figure 2:** Content repost by Rolf: response shows divergent language choice.[9]

# 5 Code-switching and code play

Code-switching (CS) in different modes of CMD has been described as a structural manifestation of linguistic playfulness (Danet 2001; Ifukor 2011; Jaworska 2014) and, more broadly, as a creative way in which users of online media capitalize on the relaxed formality regimes that characterize many born-digital modes of interaction: many CMD contexts leave behind the demand for monolingualism that is integral to the conventions of most traditional, paper-based text types (Hinrichs 2006a). A sociolinguistic approach to online CS sees instances of language (or code) alternation in discourse as meaningful at the meta-pragmatic level: message content can be framed in non-referential ways when the message is delivered in a code that differs from that of preceding or surrounding discourse, or when the code changes within the message. Thus, CS functions as a "contextualization cue" (Auer 1992; Gumperz 1982; Gumperz 1992).

Many studies of multilingual CMD have reported and studied CS. The dominant methodological paradigm is interpretive qualitative analysis (Androutsopoulos 2013; Dorleijn and Nortier 2009; Leppänen and Peuronen 2012). In the immediate research context of this study, Androutsopoulos (2014) finds rich evidence of CS, often intrasententially, among the adolescent Facebook users

---

[9] Post and response reproduced with the permission of the writers.

he studies. In his (2014: 66) data, stretches of English are embedded into other-language discourse in uses that he describes as "short, formulaic and intertextually saturated."

Remarkably, there is no evidence at all of post-internal CS in the Facebook data analyzed here. Even the rare instances of formulaic intertextuality, described in section 3.2., fail to trigger CS. If we broaden the perspective from CS in particular to linguistic playfulness in general, we observe, similarly, that none of the practices that are known to constitute linguistic playfulness are frequent in these data. Among the few examples are the four intertextual references to pop songs cited in 3.2., and the additional case of one participant who occasionally uses a third language (in addition to English and German) *outside of* any dynamic that is described by audience design: user Ann-Marie occasionally writes in Swedish. In some cases, she elicits responses in Swedish from a member of her network, another native speaker of German who, like her, speaks Swedish "as a hobby," as she wrote in a message when I interviewed her. In fact, Ann-Marie and this friend met during their time as students at the same university in Germany, when over the course of three years they both took Swedish courses purely out of interest in Swedish language and culture, but without the goal of fulfilling a curricular requirement or any other practical need. In one example of such a playful interaction between the two, Ann-Marie makes an original photo post with a short comment in German; the photo shows four Swedish-language books that she has bought on her recent trip to Stockholm. As such, the photo updates all German-speaking members of her network about the fact that she has returned from her trip and brought some enjoyable souvenirs for herself. In her first responding post, Caro selects Swedish:

(6)
Caro:      Svartsjuk!
           Jealous!
Ann-Marie: Du får gärna låna några!
           You're welcome to borrow some!
Caro:      Tack!
           Thanks!
(Thread of responding posts from Ann-Marie's wall, 01 November 2014)

Clearly, it is neither the configuration of audience nor the language choice of the initial post that prompts Caro's choice and Ann-Marie's subsequent shift to Swedish. Instead, the topic of the post (Swedish books) has functioned as a prompt for the two friends to briefly engage in their established friendship practice of conversing in Swedish, an activity that is only partly designed for the exchange of any propositional message content. It is a performance of friendship that operates almost entirely through the choice of language itself. It is playful, as evidenced by the lack of any pragmatic explanation for the choice of language, and it is unique in these data since there are practically no other instances of language choice becoming "part of the main action" in a similar way (Rampton 1998: 309).

# 6 Discussion and Conclusion

The findings from sections 3 to 5 can be summarized in five points:

1. The online writers in this study use their multilingual repertoires flexibly, according to the linguistic demands of a given interaction in their social network – which are shaped essentially by the linguistic needs of the intended target audience for each given post or response.
2. In initial posts by the participants in this study, language choice can be neatly and consistently explained as a function of pragmatic considerations. A hierarchy of choice emerges in which German as participants' primary language of interaction in daily life is preferred. When English is chosen over German, this is motivated by a desire to maximize the audience for a given post. Choices of languages other than German or English can be consistently explained as acts of audience specification. Exceptions are extremely rare, and all those that occur in the dataset were addressed in this paper (cf. use of content repetition in multiple languages as an alternate strategy for audience maximization, and language choice governed by formulaic intertextuality).
3. In responding posts, we found that language choice as audience design places greater importance on the primary addressee: responders think of their comment as directed primarily at the initial poster, and hardly (if at all) at the secondary audience of auditors. Since all participants in this study are dominant native speakers of German, we can conclude that the selection of English is a dispreferred choice, especially in cases where choosing English would imply a divergence from the initial poster's choice of language (i.e., in threads that were started with an initial post in German).
4. Code-switching within sentences or even within posts is entirely absent from the data: it occurs only within threads, i.e., across post boundaries.
5. Other instances of playfulness, role play, double voicing (Bakhtin 1984; Hinrichs 2006b; Rampton 1998), etc. are extremely rare. The example that contradicts this observation, the case of Swedish used as a friendship code between one participant and a member of her network, was discussed in section 5.

Most relevant to the initial questions asked in this paper, there is no evidence of any symbolic values that are invoked through the use of English, nor is English chosen in any higher-order indexical work. This is significant because extant studies of English use in German public texts frequently posit higher-order indexicality as adhering to the choice of English. For example, Piller (2001), having observed a prominent role of English in a corpus of German advertising, offers a conclusion that highlights the positive symbolic value of English (182). Androutsopoulos (2012), writing about the use of English in German advertising and other public texts, suggests that "English on top" – the use of English loan material in textually prominent positions – is a strategy of infusing texts with positive associations not only symbolically, but through the construction of *indexical* links between the text at hand and international communities. For example, a German commercial website about hip hop music uses English-language insertions to create indexical links to the international hip hop community. This kind of connection is a higher-order indexical link involving a degree of abstraction because, rather than indexing *all* speakers of English, it invokes a very specific characterological (Agha 2005) type of English speaker: one who is characterized by his or her membership in the North American hip hop community. In the semi-public data at hand that comes from adult German Facebook users, no such specific and positive valuation can be attested. Rather, English is chosen for practical reasons: in order to bridge communicative gaps among individuals who do not share a common first language, and while the link that is thus created between an English-language communicative act on Facebook and the thus enlarged group of auditors can certainly be considered indexical, this is a basic, first-order, non-abstract kind of indexicality, one which does not invoke specific character traits or memberships in specific communities of practice.

As the de facto lingua franca of Europeans, English certainly has a special place among the different languages encountered in the data. But despite its association with international groups of speakers, participants in this study do not show a more positive evaluation of the language as such. They never use it for symbolic or indexical contextualization of their writing and they do not integrate English loans into their discourse in a way that even remotely resembles what has so frequently been described for the language of advertising (Piller 2001) and other public texts (Androutsopoulos 2012).

In data from a different, younger group of users, Androutsopoulos (2014) did find orientations toward English as an exceptional, positively evaluated language. The adolescents in his study did frequently code-switch into and out of English, and audience maximization was not nearly a discernible objective in every instance. Social differences between that group of writers and the participants in the present study may help us contextualize these linguistic differences: all of the individuals whose Facebook walls were studied for this paper are over thirty years old; they are adults who have made several of those kinds of life choices that bring about the end of "emerging adulthood" (Arnett 2004) and initiate adulthood: commitment to a profession or career, a life partner, and a relatively permanent place of residence. They are all university-educated and employed in positions that utilize their specific training. In other words, the individuals in this study have stable and fairly privileged existences – in obvious contrast to adolescents such as those studied by Androutsopoulos. As is becoming increasingly clear from research on language use in late modernity, it is especially individuals with less stable, less privileged identities who use multiethnolects and who engage in playful linguistic practices such as crossing (Cutler 2015; Kerswill 2014; Rampton 1995, 1998) or other kinds of CS (Jaworska 2014). As Bakhtin wrote, "[our] speech, that is, all our utterances (including our creative works), is filled with others' words, *varying degrees of otherness* or *varying degrees of 'our-own-ness'*" (Bakhtin 1986: 89, emphases added). I suggest that the less stable an individual's identity is, the more likely they will be to use language playfully, as they try on identities other than their own. Thus, "otherness" of voice is more frequently found in the words of younger and more disenfranchised people than it is in the words of privileged, stable individuals. Of course, the notion of *stable* identities is more important than *adult* identities: it happens to be the case that adults more frequently show the psychological characteristics that constitute stable identities than young people do. But there are counterexamples too, i.e., accounts of adults who highlight adaptability and fluidity of identity (Podesva, Roberts, and Campbell-Kibler 2001 show how adults adapt their linguistic styles to quite different, situationally conditioned aspects of their identities). Yet as a general tendency, linguistic play and voicing are more frequent in the usage of young people.

It is therefore also plausible that the participants of this study make their language selections mostly in aid of their communicative needs, but only rarely in playful games of language contrasting, in which different languages transport different voices. In short, the writers who were analyzed here tend to write in their own voices more frequently than adolescents have been suggested to do.[10]

The participants' matter-of-fact approach to code choice shines through even in their use of intertextuality. The pop songs that are referenced are completely mainstream and historicized. These findings on the participants' language choice strategies thus seem to illustrate the notion of Facebook as the

---

**10** As noted in a reviewer's comment, the question of whether adolescents even *have* an unmarked, base voice of their own yet might deserve separate investigation.

most mainstream, least underground social network platform. While my conclusions rest in large part on the comparison with Androutsopoulos's younger participants, who were equally observed on Facebook, promising follow-up work would consist in a study of the same participants' language selection patterns on different, less canonical social media platforms such as Tumblr, Instagram, or others.[11]

In spite of the relative stability of participants' identities and the relative orderliness that underlies language choice in these data, we are seeing globalization making its mark upon the way that participants deploy their multilingual resources. It is (partly) through pragmatically adaptive language choice that this group of users addresses the problem of "context collapse," i.e., the "collapse of multiple audiences into single contexts" in electronic environments (Marwick & boyd 2011: 114; see also Androutsopoulos 2014). The outcome of this process is a fairly conservative multilingual usage profile, free of intrasentential or even utterance-internal CS, but multilingual nonetheless. It shows a complete and comfortable departure from modernist idealizations of monolingualism. The status of English in these multilingual mixes is enhanced only by its role as lingua franca, but English does not hold an *ideologically* privileged position among the linguistic resources of these writers. Rather than referring to their linguistic repertoires as "stratified" (Androutsopoulos 2015: 17), I therefore propose the descriptor *modular repertoires*: repertoires that are organized into individual elements which are activated according to the demands of each interaction and its audience.

# 7 References

Agha, Asif. 2005. Voice, footing, enregisterment. *Journal of Linguistic Anthropology* 15(1). 38–59.
Androutsopoulos, Jannis. 2012. English "on top": Discourse functions of English resources in the German mediascape. *Sociolinguistic Studies* 6(2). 209–238.
Androutsopoulos, Jannis. 2013. Code-switching in computer-mediated communication. In Susan Herring, Dieter Stein & Tuija Virtanen (eds.), *Pragmatics of computer-mediated communication* (Handbooks of Pragmatics 9), 667–694. Berlin: de Gruyter.
Androutsopoulos, Jannis. 2014. Languaging when contexts collapse: Audience design in social networking. *Discourse, Context & Media* 4-5. 62–73.
Androutsopoulos, Jannis. 2015. Networked multilingualism: Some language practices on Facebook and their implications. *International Journal of Bilingualism* 19(2). 185–205.

---

[11] I am indebted to an anonymous reviewer, who added the perspective that I summarize in this paragraph.

Arnett, Jeffrey J. 2004. *Emerging adulthood: The winding road from the late teens through the twenties*. Oxford et al.: Oxford University Press.

Auer, Peter. 1992. Introduction: John Gumperz' approach to contextualization. In Peter Auer & Aldo di Luzio (eds.), *The contextualization of language*, 1–37. Amsterdam: John Benjamins.

Bakhtin, Mikhail M. 1984. *Problems of Dostoevsky's poetics*. Ed. Caryl Emerson. (Theory and History of Literature 8). Minneapolis: University of Minnesota Press.

Bakhtin, Mikhail M. 1986. *Speech genres and other late essays*. Eds. Mikhail Holquist & Caryl Emerson. Austin: University of Texas Press.

Bell, Allan. 1984. Language style as audience design. *Language in Society* 13(2). 145–204.

Bell, Nancy. 2012. Formulaic language, creativity, and language play in a second language. *Annual Review of Applied Linguistics* 32. 189–205.

Blommaert, Jan. 2010. *The sociolinguistics of globalization* (Cambridge Approaches to Language Contact). Cambridge: Cambridge University Press.

Blommaert, Jan. 2012. Supervernaculars and their dialects. *Dutch Journal of Applied Linguistics* 1(1). 1–14.

Cheshire, Jenny, Paul Kerswill, Sue Fox & Eivind Torgersen. 2011. Contact, the feature pool and the speech community: The emergence of Multicultural London English. *Journal of Sociolinguistics* 15(2). 151–196.

Coupland, Nikolas. 2003. Introduction: Sociolinguistics and globalisation. *Journal of Sociolinguistics* 7(4). 465–472.

Cutler, Cecelia. 2015. White Hip-hoppers. *Language and Linguistics Compass* 9(6). 229–242.

Danet, Brenda. 2001. *Cyberpl@y: Communicating online*. Oxford: Berg.

Danet, Brenda & Susan C. Herring (eds.). 2007. *The multilingual Internet: Language, culture, and communication online*. Oxford: Oxford University Press.

Davenport, Shaun W., Shawn M. Bergman, Jacqueline Z. Bergman & Matthew E. Fearrington. 2014. Twitter versus Facebook: Exploring the role of narcissism in the motives and usage of different social media platforms. *Computers in Human Behavior* 32. 212–220.

Dorleijn, Margreet & Jacomine Nortier. 2009. Code-switching and the internet. In Barbara E. Bullock & Almeida Jacqueline Toribio (eds.), *The Cambridge handbook of linguistic code-switching*, 127–141. Cambridge: Cambridge University Press.

Ellison, Nicole B., Charles Steinfield & Cliff Lampe. 2007. The benefits of Facebook "friends:" Social capital and college students' use of online social network sites. *Journal of Computer-Mediated Communication* 12(4). 1143–1168.

Gerritsen, Marinel, Catherine Nickerson, Andreu van Hooft, Frank van Meurs, Ulrike Nederstigt, Marianne Starren & Rogier Crijns. 2007. English in product advertisements in Belgium, France, Germany, the Netherlands and Spain. *World Englishes* 26(3). 291–315.

Gumperz, John J. 1982. *Discourse strategies* (Studies in Interactional Sociolinguistics 1). Cambridge: Cambridge University Press.

Gumperz, John J. 1992. Contextualization and understanding. In Alessandor Duranti & Charles Goodwin (eds.), *Rethinking context: Language as an interactive phenomenon*, 229–252. Cambridge: Cambridge University Press.

Herring, Susan C. 2012. Grammar and Electronic Communication. *The Encyclopedia of Applied Linguistics*, 2338–2346. Hoboken, NJ: Wiley-Blackwell.

Hinrichs, Lars. 2006a. *Codeswitching on the Web: English and Jamaican Creole in e-mail communication* (Pragmatics and Beyond New Series 147). Amsterdam: John Benjamins.

Hinrichs, Lars. 2006b. Creole on the Internet: New types of evidence in the study of written vernacular language use among young people. In Christa Dürscheid & Jürgen Spitzmüller (eds.), *Perspektiven der Jugendsprachforschung/Trends and developments in youth language research*, 183–200. Berne: Peter Lang.

Hinrichs, Lars. 2015. Review: Jan Blommaert. Ethnography, superdiversity and linguistic landscapes: Chronicles of complexity (Critical Language and Literacy Studies 18). Bristol, U.K.: Multilingual Matters. 2013. 144 pp. *Journal of Sociolinguistics* 19(2). 260–265.

Ifukor, Presley. 2011. Linguistic marketing in "... a marketplace of ideas." *Pragmatics and Society* 2(1). 110–147.

Jaworska, Sylvia. 2014. Playful language alternation in an online discussion forum: The example of digital code plays. *Journal of Pragmatics* 71. 56c68.

Joinson, Adam N. 2008. Looking at, looking up or keeping up with people? Motives and use of Facebook. *Proceedings of the SIGCHI conference on Human Factors in Computing Systems*, 1027–1036. New York: ACM.

Jonsson, Carla & Anu Muhonen. 2014. Multilingual repertoires and the relocalization of manga in digital media. *Discourse, Context & Media* 4–5. 87–100.

Kachru, Braj B. 1985. Standards, codification and sociolinguistic realism: The English language in the outer circle. In Randolph Quirk, Henry G. Widdowson & Yolande Cantù (eds.), *English in the world: Teaching and learning the language and literatures: Papers of an international conference entitled "Progress in English Studies" held in London, 17–21 September 1984 to celebrate the fiftieth anniversary of the British Council and its contribution to the field of English studies over fifty years*, 11–30. Cambridge: Cambridge University Press for the British Council.

Kerswill, Paul. 2014. The objectification of "Jafaican": The discoursal embedding of Multicultural London English in the British media. In Jannis Androutsopoulos (ed.), *Mediatization and sociolinguistic change* (linguae & litterae 36), 428–455. Berlin: de Gruyter.

Kytölä, Samu. 2012. Researching the multilingualism of web discussion forums: Theoretical, practical and methodological issues. In Mark Sebba, Shahrzad Mahootian & Carla Jonsson (eds.), *Language mixing and code-switching in writing: Approaches to mixed-language written discourse* (Routledge Critical Studies in Multilingualism 2), 106–127. New York: Routledge.

Lang, Nico. 2015. Why teens are leaving Facebook: It's "meaningless." *Washington Post*, The Intersect. http://www.washingtonpost.com/news/the-intersect/wp/2015/02/21/why-teens-are-leaving-facebook-its-meaningless/ (accessed 10 June 2015).

Leppänen, Sirpa & Saija Peuronen. 2012. Multilingualism on the internet. In Marilyn Martin-Jones, Adrian Blackledge & Angela Creese (eds.), *The Routledge handbook of multilingualism*, 384–402. London: Routledge.

Leppänen, Sirpa, Anne Pitkänen-Huhta, Arja Piirainen-Marsh, Tarja Nikula & Saija Peuronen. 2009. Young people's translocal new media uses: A multiperspective analysis of language choice and heteroglossia. *Journal of Computer-Mediated Communication* 14(4). 1080–1107.

Martin, Elizabeth. 2002. Mixing English in French advertising. *World Englishes* 21(3). 375–402.

Marwick, Alice E. & danah boyd. 2011. I tweet honestly, I tweet passionately: Twitter users, context collapse, and the imagined audience. *New Media & Society* 13(1). 114–133.

Pennycook, Alastair. 2007. *Global Englishes and transcultural flows*. London: Routledge.

Piller, Ingrid. 2001. Identity constructions in multilingual advertising. *Language in Society* 30(2). 153–186.

Podesva, Robert J., Sarah J. Roberts & Kathryn Campbell-Kibler. 2001. Sharing resources and indexing meanings in the production of gay styles. In Kathryn Campbell-Kibler, Robert J.

Podesva, Sarah J. Roberts & Andrew Wong (eds.), *Language and sexuality: Contesting meaning in theory and practice*, 175–189. Stanford, CA: CSLI.

Rampton, Ben. 1995. *Crossing: Language and ethnicity among adolescents*. London: Longman.

Rampton, Ben. 1998. Language crossing and the redefinition of reality. In Peter Auer (ed.), *Code-switching in conversation: Language, interaction and identity*, 290–320. London: Routledge.

Seargeant, Philip & Caroline Tagg. 2011. English on the internet and a "post-varieties" approach to language. *World Englishes* 30(4). 496–514.

Seargeant, Philip, Caroline Tagg & Wipapan Ngampramuan. 2012. Language choice and addressivity strategies in Thai-English social network interactions. *Journal of Sociolinguistics* 16(4). 510–531.

Silverstein, Michael. 2003. Indexical order and the dialectics of sociolinguistic life. *Language & Communication* 23(3-4). 193–229.

Silverstein, Michael. 2006. Pragmatic indexing. In Keith Brown (ed.), *Encyclopaedia of Language and Linguistics*, vol. 6, 14–17. Amsterdam: Elsevier.

Squires, Lauren. 2014. From TV personality to fans and beyond: Indexical bleaching and the diffusion of a media innovation. *Journal of Linguistic Anthropology* 24(1). 42–62.

Stanlaw, James. 1992. English in Japanese communicative strategies. *The other tongue: English across cultures*. 178–208. Urbana, IL: University of Illinois Press.

Swaan, Abram de. 2010. Language systems. In Nikolas Coupland (ed.), *The handbook of language and globalization*, 56–76. Malden, MA: Blackwell.

Tagg, Caroline & Philip Seargeant. 2014. Audience design and language choice in the construction and maintenance of translocal communities on social network sites. In Philip Seargeant & Caroline Tagg (eds.), *The language of social media: Identity and community on the internet*, 161–185. Basingstoke, UK: Palgrave Macmillan.

Takashi, Kyoko. 1990. A sociolinguistic analysis of English borrowings in Japanese advertising texts. *World Englishes* 9(3). 327–341.

Vertovec, Steven. 2007. Super-diversity and its implications. *Ethnic and Racial Studies* 30(6). 1024–1054.

West, Laura & Anna Marie Trester. 2013. Facework on Facebook: Conversations on social media. In Deborah Tannen & Anna Marie Trester (eds.), *Discourse 2.0: Language and new media* (Georgetown University Round Table on Languages and Linguistics Series), 133–154. Washington, DC: Georgetown University Press.

Wiese, Heike. 2009. Grammatical innovation in multiethnic urban Europe: New linguistic practices among adolescents. *Lingua* 119(5). 782–806.

Taylor Jones
# Tweets as graffiti: What the reconstruction of Vulgar Latin can tell us about Black Twitter

## 1 Introduction

Accompanying the burgeoning of computer-mediated communication in past years comes a variety of approaches to compiling and interpreting corpora, and to the study of social and linguistic factors related to computer-mediated communication.

One approach that has generally been overlooked, but will be demonstrated below, is the exploitation of computer-mediated communication as a rich source of phonological information about nonstandard Englishes. The focus of this chapter is the intersection of real-world (i.e., *not* computer-mediated) spoken-language phonology and orthography in computer-mediated communication. Historical linguists have long used nonstandard spelling in conjunction with other sources of information to aid in reconstruction and analysis, even as linguistics was still a fledgling science not yet differentiated from philology (e.g., Jones 1806). Here, it will be shown that the same approaches used for centuries in historical linguistics, applied to the microblog platform Twitter and cross-validated with other media, are applicable to the analysis of innovative orthographic representations of African American English (AAE). Moreover, for many speakers of AAE who use Twitter, such spellings are not misspellings, but rather intentional representations of users' native phonology. The chapter will proceed as follows: Section 2 introduces previous analyses and the microblog platform Twitter. Section 3 challenges the common notion that spelling variation on social media is a problem for computational analysis that needs to be solved. Section 4 discusses the reconstruction of Vulgar Latin, with particular focus on the role of nonstandard written material. Section 5 draws parallels between AAE on Twitter, and the *sermo vulgaris*. Sections 6 and 7 are phonological case studies; the first on liquids, the second on glottal stops. Finally, the chapter concludes with a review of the findings and discussion of future directions for research.

---

**Taylor Jones**, University of Pennsylvania

## 2 Background

Previous approaches to the analysis of social media and CMC data have focused on discourse practices and legitimacy (Androutsopoulos 2011; Jaffe 2000; Jaffe 2012), categorizing nonstandard orthographic choices (Anis 2007; Eisenstein 2013b; Squires 2012; Tagg 2009; Van Halteren and Oostdijk 2012), and tracking the geographic spread of CMC forms (Eisenstein 2014). Particular focus has been given to sentiment analysis, and whether data mining techniques can be used to accurately gauge public sentiment – and therefore predict anything from box office earnings to the outcome of elections or even the stock market (Asur and Huberman 2010; Bollen, Mao, and Zeng 2011; Kouloumpis, Wilson, and Moore 2011; O'Connor et al. 2010; Pang and Lee 2008; Tumasjan et al. 2010). Similarly, there has been a strong interest from both computer scientists and some sociolinguists in detecting gender or other "latent variables" such as social media users' political orientation, socioeconomic status, or incidence of heart disease mortality (Bamman, Eisenstein, and Schnoebelen 2014; Eichstaedt et al. 2015; Rao and Yarowsky 2010; Shapp 2015). The inherent difficulty of automated sentiment analysis, computers' fundamental lack of human pragmatic competence, has led to an interest in automated detection of irony and sarcasm in social media (Barbieri and Saggion 2014; González-Ibánez, Muresan, and Wacholder 2011; Reyes, Rosso, and Veale 2013).

Linguistic analyses of CMC have generally been limited to lexical variation and morphosyntax (Doyle 2014; Eisenstein 2013a). In fact, most large-scale treatments of orthography in CMC are focused on eliminating noise and normalizing spelling to facilitate analysis by grouping various "misspellings" as the same lexical item (Kobus, Yvon, and Damnati 2008; Van Halteren and Oostdijk 2012). However, there is a growing amount of research on how people employ nonstandard spelling to construct identity, both their own, through allegro forms (e.g., *gonna* for 'going to') and prosodic respelling, and that of others, in transcription through eye-dialect[1] and dialect respellings (Jaffe 2012).

### 2.1 Twitter and Black Twitter

Twitter is a microblogging platform launched in 2006. Users of Twitter author and publish posts of 140 characters or fewer, called *tweets*, with the option of embedding images, using emoticons/emoji, and embedding hyperlinks to other

---

[1] Nonstandard respellings that do not reflect linguistic variation, like *sez* for 'says.'

websites or platforms, like the photosharing site Instagram, or the video microblog site Vine.

Roughly 500 million tweets are sent per day, by over 300 million active monthly users. As of 2013 just under 20% of the online adult population of the United States used Twitter (roughly 65 million people), with 23% of active users tweeting from inside the United States.[2] Twitter's usership in the United States skews young and black, with 29% of non-Hispanic Black Americans using Twitter compared to 16% of non-Hispanic Whites and 16% of Hispanics, and 31% of 18–29 year olds of all ethnicities (Duggan and Smith 2013). These numbers are all likely higher for the 13–18 age group, although Duggan and Smith's numbers on Twitter use are based on polls of adults. Furthermore, while roughly 20% online adults uses Twitter, fully 87% of American adults use the internet. Of those, 74% (i.e., 64% of American adults) are on some social media platform – if not Twitter, then some other platform such as Facebook, or Tumblr.[3]

The concept of a "Black Twitter" distinct from the rest of the social media platform dates to just a few years after Twitter's inception (Sicha 2009), but it has become a hot topic in both academic literature (Brock 2012; Clark 2014) and in popular media (Choney 2012; Ellis 2010; Hoffberger 2012; Jones 2013; Manjoo 2010; McDonald 2014; Ramsey 2015). It is generally taken to mean a network or set of networks that are a distinct subset of the larger "Twittersphere" which is uniquely *black*, although nailing down what precisely that means is problematic.

The discussion around Black Twitter has primarily been about the extent to which it is or is not monolithic (Clark 2014; Ramsey 2015), and has treated it as a locus of the Black American tradition of *signifyin'* and of social activism (Jones 2013). For the purpose of this chapter, however, *Black Twitter* is defined by use of AAE on Twitter.

This means that the Black Twitter discussed here may be significantly different from that discussed elsewhere: inner city teenagers using Twitter as a free analog to text messaging and rural AAE speakers engaging in wordplay will be represented, but social activists and critical race theorists discussing current events – people traditionally thought of as most representative of Black Twitter – may not be represented, insofar as they may be less likely to use AAE in their tweets. This approach has the benefit of ensuring linguistic relevance to discussion of AAE (especially when focusing on basilectal forms) as well as that of being immediately operationalizable: tweets using some combination of AAE features like habitual *be*, stressed *been* (*BIN* in the academic literature) (Rickford

---

[2] Statistics are from Twitter: http://about.twitter.com/company.
[3] Tumblr is a microblogging platform now owned by Yahoo!, which is similar to Twitter but without the 140 character limit. As of 2015, it hosted 248 million blogs. http://www.tumblr.com

1999), negative auxiliary inversion (Green 1998, 2002), modal *finna*, preterite *had* (Rickford 1999), grammaticalized use of *nigga* (Jones and Hall 2015), negation and nonveridical constructions using *eem* (Jones 2015a), indignant *come* (Spears 1982), modal *tryna* (Lane 2014), and so on can be reliably taken to be AAE. This is especially useful insofar as such constructions are not used by Mainstream English (ME) speakers, are grammaticalized in AAE, and are stigmatized or generally not understood by ME speakers, as in the case of camouflage constructions. This operationalization is of course not a comment on the authenticity of any Twitter users, but is simply a reflection of engagement with the norms of spoken AAE in their use of the platform, and should not be taken as a definitive description of Black Twitter. In fact, this definition's inclusion of the rare native AAE speaker who does not identify as "Black" may be potentially unsettling to those more used to thinking of Black Twitter as a cultural, and not a linguistic, phenomenon. Here, *Black Twitter* is functioning as a shorthand for the more unwieldy "use of African American English in computer-mediated (public) communication."

## 3 Data collection and analysis

There were two main approaches to gathering the data presented here. The first is the use of a small corpus of tweets (17,273 tokens) compiled by the author in January of 2015, primarily to facilitate research into regional patterns in AAE (Jones 2015b). The corpus was compiled using the {twitteR} package (Gentry 2015) using the R statistical programming language (R Core Team 2015). Tokens were selected based on their containing relevant search strings (e.g., <sholl>), and the focus was primarily finding words with the highest volume of use and the highest degree of regional differentiation. Specific attention was paid to phonological relevance, but quantity was also a deciding factor for inclusion.

The second method was to use the code developed above in conjunction with simple queries to Twitter through a web browser. Rates of use were determined by querying Topsy, a Twitter analytics website.[4] Material from other sources (i.e., YouTube, Vine, etc.) was not automated like the sampling of tweets, and was performed using a web browser.

Queries were based on intuition developed from online participation, as well as information gleaned from recursive searches. For instance, hypothetically having searched for <nuttin> and <nuffin> ('nothing'), one might later add <nun> to the list based on the results of searching for <yeen> ('you ain't') turning

---

4 http://www.topsy.com

up <yeen seen nun yet> ('you ain't seen nothing yet'). The author's native speaker intuition was also helpful, as some forms that occur with a low, but steady, rate may not immediately spring to mind for non-native speakers (e.g., <dis hyuh> for 'this here'). Furthermore, anecdotally, non-speakers of AAE seem to find parsing orthographic representations of more divergent AAE extremely difficult.

Because the focus of this chapter is on the relationship between phonology and orthography in individual posts, examples are generally tweets with the maximum possible difference from standard orthography. In the interest of transparency, glosses are provided below.

## 4 Nonstandard orthography is a feature, not a bug

Much of the AAE on Twitter uses nonstandard orthography, which can vary from minimal (1), to extreme (2, 3):

(1) The thirst be real outchea
'The thirst is real out here'
(i.e., 'People are generally (unwantedly) lustful out here')
(@PRECIOUSPARIS, May 26, 2015, Twitter)

(2) Country dennabissh and ioneem much curr lol
'I'm country-er than a bitch and I don't even much care'
(i.e., 'I'm extremely provincial...')
(@iAYoshie, April 7, 2013, Twitter)

(3) Aint eem much talmbout the jits fam
'I'm not really talking about the kids, friend' (where *jit* < *idiot*)
(@NamasteMarley, March 4, 2015, Twitter)

In much of the computer science literature, a standard approach is to treat such written material as "strings" of characters. The usual approach to strings like the above is to treat them as misspellings, ill-formed words, and typos which pose problems for analysis; the goal is then to group them under standard or normalized spellings so both *out hyuh* and *outchea* would be treated as variants of the same standard form: "out here" (Han and Baldwin 2011; Kobus, Yvon, and Damnati 2008; Van Halteren and Oostdijk 2012; Vosse 1992).[5] This way of looking at things would seem to be supported by some of the literature on literacy

---

[5] For other, more idiosyncratic variants, like *dennabissh* for "than a bitch" this approach becomes exponentially more time intensive and tedious, as it is difficult to automate.

and AAE (Harber 1977; Hart, Guthrie, and Winfield 1980; Melmed 1970; Simons and Johnson 1974; Thompson, Craig, and Washington 2004). Hart et al. (1980), for instance, find that black children of low socioeconomic status are more likely to suffer from false positives when asked to match written words to spoken words when the written form lacked final consonants present in ME, and that AAE phonology poses problems for the acquisition of ME orthography in primary education.

Indeed, we do find what looks *prima facie* to be the same phenomenon with tweets saying things like *I was juss confuse* for "I was just confused." Thompson (2004:280) argues, just before the advent of Twitter,

> African American students have models for spoken AAE; however, children do not have models for written AAE like they have for spoken AAE. Whereas AAE is an oral linguistic system and not a written system, students likely have minimal opportunities to experience AAE in print.

However, now there are emerging *de facto* standards on Twitter, Facebook, and other social media for representing AAE orthographically, although they are generally stigmatized by non-speakers of AAE and are definitely not recognized as valid in primary education (Hudley and Mallinson 2011). That said, users of Twitter are conscious of their choices, often explicitly so, with tweet after tweet saying "*I tweet how I speak*," and users exasperatedly explaining they know how things are spelled in standard orthography, but they choose to represent their speech with nonstandard orthography (4, 5). The existence of such tweets points to an ongoing tension between standard and nonstandard language in computer-mediated communication, as even users committed to tweeting in their vernacular feel a pull from 'standard' English ideologies.

(4) I tweet how I speak. I know how shit is spelled Muhfuckas I had a 4.0 throughout high school…
(@AlecStxrm, April 14, 2015, Twitter)

(5) I can spell…some tweets just work better with ebonics and urban street slang.
(@MontanaOn10, May 28, 2014, Twitter)

Moreover, even papers about normalizing tweets concede that "most ill-formed words are based on morphophonemic variation" (Han and Baldwin 2011), and that orthographic errors

> are known, also in more traditional text, to be strongly related to pronunciation. This relation is even more pronounced in tweets because of the more informal nature of tweets and the fact that Twitter language tends to be much closer to spoken language. (Van Halteren and Oostdijk 2012)

In fact, in possibly the only large analysis of phonological factors in social media writing, Eisenstein (2013a) finds that:

> ...phonology impacts social media orthography at the word level and beyond...Both consonant cluster reduction and th-stopping are significantly influenced by the phonological context: their frequency depends on whether the subsequent segment begins with a vowel. This indicates that when social media authors transcribe spoken language variation, they are not simply replacing standard spellings of individual words.

It should be clear from the above that variation in spelling and nonstandard orthographic choices are not just affected by considerations like the construction of identity, but also vary along phonological parameters. As such, spellings that diverge from standard orthography are interesting in their own right, not just because they pose problems for tweet normalization that interfere with sentiment analysis and similar endeavors, but precisely because such divergence has the potential to tell readers something about how the tweet's author speaks, in many cases, deliberately so.[6] While the volume of data is unprecedented, the problem of extracting phonological information from text and corroborating the findings is not a new problem for linguists, and the tools and approaches used by historical linguists are particularly useful in this regard. In this way, the phonological analysis of Twitter data can been seen as similar to the reconstruction of Middle English phonology or that of Vulgar Latin, except that in the case of Twitter data linguists can also make use of a wide variety of media to corroborate their hypotheses with living speakers of the language variety under investigation.

## 4 How we know what we know about Vulgar Latin

Here, *Vulgar Latin* (VL) is taken to be more or less equivalent to Latin as actually spoken, defined in opposition to the highly artificial literary language generally referred to as *Classical Latin* (CL). The issues of register, level of education, and rough date of Latin language material are set aside for the moment, and an informal, quotidian definition of Vulgar Latin will suffice for the purposes of this chapter. A thorough treatment of social variation in spoken Latin and the difficulty in pinning down *precisely* what *Vulgar Latin* is (and when various aspects of it can be reliably dated to) can be found in Adams (2013). It will

---

6 Example (2) above, incidentally, prompts Twitter to offer *View Translation*, which then results in the message: *Unable to translate this Tweet. Please try again later.*

suffice to note that the appellation *vulgar* does not carry judgement about class or education here. As Grandgent (1907) notes, it is not "the dialect of the slums or of the fields...It is distinct from the consciously polite utterance of cultivated society, from the brogue of the country, and from the slang of the lowest quarters of the city, though affected by all of these."

**Vulgar Latin** differs from the classical written language in many respects, including lexicon, derivational morphology, word order, use of prepositions and demonstratives, and case marking (Adams 2013; Kent 1945; Grandgent 1907; Pope 1934; Solodow 2010).

Some of what we know about VL comes from reconstruction, through application of the comparative method. We know, for instance, that *cavallus* was used in VL, and not just CL *equus*, through attestation *and* through evidence from French *cheval*, Italian *cavallo*, Spanish *Caballo* and Portuguese *cavalo*. In fact, there are some words we know "must have existed," but are not attested at all (Grandgent 1907), such as *refusare*, *miaulaure*, and *gentis* (Fr. *gent*, It. *gente*).

However, the comparative method is not by any means the only evidence used by historical linguists. Textual resources played a large role in the reconstruction of VL. These include evidence from statements of the grammarians, from a long list of corrections of common errors called the *Appendix Probi*, from transcription of other languages and borrowings into other languages, from (misspellings in) inscriptions such as the graffiti at Pompeii, and from puns, rhymes, and poetic meter in written sources. Each are examined here in turn.[7]

The explicit statements of various authors of CL tell us a great deal about Latin pronunciation. For instance, Quintilian (35–100 CE) tells us *b* is pronounced as *p* before *s*, so <urbs> ('city') would have been /urps/. Quintilian also tells us that word final *m* was "hardly perceptible" before a vowel (Solodow 2010). In function words, /m/ was assimilated to a following consonant. As Adams (2013) notes, "Cicero twice (*Orat*. 154, *Fam*. 9.22.2) says that the combination *cum nobis* should be avoided because it is open to an obscene interpretation (*cunno*...)...he also suggests that the combination *illam dicam* once uttered in the senate (probably by Cicero himself) might have been taken as obscene (=*landicam* 'clitoris')." Similarly, Catullus (d. 54 BCE) makes fun of a man who adds /h/ to words through hypercorrection (e.g, *hinsidias* for *insidias* 'ambush') – suggesting that deletion of /h/ had already become widespread by the first century BCE.

---

7 A thorough treatment of the sources of our phonological knowledge about Latin can be found in Adams (2013).

A particularly useful document is the *Appendix Probi*, a third (or possibly fourth) century palimpsest that is a long list of common orthographic errors in Latin, all in the style *X, not Y*. Examples, in keeping with the theme set above, include *numquam non numqua* and *idem non ide* for 'never' and 'same' respectively. Similarly, *hostiae, non ostiae* 'sacrificial animals.' Recalling Quintilian's discussion of *urbs*, the *Appendix Probi* tells us *plebs non pleps* when discussing 'commoners.' Even things that escape note by the grammarians and by the *Appendix* are informative: Carthage is frequently found spelled both as *Carthāgō* and *Karthāgō*, without comment (Kent 1945).

Translation from Latin is also helpful in determining the sounds of Latin from orthographic evidence. For instance, Greek transliterations always use *kappa*, Latin *Cicerō* is rendered as K, *Caesar* is rendered as K, and so on. Similarly, Welsh and Germanic borrowings from Latin, from the first through fifth centuries CE, all have /k/ for Latin <c>, as in Welsh *cwyr* for Latin *cēra*, or Gothic *lukarn* and *kaisar* for Latin *lucerna* and *Caesar*.[8] It is clear <c> always represented /k/.

One of the best-known sources of our knowledge of VL pronunciation is the wealth of written attestations across the former empire, most famously the graffiti at Pompeii – famous, no doubt, in part because of their frequent lewdness (e.g., 'The one who buggers a fire burns his penis').[9] Because of their brevity, the very informal tone, and the often unorthodox spelling,[10] graffiti are a sort of analog microblog *ab antiquo*, a comparison that will prove fruitful in the next section.

Finally, puns, rhymes, and meter have been extremely enlightening. A famous example comes from Cicero's *On Divination*: Marcus Crassus, before leading a failed military expedition to Parthia, heard a fig seller shouting *Cauneas!* (the name of a type of fig). Cicero tells us "We may say, if we please, that Crassus was warned by [the fig seller], *cave ne eas* ('Beware, don't go!'), and that [Crassus] would not have perished if he had obeyed the omen" (Sturtevant 1920). The point here is that from this story we know that *cauneas* and *cave ne eas* would have been pronounced alike, and that in conjunction with other sources we can say a number of things about the phonology of Latin at the time Cicero was writing: <v> represented /w/, the word final <e> in *cave* would have been deleted in speech, and there would have been liaison between *ne* and *eas*. The usefulness of rhyme here is obvious, and will be picked up in the next section. Meter has also been enlightening. A verse by Catullus, for instance,

---

8 Examples from Kent (1945), page 53.
9 Translated inscriptions all from Brian Harvey's website: http://www.pompeiana.com
10 Adams (2013) refers euphemistically to "persons of humble education."

suggests an "impossibly long" (Solodow 2010) eighteen syllables for the thirteen syllable meter: *quam modo qui ne me unum atque unicum amicum habuit* ('...as he who recently had me as his one and only friend'). However, there are five elisions (which are not prevented by word final /m/ or word initial /h/), making the verse the appropriate length. Solodow (2010) conveys the way it would have been pronounced: *quam modo qui m' un' atqu' unic' amic' abuit*.

To summarize, we have a relatively firm grasp of the sounds of Vulgar Latin despite reliance solely on text, because we have a large number of sources and tools for analysis at our disposal, and can triangulate the phonology. This is done not just through linguistic reconstruction using the comparative method, but through careful consideration of the complaints of grammar peeves, analysis of translation and transcription, analysis of graffiti, and analysis of information gleaned through puns, rhymes, and meter.

## 5 Twitter parallels to Vulgar Latin graffiti

As alluded to above, tweets can be thought of as parallel in many ways to graffiti. They are short, informal, often ribald, and public. Classroom standards of spelling and academic writing style, while definitely used by some, are not even remotely universal. A now cliché quip about the perceived navel-gazing of Facebook and Twitter users is "I don't care what you made for lunch," suggesting contemporary youth are particularly self-absorbed – yet in Pompeii we find "On April 19th, I made bread" in the gladiator barracks. Much of what is tempting to consider new opportunities or challenges posed by computer-mediated communication has a much longer history than is immediately apparent: We find parallels in Pompeiian graffiti for FourSquare[11] check-ins ("Satura was here on September 3rd"), Yelp[12] reviews ("Two friends were here. While they were, they had bad service in every way from a guy named Epaphroditus.") and spiteful *subtweets* ("Samius to Cornelius: go hang yourself!"). While the medium is different, the message is often the same. Moreover, while the language and medium differ, the authors' interaction with orthography is often similar.

For instance, *rebus*-like forms and syllabic spelling (e.g., <b4> for 'before', <c u l8r> for 'see you later' etc.) are often taken to be the product of character

---

[11] FourSquare is a "local search and discovery app" that maps localized search results. It formerly had a functionality allowing users to "check in" at a particular location and write a comment. That functionality is now a separate app, called *swarm*, though "check in" is still used colloquially. http://www.foursquare.com
[12] Yelp is a platform for crowd-sourced reviews of local businesses. http://www.yelp.com

limits on tweets, considerations of economy given the keyboards on mobile devices, or holdovers from character limits in SMS messages combined with the tedium of keypad typing on older devices (Han, Cook, and Baldwin 2013; Kobus, Yvon, and Damnati 2008; Tagg 2009; Van Halteren and Oostdijk 2012). However, there are no such restrictions on graffiti,[13] where we still find that "in all parts of Italy, there is found at times a tendency to syllabic writing, in which a letter has the value of a syllable, usually of the name of the letter" (Kent 1945). So, for instance, we find MISC for *misce* and LVBS for *lubens* at Praeneste, DECMB for *decembres* in Latium. Grammarians mention spellings like <krus> for *cārus* (Kent 1945).[14] While syllabic spellings like <c u 18r> are widely known, some AAE speakers on Twitter liberally employ such forms, including in situations where they would not be used in other dialects of English. For instance, <b> for habitual *be*, or <d> for a flapped *t/d*:

(6) I **b** press for shaw**d**, so WHAT!
I be pressed for shorty, so what?
(i.e., I am often (over-)enthusiastic about seeing (my) beau, so what?)
(@avonnadeche, January 18, 2014, Twitter)

Similarly, clippings (like *legit* for 'legitimately' or *delish* for 'delicious') are sometimes taken to be new and platform specific (Chow 2014; Reddy 2014), but there is strong evidence they are phonological, not orthographic, in nature, and are more properly described as wordplay in the spoken language that is then represented orthographically (Jones 2014; Spradlin 2015). An excellent counterexample to the clippings-as-shortening argument is the common (on Twitter) use of forms like *beeteedubs* for the shorter <BTW> (for 'by the way'). Clipped forms on Black Twitter include *bruh*, *mofo*, and *belee* for 'brother,' 'motherfucker,' and 'believe,' respectively. Similar to *beeteedubs*, <OD>, of questionable etymological origin but likely from *overdose* (Eisenstein 2014), is sometimes now <odee>:

(7) I'm odee bored
'I'm very bored'
(@selfmade27, May 29, 2015, Twitter)

---

**13** Or on magazine articles, where we also see this phenomenon (Androutsopoulos 2000).
**14** Further counterevidence for the character limit hypothesis comes from online Chinese, where Chinese netizens will use roman letters because they're perceived as cool or for taboo avoidance, for instance <B> for *bī* 'vagina,' where the single character <B> replaces another single character.

Another CMC parallel to VL is the fact that pedants and self-styled grammarians find voice discussing the *sermo vulgaris*. Complaints about popular usage, with varying degrees of phonological sophistication, are common online. The author of the *Appendix Probi* finds kindred souls in the authors of various listicles about 'grammar peeves' and 'common errors.' The speech of commoners and slaves as represented by Petronius in the *Satyricon*, and rustic speech as written by Plautus and Terence, finds a rough equivalent online in the writing of *Mock Ebonics* (Hill 2009; Ronkin and Karn 1999), as on racist white nationalist message boards, like the 'chimpire' network of vitriolically racist subreddits,[15] although such evidence should obviously be taken as more indicative of dialect *perception* rather than the reality of linguistic use (e.g., the racist caricature *Dindu Nuffin* illustrates the salience of *th-fronting* in some varieties of AAE to online white supremacists).

Lastly, there is an enormous variety of pronunciation spellings in both Vulgar Latin, in which authors, intentionally or not, respell words in a orthographically transparent manner. An enormous volume of Latin material with idiosyncratic spellings, especially in inscriptions have been "especially valuable" in reconstructing VL phonology (Kent 1945), and these find parallels in Twitter, especially Black Twitter. Two case studies, users' representations of liquids and glottal stops, are taken up in the next sections.

# 6 Case study: Liquids

AAE is generally /r/-less and /l/-less postvocalically (Bailey & Thomas 1998; Green 2002; Labov and others 1968; Labov 1972; Labov, Ash, and Boberg 2005; Rickford 1999; Wolfram 1969; Wolfram 1994). That is, /r/ and /l/ can be deleted in syllable codas when not followed by a vowel, and can be deleted word-finally even when followed by a word that begins with a vowel. There is evidence that /r/ can be deleted intervocalically, too (Green 2002).

Plenty of examples of word-final deletion of /r/ can be found represented orthographically on Black Twitter, including <mova> for *mother*, <ova> for *over*, <neva> for *never*, <wea> for *where*, and <outchea> for *out here*. It should be noted that some have become lexicalized, so we should take care to distinguish words like *nigga*, *hoe*, *brotha*, and so forth, which may have been reanalyzed as simply

---

[15] *Reddit* is a popular website that styles itself the "front page of the internet," and a *subreddit* is a more or less self-contained online community in which members can post links to other content or can write posts directly. Users then comment on the submission, and can comment on and reply to the comments *ad nauseum*. It skews young, white, male, and middle-class. http://reddit.com

not having a word final /r/, from those which have an underlying /r/ that is reduced (cf. Callier, this volume; Childs, this volume).

Similarly, Twitter furnishes plenty of examples of deletion of word-medial /r/ in syllable codas, where we find <halem> for *Harlem*, <bode> for *bored*, <wodie> for *wardie* (originally, someone who comes from the same *ward* of New Orleans, by analogy with *roomie*, *homie*, etc.), and <patna> for *partner*.

(8) I neva had no real patnas fuck these niggas outchea
'I never had no real partners, fuck these people out here'

Word-finally, /l/ is deleted, just like /r/, so we find strings like <coo> and <koo> for *cool*, <skoo> for *school*, <foo> for *fool*, <bow> for *bowl*, and <go> *gold*, and <fawt> for *fault*. However, while /l/ is deleted following any kind of vowel, given that it is often replaced by an offglide – usually either /w/ or /ʊ/ – word-final /l/ seems to be retained orthographically except following non-low back vowels, though here more research is needed.[16]

Sometimes, Black Twitter runs counter to expectations, and we find word-final liquids reversed. At the time of writing, <drawls> had been tweeted for ME *drawers* (i.e., underpants) 4.4 thousand times in the previous 30 days, <sholl> had been tweeted for ME *sure* 9.2 thousand times, and <nawl> for *no* or *naw* had been tweeted 22 thousand times.[17] These spellings reflect regional patterns in AAE use on Twitter and are not indicative of AAE on the whole (Jones 2015b, 2015c). More importantly, they are phonologically transparent: for users writing <sholl> the word they intend is *sholl*, with underlying /l/, not *sure* (no doubt the etymological origin of *sholl*). The benefit that we have over historical linguists is that because the object of our study is contemporary language use, we can immediately corroborate hypotheses. Native speakers of AAE in Harlem, originally from the south, corroborate that *sholl* is used, is pronounced /ʃoʊl/, is stereotypically used by older people, and indexes rural, Southern identity.[18] The fact that it indexes rural, Southern identity is also evident from Twitter alone:

(9) Trust me if I cuda got 400 followers wit jus a egg I dam sholl wuda tried ... did I say sholl...im officially a bama
'Trust me, if I could've gotten 400 followers with just an egg, I damn *sholl* would've tried. Did I say *sholl*? I'm officially a hick.'
(@lennydevito, September 13, 2012, Twitter)

---

16 This is in keeping with the findings in Eisenstein (2013b).
17 Data are from the Twitter Analytics service, Topsy: http://topsy.com/
18 Speakers asked were from Dallas, Texas; Corsicana, Texas; and Atlanta, Georgia.

Here, *bama* is stereotypically Washington DC slang for a country rube.[19]

The pronunciation of *sholl* can be corroborated through other technological means as well. Rappers disseminate music online using media like YouTube and SoundCloud,[20] and searching online turns up songs like *sholl iz* by Dirty (2003), where *sholl iz* is unambiguously pronounced as /ʃoʊlɪz/. It can be further corroborated in less stylized speech through recourse to Vine and other video platforms.[21] For instance, in the user @irrelevantesteban's post, stating:

(10) Chuck, I'm'one tell ya and I'm'one tell ya good. Mmm-hmm, sholl is: get all the sleep you can...

Because there is no background music and the sound quality is sufficiently high, the audio content of the video is amenable to analysis in Praat, which reveals a formant pattern typical of [ɨ] with secondary lip rounding: [ʃo̞ʊʷɬɪə].[22] Moreover, because the speaker is speaking clearly and looking at the camera, his tongue is visible and he clearly makes a gesture toward coronal contact with the alveolar ridge.[23] It is important to note that in tweets like this one, and the above ("I tweet how I speak") we are finding metalanguage discussing lexical and phonological patterns and their social meanings.

Similar to *sholl*, there is evidence that the <l> in <drawls> is actually pronounced. Just as rhymes and puns provided evidence for the pronunciation of Vulgar Latin, ribald rhymes furnish evidence here. For instance,

(11) 'suck my balls through my drawls'

(12) 'in the hall in just my drawls'

While it's plausible that /l/ is reduced or deleted in both *balls* and *drawls*, again, video corroborates our hypothesis that at least some speakers pronounce the /l/. See, for instance, Vine user @ig:nsidebeauty, who posted a video stating:[24]

---

**19** This conforms to the author's personal experience, and is verified by the Language & Communication in Washington, DC project, through the Georgetown University Department of Linguistics. http://lcdc.georgetown.edu
**20** Sound Cloud is an online audio sharing platform founded in 2007. http://www.soundcloud.com
**21** Vine is a video sharing platform that allows users to share videos of up to 9 seconds. http://www.vine.co
**22** Deletion of the word final voiced sibilant is a separate process not relevant to the discussion here.
**23** https://vine.co/v/MPT0a9vUFjw
**24** NB: Orthographic choices like *nem* were informed in part by the author's text post accompanying the video, and are not *eye-dialect*.

(13)  Niggas stay holla talmbout they just tryna be yo friend. No, dey tryna drop it off nem drawls
'Men often flirt saying they just want to be your friend. No, they want to have sex.' (*lit.* 'drop it off in them drawers')

In the video,[25] the user is speaking directly to the camera, and clearly gestures toward /l/, which is corroborated by spectrogram analysis of the audio, and made easier by the fact she deletes the word final /z/, yielding [dɹɑwɫ]. Similarly, a video clip from the Steve Harvey Show, uploaded to YouTube from Steve Harvey's official YouTube channel, not only has *drawls* in the title ("Ask Steve: Wear The Same Drawls Everyday!"), but features the host clearly saying *drawls*: not only is his tongue movement visible, but the audio – being studio qualty – is good enough that spectrogram analysis confirms of 104 milliseconds (the length is because he is speaking emphatically).[26] The same approaches work for <nawl>, which once again can be shown to be a faithful representation of pronunciation.

Some of these forms are increasingly enregistered, and they all index Southern identity, so for instance when @freakyfootbruh tweets a photograph of an enormous crustacean pulled from the Gulf of Mexico, accompanied by the text

(14)  eaux hayle nawl
'Oh hell no'
(@freakyfootbruh, April 2, 2015, Twitter)

The spelling of each word indexes southern, black identity: <nawl> is used only in AAE and primarily in the south, <hayle> is a transparent representation of the Southern Vowel Shift applied to *hell* (i.e., [heːˑɫ]), and <eaux> for /oʊ/ is an enregistered marker of Louisiana identity, by analogy with the slogan for the New Orleans Saints football team, *'Let's Geaux Saints!'* The text therefore communicates not just displeasure with the image, but that the author is Southern, Black, oriented positively toward Louisiana, and conscious of their use of a regional vowel system. Far from misspelling, it's a demonstration of the phonological genius and intellectual playfulness of some users of AAE on Twitter. A summary of the relevant phenomena is presented in Table 1.

---

25  https://vine.co/v/M0jOXVtK76J
26  https://www.youtube.com/watch?v=rs8P5b0pl-0

**Table 1:** Deletion and vocalization of liquids by position in word

| Phonological Phenomenon | Position | Orthography | Example |
|---|---|---|---|
| /r/-deletion | final | ‹do›, ‹wea›, ‹hea›, ‹ova›, ‹mo›, ‹patna› | *ur mova said you comin ova* |
| /r/-deletion | medial | ‹Halem›, ‹bode›, ‹wodie›, ‹patna› | *luh you too wodie* |
| /l/-deletion | final | ‹coo›, ‹bow› | *smoke a bow, bow of cereal* |
| /l/-deletion | medial | ‹fawt›, ‹go› | *you a go digga* |
| /l/-for-/r/ | final | ‹sholl› | *sholl ain't!* |
| /l/-for-/r/ | medial | ‹drawls› | *goin' on a date; gonna get dem drawls* |
| intrusive /l/ | final | ‹nawl› | *Nawl, it wasn't important* |

# 7 Case study: Glottal stops

While liquids have conventional representations in English orthography but can be dropped in spoken AAE, the situation with respect to glottal stops is the opposite. While glottal stops are not phonemic in AAE, they are highly salient. They also lack a standard orthographic representation, making them problematic. While academic writing often deploys apostrophes to represent a glottal stop, this is not the practice, in general, on Black Twitter. This is the one situation for which the traditional explanations about CMC being constrained by the types of devices used is most plausible: apostrophes are harder to get to on nearly all mobile devices. For some, but not all, speakers of AAE, casual pronunciation of *something* and *nothing* are subject to *th-stopping*.[27] If we adopt an ordered rule approach, we may say that those forms then *feed* other rules, for instance, the replacement of /t/ with a glottal stop. The below spectrograms are typical for such speakers, where *something* and *nothing* realized as [sʌ̃ʔn̩] and [nʌ̃ʔn̩] respectively.[28]

For such speakers, choosing to represent how they speak means choosing an orthographic representation of a glottal stop. In general, Twitter users solve this problem in two ways, neither of which is the *a priori* expected apostrophe,

---

[27] For others, labiodental fricatives are subject to *th-fronting*, which yields forms like [sʌmfɪn] and [nʌfɪn].
[28] Spectrograms of *something* and *nothing* are from interviews the author performed with friends in Harlem; shared with their express permission.

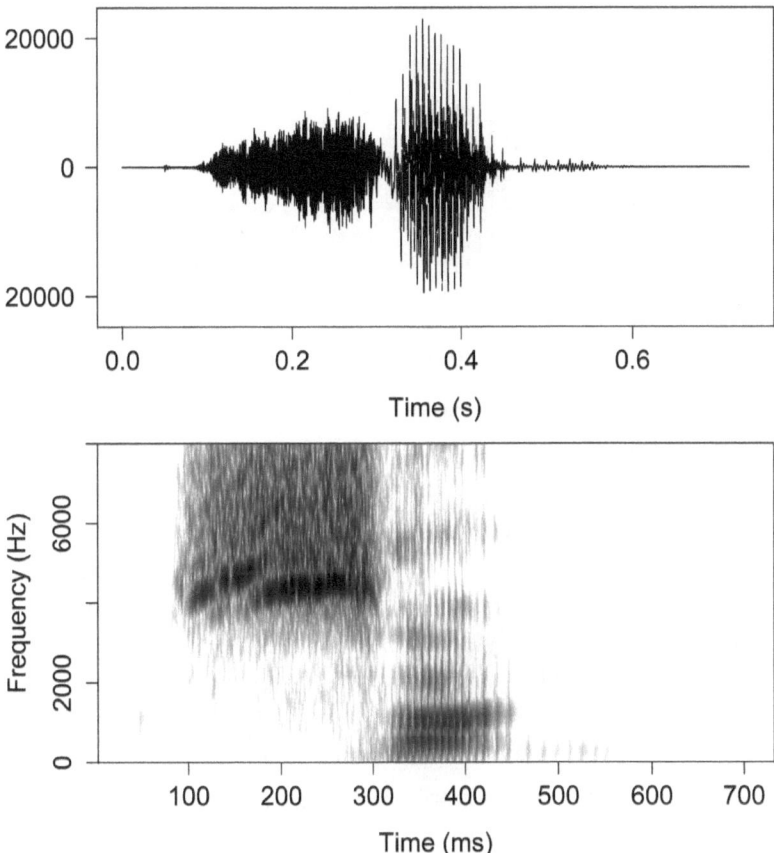

**Figure 1:** [sʌ̃ʔn̩] 'something'; note the syllabic nasal

as in <nu'in>. Instead, authors choose to either delete the stop completely, or to represent it with a stop that shares the place of articulation of an adjacent segment, whether that underlying segment is realized as such in the surface output of speech or not.

For *something*, this yields forms like <sumn> (by far the most popular, written 83,000 times in the previous 30 days at time of writing), <suttin>, <sutn>, <supm>, <sumpm>, and <sumpn>. Note that in <sumn>, the <m> may indicate nasalization on the preceding vowel (as in Vulgar Latin, and French and Portuguese). The same is true of <sumpn>, where the underlying /m/ is not usually phonetically realized as a distinct segment, but contributes to the orthographic representation of the glottal stop as <p>. For *nothing*, we find <nuttin>,

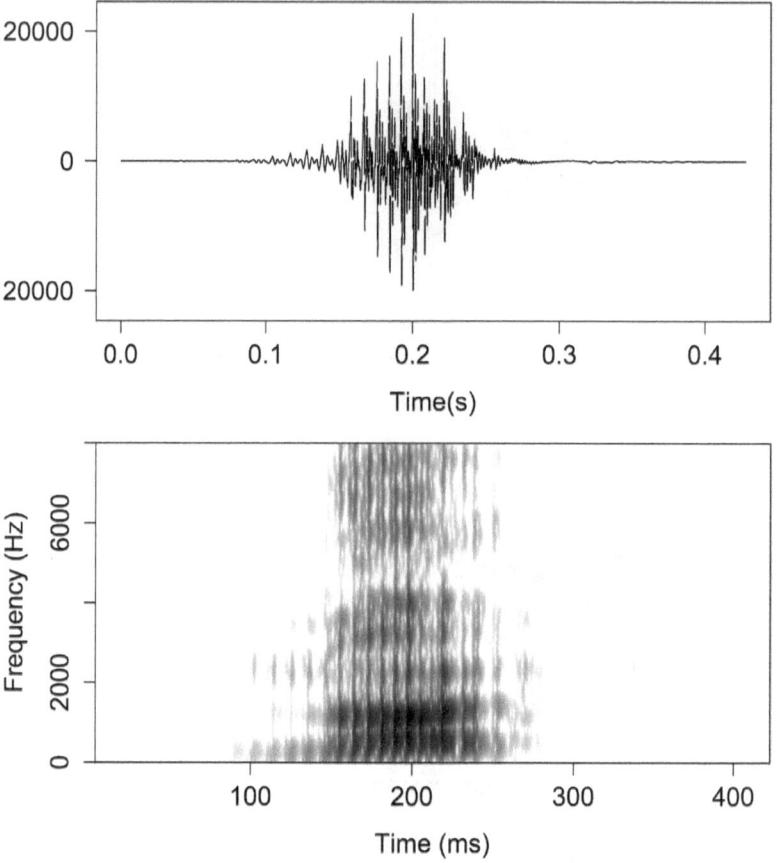

**Figure 2:** [nʌ̃ʔn̩] 'nothing'

<nutn>, <nuin>, and <nun>. In the case of the last of these, parallel to reconstruction of Vulgar Latin, context and poetic meter provides evidence:

(15)   nigga I ain't worried bout nun

Variations of (15) were extremely common in 2013 when French Montana's song "Ain't Worried About Nothin," was a hit, and are still quite common two years later.[29] The key here is that both context and meter give clues as to the meaning and pronunciation of <nun>. While context makes it clear it means *nothing*, and

---

[29] The *exact* string cited in (15) was tweeted 79 times in the 30 day period between May 3 and June 7, 2015.

not that thousands of people are suddenly expressing lack of concern about (monastic) sisters, the meter of the song they're quoting makes it clear <nun> is two syllables, not one, as a sort of inverse example to the Catullus cited above.

In some varieties of AAE, glottal stops also occur at the end of words, as secondary glottalization on (unvoiced or devoiced) word final stops. While this phenomenon is understudied, native speakers are aware of it, and it seems to be salient to at least some non-speakers of AAE.[30] Where speakers want to explicitly convey their pronunciation of secondary glottalization on a word final consonant, they represent it with a voiceless stop that shares place of articulation with the preceding segment, resulting in forms like <goodt>, <badt>, and <thangk> for *thing*:

(16) Gotdamn this mac n cheese is GOODT
     (@_Tamsey, Dec 25, 2012, Twitter)

(17) Badt Bitch. Attitude nesty.
     (@WhoseNELSON, May 25, 2015, Twitter)

(18) It's a brother nd sister thangk
     (@BobbyReefha, April 21, 2015, Twitter)

Note also, the orthographic representation of stereotypically 'Southern' vowels as well, in <nesty> for *nasty*,[31] and <thangk> for *thing*, as in <hayle> above. That speakers choose to represent their speech orthographically, and choose to do so in ways that serve to construct identity (cf. Childs, this volume), is not necessarily surprising.[32] That they have the phonological awareness to encode a regional vowel shift and to encode a speech sound that both lacks its own orthographic representation and is not phonemic – and to do so in a consistent and principled way – is impressive. A summary of the choices made by speakers is presented in Table 2.

---

**30** For instance, one of the more phonologically astute of the overtly racist definitions of *ebonics* on Urban Dictionary explains that to speak *ebonics*, one should "In a word ending in 'd,' substitute 'dt' or 'oodt.'" It goes on to dicuss r-deletion in non-rhotic varieties and consonant cluster reduction, in convoluted layman's terms. Url: http://www.urbandictionary.com/define.php?termebonics&defid661003

**31** The popular term *ratchet*, meaning 'uncouth' potentially originated hypercorrection from a southern pronunciation of *wretched*, although this is hotly contested, as by Palmer (2012; Warner 2015). There hasn't yet been an academic treatment of the word.

**32** It should be noted that one should expect a deegree of stylization and play. For some users, speech represented may be different than their "natural" speech, although the more data from a variety of sources one has, (i.e., video or audio of the person in question), the more confident one can be of the relationship between informal speech and informal writing for that person.

Table 2: Orthographic representations of glottal stops, by position in word

| Position | Choice | Orthography | Example |
|---|---|---|---|
| medial | deletion | <sumn>, <nuin>, <nun> | *I ain't worried bout nun* |
| medial | homorganic stop | <sumpn>, <sutn>, <suttin>, <nutn> | *shoulda grabbed sutn ta eat* |
| final | homorganic stop | <goodt>, <badt>, <thangk>, <lordt>, <cribp> | *Jus got to da cribp; Oh lordt!* |

Finally, it should be noted that there are instances where word final stops, usually the past -*ed* may be devoiced in AAE, and that care should be taken to separate the two phenomena when performing an analysis. So, <killt> for *killed*, <callt> for *called*, and <delivert> for *delivered* have unvoiced final stops, but may or may not have secondary glottalization. One finds both in the same text, as in:

(19)   LORDT. I am delivert!
       (@quigood, May 26, 2015, Twitter)

Both orthographic representation of word final devoicing and representation of secondary glottalization, it should be noted, seem to be highly salient to some speakers, and increasingly enregistered. While more research is needed, both can be described in broad strokes as indexing southern, church-going identity, even ironically as in (19), which is accompanied a risque image of a woman, and is reference to a popular video of a churchgoer claiming he's been *delivert* from homosexuality.[33]

# 8 Conclusions

Given the radical transformations in methods in linguistics in the past half century that accompanied the rise of generative and quantitative sociolinguistic approaches, and given the recent explosion in computer-mediated communication, it is practically *de rigeur* to formulate ever newer approaches to linguistic inquiry. However, it may be that we find ourselves in some ways tempted to reinvent the wheel. Perhaps because of CMC's relative recency and the fact that computational techniques are sometimes privileged when performing analyses of computer-mediated data, older methodologies have yet to be fully exploited.

---

[33] https//www.youtube.com/watch?v=OFtMVY-uD-0

CMC continues to be intensely studied by linguists and by computer scientists interested in language use, though there has been relatively little direct work on phonology, and the work examining orthography has typically been concerned with grouping orthographic strings to facilitate quantitative analyses. However, much of what has historically been treated as a problem to be solved can be seen as a gift to linguists in the form of a rich source of phonological information, albeit one that resists recent computational approaches.

As was shown above, we have the tools to evaluate CMC as a rich source of phonological information, and they have been validated by historical linguists and relied on for centuries. Here, they were applied to AAE on Twitter, because it is amenable to such an analysis, with a focus on parallels between AAE Tweets and Vulgar Latin graffiti. It was demonstrated that appeal to misspellings, puns, rhymes, poetic meter, borrowings, and complaints of pedants (where phonologically perceptive but sociolinguistically uninformed complaints on Urban Dictionary,[34] Reddit, and elsewhere serve as a parallel to the *Appendix Probi* and statements of the grammarians) can all provide information and corroborate phonological hypotheses. Moreover, linguists investigating CMC and textual communication are not limited to text, and can investigate the relationship between text and speech with other means, like video microblogs, where users can both write their words and speak them aloud. The value of such approaches was demonstrated with two case studies, focusing on liquids and glottal stops in computer mediated AAE. These principles are extendable to other dialects. For instance, Scottish English speaking users of Twitter writing *cannae*, etc. What's more, such tools can be used on other languages. As this chapter demonstrates, digital media don't just provide sociolinguists with rich texts for analysis of discourse and legitimacy practices, but informal CMC is also full of phonological data that linguists are only just beginning to explore.

# 9 References

Adams, James Noel. 2013. *Social variation and the Latin language*. Cambridge: Cambridge University Press.
Androutsopoulos, Jannis. 2011. Language change and digital media: A review of conceptions and evidence. In Tore Kristiansen & Nikolas Coupland (eds.), *Standard languages and language standards in a changing Europe*, 145–161. Novus: Oslo.
Androutsopoulos, Jannis K. 2000. Non-standard spellings in media texts: The case of German fanzines. *Journal of Sociolinguistics* 4(4). 514–33.

---

[34] Urban Dictionary is an online, "crowd-sourced" slang dictionary founded in 1999. http://wwww.urbandictionary.com

Anis, Jacques. 2007. Neography: unconventional spelling in French SMS text messages. In Brenda Danet & Susan C. Herring (eds.), *The multilingual internet: Language, culture, and communication online*, 87–115. New York: Oxford University Press.
Asur, Sitaram & Bernardo A. Huberman. 2010. Predicting the future with social media. In *Web Intelligence and Intelligent Agent Technology (WI-IAT), 2010 IEEE/WIC/ACM International Conference on*, vol. 1, 492–99. IEEE.
Bailey, Guy & Erik Thomas. 1998. Some aspects of African-American Vernacular English phonology. In Salikoko S. Mufwene, John R. Rickford, Guy Bailey & John Baugh (eds.), *African American English: Structure, history, and use*, 85–109. London/New York: Routledge.
Bamman, David, Jacob Eisenstein, & Tyler Schnoebelen. 2014. Gender identity and lexical variation in social media. *Journal of Sociolinguistics* 18(2). 135–60.
Barbieri, Francesco & Horacio Saggion. 2014. Modelling irony in Twitter. In *Proceedings of the Student Research Workshop at the 14th Conference of the European Chapter of the Association for Computational Linguistics*, 56–64.
Bollen, Johan, Huina Mao & Xiaojun Zeng. 2011. Twitter mood predicts the stock market. *Journal of Computational Science* 2(1). 1–8.
Brock, André. 2012. From the blackhand side: Twitter as a cultural conversation. *Journal of Broadcasting & Electronic Media* 56(4). 529–49.
Choney, Suzanne. 2012. It's a black Twitterverse, white people only live in it. *Today*. http://www.today.com/money/its-black-twitterverse-white-people-only-live-it-394051.
Chow, Kat. 2014. Researchers are totes studying how ppl shorter words on Twitter. *NPR's All Tech Considered*. http://www.npr.org/sections/alltechconsidered/2014/01/16/263096375/researchers-are-totes-studying-how-ppl-shorten-words-on-twitter
Clark, Meredith. 2014. To tweet our own cause: A mixed-methods study of the online phenomenon "Black Twitter." Chapel Hill: UNC Dissertation.
Doyle, Gabriel. 2014. Mapping dialectal variation by querying social media. In *Proceedings of EACL*, 98–106.
Duggan, Maeve & Aaron Smith. 2013. Social media update 2013. *Pew Internet and American Life Project*. http://www.pewinternet.org/2013/12/30/social-media-update-2013/
Eichstaedt, Johannes C., Andrew Schwartz Hansen, Margaret L. Kern, Gregory Park, Darwin R. Labarthe, Raina M. Merchant, Sneha Jha, et al. 2015. Psychological language on Twitter predicts county-level heart disease mortality. *Psychological Science* 26(2). 159–169.
Eisenstein, Jacob. 2013a. Phonological factors in social media writing. *Proceedings of the Workshop on Language Analysis in Social Media*, 11–19.
Eisenstein, Jacob. 2013b. What to do about bad language on the internet. In *Proceedings of HLT-NAACL*, 359–69.
Eisenstein, Jacob. 2014. Identifying regional dialects in online social media. Georgia Institute of Technology. http://www.cc.gatech.edu/~jeisenst/papers/dialectology-chapter.pdf
Ellis, Kimberly C. 2010. Why 'they' don't understand what black people do on Twitter. http://drgoddess.com/2010/08/blacktwitter/.
Gentry, Jeff. 2015. *TwitteR: R Based Twitter Client*. http://CRAN.R-project.org/package=twitteR.
González-Ibánez, Roberto, Smaranda Muresan & Nina Wacholder. 2011. Identifying sarcasm in Twitter: A closer look. *Proceedings of the 49th Annual Meeting of the Association for Computational Linguistics: Human Language Technologies: Short Papers-Volume 2*, 581–86. Association for Computational Linguistics.
Grandgent, Charles Hall. 1907. *An introduction to Vulgar Latin*. Boston: D.C. Heath & Company.

Green, Lisa. 1998. Aspect and predicate phrases in African-American Vernacular English. In Salikoko S. Mufwene, John R. Rickford, Guy Bailey & John Baugh (eds.), *African American English: Structure, history, and use*, 37–68. London: Routledge.

Green, Lisa J. 2002. *African American English: A linguistic introduction*. Cambridge: Cambridge University Press.

Han, Bo & Timothy Baldwin. 2011. Lexical normalisation of short text messages: Makn sens a# Twitter. *Proceedings of the 49th Annual Meeting of the Association for Computational Linguistics: Human Language Technologies-Volume 1*, 368–78. Association for Computational Linguistics.

Han, Bo, Paul Cook & Timothy Baldwin. 2013. Lexical normalization for social media text. *ACM Transactions on Intelligent Systems and Technology (TIST)* 4(1). 5.

Harber, Jean R. 1977. Influence of presentation dialect and orthographic form on reading performance of Black, inner-city children. *Educational Research Quarterly*.

Hart, Jane T., John T. Guthrie & Linda Winfield. 1980. Black English phonology and learning to read. *Journal of Educational Psychology* 72(5). 636.

Hill, Jane H. 2009. *The everyday language of White racism*. West Sussex: John Wiley & Sons.

Hoffberger, Chase. 2012. The demystification of Black Twitter. *The Daily Dot*. http://www.dailydot.com/society/black-twitter-dr-goddess/.

Hudley, Anne H. Charity & Christine Mallinson. 2011. *Understanding English language variation in US schools*. New York: Teachers College Press.

Jaffe, Alexandra. 2000. Introduction: Non-standard orthography and non-standard speech. *Journal of Sociolinguistics* 4(4). 497–513.

Jaffe, Alexandra. 2012. Transcription in practice: Nonstandard orthography. In Alexandra Jaffe, Jannis Androutsopoulos, Mark Sebba, & Sally Johnson (eds.), *Orthography as social action: Scripts, spelling, identity and power*, 203–224. Boston/Berlin: Walter de Gruyter.

Jones, Feminista. 2013. Is Twitter the Underground Railroad of activism? *Salon*. http://www.salon.com/2013/07/17/how_twitter_fuels_black_activism/.

Jones, Taylor. 2014. Obvs is phonological and it's totes legit. http://www.languagejones.com/blog-1/2014/5/26/obvs-is-phonological-and-its-totes-legit.

Jones, Taylor. 2015a. *Eem* negation in AAVE: A next step in Jespersen's cycle. In *Penn Linguistics Conference 39*.

Jones, Taylor. 2015b. Towards a description of AAVE dialect regions using "Black Twitter." *American Speech* 90(4). 403–440.

Jones, Taylor. 2015c. 'Yeen kno nun bout dat': Using Twitter to map AAVE dialect regions. Presentation at the Annual Meeting of the American Dialect Society, 2015. Portland, Oregon.

Jones, Taylor W. & Christopher S Hall. 2015. Semantic bleaching and the emergence of new pronouns in AAVE. In *LSA Annual Meeting Extended Abstracts* (6). 10–11.

Jones, William. 1806. A dissertation on the orthography of Asiatick words in Roman letters 1.

Kent, Roland Grubb. 1945. *The sounds of Latin: A descriptive and historical phonology*. Linguistic Society of America.

Kobus, Catherine, François Yvon & Géraldine Damnati. 2008. Normalizing SMS: Are two metaphors better than one? In *Proceedings of the 22nd International Conference on Computational Linguistics-Volume 1*, 441–48. Association for Computational Linguistics.

Kouloumpis, Efthymios, Theresa Wilson & Johanna Moore. 2011. Twitter sentiment analysis: The good the bad and the omg! *ICWSM* 11. 538–41.

Labov, William. 1972. *Language in the inner city: Studies in the Black English Vernacular*. Vol. 3. Philadelphia: University of Pennsylvania Press.

Labov, William & others. 1968. *A study of the non-standard English of Negro and Puerto Pican speakers in New York City. Volume I: Phonological and grammatical analysis.* ERIC.

Labov, William, Sharon Ash & Charles Boberg. 2005. *The Atlas of North American English: Phonetics, phonology and sound change.* Boston/Berlin: Walter de Gruyter.

Lane, Austin. 2014. 'You tryna grammaticalize?': An analysis of 'tryna' as a grammaticalized semi-auxiliary. *The Eagle Feather Undergraduate Research Journal.* The Honors College, University of North Texas.

Manjoo, Farhad. 2010. How black people use Twitter. *Slate.* http://www.slate.com/articles/technology/technology/2010/08/how_black_people_use_twitter.single.html.

McDonald, Soraya Nadia. 2014. Black Twitter: A virtual community ready to hashtag out a response to cultural issues. *The Washington Post.* http://www.washingtonpost.com/lifestyle/style/black-twitter-a-virtual-community-ready-to-hashtag-out-a-response-to-cultural-issues/2014/01/20/41ddacf6-7ec5-11e3-9556-4a4bf7bcbd84_story.html.

Melmed, Paul Jay. 1970. Black English phonology: The question of reading interference. ERIC.

O'Connor, Brendan, Ramnath Balasubramanyan, Bryan Routledge & Noah A Smith. 2010. From Tweets to polls: Linking text sentiment to public opinion time series. *ICWSM* 11. 122–29.

Palmer, Tamara. 2012. Who you calling ratchet? *The Root.* http://www.theroot.com/articles/culture/2012/10/where_the_word_ratchet_came_from.html.

Pang, Bo & Lillian Lee. 2008. Opinion mining and sentiment analysis. *Foundations and Trends in Information Retrieval* 2(1–2). 1–135.

Pope, Mildred Katharine. 1934. *From Latin to Modern French with especial consideration of Anglo-Norman: Phonology and morphology.* Manchester: Manchester University Press.

R Core Team. 2015. *R: A Language and Environment for Statistical Computing.* Vienna, Austria: R Foundation for Statistical Computing. https://www.R-project.org/.

Ramsey, Donovan X. 2015. The truth about Black Twitter: Complex, influential, and far more meaningful than the sum of its social justice-driven hashtags. *The Atlantic.* http://www.theatlantic.com/technology/archive/2015/04/the-truth-about-black-twitter/390120/.

Rao, Delip & David Yarowsky. 2010. Detecting latent user properties in social media. In *Proceedings of the NIPS MLSN Workshop.*

Reyes, Antonio, Paolo Rosso & Tony Veale. 2013. A multidimensional approach for detecting irony in Twitter. *Language Resources and Evaluation* 47(1). 239–68.

Rickford, John R. 1999. *African American Vernacular English: Features, evolution, educational implications.* Malden, MA: Blackwell.

Ronkin, Maggie & Helen E Karn. 1999. Mock Ebonics: Linguistic racism in parodies of Ebonics on the internet. *Journal of Sociolinguistics* 3(3). 360–80.

Shapp, Allison. 2015. Gender variation in the pragmatic uses of Twitter hashtags. Presentation at the LSA Annual Meeting. Portland, OR.

Sicha, Choire. 2009. What were black people talking about on Twitter last night? *The Awl.* http://www.theawl.com/2009/11/what-were-black-people-talking-about-on-twitter-last-night.

Simons, Herbert D & Kenneth R Johnson. 1974. Black English syntax and reading interference. *Research in the Teaching of English* 8. 339–58.

Solodow, Joseph B. 2010. *Latin alive: The survival of Latin in English and the Romance languages.* Cambridge: Cambridge University Press.

Spears, Arthur K. 1982. The Black English semi-auxiliary *come. Language* 58(4). 850–72.

Spradlin, Lauren. 2015. OMG the word-final alveopalatals are cray-cray prev: A morphophonological account of totes constructions in English. *University of Pennsylvania Working Papers in Linguistics* 22(1). 30.

Squires, Lauren. 2012. Whos punctuating what? Sociolinguistic variation in instant messaging. In Alexandra Jaffe, Jannis Androutsopoulos, Mark Sebba, & Sally Johnson (eds.), *Orthography as social action: Scripts, spelling, identity and power* (Language and Social Processes), 289–324. Berlin: Walter de Gruyter.

Reddy, Sravana, James Stanford & Joy Zhong. 2014. A Twitter-based study of newly formed clippings in American English. Presentation at the Annual Meeting of the American Dialect Society. Minneapolis, MN.

Sturtevant, Edgar Howard. 1920. *The pronunciation of Greek and Latin: The sounds and accents*. Chicago: University of Chicago Press.

Tagg, Caroline. 2009. A corpus linguistics study of SMS text messaging. Birmingham, UK: The University of Birmingham PhD dissertation.

Thompson, Connie A., Holly K. Craig & Julie A. Washington. 2004. Variable production of African American English across oracy and literacy contexts. *Language, Speech, and Hearing Services in Schools* 35(3). 269–82.

Tumasjan, Andranik, Timm Sprenger, Phillip G. Sandner & Isabelle Welp. 2010. Predicting elections with Twitter: What 140 characters reveal about political sentiment. *ICWSM* 10. 178–85.

Van Halteren, Hans & Nelleke Oostdijk. 2012. Towards identifying normal forms for various word form spellings on Twitter. *CLIN Journal* 2. 2–22.

Vosse, Theo. 1992. Detecting and correcting morpho-syntactic errors in real texts. In *Proceedings of the Third Conference on Applied Natural Language Processing*, 111–18. Association for Computational Linguistics.

Warner, Kristen J. 2015. They gon' think you loud regardless: Ratchetness, reality television, and black womanhood. *Camera Obscura: Feminism, Culture, and Media Studies* 30(1). 129–53.

Wolfram, Walt. 1994. The phonology of a sociocultural variety: The case of African American Vernacular English. In John E. Bernthal & Nicholas W. Bankson (eds.), *Child phonology: Characteristics, assessment, and intervention with special populations*, 227–44. New York: Thieme Medical Publishers.

Wolfram, Walter A. 1969. *A sociolinguistic description of Detroit Negro Speech*. Urban Language Series, No. 5. ERIC.

Cecelia Cutler
# "Ets jast ma booooooooooooo": Social meanings of Scottish accents on YouTube

## 1 Introduction

Following the release of the animated American film *Brave* in 2012, I asked my American friend's eleven-year-old daughter how she would feel about the female lead, Merida, having an American accent instead of a Scottish one. Without pause, she replied "no," because she hears American accents "all day long" and finds them "boring." Like many Americans, she may not even be able to distinguish Scottish accents from Irish or other British accents, but experiences them as a welcome departure from the everyday.

Starting with the epic success of the *Shrek* films featuring a large green ogre with a mild Scottish accent (*Shrek*, 2001; *Shrek 2*, 2004; *Shrek the Third*, 2007; and *Shrek Forever After*, 2010), Scottish-accented characters have made a string of appearances in a few other recent American children's animated films: Scottish accented Vikings in *How to Train Your Dragon* (2010) and *How to Train Your Dragon 2* (2014), and the Scottish accented Cornish sea Captain (Haddock) in *Tintin* (2011). Most recently the film *Brave* (2012) took the fascination with Scottish-ness to a new level by setting the film in medieval Scotland and giving all of the characters Scottish accents.[1] Disney executives, according to Cornwell (2012: 15), initially rejected the use of heavy Scottish accents in *Brave*, worrying that Americans wouldn't understand them, but these fears were eventually overcome by the pleas of the animation studio (Pixar) to strive for authenticity and realism. Reportedly, the desire for something "honest" trumped the fear that American audiences would be confused (Cornwell 2012: 15).

This chapter examines metalinguistic commentary and performances of Scottish accents in comments posted on YouTube in response to clips from three animated children's films: *How to Train Your Dragon* (2010), *Tintin* (2011), and *Brave* (2012). The comments contain non-standard orthography, metalinguistic/

---

[1] A longer list of films, novels, literature, table games, theater, TV shows, and video games featuring Scottish characters and associated tropes can be found at: http://tvtropes.org/pmwiki/pmwiki.php/Main/BraveScot

**Cecelia Cutler,** City University of New York, Lehman College

metapragmatic assessments, performances, and stylizations of Scottish accents (Androutsopoulos 2013a; Jaspers 2010; Rampton 2009). The analysis focuses on how Scottish accents are constructed and what kinds of social meanings are conveyed and spread through reflexive commentary on YouTube as a form of CMC.

Giroux (1997: 53) has argued that animated films are "teaching machines" and "producers of culture," "controlling fields of social meaning through which children negotiate the world" (cited in Lacroix 2004: 217). In animated films, language is used as a quick way to build character, getting viewers to "associate particular characters and life styles with specific social groups, by means of language variation" (Lippi-Green 1997: 85). Some prime examples in popular American animated films cited in Lippi-Green (1997) include the frequent use of Received Pronunciation (RP) and foreign accents for malevolent characters (e.g., the Arabic-accented characters in *Aladdin* 1992, and the RP speaking Cruella de Ville in *101 Dalmatians* 1961, 1996, 2000).[2] In her analysis of these and other films, Lippi-Green (1997: 85) concludes that accents in children's animated films reinforce stereotypes about particular groups of people, teaching children from a young age to form essentialized conceptions of people whose speech falls outside of the unmarked, mainstream variety.

Accents in films can have divergent functions. Giving characters different accents can simply be a way to indicate that they come from somewhere else (Androutsopoulos 2012 cited in Queen 2015: 157). However, it is also possible for actors to manipulate accents in the "construction of character" (Lippi-Green 2012: 208) which can potentially bring into play long-standing, essentialized stereotypes about groups of people. This is particularly noticeable in children's animated films, such as *Beauty and the Beast* (1991), in which stereotyped characters have French accents while "normal" characters have American accents even though the story is set in France. Accents can also mark differences in class and status. Brock (2011: 270) observes that the lower a character is on the social spectrum, the more pronounced his/her regional accent/dialect will often be.

To date, there has been no empirical attitudinal research on Americans' attitudes towards Scottish accents in YouTube comments.[3] This study examines

---

[2] It is important to note that RP accents are perceived as standard and authoritative for people outside of the US and do not generally index malevolent characters.

[3] It is not possible to definitively ascertain the nationality, ethnicity, gender, or age of any person who posts a comment on YouTube because users may not represent themselves truthfully or reveal anything about themselves at all, but the content of many of the comments analyzed here suggests and a good number are young, native speakers of English from the US.

the following questions: What role is YouTube playing in allowing viewers to engage with and respond to the filmic representations of Scottish accents and as a space where social meaning is negotiated? Secondly, taking YouTube viewers' perspectives into account, what language attitudes and ideologies are evident in the content of YouTube comments and in orthographic re-presentations of Scottish accents?

## 2 Language attitudes vis-à-vis Scottish accents

Research on attitudes towards varieties of English in the US and the UK focuses on a range of dimensions such as social attractiveness, pleasantness, prestige, likeability, friendliness, correctness, and status (Bishop, Coupland, and Garrett 2005; Cheyne 1970; Coupland and Bishop 2007; Giles 1970; Ladegaard 1998; Menzies 1991; Niedzielski and Preston 2003; Romaine 1980). This work suggests that most English speakers rank the standard variety highest in terms of correctness, prestige, and status, and their own variety (whether stigmatized or not) favorably in terms of likeability and pleasantness.

The same body of work shows that in the U.K., Scottish accents are evaluated very highly on measures of social attractiveness such as friendliness, but rather low in terms of status. Scottish English follows RP in trustworthiness and competence, but outscores it by a wide margin in terms of likeability (Giles 1970). Similar to the previous findings, Coupland and Bishop (2007) found that Scottish English along with Southern Irish English, and Edinburgh English in particular enjoy high ratings of social attractiveness *and* prestige. More recently, Hall-Lew, Fairs, and Lew (2015: 108) have shown that tourists experience Scottish accents as "pleasant, warm, and authentic" and that heavy Scottish accents in particular are associated with authenticity.

Articles in the mainstream print media in the U.K. discuss the desirability of Scottish accents in business and advertising. Rennie (2005) reports that more than half of British bosses regard someone with a Scottish accent as a high achiever, and as hardworking, industrious, and reliable. Not only do Scottish accents convey positive attributes of potential employees, they also help sell products. Advertisers in the UK and the US have been using Scottish accents for at least the past two decades to convey traditional attributes of honesty and reliability for a range of products including cars, lawn care products, incontinence pads, cell phone service, computers, and insurance (Elliott 2012; O'Shea 1999).

Scottish accents in English-language films and video games reveal a range of potential associations which largely corroborate previous empirical work on

English speakers' perceptions of Scottish as a socially attractive accent. Bratteli (2011) cites the Scottish-accented dwarves in *Lord of the Rings*, the fantasy game franchise *Warhammer* in the 80s and 90s, and the popular *World of Warcraft* (cf. Collister, this volume), linking the accent with mythical, temperamental mountainfolk, who are fond of beer, and spend their days mining ore and precious metals (36). However, in *Harry Potter* films, they index sophistication (Lundervold 2013: 63). An analysis of the attitudes towards Scottish in *Shrek* shows how the green ogre initially comes across as a scary outsider, but over the course of the film emerges as goodhearted, clever, and friendly (Harvey, Pretzsch and Snowman 2007: 58). Finally, Williams (1999), in line with Hall-Lew, Fairs, and Lew (2015), claims that Scottish accents in the films *Shrek* and in *Trainspotting* (1993) lend authenticity and realness to the characters who use them.

In sum, research on language attitudes shows that Scottish accents are seen as likeable, trustworthy, reliable, pleasant, warm and authentic, but lower status (vis-à-vis RP). In films, they may connote a slightly different set of meanings including emotional volatility, or high status and prestige. This chapter shows how YouTube comments are a bridge between people's perceptions as measured by the various studies on language attitudes cited above and media representations/products such as children's animated films, allowing us to observe viewers' self-generated responses to accents in "natural" settings, and giving a different perspective on the social meanings of Scottish English (ScE) accents.

## 3 Scottish English features

A range of ScE phonological features identified by Wells (1982), Stuart-Smith (2004), and Scobbie and Stuart-Smith (2008) is observable in the speech of Scottish-accented characters in the three films. The description of features below is not exhaustive, nor does it paint a complete picture of regional or social variation, or on-going changes in ScE (cf. Stuart-Smith, Timmins and Tweedie 2007). Rather, this cluster of features should be thought of as iconic or stereotypical of ScE, particularly for outsiders (i.e., non-Scots). These features include a range of rhotic variants: the now quite rare trilled [r], the post-alveolar approximant [ɹ], the retroflex approximant [ɻ], and tapped [ɾ] (Stuart-Smith 2004; Wells 1982: 410f).[4] The velar fricative /x/ (although rare in terms of its distribution) is another highly iconic feature used by characters in the films, occurring in words such as *loch* ('lake') and names like *Enoch*, although it is diminishing in the

---

4 Andersson (2009:12) observes that the hobbit Pippin and Gimli the dwarf in the film *Lord of the Rings* both use a clear Scottish accent, notable for its rhoticity and trilled /r/.

speech of younger Scots (Stuart-Smith, Timmins and Tweedie 2007) and even rural Scots (Marshall 2004, cited in Scobbie and Stuart-Smith 2008: 94).

Some of the stereotypical features of ScE tend to be working-class features. One example is /t/-glottaling in stressed intervocalic environments (*let it go*; [lɛʔ ɛt go]) (Stuart-Smith 2004). Another is the vowel in *foot* and *goose* which are both typically realized as [ʉ] in ScE, rather than the /ʊ/ – /uː/ distinction in American English (cf. Stuart-Smith 2004:60). The range of features used in the films also includes dark /l/, lowering and backing of /ɪ/ (towards /ɛ/), a centralized /au/ diphthong, monophthongal /e/ and /o/, and the realization of the first vowel in *person* as [ɛ]. There is also a non-phonemic pattern of vowel lengthening in pre-pausal position, before /r/, and before voiced fricatives (Aitkins law, cited in Wells 1982: 400), a feature that appears to be in decline among middle-class speakers (Stuart-Smith 2008: 58).

Miller (2008: 300) cites a number of "typical" ScE morphological and syntactic features, some of which are listed here. They include past tense verb forms that take regular endings (eg. *tell – tellt – tellt, sell – sellt – sellt* vs. *tell-told-told* and *sell-sold-sold*), past participle forms that are used to indicate past tense (*I seen it*; *He done it*), and preterite forms used in place of the past participle (*has broke*; *has went*). Additionally, the personal pronoun *yous* can be used as a plural of *you* (Miller 2008: 301). ScE negative forms may include the enclitic *-nae* (and its dialectal variants [ne], [nɪ] or [nɛ]) such that sentences like *He isn't coming, I can't go* and *It didn't help* are realized as *He isnae coming, I cannae go* and *It didnae help* (Miller 2008: 307). There is also a tendency in ScE speakers to use progressive verb forms more often with verbs of perception and verbs of mental activity than in other varieties of English (I *was hearing* you were late for school this morning; She's *knowing* the answer; He's *liking* this book) (Miller 2008: 307). Finally, there are a number of colloquial forms such as the use of singular nouns where other varieties of English require plural forms: *he weighs fifteen stone, five year ago, it's two meter long* (Miller 2008: 302).

There are also numerous recognizable Scottishisms (at least to North Americans) such as *wee* (small) *lassie/laddie* (boy/girl). Less well-known terms terms like *kirk* (church), *bairn* (small child) and *ken* (know) can still be heard in spoken ScE although they are becoming more rare (Corbett and Stuart-Smith 2012: 79–80). In the film *Brave* there were several more obscure Scottish expressions like *gobblywobbles* (nausea), *galoot* (oaf), and *numpty* (idiot), and exclamations such as "*Jings crivins, help ma boab!*" ('goodness gracious').[5]

---

[5] In their analysis of the Scottish Corpus of Text and Speech (Douglas 2003), Corbett and Stuart-Smith (2012) note that *bairn, kirk, lass*, and *ken* are used less often in spoken Scottish than their synonyms (child, church, girl, and know). Only *numpty* and *Help ma boab* appear in the Scottish Corpus of Text and Speech (http://www.scottishcorpus.ac.uk/).

In sum, film actors, dialect coaches, and directors can avail themselves of a large number of ScE features to index Scottish-identified characters or in other cases, traits and behaviors stereotypically associated with Scottishness. As mentioned earlier, film audiences in the US might not be aware that they are hearing ScE features, nor are the links to Scottish identities necessarily important in terms of the story. The analysis of YouTube comments will show that Scottish accents which already enjoy high ratings in terms of likeability, warmth, trustworthiness among English speakers, acquire additional albeit closely related social meanings for the mostly young, American audience posting comments on YouTube.

# 4 Theoretical orientation

Understanding the social meanings of Scottish accents for readers and writers of YouTube comments requires an analysis rooted in language ideologies (Schieffelin, Woolard and Kroskrity 1998; Irvine and Gal 2000) and indexicality (Ochs 1992). It also calls for an examination of stances or positions speakers take up with respect to the form or content of an utterance, and how stances are reflective of language attitudes. Higgins (2014) writes that "stance-taking towards languages and their speakers is an effective way of examining language attitudes since it allows us to see how individuals articulate their ideological convergences with respect to others" (18). A language ideology approach coupled with an examination of stance-taking can help explain how certain beliefs concerning people's behavior and language practices shape attitudes towards language varieties. Languages and linguistic features themselves can be vessels for a whole range of social meanings because of their indexical links to groups of people and groups' perceived traits and characteristics (Silverstein 2003). Thus, the alveolar variant of *-ing* in American English (e.g., *goin'*, *laughin'*), can convey low educational attainment and a "redneck" identity (Campbell-Kibler 2007: 32), but in other cases may simply index informality.

Ochs (1992) uses the terms *direct* and *indirect indexicality* to illustrate the ways in which linguistic forms are associated with social categories, stances, and the like. Her example is sentence-final particles in Japanese, which signal a stance of deference, but have come to be regarded as women's language because women are more likely than men to be deferential and use such forms. Thus, deference particles only indirectly index gender because the intermediate step from stance to identity is obscured (Bucholtz and Hall 2004; Ochs 1992). The process through which a particular language style such as "women's language" enters our social consciousness has been called "enregisterment" (Agha

2003; Johnstone 2008). Johnstone (2011: 4) observes that "[i]ndexical links between forms and meanings can be fleeting, idiosyncratic, and changeable," yet they are often created "in the context of already available cultural schemata." Animated films play a role in this process by building on prior conceptual links between accents and particular kinds of social traits and behaviors and by adding on new layers of social meaning.

Much of the uptake and replay of Scottish accents in YouTube comments focuses on how funny they sound, which makes them analyzable as speech play (cf. Jones and Schieffelin 2009: 1053). Speech play is a type of ludic performance in which elements of language are consciously manipulated in ways that push boundaries of what is "socially, culturally and linguistically possible" (Sherzer 2002: 1). Playful dialect performances and metalinguistic commentary are part of the enregistering process, further fixing viewers' associations between Scottish accents and particular social attributes. As Jones and Schieffelin (2009:1075) write, YouTube is an "inherently dialogic forum in which young people...can display, develop, and co-construct the meaning of preferential stylistic and communicative practices." Given that many Americans may struggle to distinguish different types of British accents (e.g., Irish vs. Scottish English), YouTube comments also work collectively to make Scottish accents more readily identifiable.

In the first two sections above, we saw that many people associate Scottish accents with authenticity, a concept that requires a bit of unpacking. Bucholtz and Hall (2004) note that authenticity may entail the idea that some identities are more "real" than others (385). Another way to think of authenticity is in terms of place, specifically a person's ties to a physical and/or "imagined" space. This involves the ability to claim that one's heritage and primary socialization has occurred in a specific community or geographical location, something that may be conveyed quite directly through one's accent or other dialectal features. Johnstone (2013: 13) discusses the link between cultural authenticity and place or the rootedness of generations in a particular geographic area: "Older social practices last longer in isolated places, where it is less likely that new practices will be imported" leading to the idea that some cultures are more authentic than others (2013: 4). Place also plays an important role in a number of subcultures, particularly in Hip Hop, where the "street" figures so prominently in the construction of authenticity (Alim 2002: 289; Cutler 2014: 41). Thus, a person's accent can potentially index a very specific place identity, entailing that he or she is a veritable representative of that place.

However, unlike stigmatized or undesirable accents like Cockney or Brooklynese which are also linked to specific places and groups of people (e.g. East London, working class, or Brooklyn, immigrant background, etc.), Scottish accents are linked to a highly desirable place that has been a destination for travellers for over three centuries (Rackwitz 2007). The Wikipedia entry for "Tourism in Scotland" describes it as "a clean, unspoilt destination with beautiful scenery which has a long and complex history, combined with thousands of historic sites and attractions." Consequently, Scottish accents are seen as authentic and desirable at least in part because of the way Scotland is conceived in the popular imaginary as ancient, pristine, and exotic. Scottish accents also index another set of social meanings linked to popular images of the Scots as warlike (*Braveheart*), sexually desirable (Sean Connery's role in the *James Bond* films, and the *Outlander* book series), culturally distinct practices like playing bagpipe music, wearing kilts and tartans, eating haggis, and sporting events like the Highland Games.

Lastly, this chapter draws on Jones and Schieffelin (2009) as a starting point for understanding how YouTube provides opportunities for "extending the media life of visual and verbal artifacts" and how this process provides "additional routes for entering into the public and popular circulation of ideas, images and talk" (Jones and Schieffelin 2009: 1060). Part of the reason that YouTube commenting forums are so effective at doing this is that they are relatively egalitarian, "democratic spaces" where metalinguistic views can be exchanged (Jones and Schieffelin 2009: 1062). At times, comments involve the policing of linguistic norms in ways that "reinforce the social meaning of variant forms" (Jones and Schieffelin 2009: 1074), but in the present data, most of the commentary is either performative or metalinguistic, pointing to the ways in which YouTube is implicated in the spread of language attitudes about English varieties.

## 5 Data and methodology

Exploring the relationship between speech forms or varieties and their social meanings involves tapping into people's overt and covert beliefs and attitudes about language. These can be gauged via direct and indirect approaches which either employ direct questioning about the meaning of linguistic variables or seek to tap into unconsciously-held beliefs (Garrett 2010). The present study employs an indirect approach, drawing on unsolicited, spontaneous metalinguistic and metapragmatic comments and performances of Scottish accents posted on YouTube in response to video clips from three animated films. This approach is similar to what Androutsopoulos (2013b) refers to as "screen based," involving qualitative analysis of YouTube videos and comment threads. As recommended by Androutsopoulos and Tereick (2015: 23), the analysis takes the videos as starting point, and then "oscillates between videos and comments in a circular manner."

The three films (*Brave*, *How to Train Your Dragon*, and *Tintin*) were initially chosen because they all featured at least one Scottish-accented character. The plots of these films are briefly described in Table 1.

Apart from Captain Haddock and Queen Elinor, these characters are highly exoticized through their dress, behavior, and speech patterns. The male figures,

**Table 1:** Film plot summaries

| Film | Storyline and accents |
|---|---|
| *How to Train Your Dragon* (2010) | The film takes place in a Viking island village plagued by dragons which the Vikings eventually domesticate and train; adults (Stoick the Vast, pictured on the extreme left and Gobber, on the right) have Scottish accents (voiced by Craig Ferguson, Gerard Butler). The lead character (Hiccup, pictured center left with father, Stoick) and other young people all have mainstream American accents. |
| *The Adventures of Tintin* (2011) | The story of young journalist, Tintin (right), who meets Captain Haddock (left) and discovers the lost treasure of the Unicorn. Captain Haddock, a Cornish sea captain (in the English language version), has a Scottish accent and is voiced by the English actor Andy Serkis. The lead character, Tintin, has an RP accent. |
| *Brave* (2012) | The story of a young Scottish princess, Merida, (pictured above) and her efforts to resist being married off to the son of one of her father, King Fergus' (pictured below left) allies. The entire cast, including the protagonist Merida, have Scottish accents. The lead actors are Scottish (Kelly MacDonald, Billy Connolly, Craig Ferguson, Robbie Coltrane), except Queen Elinor (below right) who is voiced by the English actress Emma Thompson. |

Stoick the Vast, Gobber and King Fergus, are physically imposing warriors sporting furs, leather, helmets and weapons and heavy Scottish accents (trilled and tapped /r/s, monophthongal, lengthened vowels, ScE phrasing and lexis). The main female character embodied by young Merida is self-confident and boyish with a giant mop of unruly red curls and world-class archery skills. Her accent is notable for its lengthened vowels, tapped /r/, and unique lexical expressions (*Jings crivins, help ma boab*!). Queen Elinor makes minimal use of ScE features (dark /l/, softly tapped /r/, and slight vowel lengthening) which helps to establish her role as a model of proper speech and behavior for her daughter Merida. Like Queen Elinor, Captain Haddock in *Tintin* is voiced by a non-Scottish actor who uses ScE features less frequently and more subtly than Stoick, Gobber, and Fergus (tapped /r/ and slightly lengthened monophthongal vowels). Compared with his Scottish-accented counterparts in *How to Train Your Dragon*, Captain Haddock dresses in a more conventional way, but embodies similar traits like gruffness, valor, and loyalty. Part of Haddock's appeal is his crusty exterior and alliterative but inoffensive cursing. On the whole, these are appealing characters whose allure lies in their good-heartedness, loyalty, bravery, and charm.

There are hundreds of clips from these films posted on YouTube accompanied by thousands of YouTube comments. A number of keyword searches in the comments sections following various video clips from the films turned up five YouTube video clips containing metalinguistic and metadiscursive commentary and other responses to, and/or performances of Scottish accents (see Table 2). These five video clips generated a total of 754 comments, 80 of which make specific mention of Scottish accents or identities, or performances of Scottish accents. All of the comments were collected in September, 2013.

The two clips from *Brave* include a dinner scene in which the heroine Merida is admonished by her mother for laying her bow on the table; the second clip features an archery contest in which several suitors vying for her hand in marriage are defeated by Merida. The clip from *Tintin* is one in which Captain Haddock and Tintin have just met aboard a ship and are trying to escape the mutinous crew. The clips for *How to Train Your Dragon* (*HTTYD*) are not actually from the film itself: one contains interviews with the lead actors including Gerard Butler who voices the Viking village chief Stoick the Vast; the second clip shows the actors from the same film rehearsing a scene in a sound studio.

Within the 80 YouTube comments, six groups of closely related comments were identified which I have termed "speech chains" (Agha 2003) because they involve the transmission of accent values via accent metadiscourse from the "sender" or writer of the comment to the various "receivers" who read it (Table 3). Although these comments were posted by individuals separated by time and space and are non-sequential in the longer list of comments, they build on

**Table 2:** List of video clips and YouTube comments

| Film/Clip | Comments relating directly to Scottish accents N = | Total # of comments N = |
|---|---|---|
| *Brave* – Dinner scene http://www.youtube.com/watch?v=-p14unwrao | 19 | 80 |
| *Brave* – Archery scene https://www.youtube.com/watch?v=5ZDRjblUHJg | 3 | 72 |
| *The Adventures of Tintin* – Captain Haddock and Tintin escaping captivity on the ship http://www.youtube.com/watch?v=Er3IkyPus9o | 2 | 61 |
| *How to train your dragon* – Rehearsal clip http://www.youtube.com/watch?v=MCQGPwssinc | 43 | 225 |
| *How to train your dragon* – Interviews with actors clip https://www.youtube.com/watch?v=J-M6hR6ihF0 | 13 | 316 |
| TOTAL | 80 | 754 |

one another to enregister ScE with a range of social meanings. The individuals who wrote the comments constitute a "speech chain network" (Agha 2003: 248) insofar as they "have something common" in their discursive history, namely having viewed the same YouTube video clip and having read many of the same comments. The six speech chains selected for analysis all contain direct references to ScE as an accent or speech variety, whether to perform it for the enjoyment of others in the YouTube speech chain network, negotiate its status, and/or instill it with various social meanings.

**Table 3:** Speech chains

| Speech chain | Examples |
|---|---|
| 1. Dialect performances | 2–16 |
| 2. Accent confusion | 17–21 |
| 3. Sociolinguistic disorder | 22–32 |
| 4. Scottish accents as desirable | 33–36 |
| 5. Scottish accents as sexy | 37–44 |
| 6. Scottish accents as cute | 45–48 |

Each comment can be thought of as a "small story" (Georgakopoulou 2006) or a "small performance" (Deumert 2014: 110–111), allowing authors to share thoughts and opinions, display special knowledge, take stances, project their identities, and/or perform their linguistic skills for an audience (Androutsopoulos and Tereick 2015; Chun and Walters 2011). One salient feature of many of these YouTube comments is their poetic aspect as performances of a dialect (Androutsopoulos 2013a). Many contain unconventional spelling patterns that reflect a number of functions identified in previous work on CMC writing: creativity, expressions of personality, affect, emotional involvement, and informality (Danet et al. 1997; Darics 2013; Jones and Schieffelin 2009; Peuronen 2011). Some examples appear to be attempts to render spoken words (cf. Cho 2010; Herring 2012; Soffer 2010) while others seem to stereotype and position ScE in contrast to commenters' own speech or what they conceive of as standard (American) English (cf. Hinrichs and White-Sustaíta 2011; Jaffe and Walton 2000). These performances are not only entertaining; they also provide what Jones and Schieffelin (2009) call "resources for further verbal play" as well as "an impetus for metalinguistic commentary and assessment" (1075).

Dialect performances are often rendered via non-standard orthography which includes prosodic spellings, letter repetitions, expressive respellings, capitalization, and serial punctuation. Strategies like prosodic spelling (the use of capitalization or serial graphemes) are sometimes used as a way to draw attention to the words on the page rather than accurately represent vowel quality or vowel length in the spoken words themselves (Androutsopoulos 2013a; Darics 2013). Indeed, Darics (2013: 144–145) has argued that letter repetition is often a contextualization cue that signals how the reader/receiver should interpret the message rather than as an attempt to render pronunciation. Shaw (2008: 2) uses the term "expressive respellings" for visually iconic but unpronounceable forms like <luvvvv> and <yhuu>. Some additional features that CMC researchers have examined include the use of capitalization, reduplicated letters, and exclamation points to encode increased volume, pitch emphasis, or strong affective stances (Chun and Walters 2011: 264).

Besides non-standard spelling and punctuation, YouTube comments have been shown to exploit a range of affective markers such as laughter variants (e.g., *lol, haha*) and emoticons (e.g., smile emoticons like : D) (Squires, this volume; Jones and Schieffelin 2009). Emoticons, thought to be more characteristic of female CMC users (Baron and Ling 2011), are often described as tools for conveying facial expressions that are typical of face-to-face communication. However, others have pointed out that there may also be a range of illocutionary functions such as downplaying the force of an utterance or altering its pragmatic meaning (Dresner and Herring 2010).

# 6 Analysis

## 6.1 Dialect performances: *It's just ma bow!* meme

The examples analyzed in (2)–(15) below illustrate how non-standard orthography in YouTube comments is used as a resource for expressing performing and expressing stances towards ScE (cf. Childs, this volume). The first set of examples comes from a speech chain of 14 comments posted in response to a scene from *Brave* in which the adolescent heroine (and expert archer) Merida emphatically protests her mother's request that she remove her bow from the dinner table in deference to proper ladylike behavior. A transcript of the exchange appears in example (1). Merida's utterance is transcribed in IPA because her words (not Queen Elinor's) are the subject of a series of YouTube comments in examples (2)-(15).

(1) Scene from *Brave* (2012)
  Queen Elinor: Merida, a princess does not place her weapons on the table.
  Merida: Mom, it's just my bow!
  [mö:::m ɛts dʒʌs mɑ bə:::]

The comments posted in response to this clip (and all of the others discussed below) are listed in reverse chronological order from oldest to newest. They are non-contiguous in the longer list of comments but are often clearly dialogic in terms of content and style and retain a high degree of topic coherence and responsive turn-taking (Jones and Schieffelin 2009: 1063).

The first speech chain, in (2)–(15), consists of increasingly exaggerated renditions of Merida's utterance, "it's just my bow." The first comment, shown in (2), establishes a humorous key that frames subsequent comments with the laughter variant <Haha> and the smile emoticon <:D>.

(2) Ryan Frankland
  Haha "Mom, it's just my bow" I laughed for five minutes after that :D

Subsequent comments are increasingly ludic and experimental, showing how YouTubers engage in hyperbolic one-upmanship in their increasingly lengthy renditions of *bow*. Together, they co-construct Scottish English as funny-sounding, but also aesthetically pleasing as each author "tries on" the accent, and attempts to "create the experience of the spoken word" (Soffer 2010: 313, cited in Darics 2013: 143).

(3) Loserlykewhoaa
"booohhhhhhhww."

(4) clamchowder138
MOOOOOM, es jus' mah BOOO.
Best part of the movie.

(5) cplanner87
Mum* not mom

(6) bryan collado
MUUUUUUUUUUUUMMMMMMMMMMM.........ITSSSSSSSSSSSSSSS
JUSSSSSSSTTTTTTTTTT MYYYYYYYYYYYYYYY
BBBBBBBBBUUUUUUUUWWWWWWWWWWWW!!!!!!!!!!!!!!!!!!!!!

Viewed as dialect performances, most of the comments concentrate on Merida's lengthened monophthongal realization of the vowels in *mom*, *my*, and *bow*, using serial vowels, capitalization, and letter repetition to represent perceived vocalic and prosodic contrasts. Respelling the sounds one hears is an inexact and highly subjective art, and spelling conventions interfere with what people think they are hearing (cf. Garley 2014), so it is perhaps not surprising to see seven different variants in the spelling of *mom* (<mom>, <moOOOOM>, <Mum>, <MUUUUUUUUUUUUMMMMMMMMMMM>, <mooom>, <Maaaaam>, and <maaaaam>). In (5), we see an example of policing of British orthographic conventions in the assertion that the word should be written as <mum> instead of <mom>, a repair that cplanner87 mitigates with a <*>. The rising number of vowels in subsequent renditions of *mom* across the speech chain suggests that non-standard spellings also serve a visual function by grabbing other YouTubers' attention with longer and longer strings of vowels and consonants. The repetition of these creative spellings creates "an aesthetic or stylistic coherence" by mirroring the content and genre of other comments (Jones and Schieffelin 2009: 1063).

(7) DerpyEponine
"Merida a princess does not place her awards on the table." "Mooom,
It's just mah glooooobe."

(8) DMTfan
Mah booooo – sexy!

(9) PsychedelicSouljam29
Booohhhwwww

(10) TheMrsGaskarth1
Maaaaam et's just ma boooooohw.

(11) armedana
I'ts just my booooohhww

(12) JacksonKovacs
mum its just me booooooooooooooohhhhhhhwwwwwwww

(13) KingRaven101
maaaaam es jes ma booooooooooooo

(14) BlackAndWhite9999
ets jast ma booooooooooooo

(15) Naithon Rodriguez
it hust my booooowwwww

Non-standard spellings of *bow* range from 3–15 <o>s and/or <u>s. The use of serial vowels may again reflect an auditory perception of the monophthongal, lengthened quality of the vowel in *bow*, and the addition of multiple <h>s and <w>s – as (3), (6), (9)–(12), and (15) – may be an effort to symbolize the fronting of /o/. Posters also highlight the lowering of /ɪ/ in *it's* which is spelled <es> or <ets> in (4), (10), (13), and (14). These attempts to render ScE vowels point to the limitations of standard orthography to map directly onto the sounds of these words (cf. Jones, this volume). Yet the resulting playful spellings often go beyond attempts to represent unfamiliar sounds, encoding affective responses that frame ScE as a humorous, delightful, and desirable language. The recurring performances of "it's just my bow" show how participants align themselves with Merida in their dialectal revoicings of her utterance, but also provide a means for participants to signal stances towards this way of speaking.

Another locus for dialect performance is the first person possessive pronoun which takes a variety of forms in these comments: <mah>, <ma>, <MYYYYYYYYYYYYYYY>, and <me>. The first two variants, <mah> and <ma> ((7), (8), and (10)), come closest to the actor's monophthongal realization of the /aɪ/ diphthong in *my* ([mɑ]). The third variant, in (6), <MYYYYYYYYYYYYYYY>, appears to be another example of prosodic spelling, but on closer examination there is no relationship between the spelling and the monophthongal, unstressed realization in the video. Rather, it seems to serve a playful, visual, and aesthetic function like the other words in the utterance which all contain multiple and thus unpronounceable consonants. The fourth variant, <me>, in (12) picks up on a feature of northern British varieties that use the objective rather than the possessive pronoun (e.g., *Me* house) (Schneider 2011: 75). Here, the use of <me> lumps ScE in with regional varieties, marking them as collectively deviant and erasing differences between them.

The sociopragmatic function of the prosodic spelling patterns we see here could be what Androutsopoulos (2000: 517) has dubbed "graphemic contextualization cues," or devices for cuing various affective stances towards an utterance (cf. Darics 2013). In this data, creative spellings such as <moOOOOM> or <Booohhhwwww> contextualize YouTube comments as an informal space for playful experimentation with language. Capitalization as in (4) and (6) may encode word stress, but perhaps also volume or emphatic delivery. Serial punctuation as in (6) plays a similar role, but may also reveal an authorial stance of delight and aesthetic pleasure, possibly substituting for facial expressions (Bieswanger 2013). This stance is reinforced in the content of (7), where DerpyEponine recontextualizes the exchange between Merida and her mother as an imaginary awards ceremony, thus positioning Merida's linguistic performance as worthy of a <glooooobe> award.

A similar instance of vowel lengthening appears in a viewer comment responding to a YouTube clip of Gerard Butler rehearsing his lines for *HTTYD* in (16). Rather than repeat the actor's lines, however, the comment is a first person utterance, commending Gerard Butler on his performance, with a Scottish twist. Using prosodic spelling, the lengthened, monophthongal vowel in *best* is represented via serial vowel graphemes that seem to map backwards onto the spelling of *the*. Smile emoticons accompany the utterance, establishing a humorous key and cuing other readers that this is a dialect performance.

(16)  Raudifan 2 years ago
      Ohh Gerard! :D Yorue thee beeest :)

In sum, prosodic and creative respellings, serial punctuation, capitalization and other affective markers show how YouTubers are fascinated by the unfamiliar accents they hear in the video clips and how they resort to a range of creative attempts to represent and perform them for their own pleasure and for the enjoyment of others. YouTubers respond to each other's posts dialogically, each attempting to make his or her own version more visually and auditorily distinctive. Collectively, they paint a picture of Scottish accents as strange-sounding, exotic, and even sexy. The comments in the speech chain show how YouTubers feel about ScE; they embrace the accent and align themselves with it in their performances. Their orthographic representations of ScE signal positive affective stances towards ScE and its speakers as YouTubers celebrate and delight in the pleasure of revoicing memorable lines from the film. As in the playful reworkings of texting language described by Jones and Schieffelin (2009), young people engage with the content of YouTube videos through speech play and performance, co-constructing ScE, in the present data, as an oddly intriguing, but also cool, accent.

## 6.2 Accent confusion: Scottish or Irish?

The previous section focused on how YouTubers represent Scottish accents orthographically and the kinds of stances these creative orthographies reveal vis-à-vis ScE. The next three sections look at the ways in which metalinguistic and metapragmatic comments reveal the kinds of social meanings being enregistered. In (17)-(21), there was confusion between Irish and Scottish accents. In (17), 1PSYTEX1 exclaims in all uppercase letters emphatic enthusiasm for the Irish accent, but is corrected by 1clackie in (18) and admonished by Jack Bosworth in (19). In (20) and (21), FireWrathAK riffs on the "It's just my bow" meme, to express a desire to visit Ireland to which Merel Dongelmans replies <*Scotland> where the star symbol functions to soften the repair (Collister 2012).

(17) 1PSYTEX1
Irish = THE MOST BADASS AXCENT/LANGUAGE EVER!

(18) 1clackie
in reply to 1PSYTEX1
@1PSYTEX1 it's scottish

(19) Jack Bosworth
in reply to 1PSYTEX1
@1PSYTEX1 Irish? what are you on...?

(20) FireWrathAK
it's jus mah bauh. I love the accent. Someday I will go to Ireland.

(21) Merel Dongelmans
in reply to FireWrathAK
*Scotland

These examples also illustrate what Martin and White (2005) call "stances of appreciation" in which speakers evaluate aesthetic and social value of a speech variety. Statements such as <THE MOST BADASS AXCENT LANGUAGE EVER!> and <I love the accent.>, although mistakenly referring to Irish, are further instantiations of stances that place value on ScE as an aesthetically pleasing language and as a commodity linked to tourism.

## 6.3 Sociolinguistic disorder

The sociolinguistic distribution of Scottish and American accents is great fodder for commentary in the next two speech chains. The fact that Vikings in *HTTYD* are given Scottish accents provides an opportunity for bemused metalinguistic remarks. In (22)-(25), okcatluv, badboy69yoda and chillaxtv use laughter (<D:>), affect markers (<lol>), an elongated discourse marker (<sooooooooo>), and serial punctuation (<???>) to express bewilderment about Vikings having Scottish accents. Bloodthirst1101, who might be Scandinavian judging from his comment, takes the opportunity to bash Americans for their ignorance of geography and culture outside of the US.

(22) okcatluv
Love Scottish accents...but...since when were the Vikings Scottish???

(23) gamesaddict
lol scottish vikings

(24) badboy69yoda
sooooooooo why do vikings always have Scottish accents????

(25) chillaxtv
Whats with all the Scottish actors doing the Vikings D:

(26) Bloodthirst1011
because Americans think all Scandinavian people are the same. Hell i take that back, they dont even know what Scandinavia is.
in reply to chillaxtv

Using Standard American accents for protagonists is a common strategy in American children's animated films while antagonists are given other accents (Queen 2015: 160). In *HTTYD*, Scottish accents index an exotic (non-Scottish) European ethnicity, but they also signal the generational divide between adolescents and adults. In (27)–(32), YouTubers find it jarring that the adult Vikings have Scottish accents, while the adolescents sound American. While willkillyoulast appears not to mind, the others find it difficult to suspend belief about this sort of accent variation, noting that it defies logic that most people have the same ethnic and/or geographical accent as their parents. Mark Boston finds that American accents are somehow inappropriate and inauthentic for representing Viking characters (28). These comments show that filmgoers do not always agree with the ways in which accents are distributed in films, even when the characters they are meant to identify with are given familiar (American) accents.

(27) pyradragon
Why do the adult characters have a Irish/Scottish accent and the tenns are american?

(28) Mark Boston
Notice how all the younger vikings were strangely american. Ruins the effect of the Vikings for me.

(29) anaHajar
Why does hiccup and his girlfriend do not speak in scottish accent?

(30) axlis123
you know whats weird? the adults have the accent but the kids dont.

(31) oneworldfamily
I love this film just as much as anyone. But at what point in the child characters' life do they lose the American accents and gain Scottish ones? That was the weirdest and most constantly unavoidable thing about this film.

(32) willkillyoulast
Yeah that got to me too...I mean, Hiccup grew up surrounded byt adults with very thick Scottish accents, yet he has a full-blown American one...as do some of the others. But I don't care somehow haha, it annoyed me at the start, but I enjoyed the movie so much I eventually forgot all about that.

## 6.4 Scottish accents as desirable, sexy and cute

The next three speech chains contain metalinguistic expressions of longing and desire for Scottish accents and Scottish identities, often closely tied to the appeal of Scottish-born actors like Gerard Butler (Stoick the Vast in *HTTYD*) and Kelly MacDonald (Merida in *Brave*), but also in ways that commodify Scottish accents and Scotland. The success of *Brave* has generated a flurry of tourism to Scotland, thanks to a joint venture between the Scottish tourist board (VisitScotland) and Disney (McKenzie 2013). The post-*Brave* rage for things Scottish and the commodification (cf. Heller 2010; King and Wicks 2009) of Scottish accents are reflected in the fourth speech chain in (33)–(36). scottduddy claims a Scottish identity, but tries to show humility via an affect emoticon (<-.->) which connotes shame or embarrassment to which jennifer marion replies <Lucky!>. The last two comments fetishize Scottish accents as cool and unique and downgrade American and Australian accents as <old> and indistinctive (<my whatever-the-hell-it-is accent>). Again we see stances of appreciation in the social valuing of Scottish identities accents as something desirable (<cool>, <I wish I had one...>) and even consumable (<I really can't wait to hear their accents>) (cf. Collister, this volume).

(33)  scottduddy
      I'm Scottish -.- ....

(34)  jennifer marion
      Lucky! in reply to scottduddy

(35)  BekahIris
      I'm actually traveling to Scotland in about a week, and I really can't wait to hear their accents. I wish my American/Texan/whatever-the-hell-it-is accent was as cool as theirs! D:

(36)  jeramahia123
      I love scottish accents. I wish I had one and not my old Australian accent.

In the fifth speech chain, shown in (37)–(44), commenters enregister ScE with even stronger emotions, at times conflating the allure of well-known actors like Gerard Butler and Craig Ferguson in *HTTYD*, with the appeal of their accents. As noted above, the "sexy Highlander" has been a long-standing fixture of romance novels at least since the Outlander series which first appeared in 1991. This may partly explain why Scottish actors and Scottish accents are seen as sexy even though the characters they voice do not dress or behave in seductive ways. jonnyjumpsalot frames Butler's and Ferguson's performances as a turn on for women of any age (up to 54), and le tiff implies that Craig Ferguson's Scottish accent causes (possibly homoerotic?) sexual arousal. KaZhKaZ aligns his own voice with that of a Scottish-accented speaker via non-standard orthography (<Foking>, <luv>, and <tha'>) to signal a ribald approval in a uni-directional double-voicing sense (Bakhtin 1984), and dtcgirly does something similar with the Scottish lexical form <aye> to express affirmation and approval. Ruennie bestows the honor of <sexiest vikings ever> on Gerard Butler and Craig Ferguson, and the last four posts give props to Scottish accents with the smile (<: D>) and surprise (<O O>) emoticons. As in previous speech chains, YouTubers express positive affective stances towards Scottish accents in their lexical choices (ie. various forms of 'love' in (39), (41), and (43)) and temporal markers like <now> as in (41) which convey a newfound appreciation for ScE.

(37) jonnyjumpsalot
This video is most popular with:
Gender Age
Female 13–17
Female 18–24
Female 45–54

(38) le tiff
Craig with heavy accent…be still my pants.

(39) KaZhKaZ
2:36–3:30 the best! Foking luv tha' accent :D

(40) Ruennie
Gerard and Craig…sexiest vikings ever! :D

(41) peaceluvfever825 2 years ago
Totally in love with Scottish accents now.

(42) Nizzie Fino
Lovethe accent.

(43) MissBananaHappy
Scottish accent O O

(44) dtcgirly
Aye on the Scottish accents!

In the last speech chain in (45)–(48), a Swedish girl and two other young women construct ScE as an asset that can transcend objectionable traits like drinking too much. lotten1992, voices uncertainty about the origin of Captain Haddock's accent in *Tintin* and satisfaction that she has seen the film in the original English version. (He was given a Gothenburg or Skåne accent in the Swedish language version.[6]) She then asks if it is wrong that she finds Captain Haddock <attractive> which she says is partly due to his accent. She is reassured by CaptainHooksGirl who finds Haddock <cute> for the same reason.

---

6 The use of the Skåne dialect in the Swedish language version to voice Haddock lends a regional, slightly lower status and vernacular flavor to his speech that parallels the position of Scottish vis-à-vis RP in the U.K. (Unn Røyneland, personal communication).

(45) lotten1992
Andy Serkis was THE perfect choice for Capt. Haddock
He's right now my fav-actor, and Capt. Haddock is my fav-character in this movie
i can't wait for the sequel, i'm all on pins and needles.
i'm very thankful to have seen this movie in original-language, not in Swedish, 'cause Capt. Haddock
doesn't have a Gothenburg-dialect, though i'm curious. *What accent does he have in this movie?* [my emphasis]

(46) Hanna
*Capt. Haddock has a Scottish accent* [my emphasis] in this movie (from Scotland, United Kingdom).
I can't wait for the sequel either! :) Jamie Bell and Andy Serkis were both amazing in their roles as Haddock and Tintin.

(47) lotten1992
*is it wrong that i find Capt. Haddock attractive? I think it must be the accent* [my emphasis], beard, Andy Serkis voice and that he's a captain (if i look away the fact that he drinks alot), but i think i'm the only one.

(48) CaptainHooksGirl
No, you're not the only one.... Though Hook will always be my favorite captain, Haddock is definitely a very close second. ;) *I think it's the accent combined with the fact that he's just so clueless sometimes that makes him cute.* [my emphasis] · in reply to lotten1992

The previous four sections show how YouTubers expressive positive affective stances towards ScE in their hyperbolic performances of the dialect and in their metalinguistic expressions of appreciation and desire for ScE. The final section offers a discussion of the significance of these observations in terms of the research questions.

# 7 Discussion and conclusion

The foregoing data and analysis point to the role that YouTube is currently playing in allowing viewers to engage with and respond to language variation. The YouTube comment space has emerged as a site where the social meaning of languages and language varieties is negotiated. Attitudes and ideologies vis-a-vis Scottish accents appear in YouTubers' performative renditions of ScE utterances and in their metalinguistic commentary. The "small stories" contained in the

YouTube comments shown above provide a rich source of user-generated attitudinal data that can complement matched guise tests and large-scale language attitude surveys by giving us a window into unsolicited, spontaneous responses to accents. Broadly speaking, the data reinforce stereotyped perceptions of ScE as a socially attractive dialect. We saw these attitudes displayed in the use of creative orthography and various CMC conventions such as prosodic and expressive respellings, capitalization, serial punctuation, laughter variants, and emoticons. We observed how YouTubers' re-presentations of ScE are particularly attuned to the differences in vowel quality that distinguish Scottish accents from their own (presumably mostly American) vowel systems. Yet the function of these performances seems to be to create a visual impact rather than to faithfully render the accent. Hyperbolic letter repetition, smile and laughter emoticons, and affective comments signal highly affirmative stances which replicate the high ratings given to ScE in terms of prestige and social attractiveness in previous attitudinal research. These performances also help construct YouTube as a space for language and metalinguistic play (Jones and Schieffelin 2009: 1063) where young people can "display, develop, and co-construct" the meaning of styles and communicative practices (Jones and Schieffelin 2009: 1075; Sherzer 2002). In this creative space, participants can manipulate elements of language, try on accents, experiment with creative spelling, and draw on a growing repertoire of affective markers to lend their comments greater expressivity.

Dialect performances and the stances they embody are ideological, drawing on and reshaping ideas about a speech variety and its social meanings (Johnstone and Baumgardt 2004). The didactic and enregistering functions of the YouTube comment space are apparent in the second speech chain as commenters sort out what kind of accent they are hearing and express a newfound awareness of Scottish accents in affective comments such as <Totally in love with Scottish accent now>. The temporal marker <now> shows how attitudes towards ScE spread from user to user, highlighting the role of YouTube in the dissemination of language attitudes more broadly. The confusion between Scottish and Irish accents gets worked out in overt "corrective feedback" (Lyster and Ranta 1997), helping to make Scottish accents more recognizable and more readily identifiable for YouTube viewers. The enregisterment of the accents in this identification phase establishes a platform onto which social meanings can be layered in other speech chains.

The YouTube comment space is also a forum for metalinguistic and metapragmatic discussions about language norms and expectations. Some YouTubers found it <annoying> and <weird> that the adult characters in *HTTYD* have Scottish accents while the younger Vikings sound <strangely American>. Although they express positive stances towards ScE accents on the whole, they have quite negative reactions to the mixing of accents within onscreen families in *HTTYD*. However, other work has shown that the violation of sociolinguistic norms is not always met with disapproval. Jones and Schieffelin (2009) describe the delight that YouTubers expressed upon viewing a similar violation of everyday language conventions such as a grandmother who texts <ONUD> ('Oh no you didn't') in an AT&T television commercial (1072). Thus, there is no way to generalize about how YouTubers will respond to unexpected language use or other sociolinguistic patterns. YouTube has simply become a space where accents, norms, trends, and the like can be discussed, flaunted, policed, and/or celebrated.

Finally, YouTube is a place where languages and accents can undergo commodification. This was evident in the fourth speech chain where ScE was enregistered with meanings related to Scotland as a desirable tourist destination where people have interesting accents (Hall-Lew, Fairs, and Lew 2015; Heller 2010; King and Wicks 2009). We also saw how some YouTubers long to possess Scottish accents. The framing of Scottish accents as <sexy> and <cute> is linked to the appeal of the actors who voiced them while also referencing older, well-established meanings like the "sexy Highlander." Here, the sexiness of ScE gets mapped onto the unbridled masculinity of Stoick the Vast, Gobber, and King Fergus, the inebriated bravado of Captain Haddock, and the gamine assertiveness of Merida. These social meanings are repeated and reworked in various ways throughout the various speech chains, constructing and reinforcing a collective understanding of ScE among YouTubers.

User-generated content such as comments posted on YouTube represent a confluence of mass media and the online digital world, giving ordinary people a chance to broadcast their own interpretations and performances of mass media content and language use. Here, the dialogic potential of YouTube is a vast marketplace for language-related activity (language teaching and learning, language play, dialect and second language performance, mash-ups, redubbings, etc). Video clips containing non-standard or non-local accents frequently elicit metalinguistic and metapragmatic commentary as well as attempts to represent or perform them (cf. Androutsopoulos 2013a). Importantly, the YouTube comment space is a site where dialect features and accents become "socially noticed" or enregistered (Agha 2003) and where social meanings are shaped and language attitudes spread (cf. Heyd, this volume). In the comments discussed here, orthography is a principal means through which social meanings are conveyed; it is used to signal the otherness of ScE but also a range of positive affective stances. Building on long-standing associations with a range of positive attributes such as warmth, attractiveness, and authenticity, YouTubers collectively frame and commodify Scottish accents, Scottish bodies, and Scotland itself as objects of longing and desire.

# 8 Acknowledgements

I wish to thank Miriam Meyerhoff, Lauren Squires and the anonymous reviewers for their careful reading and perceptive comments on earlier drafts of this paper. All the weaknesses are my own.

# 9 References

Agha, Asif. 2003. The social life of cultural value. *Language and Communication* 23(3/4). 231–273.
Alim, H. Samy. 2002. Street-conscious copula variation in the Hip Hop Nation. *American Speech* 77(3). 288–304.
Andersson, Niklas. 2009. Stereotypes of English in Hollywood movies: A case study of the use of different varieties of English in *Star Wars*, *The Lord of the Rings* and *Transformers*. Stockholm: Stockholm University B.A. Thesis.
Androutsopoulos, Jannis. 2000. Non-standard spellings in media texts: The case of German fanzines. *Journal of Sociolinguistics* 4(4). 514–533.
Androutsopoulos, Jannis. 2013b. Online data collection. In Christine Mallinson, Becky Childs, Becky & Gerard Van Herk (eds.), *Data collection in sociolinguistics: Methods and applications*, 236–249. London: Routledge.
Androutsopoulos, Jannis. 2013a. Participatory culture and metalinguistic discourse: Performing and negotiating German dialects on YouTube. In Deborah Tannen & Anna Marie Trester (eds.) *Discourse 2.0: Language and New Media*, 47–71. Washingtoin, DC: Georgetown University Press.
Androutsopoulos, Jannis & Jana Tereick. 2016. YouTube: Language and discourse practices in participatory culture. In Alexandra Georgakopoulou & Teresa Spilioti (eds.), *The Routledge handbook of language and digital communication*, 354–370. Abingdon/New York: Routledge.
Bakhtin, Mikhail M. 1984. *Problems in Dostoevsky's Poetics*. Minneapolis, MN: University of Minnesota Press.
Baron, Naomi S. & Rich Ling. 2011. Necessary smileys and useless periods. *Visual Language* 45 (1/2). 45–67.
Bieswanger, Markus. 2013. Micro-linguistic structural features of computer-mediated communication. In Susan Herring, Dieter Stein & Tuija Virtanen (eds.), *Pragmatics of computer-mediated communication*, 463–88. Berlin: Walter de Gruyter.
Bishop, Hywel, Nikolas Coupland & Peter Garrett. 2005. Conceptual accent evaluation: Thirty years of accent prejudice in the UK. *Acta Linguistica Hafniensia – International Journal of Linguistics* 37. 131–155.
Bratteli, Anders. 2011. World of speechcraft: accent use and stereotyping in computer games. Bergen: University of Bergen M.A. Thesis.
Brock, Alexander. 2011. Bumcivilian: Systemic aspects of humorous communication in comedies. In Roberta Piazza, Monika Bednarek & Fabio Rossi. (eds.). *Telecinematic discourse: Approaches to the language of films and television series*, 263–280. Amsterdam: John Benjamins Publishing.

Bucholtz, Mary & Kira Hall. 2004. Language and identity. In Alessandro Duranti (ed.), *A Companion to Linguistic Anthropology*, 369–94. Malden, MA: Blackwell.

Campbell-Kibler, Kathryn 2007. Accent, (ING), and the social logic of listener perceptions. *American Speech* 82(1). 32–64.

Cheyne, William M. 1970. Stereotyped reactions to speakers with Scottish and English regional accents. *British Journal of Social and Clinical Psychology* 9. 77–79.

Cho, Thomas. 2010. Linguistic features of electronic mail in the workplace: a comparison with memoranda. *Language@Internet* 7(3). http://www.languageatinternet.org/articles/2010/2728 (accessed 22 February 2015).

Chun, Elaine & Keith Walters. 2011. Orienting to Arab orientalisms: Language, race, and humor in a YouTube video. In Crispin Thurlow & Kristine Mroczek (eds). *Digital Discourse: Language in the New Media*, 251–273. Oxford: Oxford University Press.

Collister, Lauren B. 2012. The discourse deictics ∧ and <– in a World of Warcraft community. *Discourse, Context & Media* 1(1). 9–19.

Corbett, John & Jane Stuart-Smith. 2012. Standard English in Scotland. In Raymond Hickey (ed.), *Standards of English: Codified varieties around the world*, 72–95. New York: Cambridge University Press.

Cornwell, Tim. 2012. Hang on tae your hurdies, Hollywood. *The Scotsman*. June 2, 2012, Saturday, p. 15.

Coupland, Nikolas & Hywel Bishop. 2007. Ideologized values for British accents. *Journal of Sociolinguistics* 11(1). 74–93.

Cutler, Cecelia. 2014. *White hip-hoppers, language and identity in post-modern America*. New York: Routledge.

Danet, Brenda, Lucia Ruedenberg & Yehudit Rosenbaum-Tamari. 1997. "HMMM...WHERE'S THAT SMOKE COMING FROM?" Writing, play and performance on internet relay chat. *Journal of Computer-Mediated Communication* 2(4). http://onlinelibrary.wiley.com/enhanced/doi/10.1111/j.1083-6101.1997.tb00195.x/ (accessed 2 February 2015).

Darics, Erika. 2013. Non-verbal signaling in digital discourse: The case of letter repetition. *Discourse, Context & Media* 2(3). 141–148.

Deumert, Ana. 2014. *Sociolinguistics and mobile communication*. Edinburgh: Edinburgh University Press.

Douglas, Fiona M. 2003. The Scottish corpus of texts and speech: Problems of corpus design. *Literary and Linguistic Computing* 18(1). 23–37.

Dresner, Eli & Susan C. Herring. 2010. Functions of the nonverbal in CMC: Emoticons and illocutionary force. *Communication Theory* 20(3). 249–268.

Elliott, Stuart. 2012. Playing up a Scotsman's lawn expertise. *New York Times*, March 12, 2012. http://www.nytimes.com/2012/03/13/business/media/playing-up-the-lawn-ken-of-a-scotsman.html?r=0 (Accessed 12 June 2015).

Garley, Matt. 2014. Seen and not heard: The relationship of orthography, morphology, and phonology in loanword adaptation in the German hip hop community. *Discourse, Context and Media* 3. 27–36.

Garrett, Peter. 2010. *Attitudes to language*. Cambridge: Cambridge University Press.

Georgakopoulou, Alexandra. 2006. Thinking big with small stories in narrative and identity analysis. *Narrative Inquiry* 16(1). 122–130.

Giles, Howard. 1970. Evaluative reactions to accents. *Educational Review* 22(3). 211–227.

Giroux. Henri A. 1997. Are Disney movies good for your kids? In Steinberg, Shirley R. & Joe L. Kincheloe (eds.), *Kinderculture: The corporate constitution of childhood*, 53–62. Boulder, CO: Westview.

Hall-Lew, Lauren, Amie Fairs & Alan A. Lew. 2015. Tourists Attitudes towards linguistic variation in Scotland. In Eivind Torgersen, Stian Hårstad, Brit Mæhlum & Unn Røyneland (eds.), *Language variation – European perspectives V, Studies in language variation* (SILV) series, 99–110. Amsterdam/Philadelphia: John Benjamins Publishing Company.

Harvey, Kathrine, Sabine Pretzsch & Katrine Snowman. 2007. Language variation in *Shrek*. Denmark: Roskilde University. Unpublished manuscript. http://hdl.handle.net/1800/2254 (Accessed 12 February 2015).

Heller, Monica. 2010. The commodification of language. *Annual Review of Anthropology* 39. 101–114.

Herring, Susan. 2012. Grammar and electronic communication. In Carol A. Chapelle (ed.), *Encyclopedia of applied linguistics*. Wiley-Blackwell. http://onlinelibrary.wiley.com/doi/10.1002/9781405198431.wbeal0466/full (accessed 16 February, 2015).

Higgins, Christina. 2014. Language attitudes as stance-taking: An interview-based study on intergenerational transmission among Native Hawaiians. Paper presented at ICLASP (International Conference on Language and Social Psychology), May 22, Honolulu.

Hinrichs, Lars & Jessica White-Sustaíta. 2011. Global Englishes and the sociolinguistics of spelling: A study of Jamaican blog and email writing. *English World-Wide*. 32(1). 46–73.

Irvine, Judith & Susan Gal. 2000. Language ideology and linguistic differentiation. In Paul V. Kroskrity (ed.), *Regimes of language*, 35–84. Santa Fe, NM: School of American Research Press.

Jaffe, Alexandra & Shana Walton. 2000. The voices people read: Orthography and the representation of non-standard speech. *Journal of Sociolinguistics* 4(4). 561–587.

Jaspers, Jürgen. 2010. Introduction. Society and language use. In Jaspers, Jürgen, Jef Verschueren & Jan-Ola Östman (eds.), *Society and Language use*, 1–20. Amsterdam: John Benjamins.

Johnstone, Barbara. 2008. Pittsburghese shirts: Commodification and the enregisterment of an urban dialect. *American Speech* 84(2). 157–75.

Johnstone, Barbara. 2011. Dialect enregisterment in performance. *Journal of sociolinguistics* 15(5). 657–679.

Johnstone, Barbara. 2013. "100% Authentic Pittsburgh": Sociolinguistic authenticity and the linguistics of particularity. Barbara Johnstone. In Véronique Lacoste, Jakob Leimgruber & Thiemo Breyer (eds.), *Sociolinguistic authenticity and the linguistics of particularity*, 96–112. Berlin: De Gruyter.

Johnstone, Barbara & Dan Baumgardt. 2004. "Pittsburghese" online: Vernacular norming in conversation. *American Speech* 79. 115–145.

Jones, Graham M. & Bambi B. Schieffelin. 2009. Talking text and talking back: "My BFF Jill" from boob tube to YouTube. *Journal of Computer-Mediated Communication* 14(4). 1050–1079.

King, Ruth & Jennifer Wicks. 2009. "Aren't we proud of our language?": Authenticity, commodification, and the Nissan Bonavista television commercial. *Journal of English Linguistics* 37(3). 262–283

Lacroix, Celeste. 2004. Images of animated others: The orientalization of Disney's cartoon heroines from *The Little Mermaid* to *The Hunchback of Notre Dame*. *Popular Communication* 2(4). 213–229.

Ladegaard, Hans J. 1998. National stereotypes and language attitudes: The perception of British, American and Australian language and culture in Denmark. *Language & Communication* 18. 251–274.

Lippi-Green, Rosina. 1997. *English with an accent: Language, ideology, and discrimination in the United States*. New York: Routledge.

Lippi-Green, Rosina. 2012. *English with an accent: Language, ideology, and discrimination in the United States*. 2nd edn. New York: Routledge.

Lundervold, Lene. 2013. Harry Potter and the different accents. A sociolinguistic study of language attitudes in Harry. Bergen: University of Bergen M.A. thesis.

Lyster, Roy & Leila Ranta. 1997. Corrective feedback and learner uptake. *Studies in Second Language Acquisition* 19(1). 37–66.

Marshall, Jonathan. 2004. *Language change and sociolinguistics: Rethinking social networks*. Basingstoke: Palgrave Macmillan.

Martin, James R. & Peter R. White. 2005. *The language of evaluation: Appraisal in English*. Houndmills, NY: Palgrave Macmillan.

McKenzie, Steven. 2013. Pixar's Brave forecast to generate £120m in five years. BBC News. http://www.bbc.com/news/uk-scotland-highlands-islands-24014661 (accessed 6 June 2014).

Menzies, Janet. 1991. An investigation of attitudes to Scots and Glasgow dialect among secondary school pupils. *Scottish Language* 10. 30–46.

Miller, Jim. 2008. Scottish English morphology and syntax. In Bernd Kortmann & Clive Upton (eds.), *Varieties of English: The British Isles*, 299–327. Berlin: Mouton de Gruyter.

Niedzielski, Nancy A. & Dennis R. Preston. 2003. *Folk linguistics*. Berlin: Walter de Gruyter.

O'Shea, Suzanne. 1999. Scots tones accentuate the positive. *Scotland on Sunday*. April 25, p. 11.

Ochs, Elinor. 1992. Indexing gender. In Alessandro Duranti & Candace Goodwin (eds.), *Rethinking context: Language as an interactive phenomenon*, 335–358. Cambridge: Cambridge University Press.

Peuronen, Saija. 2011. Ride hard, live forever: translocal identities in an online community of extreme sports Christians. In Crispin Thurlow & Kristine Mroczek (eds.), *Digital discourse: Language in the new media*, 154–176. Oxford: Oxford University Press.

Queen, Robin. 2015. *Vox popular: The surprising life of language in the media*. West Sussex: Wiley-Blackwell.

Rackwitz, Martin. 2007. *Travels to terra incognita: The Scottish Highlands and Hebrides in early modern travellers' accounts C. 1600 to 1800* (Vol. 472). Waxmann Verlag.

Rampton, Ben. 2009. Interaction ritual and not just artful performance in crossing and stylization. *Language in Society* 38(2). 149–176.

Rennie, Jonathan. 2005. Why Scots can help put the accent on success; Survey reveals Scottish tongue is popular in business. *Evening Times* (Glasgow). December 29, 2005, p. 23.

Romaine, Suzanne. 1980. Stylistic variation and evaluative reactions to speech: problems in the investigation of linguistic attitudes in Scotland. *Language and Speech* 23(3). 213–232.

Schieffelin, Bambi B., Kathryn Ann Woolard & Paul V. Kroskrity, (eds.) 1998. *Language ideologies: Practice and theory*. Oxford: Oxford University Press.

Schneider, Edgard W. 2011. *English around the world: An introduction*. Cambridge: Cambridge University Press.

Scobbie, James M. & Jane Stuart-Smith. 2008. Quasi-phonemic contrast and the fuzzy inventory: Examples from Scottish English. In Peter Avery, Elan B. Dresher & Keren Rice (eds.), *Contrast: Perception and Acquisition: Selected Papers from the Second International Conference on Contrast in Phonology*, 87–113. Berlin: Mouton de Gruyter.

Shaw, Philip. 2008. Spelling, accent and identity in computer-mediated communication. *English Today* 24(2). 42–49.

Sherzer, Joel. 2002. *Speech play and verbal art*. Austin: University of Texas Press.
Silverstein, Michael. 2003. Indexical order and the dialectics of sociolinguistic life. *Language & Communication* 23(3). 193–229.
Soffer, Oren. 2010. "Silent orality": toward a conceptualization of the digital oral features in CMC and SMS texts. *Communication Theory* 20(4). 387–404.
Stuart-Smith, Jane, Claire Timmins & Fiona Tweedie. 2007. Talkin' Jockney: Accent change in Glaswegian. *Journal of Sociolinguistics* 11(2). 221–261.
Stuart-Smith, Jane. 2004. Scottish English: Phonology. In Bernd Kortmann & Edgar W. Schneider (eds.), *A handbook of varieties of English, volume 1: Phonology*, 47–67. Berlin: De Gruyter.
Tourism in Scotland (Wikipedia page). https://en.wikipedia.org/wiki/Tourism_in_Scotland (Accessed 22 June, 2015).
Wells, John C. 1982. *Accents of English*. Vol. 2. Cambridge: Cambridge University Press.
Williams, Nicholas M. 1999. The Dialect of authenticity: The case of Irvine Welsh's *Trainspotting*. In Ton Hoenselaars & Marius Buning (eds.), *English literature and the other languages*, 221–230. Amsterdam: Rodopi.

## II Contact, Spread, and Innovation

Theresa Heyd
# Global varieties of English gone digital: Orthographic and semantic variation in digital Nigerian Pidgin

## 1 CMC and globalizing varieties: Contact, change, and spread

### 1.1 CMC and language change

The question of whether and how computer-mediated communication (CMC) is a factor in processes of language variation and change has prompted eager debate from early on. Does the internet act as a site of language contact and spread? Can it be a motor of linguistic innovation and change, or does it merely mirror processes that are ongoing in a given language ecology? Do linguistic innovations from 'real-life' usage migrate into the digital domain, or is it possible that indigenously digital forms of language use spread into the non-digital realm?

Debates about language and the media are still very much ongoing, as evidenced by recent publications such as Androutsopoulos (2012) and Sayers (2014). While the approaches to the topic are still varied, the on-record nature of this discussion does indicate that mediated language has become a substantial topic in variationist approaches.

In parallel to these fundamental and more programmatic debates, the recent years have seen a constant and growing stream of research output that is centered on the analysis of computer-mediated discourse. In these approaches, the high variability of digital language use itself is taken for granted, and patterns of innovation and variation have been studied with increasing methodological and empirical sophistication. These second-generation CMC studies, following the early approaches of charting the field, are thus committed to "highlighting the social diversity of language use in CMC," as Androutsopoulos (2006a: 421) remarks in his seminal introduction to the sociolinguistics of CMC.

Furthermore, digital language practices have become fully integrated in analyses focused on the sociolinguistics of globalization and mobility (Blommaert 2010; Coupland 2010). In these approaches, language use through digital media is simply seen as one important factor amongst others (such as global migration

---

**Theresa Heyd**, Freie Universität Berlin

and the affordability of long-distance travel) that shapes our late-modern, super-diverse societies. Thus Blommaert and Rampton (2011: 3) point out that "migration movements from the 1990s onwards have coincided with the development of the internet and mobile phones, and these have affected the cultural life of diaspora communities of all kinds" – a condition that also deeply impacts the linguistic practices in such communities. This approach is well-equipped to interpret new technological realities such as ubiquitous computing through mobile devices and the gradual disappearance of the online/offline dichotomy. Thus as early as 2007, Coupland (2007: 28) notes that "the media are increasingly inside us and us in them." These emerging new conditions are sure to have an impact on the way we think about language contact, spread and change in digital usage.

## 1.2 CMC and Global Englishes

Over the course of the past two decades, the internet has gradually undergone a transformation from a predominantly Anglophone to a more diverse and multilingual environment (Danet and Herring 2007). This is the case on the macro level of individual languages, so that other languages besides English are gaining in relevance, but also extends to the micro level of varieties of English, so that nonstandard varieties are becoming more prominent in digital usage. Factors of globalization (e.g., the spread of digital technology and the gradual reduction of digital divides; the global migration and emergence of new diasporas; the appropriation of global practices to local communities; see Blommaert and Rampton 2011 for a summary) are instrumental in the emergence of more and more global varieties of English on the digital map. While research into the sociolinguistic ecology of CMC is still striving to catch up with these patterns of diversification, there is a growing body of research on several bundles of digital global Englishes, in particular Asian (e.g., Leimgruber 2015; Liu and Tao 2012; Seargeant and Tagg 2011), Caribbean (e.g., Deuber and Hinrichs 2007; Hinrichs 2006; Moll 2015), and African (e.g., Chiluwa 2013; Heyd and Mair 2014; Ifukor 2011) varieties.

Analyzing these and other global varieties of English grants many insights into growing linguistic diversity in general, and the language ecology of digitally mediated usage in particular. Two challenges and ongoing debates seem particularly prominent, and they set the framework for a number of chapters in this volume (see e.g., Jones, Cutler, and Coats). First is the question of nonstandard features and their social meanings. How does the nonstandard, marked nature of varietal features figure in digital usage? To what degree are they transposed to the digital environment, and how are they encoded in the digital medium?

Moreover, how do such regional nonstandard features interact with the overall 'nonstandardness' that has been described as typical for the digital supervernacular (Blommaert 2011), and what are the social meanings that users attribute to such features?

The second issue is more general, as it concerns the notion of mobility. Sociolinguistic theory is increasingly moving away from firm concepts of "varieties of English" that are geolocationally anchored and constrained to a specific, homogeneous speaker community (Hinrichs, this volume). Instead, we tend to think of globally available linguistic resources that are locally reproduced, for example in diasporic communities, but also by other speakers who may adopt certain features or repertoires in moves of crossing or linguistic appropriation. How do we map such deterritorialized usage in digitally mediated communication, and how does it interact with digital notions of place and space? The examination and description of such digital ethnolinguistic repertoires (Heyd and Mair 2014; Moll 2015) is an ongoing work that is likely to produce new insights into language contact, spread and change in CMC.

## 1.3 Emerging norms in digital communities

The developments outlined above are of particular interest to sociolinguists and variationists with a specific perspective: how do nonstandard repertoires such as creoles and pidgins, urban ethnolects or local languages fare in the transition from essentially oral usage in locally anchored communities to a written environment that is technologically mediated and often involves communities that recruit a global diaspora? (Androutsopoulos 2006b; Deuber and Hinrichs 2007; Heyd and Mair 2014; Hinrichs 2006; Mair and Pfänder 2013) In particular, the question as to how previously *spoken* vernaculars perform as they become routinely *written* in the context of digital usage has been of interest, as it may provide insights into both the nonstandard varieties themselves, and the linguistic practices that are prevalent in CMC.

In earlier approaches, this interest was primarily focused on the emergence of orthographic norms in relatively homogeneous communities. For example, Deuber and Hinrichs (2007) analyzed corpora of digital Jamaican Creole and Nigerian Pidgin in terms of orthographic standardization processes and their relation to the sociolinguistic situations in the respective countries of origin. In the context of super-diverse and late-modern societies, such close-knit user communities which share a common linguistic background and profile (and thus mirror the locally anchored 'speech communities' of traditional sociolinguistic inquiry) are coming to seem less important, and less indicative of typical communicative settings. Instead, we find communities and platforms where local users from countries of origin interact with diasporic users of varying generations, where spouses and friends with a mere interest in a certain culture/language may chime in, and where many users may have a super-diverse and multi-ethnic background. In such heterogeneous and polyphonous settings, the interest in orthographic variation is just as acute, but different questions need to be asked. For example, what does it mean to be an authentic user of a specific repertoire in such an environment? How do local and diasporic users tap into the linguistic resources that are in currency within a community? Which linguistic features are used to index certain personas or ethnolinguistic profiles?

## 2 Case study: Orthographic and semantic variation in digital Nigerian Pidgin

In the study presented here, the themes outlined above are explored in a Nigeria-based discussion forum which functions as an online community for both local Nigerian users and globally spread diasporic members. This heterogeneous mix of participants creates a multilingual language ecology that includes the use of relatively Standard English varieties, indigenous languages such as Hausa, Yoruba and Igbo, and other diasporic languages such as French, Dutch or Italian. Besides these, a set of nonstandard repertoires plays an important role in the community, such as influences from African American Vernacular English, the 'supervernacular' (Blommaert 2011) of digital semiotic resources, and especially Nigerian Pidgin (NigP).

Within this environment, the study presented here explores the digital linguistic practices of this heterogeneous online community with regard to emerging norms, using a corpus of digital NigP. The analytical focus is on the use of the NigP function words *dey* and *am*, and how their usage aligns with the performance of identities in the community. To assess this, two different aspects of variation are analyzed here. The first concerns patterns of orthographic variation, as they are bound to appear where a traditionally spoken vernacular migrates into the digital medium. The second concerns a pattern of distribution which is tentatively described as *semantic variation*: namely, both lexical items are homonyms which have secondary nonstandard meanings besides their primary NigP meaning. It is argued here that this semantic alternation is a form of variation that users can tap into in order to display linguistic identity online. Before the approach is described in more detail in sections three and four, the following outline sketches the social history of Nigerian Pidgin and its status in the global linguistic ecology of English.

Nigerian Pidgin is a West African contact language with a long and well-charted history (see e.g., Deuber 2005; Deuber 2006: 242–244; Faraclas 1996; Gaudio 2011: 235–237; Mann 1993). Grounded in a pre-colonial emergence within a traditionally multilingual Nigerian society, its rise began in the 15th century along the Slave Coast through Portuguese trade contact. This led to its gradual transformation to an English-lexifier contact variety which incorporates many structural, but also lexical features of tribal languages. In present-day usage, it is shaped by its longstanding role as a lingua franca in the multi-ethnic linguistic ecology of Nigeria. In this context, the "social profile of Nigerian Pidgin" (Mensah 2011: 212) is well-documented in terms of its historical evolution. It is a matter of ongoing debate whether NigP has, in more recent times, undergone creolization to act as an L1 to a considerable number of speakers;[1] however, it is safe to say that the sociocultural status, public perception and diffusion, and importantly the global spread of NigP have significantly changed throughout the 20th and early 21st centuries.

This large-scale change in the social profile of NigP can be roughly conceptualized in two (closely conjoined) phases: first, a broad destigmatization and revalorization of the vernacular within the Nigeria-based speaker community throughout the 20th century. In a second and ongoing step, NigP has caught on to the traction of globalization (Cameron 2012) and its mechanisms of linguistic super-diversity, so that we can today note effects such as commodification and mediatization in the use of NigP, and particularly its role in diasporic, deterritorialized and digital usage.

As to the first phase, the overall rise of NigP in the 20th century is summarized by Mensah (2011: 212–213):

> During the pre- and post- independence era in Nigeria, the attitude towards NP was overwhelmingly negative and degrading. It was regarded as "broken English," "unruly jargon," "vulgar" and "corrupt" form of expression. It was outlawed in schools and within government circles. The language was mainly associated with the peasants, uneducated, artisans and the general low-income population. (...) NP has come to stay with Nigerians and is acquiring new roles in every facet of the country's economic and socio-political life. It is no longer seen as the restricted mode of interlingual communication with limited lexicon but as a language with its own vitality and essence. (...) It is politically, socially and ethnically detached and has greater acceptability than any precolonially existing Nigerian language.

---

[1] Assessments and numbers vary considerably. For example, Gaudio (2011: 236) pegs NigP as "the native tongue of an estimated 3–5 million speakers"; Deuber (2006: 242) notes that it is "mostly spoken as a second language but creolization is under way"; by contrast, Mensah (2011: 210) contests these claims and manifests that "(t)here is no speaker of NP in Nigeria without a distinct mother tongue. NP merely serves as L2 to speakers without western education and L3 to speakers with such privileges."

Other accounts emphasize that this changing role of NigP is not just attributable to purely practical reasons, such as its usability as a lingua franca, but also to sociolinguistic factors of prestige and solidarity. Thus Mann, as early as 1993, notes that NigP has become a "trendy code for the young generation" (1993: 171); Deuber (2006: 244) expands on this by outlining that "younger educated Nigerians, especially university students, have increasingly adopted it as an informal medium of communication and a means of expressing (...) solidarity." In this sense, NigP has over the years acquired the status of a covert-prestigious repertoire, and the language attitudes expressed towards it by the Nigerian speaker community are expectedly ambivalent (Gaudio 2011: 236), a tendency which is not untypical for contact languages in postcolonial settings (see e.g., Schneider 2007: 67).

As to the second phase, this first wave of sociocultural change in the status of NigP has paved the way for more recent developments (see Heyd and Mair 2014 for an overview). Thus the wide use of NigP in outlets of popular media – radio and TV coverage, but in particular the rise of Nigerian pop music and the Nollywood industry – have led to a mediatization of the repertoire. It has been argued that this is bringing about concomitant sociolinguistic effects such as stylization and, ultimately, a trajectory of commodification. In addition, the large-scale global migration and the emergence of a New African Diaspora have paved the way for the deterritorialized and diasporic usage of NigP. Under these conditions, NigP exists as a (albeit often truncated) repertoire on the streets of London and New York City, but also in more unlikely locations such as Arlington, Texas; Frankfurt; or Palma de Mallorca. Finally, the digitized usage of NigP (see Mair 2013 for an overview), both by local Nigerian speakers and users across the global diaspora, is now a significant factor in the sociocultural profile of the repertoire. The leap from the streets of Lagos and its media outlets, to the global urban settings of the New African Diaspora, to Twitter and Tumblr is an unsurprising one in the mediasphere of the early 21st century.

## 3 Data and analytical framework

### 3.1 Little words: Windows onto orthographic/semantic variation and social meaning

There is a small but growing body of research on Nigerian English and NigP and their usage in mediated contexts (see e.g., Deuber and Hinrichs 2007; Chiluwa 2013; Omoniyi 2009). In previous publications investigating the corpus data discussed here, I have analyzed lexical items that are particularly semantically rich, for example labels of race and ethnicity such as *akata* or *oyibo* (Heyd 2014), or the metacommunicative lexical inventory of Nigerian Pidgin (Heyd 2015). Unsurprisingly, such items were found to be strong carriers of social meaning which facilitate "the systematic absorption of ideology into the lexicon" (Eckert 2008: 465), and which are used to mitigate identity and claims of legitimacy in this community. However, for all their symbolic power, such socially meaningful words are infrequent in absolute terms in the corpus used here. While they are highly visible "beacons" in terms of claims about authenticity and legitimacy, they have little to do with the everyday sociolinguistic fabric of the forum.

Instead, the approach taken here focuses on NigP-specific function words, on "little words" (Leow et al. 2009) such as pronouns and coordinators, prepositions and modals. The rationale for closely analyzing these forms is at least threefold:

1) The overall frequency of function words is higher, as they occur throughout all discourse contexts, whereas content words are strongly constrained by factors such as context, topic, and speaker identity.
2) Function words are a constitutive part of written NigP: items such as *dey, na, abi, o* are relatively distinct and overt features of NigP usage. Agheyisi (1988: 236) describes many of these function words as "pure pidgin words."
3) Despite this overt status, the felicitous usage of function words requires the linguistic skills of a native or near-native speaker. Using these forms in grammatical ways is a clear way of displaying NigP skills and thus performing an authenticated NigP persona. Because the social profile of NigP (Gaudio 2011; Heyd 2015; Mensah 2011) is strongly built around concepts of authenticity and legitimacy, this functionality is vital in the larger sociolinguistic context of NigP usage.

The analysis presented here focuses on two function words that are essential to the NigP repertoire, namely *am* and *dey*. Their range of orthographic and semantic variation, and how its usage reflects different forms of nonstandardness in terms of digital linguistic practice, is outlined in section 4.

## 3.2 The Nairaland data: corpus and community

The analysis provided here is part of a large-scale approach in which the assumptions made by the sociolinguistics of globalization and mobility (Blommaert 2010; Coupland 2010) are explored in a corpus setting. (See Heyd and Mair 2014; Mair 2013; Mair and Pfänder 2013 for general overviews on the approach.) In this specific case, a corpus was compiled based on the web forum http://nairaland.com, which functions as an online community and virtual meeting place for both local and diasporic Nigerians as well as anyone interested in Nigerian affairs and culture; the platform, subcategorized in subforums, covers an encompassing range of topics from political discussion and casual gossip to job postings and travel tips.[2] Forum discussions were downloaded covering the timespan 2005–2008, which yields a corpus of 17.3 million tokens. The data are not syntactically parsed;[3] however, the core users are tagged for gender and geolocation, which facilitates a differentiated analysis.

The Nairaland data consist of a diverse language ecology that includes standard varieties of English, indigenous languages such as Hausa, Yoruba and Igbo, other languages such as Italian, French and Dutch, and a number of nonstandard varieties. The most important and prominent of these is NigP, but other repertoires such as African American Vernacular Englishes or Multicultural London English (Cheshire et al. 2011) and others are also drawn upon to some extent. This heterogeneity of the dataset in terms of varieties and speaker backgrounds is not seen as a limitation or analytical drawback here; instead, in the context of globalized varieties, it can be considered a fairly representative cohort of the Nigerian language ecology.

The organization of the data into a corpus structure, together with the sheer size of the sample, allows for quantitative assessments. In addition, the corpus architecture conserves the macro structure of the forum, so that linguistic items and utterances can be analyzed in the context of user interactions, conversations and threads. This situated nature of the data allows for well-informed close readings of the data that permit insight into the forum dynamics and interactional features of the material. In this sense, the data analyzed here are also available for a close and discourse-analytical look at the beliefs, power struggles and identity concepts that the users exhibit.

By combining these two approaches – by considering the data as both corpus and community – it is possible to take a close look at patterns of variation, and at the same time to assess the associated social meanings that prevail in this community. The polyphonous nature of the corpus material poses specific challenges and opens up research questions. In particular, these questions revolve around the notion of authentic and legitimate use of linguistic resources: who are the "authentic" users of digital NigP? How can their usage be assessed, and how do other, secondary forms of usage play into this language ecology? The analysis presented here taps into the dual nature of the data to both analyze patterns of variation in usage of *am* and *dey*, and to uncover the indexicalities that are tied to such usage.

---

[2] "Naira," in the forum title, refers to the Nigerian currency.
[3] This is largely due to the fundamental challenge of syntactic annotation in nonstandard varieties.

## 3.3 Data extraction and preparation

As outlined above, NigP function words emerged as potential targets for analysis from initial evaluations of the data. This concerns a range of "little words" (Leow et al. 2009) including pronouns, conjunctions, prepositions and discourse markers. The rationale for using these items for a closer analysis is in part due to practical reasons: they are frequent and easily identifiable in a corpus approach, and their usage is likely to occur across all thematic contexts. In addition, how these function words occur is sociolinguistically relevant: their felicitous usage presupposes a highly competent user of digital NigP. Mair (2013: 269) provides an example that shows the attempted usage of NigP function words by a diasporic user with minimal NigP skills acquired through online contact:

(1) **Nah waytin** is happening in this place? **Oooh** yeah.
[It's what is happening in this place? Ooh yeah.]

As Mair points out, the usage of these forms (*nah waytin* as a focused question clause introducer; *ooh* as an utterance-final discourse marker) is evocative of NigP, but their spelling, placement and ineffective syntactic embedding unveil them as pure lexical add-ons. As a consequence, a native speaker of NigP promptly chips in with a correct, authenticated version:

(2) **wetin dey** happen hia?
[What is happening here?]

This example reveals that function words are a well-suited resource for analyzing NigP usage. For the present study, concordances for specific items were extracted from the Nairaland corpus. However, in the process of identifying these items in the corpus material, problems with precision (in the sense of false positives) and recall (in the sense of false negatives) were encountered. On the one hand, the forms exhibit a certain range of orthographic variation; thus the question word *wetin* (what) is alternatively rendered in the data as *waytin*, as above, and also *wetin*. This recall issue was to be expected, as orthographic variation is an elementary part of the norm-building process in the digitization of nonstandard vernaculars. As a consequence, alternate spellings were explored and equally extracted as concordances.

However, the results also revealed problems of precision: not all instances of these function words are used in the NigP sense in the corpus. Instead, there is a considerable amount of semantic variation in their usage. In some cases, this is due to the presence of StE cognates in the corpus; for example, the item *no* is used both in its StE meanings as a determiner and a particle, but it also occurs as the NigP negation marker as in (3a). In this latter function, it also occurs in the alternate spelling *nor*, as in (3b) – which, in turn, also occurs in the corpus as the StE conjunction *nor* in *neither/nor* constructions.

(3) a. Abeg **no** cry
 [Please don't cry]

 b. I **nor** wan argue with you today
 [I don't want to argue with you today]

In other cases, the semantic variation is based not on etymologically related cognates, but on merely incidental homography. This was found to be true in the two items analyzed here, namely *am* and *dey*. In both instances, the semantic variation includes a NigP usage (*am* as a pronoun, *dey* as a copula), but also a secondary nonstandard usage that is not specifically associated with NigP usage (*am* as a verbal form, *dey* as a pronoun). To further assess these patterns of semantic variation, the results were thus coded for NigP or non-NigP usage of the forms, similar to Deuber and Hinrichs (2007). These two datasets, consisting of annotated concordances of *am* (2,946 items) and *dey* (7,652 items), form the point of departure for the analyses outlined below.

## 4 Results

For this analysis, the function words *am* and *dey* were examined in terms of their orthographic and semantic variation. Both words are frequent in the corpus, with *am* on place 76 in the word frequency list (31,126 instances) and *dey* on place 176 (11,190 instances). *Am* is the third person gender-neutral singular object pronoun in NigP, as used in examples (4a) to (4c):[4]

(4) a. Wetin me wan no is the cause of her death. Wetin kill **am**?
 [What I would like to know is the cause of her death. What killed her?]

 b. Forget it she no worth **am**.
 [Forget it, she is not worth it.]

 c. You don hear say when one man die na one woman kill **am** but na six man dey carry **am** go to the grave.
 [Have you heard the saying: when a man dies, it is one woman who killed him, but six men will carry him to the grave.]

---

4 Unless otherwise specified, all examples given in this paper are taken from the Nairaland corpus.

*Dey* is a verbal form with two functions that are etymologically related, namely as a copula, and as a preverbal imperfective aspect marker,[5] as shown in (5a) and (5b):

(5) a. hope unano **dey** south london ooo lol
 [Hope you guys **are** not in South London lol]

 b. i sorry d guy **dey** always make me vex
 [I am sorry, the guy always makes me angry]

In this study, the semantic and orthographic variation of these items is explored in the corpus. Both lexical items show some orthographic variation in the corpus, but the spellings <am> and <dey> are clearly preferred and seem to have become the de facto orthographic standard. This is in line with the findings from Deuber and Hinrichs (2007), where in spite of some variation, NigP lexical items gravitated toward one distinct orthographic preference.

By contrast, the semantic variation between meanings of both items is more complex, and more revealing in terms of the social indexicality of the terms. The term "semantic variation" is used here to describe the distribution of sememes, or semantic variants, that pertain to a homonymous or polysemous item. Besides the distinct NigP meanings outlined above, both terms are used in a secondary nonstandard way. Thus *dey* also occurs as an orthographic representation of *they* with DH-stopping (see Callier, this volume). *Am* is also used as a contracted and/or elliptical form of <I'm>/<I am>.[6] The distribution of these nonstandard homographs is analyzed and critically discussed later in the results section. It is argued that the usage of these different nonstandard meanings is imbued with indexical meaning for these users and can signal different identities. The more typical NigP forms tend to co-occur with other clear NigP markers. By contrast, the generic nonstandard forms are used in co-occurrence with other, more general nonstandard markers (<d>, <r>, <hav>,...) that are associated with a more internationalized "Netspeak" or digital supervernacular. Thus the two identities that are often metalinguistically pitted against each other, namely the "genuine" local Nigerian vs. the diasporic, globalized user, have their corollary in this distribution of variants. The wider implications of semantic variation on identity management, and concomitant aspects of authenticity and legitimacy in language use, are revisited in the discussion.

---

**5** As practiced in Deuber and Hinrichs (2007), the analysis here collapses these two functions as both share the same orthography; for the purpose of this study, both functions are indicative of "genuine" NigP and a speaker's high command of the variety.

**6** Instances where <am> occurs as a standard form, as 1st person singular form of be in *I am* constructions, were disregarded for this study.

## 4.1 Orthographic variation

The two elements under consideration here were first analyzed for patterns of orthographic variation. Since nonstandard spellings have to be identified in an exploratory manner in a large corpus, it is possible that isolated, idiosyncratic spellings remained unidentified. However, the semi-automated search yielded robust tendencies for both lexical items.

The verbal form *dey* is present in three orthographic variants in the corpus, namely <dey>, <de> and <deh>. <dey> is by far the dominant orthographic variant, accounting for 95% of the instances in the corpus. Interestingly, the marginal spelling <deh> is the only one that is specific for this lexical item. By contrast, <de> occurs 1,899 times in the corpus, so that the 414 relevant instances are only one semantic variant of this item; <de> is a polysemous item that occurs, amongst other usages, as a nonstandard spelling of *the* and *they*, as well as in French and Hausa portions of the corpus material. Example 6 shows how <de> can occur in a NigP environment as either the definite article or the imperfective marker:

(6) a. Why una dey yab **de** girl.
 [Why are you picking on **the** girl.]

 b. I think say you don **de** colo
 [I think you **have gone** crazy.]

It is interesting to note that these results for *dey* closely match those found in Deuber and Hinrichs (2007). The distribution of <dey> (94%), <de> (5%) and <deh> (1%) found in their 90,000 token corpus of digital NigP is faithfully mirrored in the much larger sample analyzed here.

For *am* as the NigP object pronoun, orthographic variation to the dominant form <am> (961 instances) is equally sparse; some of the very few exceptions are displayed in example 7. Thus  can potentially be used as an alternate spelling; however, virtually all of the 761 instances of  in the corpus are either used as an interjection, or as the shortened form of *them*. Surprisingly, another contender is the spelling <I'm>, as shown in (7b): there are 484 cases of pronominal *I'm* in the corpus, which seems remarkable, given that this usage is somewhat counterintuitive.[7] However, the item is primarily used as a 3rd person possessive pronoun, i.e., in the sense of *his* (see "I'm mama" in example 7c).

---

[7] Interestingly, these are not cases of autocorrection. The data predate the era of widely available mobile devices. This spelling pattern is also found in NigP usage outside of the corpus examined here, suggesting that it is a somewhat popular usage.

Finally, clitic spelling is a possible orthographic variation, where the pronoun is fused to the preceding verb. While this variant is somewhat to be expected, given that Faraclas (1996: 234) classifies *am* as a bound pronoun with clitic status in spoken NigP, this apparently does not translate into an orthographic norm – clitic spelling occurs only in very few cases in the corpus, one of which is displayed in example (7c).

(7) a. you can lead a camel to water but you can't make **em** drink it
 [You can lead a camel to water but you can't make **it** drink.]

 b. if someone wan die put for a position, una go say make **I'm** resign
 [If someone clings to a position, you guys want **him** to resign]

 c. Monkey no fine but I'm mama **likam**
 [The monkey is ugly, but his mother likes **him** nevertheless]

It can be concluded that *dey* and *am* are cases of de facto norm-building in digital NigP; as Deuber and Hinrichs note (2007: 36), there is "a high degree of conventionalization" in particular with regard to function words in digital NigP. Deuber and Hinrichs (2007) hypothesized that spelling variation can be mitigated based on the etymology and provenience of a lexical item. In the corpus material analyzed here, some provisional findings point to word length and/or semantic richness as possible influencing factors. For example, for a semantically rich content word such as *phonetics*, over a dozen spelling variants were found in the corpus – see Heyd (2015) for a brief discussion.

## 4.2 Semantic variation

While the analysis so far shows that orthographic variation does not play a dominant role in the digital usage of NigP function words, the initial data analyses quickly revealed that the case is different with regard to the semantics of these items. Specifically, many of these "little words" display a kind of multifunctionality or polysemy. What is noteworthy about this polysemous nature is that it extends over completely disparate word classes and syntactic functions: while semantic variation is unsurprising and indeed to be expected in homophonous cognates which share an etymological root (as in the case of *no/nor* shown in example (3b)), the digital NigP corpus contains examples where one orthographic form represents two lexical items that are thoroughly distinct in their etymology, semantics, and usage.

In the case of *dey*, the NigP meaning as a copula/verbal marker is clearly dominant, as it covers 7,290 of an overall 7,652 instances. In the remaining 362 cases, <dey> is used as the 3rd person plural pronoun *they*, as shown in example 8:

(8) a. hell no if **dey** don't do their chores no food for them
 [hell no, if they don't do their chores, no food for them]

  b. datz real bad , how dare **dey** come 2 ur yard
 [that's real bad, how dare they come to your yard]

  c. Yes oh **dey** r d cause of Africas problem
 [Yes, they are the cause of Africa's problem]

The use of pronominal *dey* may not be quantitatively commanding in the corpus, but it is noteworthy. On the one hand, the spelling is clearly marked as nonstandard, as the use of <d> mimics the realization of a dental fricative as a stop. As Deuber and Hinrichs (2007: 37) point out, orthographic variants where StE <th> is replaced by <d> or <t> are common in NigP, as they coincide with the phonemic inventory of NigP, which does not have an interdental fricative. In the case of pronominal *dey*, however, this explanation falls short, as *dey* is not part of the NigP pronoun paradigm, where *dem* is used as the 3rd person plural subject pronoun. It could be said, then, that <dey> is a StE pronominal form represented through a nonstandard spelling.

This interpretation is corroborated by a look at the usage patterns of *dey* and its semantic variants in the corpus. First, the distribution of verbal *dey* vs. pronominal *dey* by user is almost complementary in the corpus. Out of 1,818 users in the corpus who use a form of *dey*, only 65 use both semantic variants at some point in their discourse. All other users are either sole users of pronominal (92) or verbal (1,661) *dey*.

In addition, the context provided in the concordance results reveals that pronominal *dey* co-occurs very frequently with general markers of digital nonstandardness, in particular abbreviated forms such as <r> for *are*, <u> for *you*, or numeric spellings such as <2> for *to*, as can be seen in example 8. By contrast, overt markers of digital NigP are virtually absent in the direct context of pronominal *dey*. It can be argued, then, that both semantic variants of *dey* tap into orthographic marking, but the resources they use and the social meanings they activate by doing so are quite distinct: whereas verbal *dey* has become a de facto orthographic standard for a NigP term whose use is accessible to highly competent speakers of NigP, pronominal *dey* is a much less situated form whose pronunciation spelling is evocative of a much more general nonstandardness – the type of nonstandard spelling that is typically enregistered as a "Netspeak" feature (in the sense of Squires 2010).

A similar dualism was found in the semantic variation of *am*. Unsurprisingly, the dominant usage of the item *am* is the StE spelling of the 1st person singular form of *be*, as in *I am* constructions, which are not relevant for the analysis here. These sociolinguistically unmarked forms make up 21,153 instances of <am> in the corpus. Once they were excluded, 2,953 cases remained where <am> was used in a nonstandard way. The analysis of these tokens again revealed two semantic variants, namely the NigP 3rd person singular object pronoun that was discussed above and shown in example 1; and the use of *am* as an elliptical form and/or pronunciation spelling for *I am*. This latter usage is displayed in example 9:

(9) a. @[username] The next time You talk to my wife in such an indecent manner, **am** going to cut off your head.
[@[username] The next time You talk to my wife in such an indecent manner, I am going to cut off your head.]

b. Sounds like d place **am** from.
[Sounds like the place I am from.]

c. You guys should tune to channel 4 for the conspiracy is being aired as **am** sending my post.
[You guys should tune to channel 4 for the conspiracy is being aired as I am sending my post.]

A first surprising finding is that this verbal usage of *am* in fact outnumbers pronominal *am* in the corpus: for 960 cases of pronominal *am*, there are 1,852 instances of the nonstandard verbal usage. This is in contrast with *dey*, where the NigP usage clearly dominated. These numbers indicate that verbal *am* is an important resource for the Nairaland community. However, interpreting its meaning and underlying rationale is surprisingly complex. One possible reading is that these are simply cases of subject ellipsis, where the first person pronoun is being dropped from the construction. Elliptical writing, and in particular subject ellipsis, has been mentioned as a potential linguistic feature of CMC frequently (see e.g., Crystal 2006: 122), because it seems to mesh well with the technologically-induced restrictions of mediated writings and a certain telegraphic style this might motivate. However, it is not clear to what degree this is an actual feature of CMC, and not just a perceived one. Regardless of this question, it seems unlikely that many or all instances in the corpus are cases of subject ellipsis. As shown in examples (9a) and (9c), many cases of verbal *am* occur in syntactically complex and well-formed contexts, so that an elided subject does in fact stand out as informal usage, rather than adapt to its context of use.

The alternative reading is that verbal <am> in the corpus is a nonstandard orthographic representation of *I'm*. This strategy would be understandable in the context of the Nigerian phonological inventory, where [aɪ] is monophthongized. <am> as a nonstandard spelling for contracted *I'm* would thus be an attempted representation of [aːm]. This second interpretation seems more likely than the reading of *am* as subject ellipsis, but it remains somewhat surprising nonetheless. This is probably due to the fact that we would expect a pronunciation spelling to be more typographically unambiguous. Also, <am> as a spelling for contracted *I'm* does not seem to be part of global digital nonstandard writing practices – in contrast to what was found for <dey>. It is possible then, that this usage of a "little word" has emerged out of this community as a kind of grassroots norm.

Despite these structural differences to the usage of *dey*, other aspects are similar in the semantic variation of *am*. Specifically, the co-occurrence with other nonstandard features follows similar patterns: whereas pronominal *am* is used in environments that are dense with other overt NigP markers, verbal *am* occurs either in stylistically unmarked situations, or together with general markers of nonstandardness. It can be concluded that *am* usage, as was the case with *dey*, exhibits a dualistic pattern of nonstandard usage: one that is highly specific and de facto standardized for digital NigP; and a second one, that is more general, deterritorialized and thus globally available in its nonstandardness.

## 4.3 Discussion: The social meaning of "little words"

The analysis of *am* and *dey* in the corpus has provided two major findings: first, there is relatively little orthographic variation – so little that it amounts to de facto norm-building (albeit in a purely grassroots manner). Secondly, with regard to semantic variation, two dominant types of usage were found for both forms. While all semantic variants are part of a nonstandard repertoire, the nature of their nonstandardness was found to differ: pronominal *am* and verbal *dey* occur as key features of the NigP lexicon; they are "pure pidgin words" in this regard. At the same time, verbal *am* and pronominal *dey* are nonstandard forms of a more general sort: rather than point to a specific, regionally anchored variety, they are evocative of nonstandard spelling practices in general such as DH-stopping (<dey>) and contraction (<am>). In a traditional sociolinguistic account, the NigP semantic variants of *am* and *dey* would probably be considered the more "authentic" usages of the forms, whereas the secondary forms might be described as "piggybacking" on legitimate nonstandardness by merely drawing on evocative spellings. In a late modern account of linguistic variation, such a variety-oriented account clearly is not able to capture the full picture. As

Mair (2013: 269) points out, "authentic use of non-standard linguistic resources in spite of (...) mimetic deficits" is not just possible, but an essential component of global varieties in a constructivist approach.

These semantic variants can thus be understood here as linguistic items that play a part in the creation and stylistic evocation of distinct identities and personas in this community. In particular, two types of persona have emerged from previous analyses of this corpus material in a qualitative (Heyd and Mair 2014) and quantitative (Heyd 2015) way. On the one hand, users tend to affiliate with an image of the true and authentic Nigerian: someone who is locally based or at least has firsthand knowledge about and experience with Nigeria, and who by consequence is well-acquainted with Nigerian affairs and practices. Very often, this also extends to the command and endorsement of NigP as a linguistic resource. On the other hand, users may identify with the notion of the "International African" – someone who is well-traveled, socially and globally mobile, and well-versed in Western affairs and cultural practices. Note that in the global setting of this community, both identities are not tied to geolocational anchoring of the users – a "Nigerian" or "diasporic" identity may be displayed by users regardless of their current geolocational affiliation.

Unsurprisingly, little words such as *am* or *dey* are not the sole carriers of such evocations; they are simply parts in the larger machinery of indexing these identities in situated discourse, together with other factors. Some of these factors are found at the lexical level, such as the use of semantically rich content words as outlined in section 3.1 and fully described in Heyd (2014) and Heyd (2015). Others are more general and discourse-oriented: in particular, users tend to display more or less overt stances in their community interactions that situate them identity-wise. In such utterances, items such as *am* and *dey* may be used – strategically or unwittingly – to reinforce and indeed index the specific persona in question. The following examples provide qualitative evidence of how the differing semantic variants of *am* and *dey* are used in context, and how they can play a part in linguistically indexing local Nigerian vs. global, diasporic identities – and the various qualities and stances that are conventionally associated with these identities.

In example (10), a user overtly embraces the use of NigP, both through the content of her metalinguistic utterance and her seasoned performance of digital NigP:

(10) (...) wettin na?! Pidgin should even become national lingo jare!! I mean who no **dey** speak brokin abeg!! SIDON DIA!!!
[What's up? Pidgin should even become our national language. I mean, who does not speak pidgin, please? Shut up!]

Similarly, we find this identity in discussions where a life in Nigeria vs. abroad are discursively pitted against each other, as in this discussion about the 2007 presidential elections:

(11)  You are not even based in nigeria and You are saying with confidence who will/will not rule lagos.guy no be yankee we **dey** ok.
[You are not even based in nigeria and You are saying with confidence who will/will not rule lagos. Man, we are not in the United States, ok?]

This local, Nigerian identity can be contrasted with a diasporic identity, which embraces global and particularly western notions. This is clearly captured in example 12, where the user (a young woman based in the UK) strongly affiliates with European club football, a quintessentially western commodity, and does so through the heavy use of expletives, digital supervernacular features such as the use of numericals (<no1>) and leetspeak-inspired replacement of letters with symbols, such as <@$$es>:

(12)  ey no1 mess with my arsenal babies! **dey** rock...**dey** just standing up..**dey** gon f*ck chelsea and Manchester United in de @$$es next
[Hey, no one mess with my Arsenal babies! They rock... They are just starting to stand up... They will fuck Chelsea and Manchester United in the asses next.]

Example 13 is reminiscent of example 11 in that it infers an opposition of home (Nigeria) vs. abroad; here however, the user is a young man living in the UK, who as a consequence affiliates with the diasporic identity:

(13)  I only hope 9jerians @ home pray too because most want to come abroad thus dey pray 4 dere dream counties
[I only hope Nigerians at home pray too because most want to come abroad, thus they pray for their dream countries]

Finally, for *am*, examples (14) and (15) show this opposition in stances and performed identities. Both are metalinguistic utterances that address notions of linguistic authenticity and properness and ways of being a legitimate language user. Example (14) is taken from a folk-linguistic discussion about linguistic accommodation in the diaspora, and criticizes a child's ability to "form jand," i.e., accommodate to a British accent:

(14) Ok but the child is 3, you think say her mama **dey** tell **am** to form jand at this age?
[Ok, but the child is three, are you implying that his mother told him to put on a British accent at this age?]

In this case, the user strongly aligns with a Nigerian identity through the heavy use of digital NigP features as well as the pro-NigP stance expressed in his utterance. The opposite is true in example (15):

(15) @[username] **am** sorry to say but your written English is quite poor!!!!!
[@[username] I am sorry to say but your written English is quite poor!!!!!]

Here, two users are in disagreement over a political debate, which prompts the metalinguistic ad hominem attack shown in example (15) – a discourse strategy which is repeatedly found in the corpus (see Heyd 2015 for an in-depth analysis). Here, the diasporic user accuses his opponent of a lack of English proficiency, referring to written StE. It is of course noteworthy that the user's utterance itself does not quite conform to StE written norms, for example regarding the excessive use of punctuation and the secondary nonstandard use of *am*. Through this move, and the stance displayed in the utterance, the user affiliates himself with a diasporic, Western identity, where StE, but also digital usage of the language, is valued.

These examples show how little words such as *am* and *dey*, despite their relative lack of semantic richness, can perform a function in the machinery of social meaning-making. In the case study described here, it can be argued that semantic variation is a more important factor in the evocation of different types of nonstandardness than orthographic variation. This finding may not be true for many other situations, but it is worth noting, because digital language use has so often been associated with and enregistered through notions of orthographic deviation (Squires 2010). This opens up room for future studies, as the notion of semantic variation in digital usage is so far an underexplored field.

# 5 Conclusion

This paper has given an overview on global contact, spread and change of English in digital settings. The language ecology of global Nigerian usage is a good model to monitor such forces at work, as NigP is simultaneously a very old and longstanding English-lexifier contact language, and at the same time strongly involved in the traction of linguistic globalization. On a larger scale, the results discussed here provide insight into a digital community and its dynamics of interaction. A community such as Nairaland shows quite clearly that the co-presence of both local and diasporically spread users in a shared digital environment has a deep impact on the digital emergence of ethnolinguistic vernaculars and similar nonstandard repertoires. The fact that such digital platforms have become a more or less natural habitat for globalized communities – and have arguably increased to do so with the global spread of social media – is certainly one of the more powerful effects in the sociolinguistics of mobility and globalization.

On a more specific scale, the case study discussed here has provided insight into patterns of orthographic and semantic variation in digital NigP. The findings showed, with surprising clarity, that orthographic heterogeneity itself is not a major factor of contestation in the digital usage of a nonstandard variety such as NigP. At least for high-frequency items as in the case of the function words *am* and *dey*, a de facto norm-buliding process can be witnessed in the digital usage of NigP. This goes against the popular notion of online language usage as chaotic and rule-resistant, and it shows that digital communities are very good environments for the evolution of shared linguistic practice. Instead, it was found here that semantic variation in the usage of nonstandard items is a much more central issue with regard to variation and change in this linguistic ecology. In particular, it was found here that different meanings of one orthographic form can be evocative of different frameworks of nonstandard language use. And these different frameworks of nonstandardness were shown to coincide with distinct identities and personas as they are negotiated in this community: the locally anchored user, immersed into Nigerian affairs and fluent in NigP, on the one hand; and the globally oriented, technology-savvy user on the other hand. In a digital community such as Nairaland, it is important to stress that these identities are not necessarily tied to the specific geolocation of a language user, quite to the contrary – through the usage of such socially charged items, these identities can be activated regardless of the offline speech community that a user moves in at a given time. In this sense, the analysis of variation and change in nonstandard spelling practices on the internet is a highly relevant angle to study global varieties of English, that goes beyond the somewhat straightforward question of norm-building and standardization; indeed, orthographic practice proves to be an important outlet for the negotiation of identities on a global scale.

In sum, this paper has argued that a fine-grained, corpus-based approach to linguistic effects of superdiversity reveals complex patterns of usage, which are not just limited to different standards of orthography, but deeply involve the negotiation of identities – and as such, the mitigation of linguistic power and prestige in a linguistic ecology. Given that the societal impact of spelling practices is still a somewhat marginalized domain in sociolinguistic analysis (Sebba 2007), issues of variation and change in digital and globalized usage of English provide an important field for investigation, and one that may provide insights about the mechanisms of language contact, spread and change in general.

# 6 References

Agheyisi, Rebecca. 1988. The standardization of Nigerian Pidgin English. *English World-Wide* 9. 227–241.
Androutsopoulos, Jannis (ed.). 2012. *Mediatization and sociolinguistic change*. Berlin: de Gruyter.
Androutsopoulos, Jannis. 2006a. Introduction: Sociolinguistics and computer-mediated communication. *Journal of Sociolinguistics* 10(4). 419–438.
Androutsopoulos, Jannis. 2006b. Multilingualism, diaspora, and the Internet: Codes and identities on German-based diaspora websites. *Journal of Sociolinguistics* 10(4). 429–450.
Blommaert, Jan. 2010. *The sociolinguistics of globalization*. Cambridge: Cambridge University Press.
Blommaert, Jan. 2011. Supervernaculars and their dialects. *Working Papers in Urban Language and Literacies* 81. 1–14.
Blommaert, Jan & Ben Rampton. 2011. Language and superdiversity. *Diversities* 13(2). 1–22.
Cameron, Deborah. 2012. The commodification of language: English as a global commodity. In Terttu Nevalainen & Elizabeth Closs Traugott (eds.), *The Oxford handbook of the history of English*, 352–361. Oxford: Oxford University Press.
Cheshire, Jenny, Paul Kerswill, Sue Fox & Elvind Torgersen. 2011. Contact, the feature pool and the speech community: The emergence of Multicultural London English. *Journal of Sociolinguistics* 15(2). 151–196.
Chiluwa, Innocent. 2013. West African English in Digital Discourse. *Covenant Journal of Language Studies* 1(1). 42–62.
Coupland, Nikolas. 2007. *Style: Language, variation and identity*. Cambridge: Cambridge University Press.
Coupland, Nikolas (ed.). 2010. *The handbook of language and globalization*. Malden, MA: Blackwell.
Danet, Brenda & Susan C. Herring (eds.). 2007. *The multilingual Internet: Language, culture, and communication online*. Oxford: Oxford University Press.
Deuber, Dagmar. 2005. *Nigerian Pidgin in Lagos: Language contact, variation and change in an African urban setting*. London: Battlebridge.
Deuber, Dagmar. 2006. Aspects of variation in educated Nigerian Pidgin: Verbal structures. In Ana Deumert & Stefanie Durrleman (eds.), *Structure and variation in language contact*, 243–261. Creole Language Library 29. Amsterdam: Benjamins.
Deuber, Dagmar & Lars Hinrichs. 2007. Dynamics of orthographic standardization in Jamaican Creole and Nigerian Pidgin. *World Englishes* 26(1). 22–47.
Eckert, Penelope. 2008. Variation and the indexical field. *Journal of Sociolinguistics* 12. 453–76.

Faraclas, Nick. 1996. *Nigerian Pidgin*. London: Routledge.
Gaudio, Rudolf. 2011. The blackness of "Broken English." *Journal of Linguistic Anthropology* 23(2). 230–246.
Heyd, Theresa. 2014. Doing race and ethnicity in a digital community: Lexical labels and narratives of belonging in a Nigerian web forum. *Discourse, Context & Media* 4/5. 38–47.
Heyd, Theresa. 2015. The metacommunicative lexicon of Nigerian Pidgin. *World Englishes* 34(4). 669–687.
Heyd, Theresa & Christian Mair. 2014. From vernacular to digital ethnolinguistic repertoire: The case of Nigerian Pidgin. In Véronique Lacoste, Jakob R. E. Leimgruber & Thiemo Breyer (eds.), *Indexing Authenticity: Perspectives from linguistics and anthropology*, 242–266. Berlin: de Gruyter.
Hinrichs, Lars. 2006. *Code-switching on the web: English and Jamaican Creole in e-mail communication*. Amsterdam: Benjamins.
Ifukor, Presley. 2011. Spelling and simulated shibboleths in Nigerian computer-mediated communication. *English Today* 27(3). 35–42.
Leimgruber, Jakob. 2015. Bah in Singapore English. *World Englishes* 35(1). 78–97.
Leow, Ronald. Héctor Campos & Donna Lardière (eds.). 2009. *Little words: Their history, phonology, syntax, semantics, pragmatics, and acquisition*. Washington: Georgetown University Press.
Liu, Jin & Hongyin Tao (eds.). 2012. *Chinese under globalization: Emerging trends in language use in China*. Singapore: Stallion Press.
Mair, Christian. 2013. The World System of Englishes: Accounting for the transnational importance of mobile and mediated vernaculars. *English World-Wide* 34(3). 253–278.
Mair, Christian & Stefan Pfänder. 2013. Using vernacular resources to create digital spaces: towards a sociolinguistics of diasporic web forums. In Peter Auer, Martin Hilpert, Anja Stukenbrock & Benedikt Szmrecsanyi (eds.), *Space in language and linguistics: Geographical, interactional, and cognitive perspectives*, 529–555. Berlin/New York: de Gruyter.
Mann, Charles. 1993. The sociolinguistic status of Anglo-Nigerian Pidgin: An overview. *International Journal of the Sociology of Language* 100/101. 167–178.
Mensah, Eya Offiong. 2011. Lexicalization in Nigerian Pidgin. *Concentric: Studies in Linguistics* 37(2). 209–240.
Moll, Andrea. 2015. *Jamaican Creole goes web: Sociolinguistic styling and authenticity in a digital yaad*. Amsterdam: Benjamins.
Omoniyi, Tope. 2009. So I choose to do am Naija style: Hip hop, language, and post colonial identities. In H. Samy Alim, Awad Ibrahim & Alastair Pennycook (eds.), *Global linguistic flows: Hip Hop Cultures, youth identities, and the politics of language*, 113–135. London: Routledge.
Sayers, Dave. 2014. The mediated innovation model: A framework for researching media influence in language change. *Journal of Sociolinguistics* 18(2). 185–212.
Seargeant, Philip & Caroline Tagg. 2011. English on the internet and a 'post-varieties' approach to language. *World Englishes* 30(4). 496–514.
Schneider, Edgar. 2007. *Postcolonial English: Varieties around the world*. Cambridge: Cambridge University Press.
Sebba, Mark. 2007. *Spelling and society*. Cambridge: Cambridge University Press.
Squires, Lauren. 2010. Enregistering internet language. *Language in Society* 39. 457–492.

Matt Garley and Benjamin Slade
# Virtual meatspace: Word formation and deformation in cyberpunk discussions

## 1 Introduction

In 2013, US government contractor Edward Snowden made public information about PRISM, a global internet surveillance program run by the US National Security Administration, in a highly-publicized case which led to his flight into exile abroad. In 2014, a group known as the Guardians of Peace, possibly sponsored by North Korean government elements, hacked into the computer systems of Sony Pictures Entertainment. In 2009, the US Secretary of Defense established a "United States Cyber Command" (USCYBERCOM), which "unifies the direction of cyberspace operations, strengthens DoD [Department of Defense] cyberspace capabilities, and integrates and bolsters DoD's cyber expertise" (U.S. Strategic Command 2015).

In a present where drone warfare is a commonplace means of international action, and corporate and government interests intersect around notions of "cyberwarfare," there are many parallels to be drawn from reality to the cyberpunk genre of science fiction. William Gibson, coiner of the term *cyberspace* and author of seminal cyberpunk works like *Neuromancer*, noted in 2012 that "Cyberpunk today is a standard Pantone shade in pop culture" (Evans 2012).

Since its inception, the cyberpunk genre of science fiction, which has instantiations in literature, cinema, and videogames, has influenced music and fashion, and has spawned a subculture of fans interested in its ideas and aesthetics. This chapter deals with the use of linguistic forms in online cyberpunk discussions. This domain is interesting precisely because this culture is digitally "native," dating to the earliest instantiations of internet communication and surviving across the intervening decades, with the locus of active discussion shifting across multiple CMC platforms. These discussions are characterized by frequent neologisms and jargon.

In an initial exploration of cyberpunk glossaries found online, we noticed a variety of formation processes for cyberpunk terms: compounding (*screamsheet* 'newspaper'), clipping (*base* 'database') and acronym formation (*DNI* 'direct neural interface'), as well as fantasized borrowings (*gomi*, Japanese 'junk'). In

---
**Matt Garley,** York College, City University of New York
**Benjamin Slade,** University of Utah

this analysis, we are motivated by the question of which methods of word-formation are most characteristic and productive within cyberpunk discussions online from the late 1980s to the present day. This research question engages with long-standing questions in sociohistorical linguistics regarding actuation, the origin of linguistic features; and transmission, the means by which such features spread. We deal with the latter question on a subculture-wide level, engaging the question of which forms are favored in this particular subculture.

In this chapter, we examine the ways in which words characteristic of cyberpunk are formed and deformed through diverse and complex processes, including blending around common sound/character sequences (*corpsicle*), re-spelling (*tek* for 'tech' or *cypx* for 'cyberpunk'), and sequential clipping-compounding (*netrode* 'network' + 'electrode'), as well as more complex creations (e.g., *teledildonics*).

We find clipping with compounding to be the most characteristically "cyberpunk" word-formation process in the data in terms of both frequency of word-formation strategy, and frequency of use of the resulting neologisms. Our data include corpora from the Virtual Meatspace forum, including posts from the years 2006–2013 (Cyberpunk Review, 2013), and the Collective Cyberpunk Community forums, spanning the years 2011–2013 (Collective Cyberpunk Community, 2013), alongside 1980s-90s Usenet data from alt.cyberpunk. We combine these analyses in order to provide a longer-term view of lexical formation/deformation within the cyberpunk subculture. Several roots, including clipped forms like *trode* 'electrode,' seem to be especially productive. Other common constructions take the form of *cyber-X*, *X-punk*, *X-jockey/jock*, and *X-boy/girl*. While some of these formation processes are well-known (see, e.g., Bauer and Renouf 2001), the large-scale use of such lexical innovations in the context of a subculture is not well-researched, and through the combination of synchronic and diachronic analysis, we make an effort to fill this research gap.

Part of the examination of the spread of neologisms must also involve analysis of the development and spread of elements more abstract than lexical items, i.e., morphological processes. The nature of online discourse – posts marked with explicit dates, threaded conversations, etc. – offers an ideal opportunity to observe and categorize the adoption of neologisms and investigate the abstract morphological means of their coinage.

# 2 Cyberpunk: A primer

Cyberpunk is an artistic genre (mainly literary) which coalesced in the early 1980s, and is most strongly associated with the early works of William Gibson, Bruce Sterling, Rudy Rucker, and John Shirley, though cyberpunk's prevailing vision of the future as non-utopian (and often dystopic) can be traced back further to authors like Philip K. Dick. Certainly the film *Blade Runner* (1982), an adaptation of Dick's *Do Androids Dream of Electric Sheep?*, did much to establish the visual aesthetics for cyberpunk, and Dick's novel indeed presages the genre with guiding questions of what constitutes "human." Gibson, Sterling, and other "cyberpunk authors" broke away from the mainstream science fiction of the time, and dealt with "marginalized people in technologically-enhanced cultural 'systems'" (Frank et al. 1998). Technology is often shown in a somewhat ambivalent light in cyberpunk depictions: both as a tool used to oppress, and as a means of escaping (or transgressing or transcending) limitations, both legal and natural.

The term *cyberpunk* was itself coined in the title of a short story by Bruce Bethke, who notes on its formation:[1]

> The invention of the c-word was a conscious and deliberate act of creation on my part. [...] I was actively *trying* to invent a new term that grokked the juxtaposition of punk attitudes and high technology. [...] How did I actually create the word? The way any new word comes into being, I guess: through synthesis. I took a handful of roots – cyber, techno, et al – mixed them up with a bunch of terms for socially misdirected youth, and tried out the various combinations until one just plain sounded right. (Bethke 1997: para. 3)

Beyond its status in literature, cyberpunk became a subculture of sorts, as people began to both identify and be identified as cyberpunks. As with many subcultural communities, gatekeeping and authenticity soon became significant. As R.U. Sirius, editor of erstwhile cyberpunk zine *Mondo 2000*, put it:

> Cyberpunk escaped from being a literary genre into cultural reality. People started calling themselves cyberpunks, or the media started calling people cyberpunks. The first people to identify themselves as cyberpunks were adolescent computer hackers who related to the street-hardened characters and the worlds created in the books of William Gibson, Bruce Sterling, John Shirley, and others. Cyberpunk hit the front page of the New York Times when some young computer kids were arrested for cracking a government computer file. The Times called the kids "cyberpunks." Finally, cyberpunk has come to be seen as a generic name for a much larger trend more or less describing anyone who relates to the cyberpunk vision. This, in turn, has created a purist reaction among the hard-core cyberpunks, who feel they got there first. (Sirius, cited in T and Maniac 2004a)

---

1 The *cyber-* of *cyberpunk* is ultimately from *cybernetic*, either via shortening/clipping or blending or both, itself introduced into English in the first half of the 20th century (based on ancient Greek κυβερνήτης 'steersman'), applied to self-regulatory automata, or mechanisms exhibiting some sort of automatic control, but by the sixies at latest coming to be associated particularly with the integration of living organisms (particularly humans) and electronic or other technological devices, as in *cyborg* (for *cybernetic organism*). (Cf. "cybernetic, adj." & "cyber-, comb. form." *OED Online*. Oxford University Press, June 2015. Web. 14 June 2015.)

Since the early 1990s, when the above quote was written, it would be increasingly rare to find anyone who identified primarily with the label "cyberpunk" – however, many fans in diverse groups or as individuals still identify themselves as being interested in cyberpunk fiction, aesthetics, media, fashion, etc. For the majority of its existence, then, cyberpunk should not be understood as a single close-knit or monolithic fan community as, for example, the online *Buffy the Vampire Slayer* community is (see, e.g., Gatson 2011; Gatson and Zweerink 2004), but rather something more diffuse and widespread than a traditional sociolinguistic community, which has as its organizing principle not a location or web address, but an informal canon of media. Furthermore, those who engage with cyberpunk media largely do so by the use of, and extension of, various lexical innovations.

The seminal cyberpunk novel is usually considered to be William Gibson's *Neuromancer* (1984), which introduced or popularized words like *deck*, *simstims*, *ICE*, *cyberspace*, and *matrix*. This is one of the first literary works to depict an alternative reality space whose existence is mediated by technology, a "matrix" that can be entered by interfacing human minds with computers. Later works like Neal Stephenson's *Snow Crash* (1992), sometimes considered the first "post-cyberpunk" novel or an almost-parody of cyberpunk, continued to develop the idea of a virtual cyber-world ("metaverse") which takes on an importance equal to that of the "real" (or "meatspace") world. Stephenson's novel popularized the term *avatar* in the sense of a user's virtual online body, or a user's alter ego in the metaverse. Neologisms are an especially prominent and noticeable linguistic feature characteristic of cyberpunk discussion, and the analysis of such neologisms will form the primary matter of the present chapter.

Cyberpunk is particularly interesting in terms of linguistic analysis for several reasons. First, it constitutes a culture that is technologically aware and has been online since the earliest days of the internet. It is thus digitally native in the sense that it primarily coalesced online. Second, it survived across several decades, with the locus of active discussion shifting across multiple CMC platforms, from Usenet groups to web forums and social media. Because of these features, cyberpunk is a domain of interest for questions regarding how neologisms are formed and spread, and more specifically, how and to what degree orthographic features influence the formation and spread of these neologisms.

## 3 Data

In order to collect a diverse set of linguistic interactions within the cyberpunk subculture, we evaluated a large number of resources from varied sources, informed by (often fairly dated) clearinghouses online like The Cyberpunk

Project (http://www.cyberpunk.ru) which collected comprehensive lists of links to cyberpunk resources and locations of communication online. The primary data we analyze were collected from the Cyberpunk Review Forums (http://cyberpunkreview.com/forums/index.php), established in January 2006, and its successor the Collective Cyberpunk Community Forums (http://cyberpunkforums.com), where the non-review forums of the Cyberpunk Review Forums were moved to in August 2011. Together, these data consist of about 90,000 threads and approximately 4.88 million words.

We also examined data from the Usenet archive of the newsgroup alt.cyberpunk, accessible via Google Groups. The earliest posts archived today date to 1987, and this newsgroup was active at least through the late 1990s. The current configuration of Google Groups prohibits full scraping of the alt.cyberpunk archive, but is fully searchable – we examined this archive manually for forms of interest, searching for terms we identified in the other corpora to provide historical perspective.[2]

In order to understand the influence of neologisms in published cyberpunk literature on neologism formation and use in cyberpunk interaction online, we additionally collected a small corpus of cyberpunk literature, comprised of 42 fiction texts (ranging from short stories to novellas to novels) published between 1980 and 2007 by 17 noted cyberpunk authors. The corpus contains 2,153,406 word tokens. The authors most frequently represented in the corpus, in light of their prominent influence in the cyberpunk genre, are William Gibson (7 sole-authored texts and one co-authored text, including the seminal *Neuromancer* trilogy), Bruce Sterling (5 texts) and Rudy Rucker (4 texts). This corpus is not intended to be exhaustive in terms of the canon of cyberpunk literature, but contains what we consider to be a core set of firmly in-genre texts, based on a combination of online lists of cyberpunk works and literature which was available online in plaintext format.

---

[2] We also collected the top 1000 "top" posts and top 1000 "controversial" posts (together with comments on the posts) of all time (as of September 2013) from reddit.com/r/cyberpunk. These data consist of approximately 831 thousand words. However, we found that the corpus we collected from reddit was largely uninteresting in lexical terms, in that vanishingly few neologisms were present. In examining these data, we found that the redditors in /r/cyberpunk weren't creating new vocabulary, or even using much pre-existing cyberpunk vocabulary. We suggest that this is part of the nature of being a subreddit – that because /r/cyberpunk is just one small piece of reddit even for /r/cyberpunk-subscribers, the community and the community interaction structure is very different from a dedicated cyberpunk forum. For these reasons, we do not cite any examples originating in these data in the present chapter.

## 4 Method

We began our investigation by creating an XML-format corpus from the combined forums, removing quoted lines (any lines reproducing material seen in the last 200 lines of forum interaction). This XML corpus was then reformatted into a second file with one line per post, ignoring usernames used in the last 10 posts, lowercasing all words, and keeping only alphanumeric characters. This corpus was 4,962,921 word tokens in size. From this file, a frequency-ranked wordlist was created from the combined forum corpus, removing words found in an aspell wordlist containing US and British spellings, created using the SCOWL tool (Atkinson 2014). After removing dictionary words, the authors jointly annotated the first 2,752 entries by frequency in the list of 85,114 remaining neologism candidates[3] (a wordlist of non-dictionary words).

The hand-annotation of the wordlist served two purposes, the first being to remove those words known to the authors to be uninteresting acronyms, proper names, brand names, typos, usernames, etc. – i.e., to filter material which included non-dictionary words but which did not represent word-formation in the cyberpunk subculture. The second purpose of hand-annotation was to categorize the remaining forms according to word-formation processes. Before annotating the wordlist, we consulted several available cyberpunk glossaries (e.g., T and Maniac 2004a) to get a feel for what members of the subculture considered cyberpunk terminology and to gauge the kind of lexical items we might find in the corpus. In advance of analysis, we also informally looked over a selection of words from the corpus, finding that several categories of words seemed to be especially relevant to cyberpunk literature or culture – in doing so, we allowed our proposed categories to emerge organically from the data. However, in performing annotation, we kept in mind that these categories were suggestions only, and subject to revision – many words seemed to be included in multiple categories, for example, *netrode* for 'networked electrode.' This example qualifies as a form produced by both clipping and subsequent compounding, or else a blend – we devote a later part of this chapter to discussion of the putative difference.

We independently hand-filtered and coded the first 2752 unknown wordforms, a list including every form occurring 10 or more times in the forum corpus (and occurring at least twice per million word tokens in the corpus). Details of the tagging scheme are discussed in the next section.

---

[3] Out of 127,762 words types in the corpus, 85,114 were not found in the aspell dictionary. 65,465 of these were hapax legomena (occuring only once in the corpus) and 10,878 were dis legomena (occuring only twice).

The annotators' lists agreed on the categorization of 140 wordforms, and 823 in total were identified as neologisms by at least one of the two annotators. In the end, we took some examples from this larger inclusive list as we recognized that one or the other of us had missed a form which, upon reflection, we both agreed was a valid neologism. However, the list of 140 was useful in that these terms certainly seemed to be the most prototypical cyberpunk neologisms of those under consideration.

After using these corpus methods to identify neologisms, we performed qualitative morphological and orthographic analysis of their formation processes, confirmed their use in context, and examined their occurrence in the other corpora. Because Google's Usenet archives of the alt.cyberpunk newsgroup date to only three years after the first publication of *Neuromancer* (1984), finding terms in use in the Usenet archive as well as in our more recent forum corpus could theoretically establish a pattern of use within cyberpunk subculture for 26 years, i.e., the time between the foundation of the Usenet archive and the collection of the internet forum corpus. Such a pattern of use would reveal continuity of use across users interested in cyberpunk, likely through re-seeding of the lexicon from primary sources (the canonical cyberpunk works).

# 5 Analysis

## 5.1 Preliminaries: the problem of compounding, clipping, and blending

In our initial identification of categories, we posited five word-formation processes:

- compounding, whereby (usually) free morphemes are compounded into a single word – e.g., *meatspace*;
- clipping, whereby part of a word, usually one or more syllables, is omitted from the beginning or end – e.g., *trode* for 'electrode' or *net* for 'network';
- respellings, whereby orthographic substitutions are made that would not alter pronunciation – e.g., *lo-tek* for 'low tech';
- acronyms/initialisms (e.g., *ICE*, 'intrusion countermeasure electronics'), whereby a word is made from the initial letters of several other words in sequence; and
- foreign borrowings, which reflect influence from a non-English language in the cyberpunk fantasy context, e.g., *gomi*, Japanese for 'junk.'

Table 1 provides a listing of 20 representative terms from the 140 on which the annotators agreed, and Table 2 presents a breakdown by category of the results of the annotation task.

Table 1: Representative neologisms found in the cyberpunk discussion forum corpus

| Wordform | Categories assigned | Freq. (raw) | Freq. per mil. words | Presence in novel corpus | Earliest use in Usenet | First/last use in forum corpus |
|---|---|---|---|---|---|---|
| cy | clipping | 439 | 88.46 | Not found | Not found | Nov. 2006–May 2013 |
| vr | acronym | 328 | 66.09 | 5 authors, earliest 1991 | Aug. 1988 | Feb. 2006–May 2013 |
| meatspace | compound | 194 | 39.09 | 3 authors, earliest 2001 | Jan. 1998 | Jan. 2006–Feb. 2013 |
| emp | acronym | 100 | 20.15 | 2 authors, earliest 1988 | Apr. 1991 | May 2007–Feb. 2013 |
| cyberware | clipping, compounding | 68 | 13.70 | Not found | Sept. 1989 | Oct. 2006–Mar. 2013 |
| cypx | clipping, compounding, respelling | 64 | 12.90 | Not found | Not found | Oct. 2011–Feb. 2013 |
| wetware | clipping, compounding | 63 | 12.70 | 5 authors, earliest 1985 | Sept. 1997 | Mar. 2006–Feb. 2013 |
| transhuman | compounding | 50 | 10.07 | 1 author, earliest 2005 | Mar. 1991 | Jan. 2007–Apr. 2013 |
| rez | clipping | 47 | 9.47 | 3 authors, earliest 1984 | Mar. 1992 | Apr. 2006–Feb. 2013 |
| cyberdeck | clipping, compounding | 31 | 6.25 | Not found ('deck' is common in this sense across authors) | Dec. 1989 | Mar. 2007–Mar. 2013 |
| transmet | clipping, compounding | 28 | 5.64 | Not found (usu. refers to Transmetropolitan, a popular comic book with cyberpunk themes) | Oct. 1998 | Jan. 2007–Mar. 2013 |
| cyberia | clipping, compounding (blending) | 26 | 5.24 | Not found (title of a 1994 nonfiction book and unrelated video game, among other usages) | Jun. 1991 | Apr. 2006–Feb. 2013 |
| razorgirls | compounding | 25 | 5.04 | 1 author, earliest 1984 | Apr. 1991 | Jan. 2007–Jun. 2012 |
| darknets | clipping, compounding | 24 | 4.84 | Not found | Not found | Jan. 2007–Feb. 2013 |
| cyberprep | clipping, compounding | 24 | 4.84 | Not found | Sept. 1987 | Aug. 2006–Jun. 2010 |
| neurofunk | clipping, compounding | 18 | 3.63 | Not found | Not found | Jul. 2008–Mar. 2013 |
| ghostnet | clipping, compounding | 13 | 2.62 | Not found | Not found | Mar. 2009–Jan. 2010 |
| utopiates | clipping, compounding (blending) | 12 | 2.42 | Not found (name of a recent comic book, but usage is attested earlier) | Not found | Aug. 2012–Oct. 2012 |
| psyborg | clipping, compounding, respelling | 12 | 2.42 | Not found | Not found | Mar. 2010–Apr. 2013 |
| cryo | clipping | 12 | 2.42 | Not found | Sept. 1989 | Feb. 2007–Oct. 2012 |

**Table 2:** Results of categorization/filtering

|                        | both annotators                          |                                    | at least one annotator                   |                                    |
|------------------------|------------------------------------------|------------------------------------|------------------------------------------|------------------------------------|
| type of neologism      | number of forms identified with label    | percent of forms with label        | number of forms identified with label    | percent of forms with label        |
| compounding            | 70                                       | 50.00%                             | 254                                      | 30.86%                             |
| clipping               | 38                                       | 27.14%                             | 168                                      | 20.41%                             |
| respelling             | 30                                       | 21.43%                             | 76                                       | 9.23%                              |
| acronym/initialism     | 32                                       | 22.86%                             | 296[4]                                   | 35.97%                             |
| foreign neologism      | 8                                        | 5.71%                              | 81                                       | 9.84%                              |
| any or multiple labels | 140                                      | 100%                               | 823                                      | 100%                               |

It quickly became evident that, for many of the items in our corpus, the compounding and clipping labels coincided—for the list of forms agreed upon by annotators, 20 forms were categorized as both clippings and compoundings (over half of all forms involving clipping, and over a quarter of all forms involving compounding). For the list of forms identified by at least one of the annotators, 70 forms were categorized as both (about 40% of clippings and over a quarter of compounds). This spurred a discussion of whether *blending* might be the more appropriate term for some of these items, e.g., *utopiates* (< *utopia+opiates*).

In addition, the frequent combination of morphologically quasi-bound components like *cyber-* and *-ware* with free morphemes might more appropriately be called *derivation*. Further complicating the analysis of such elements more generally is the problem, discussed by Arnold Zwicky, of *libfixation*, "the 'liberation' of parts of words [like '-flation' and '-naut'] to yield word-forming elements that are semantically like the elements of compounds but are affix-like in that they are typically bound" (Zwicky 2010). This problem is additionally discussed by Hock & Joseph (1996/2009), who note with regard to an initial monomorphemic form *marathon* that "once forms like bik(e)athon and telethon [...] have arisen, it is possible to reanalyze them as containing a suffix -(a)thon. Four-part analogy, then, can extend this suffix to new forms, such as *rentathon* or *saleathon*" (see also Bauer 2004, who refers to "splinters"). In the case of cyberpunk-related forms like *wetware*, the *-ware* in this case is not the (increasingly archaic) free

---

[4] The high rate of acronyms/initialisms in this column reflects one of the two annotators who included a large number of established/enregistered internet-culture acronyms, e.g., *lol*, *wtf*, *stfu* in counts.

morpheme referring to tangible trade goods. Just as *software* was created by analogy to the earlier *hardware* (in the sense of 'tools'), *wetware* and *meatware*, further discussed in the corpus context below, are formed by analogy to (specifically computer) *hardware* and *software*, and as compounding of other forms with *-ware* becomes more frequent, something more akin to an affix takes shape.

Because of these difficulties, we do not distinguish between derivation and compounding in this analysis, and consider blending prototypically a process where there is graphemic and/or phonemic overlap in the final form (e.g., *liger* from 'lion' + 'tiger,' *motel* from 'motor' + 'hotel'), and/or the semantics suggest a blend of the components (as in *liger*, *spork*, and *brunch*),[5] while continuing to treat such forms as both clippings and instances of compounding.

We examine below the different types of morphological formations observed in the neologisms in our dataset: compounding; respellings, acronyms and other orthography-centric processes; clipping; and finally forms which involve both clipping and compounding. Processes which might be labeled as *derivation* are included under compounds; all of these are cases involving putative prefixes which are either libfixes (e.g., *cyber-*) or else prefixes of somewhat limited productivity (e.g., *mega-*).

We do not claim that every one of these terms originated in the CMC environment of the cyberpunk forums/newsgroup, or even in the cyberpunk literature or subculture (although a number of them certainly did). What we do claim, however, is that these are in relatively frequent use in the texts produced by one or more of these instantiations of the online cyberpunk community, and therefore particularly characteristic of the language of cyberpunk discussion.

## 5.2 Compounding

In (1–3) below, we include examples of fairly straightforward compounding. When possible, we select in-context examples from different dates and corpora to demonstrate continuity of use. If we were additionally able to identify the term's origin or popularization in a specific work of literature, we indicate this as well.

---

[5] The examples in this paragraph are common examples, as relatively few of the forms we considered in our analysis would qualify as blending under this definition.

(1) *meatspace* (< *meat* + *space*, by analogy with *cyberspace*)
    novel corpus: 3 authors, earliest 2001
    forum corpus: 194 hits, 39.09 per million words

   a. [Usenet, 1998] If it has happened in "meatspace", absolutely nothing would be different.

   b. [forums, 2011] Currently, as soon as meatspace allows, I plan on [...]

   c. [forums, 2011] I had prepared [username]'s "Occupy Meatspace" poster but never managed to [...]

(2) *razorgirl* (< *razor* + *girl*, originating in *Neuromancer*)
    novel corpus: 1 author, earliest 1984
    forum corpus: 25 hits, 5.04 per million words

   a. [Usenet, 1993] Subject: RazorGirls [user posts story about Japanese businessmen hiring female bodyguards]

   b. [forums, 2007] Of course who couldn't love (or is it lust) razorgirls and I think the archetype that Gibson established...

(3) *datajack* (< *data* + *jack*, popularized in *Shadowrun* role-playing game)
    novel corpus: not found
    forum corpus: 19 hits, 3.83 per million words

   a. [Usenet, 1991] This is accessible by traditional terminals ('turtles') or by plugging a 'Deck' into a datajack implanted in one's [...]

   b. [forums, 2008] Doesn't sound very feasible, you'd need a DNI to affect them that much. That means trodes or access to any datajack they may have.

Other examples of compounding include *rivethead* and *cellflux*. In their form, such examples are relatively unremarkable, though the choice of compounding elements is of interest, especially in the case of *meat-*, used in opposition to *cyber-*, carrying negative connotations of impermanence of the crass physical realm and the ordure of bodily existence. It is in addition worth noting that these, and other terms, are sometimes put in scare quotes, as with *"meatspace"* in (1a). This, along with hyphenation of compounds (*trode-net* in 12a) or the use of apostrophes to indicate elided material in the case of clippings, would constitute what Squires (2014) calls *metalinguistic highlighting*, indicating that attention is being called to the term's unfamiliarity – or conversely, that the term's indexical nature is being highlighted. This, then, further underlines the social importance of these terms in the forum community, and in the subculture more broadly.

## 5.3 Respelling, acronyms, and other orthography-centric changes

We find examples of respellings like (4), a form adopted from hacker culture:

(4)  *warez* (respelling from spurious pluralization of *software*)
novel corpus: 2 authors, earliest 1992
forum corpus: 22 hits, 4.43 per million words

   a. [Usenet, 1997] [...] little kids who think they are cyberpunks because they know how to use a warez.

   b. [forums, various dates] 'malwarez', 'spywarez', 'how much warez', 'the exact piece of warez youre looking for'

Respellings of <z> for <s> and <k> for <c> (or <ch>) are relatively common in English, though their association with nonconformity, resistance, and subversion is appropriate to the sensibilities of cyberpunk – similar forms were noted by Androutsopoulos (2000) in an analysis of German punk fanzines, and the use of orthographic <z> is also common in the German hip hop community (Garley forthcoming). In both of these contexts, as in the cyberpunk subculture, stylization and dissociation from written norms is accomplished through the use of alternative orthography. Another respelling represented in our data is *lo-tek*, which fits in with well-known mainstream respellings like *hi-fi*. Additional respellings found especially in the later forum data include *w00t*, *sux*, and *skool* (primarily in the set phrase *old/new/nu skool*), along with *lulz* and *pwn*, but we believe these sorts of respellings to be fairly common across genres, and reflective more of a generalized "internet culture" set of respellings (see the chapters by Heyd and Hinrichs, this volume, for further treatment of generalized "internet culture"). Acronyms and initialisms are also found in our data, as in *ICE* 'intrusion countermeasure electronics,' from *Neuromancer*, *AR* 'augmented reality,' and *EMP* 'electromagnetic pulse.'

As these are very straightforward examples in terms of word formation process, we omit further discussion here, focusing instead on a more interesting respelling with some aspects of an acronym appearing in our data. This form, *cypx*, is not found in the novel or Usenet corpora, and was first used (and possibly coined) in 2011 by forum user "Z." In this example, we have used single capital letters as pseudonyms for forum usernames because orientation to and ratification of the new linguistic feature can be seen in detail in the forum corpus. The excerpts in (5) do not occur in the same thread, but all (except the first usage) comment metalinguistically on the form.

(5) *cypx* (alternate form of *cyberpunk(s)*)
    novel corpus: not found
    forum corpus: 64 hits, 12.90 per million words

   a. [Z, Nov 2011] re: CYPX boots

   b. [C, Feb 2012] The assumption is fine by me, I'd rather live without the term 'cp' (besides 'cypx looks much better...hehe...) than risk attracting attention over the nasty kind of 'cp'...

   c. [K, Feb 2012] I also prefer cypx; it's not much longer than cy, and looks better than cp. The x is a nice touch.

   d. [C, Oct 2012] Neither really feels that cypx (<= Z, I really like that expression)

Here, the form *cypx* is standing in as a clipping/respelling of *cyberpunk*; the clipping of *cyber-* to *cy-* represents a fairly common syllabic clipping process, but the replacement of <unk> with <x> in <-px> is part of a much rarer respelling process, presumably one in which the <x> stands as a sort of "wildcard" for variable orthographic material, rather than its usual value of [z] or [ks].

It is further possible that the final <x> is influenced by tech-culture forms like *Linux, Unix,* and perhaps even *Xerox,* all of which, however, use <x> for [ks]. The name of the markup/formatting language *LaTeX* popular in tech-culture also contains a final <X>/<χ>, which is officially pronounced [k] (or, more rarely, [x]).

This respelling process is found in, e.g., telecommunications in *Tx/Rx*, abbreviations for 'transmit' and 'receive,' or *Dxing*, listening to shortwave radio over extreme distances; as well as in medical use, where a wide range of abbreviations like *Rx* 'prescription,' *Px* 'prognosis,' *Tx* 'treatment,' and *Hx* 'history' are used in healthcare environments (between healthcare professionals, rather than with patients).

After the initial uses of the form in (5), the form becomes more common across threads and users, appearing in the forums in the inflected comparative form *cypxer* ('more cyberpunk'), the derived form *cypx'ness/cypx-ness*, in the phrase 'CYPX helping CYPX,' i.e., representing the plural noun 'cyberpunks,' and used similarly in the phrase "for you cypx I make the exception." In the latter two cases, where *cypx* is read as 'cyberpunks,' the <x> could have orthographic-phonemic correspondence to the final <-ks>. In terms of its social significance, however, we posit that the true motivation for the use of <x> in this case is like that for <x> in the German punk fanzines analyzed by Androutsopoulos (2000: 14):

> The crucial motivation for these spelling variants is not phonetic representation, but their indexical or symbolic value as cues of subcultural positioning. In other words, they act as an instruction to interpret the discourse as 'subculturally engaged' or 'hip.'

Likewise, the use and spread of *cypx* to represent both adjective/singular noun and plural forms in our present forum data is likely to have been successful precisely because the form suggests subcultural engagement. Because this becomes the autonym for the community, its relevance and success are further reinforced (cf. Gatson and Zweerink's (2004) community of "Bronzers" in the *Buffy the Vampire Slayer* fan forum). Thus, the process of clipping and respelling in this way is a central practice in constructing and maintaining the identity of the cyberpunk subculture.

## 5.4 Clipping

Clipped elements, like (6)–(8), are of course not infrequent in many registers of English, e.g., *ad, ref, sub, ad, pub, flu* etc., though many clipped items carry a sense of the modern with them (*phone, bot, fax, memo, pop, gas, fridge*, etc.) and frequently the use of clipped forms implies general familiarity with the referent. Thus the use of *trode* rather than *electrode* suggests a setting in which electrodes are more of a common, everyday sort of item than they are at present.

(6)  *trodes* (< *electrodes*, originating in *Neuromancer*)
 novel corpus: 2 authors, earliest 1984
 forum corpus: 14 hits, 2.82 per million words

   a. [Usenet, 1989] But I don't see any way that you could be stuck should someone at your physical location remove your 'trodes and thereby snap you back into your body.

   b. [forums, 2012] Another brain-wave scanner, but this one looks really nice.. 4 trodes..

(7) *stim* (< *stimulant* or *stimulation*, *Neuromancer* as *simstim*, later in trilogy as *stim*)
   novel corpus: 1 author, earliest 1984
   forum corpus: 15 hits, 3.02 per million words

   a. [Usenet, 1990] Remember, the translation device in a cyberdeck is a scaled-down stim unit

   b. [forums, 2010] When I do drink coffee, I look for the instant stuff [...] But, I'm trying to avoid stims these days

(8) *augs* (< *augmentations*)
   novel corpus: not found
   forum corpus: 27 hits, 5.44 per million words

   a. [forums, 2011] Even more interesting would to "piggyback" augs to our normal senses.

   b. [forums, 2012] computer hacking would be completely useless against a band of marauding steampunk pirates. but hey, at least we have neon hair dye and "augs" which make us look fugly.

*Augs* as a form is not found in the Usenet data or the novel corpus – it may originate in discussions of the popular cyberpunk videogame series *Deus Ex* (published in 2000), which had a particular game mechanic featuring augmentations (biotechnological implants). Again, in (8b) scare quotes metalinguistically highlight this feature, pointing to its status as not entirely integrated in the discourse.

## 5.5 Clipped compounds and derived forms

Clipped compounds are not that rare in English (e.g., *sitcom, cablegram, photo op*), and this type seems to be extremely well represented in our data. A clear example of this type is given in (9), which in fact involves clipping of both compounding elements:

(9) *trodenet* (< *electrode* + *network*, originating in *Mona Lisa Overdrive* as *trode-net*)
   novel corpus: 1 author, earliest 1988
   forum corpus: 18 hits, 3.63 per million

    a. [Usenet, 1990] When it gets to the stage where I need to bathe my trode-net in pigs blood and incant over it every full moon, then I'll begin to wonder.

    b. [forums, 2009] Trodenet's just a slang term we like to use around here for neural interface.

Other instances may represent derivation processes, if the clipped element in question has been reanalyzed as a bit of productive morphology. This may be the case for *-ware* as in (10) and (11), which appears to represent a libfix (as discussed earlier, a word part "liberated" for limited use as an affix-like morpheme) drawn from *hardware/software*.

(10)   *wetware* (< *wet* + *-ware*)
        novel corpus: 5 authors, earliest 1985
        forum corpus: 63 hits, 12.70 per million

    a. [Usenet, 1996] Listen, you've got this ultra-spiffy piece of wetware sitting between your ears that's hardwired to deal with 3D spaces

    b. [forums, 2010] even normal wiring would perform better than your wetware, providing it can mimic the overwhelming complexity of your neurons.

    c. [forums, 2008] I've heard about teledildonics since... 1995? At least? I'm not surprised it hasn't caught on... you're dealing with 'wetware.'

(11)   *meatware* (< *meat* + *-ware* by clipping/compounding or libfixation)
        novel corpus: not found
        forum corpus: 12 hits, 2.42 per million

    a. [Usenet, 1994] Neural nets operate in the same fashion whether they are made of meatware (brain) or hardware.

    b. [forums, 2007] I personally am anxious to upgrade my meatware. the sooner I could replace my body with a stronger steel chassis the better [...]

    c. [forums, 2008] Zombie cyborgs. Cyborgs infected with a data virus that leaves the cybernetics moving long after the meatware is rotting.

As mentioned in Section 5.2, the use of *meat-* in cyberpunk coinages is informative from a sociolinguistic point of view. Between cyberspace and meatspace, the former is cast as preferable to the latter; the former is the space of possibilities, the latter is the realm in which individuals are confined in "meat." The visualization of the body as "meatware" is reminiscent of one of the Old English poetic kennings for "body": *bānhūs* ('bone-house'), a picture of the body as a potentially constraining and necessarily impermanent structure. The language of cyberpunk shows a tendency to privilege the cyber-manifestations of individuals over their bodily-incarnations.

Likewise, *cyber-* itself, in examples such as (12), appears to have become a libfix, though originally its appearance would have been produced by blending *cybernetic*.

(12) *cyberprep* (< *cyber-* + *prep* [from *preparatory school* (*student*)], by analogy with *cyberpunk*)
novel corpus: not found
forum corpus: 24 hits, 4.84 per million

   a. [Usenet, 1987] The cyberprep movement (such as it is, ha ha) takes as its motto: "Whatever you do, remember, be polite".

   b. [forums, 2010] Very bland and un-gritty. More cyberprep.

In terms of subculture-building, the form *cyberprep* is additionally interesting in that it defines certain types of (presumably cyberpunk-adjacent) literature or cultural practice as an outgroup, walling off certain types of practice (those not suitably gritty or rude) as non-cyberpunk. Even further, while this form does not appear in the novel corpus, which contains the most widely-accepted canon of cyberpunk literature, it appears twenty-three years apart in online discussions, used in exactly the same way. This suggests that neologisms like this, which by dint of their existence serve to define the boundaries of the cyberpunk subculture, are coined within the community and preserved and used over time to maintain these community boundaries.

By contrast with *cyber-* libfixation, other examples seem to more clearly involve a derivational process like prefixation, as in (13) (which does, however, also involve clipping of the second element):

(13) *megacorp* (< *mega* + *corporation*)
novel corpus: not found
forum corpus: 80 hits, 16.12 per million

   a. [Usenet, 1991] It would be tough to have "the lone outsider against the megacorp" without the megacorp.

b. [forums, 2013] In a way, Seoul had more of that dynamic technological development vibe that Tokyo has lot [sic]. With the huge Megacorps truly looming all over the place.

Many other instances of clipped compounds or derived forms (esp. involving libfixes) were found in our data, including *ghostnet, darknets, microsofts, neurofunk, mil-spec, cypunk, teledildonics, simsense, biohacking, cyberdeck, cyberware, cybercide, transhuman,* and *nanosolar.*

Due to the large variety and number of these forms specifically (see Tables 1 and 2), we propose that clipping with compounding/derivation/libfixation is the word formation strategy most characteristic of language use in the cyberpunk community, followed by compounding alone and clipping alone; we discuss this further in the final section.

# 6 Discussion and conclusions

Our data show that one of the most characteristically cyberpunk word formation processes is clipping-compounding. We speculate that at least one motivating factor for this preference is the association of clipping-compounding with both futuristic/scientific naming practices on the one hand, see examples in (14), and naming practices associated with totalitarian/militaristic governments on the other, as in (15), as well as fictional portrayals of totalitarian governments, specifically in the Newspeak of George Orwell's *1984*, as in (16), and in the Nadsat language of Burgess's *A Clockwork Orange* in (17).[6]

(14)  a.  *hi-fi* 'high fidelity (sound equipment)' (1950)
      b.  *sci-fi* 'science fiction' (1955)
      c.  *cyborg* 'cybernetic organism' (1960)
      d.  *modem* 'modulator-demodulator' (1958)
      e.  *FORTRAN* 'formula translating system' (1957)
      f.  *INTELSAT* '**Int**ernational **Tel**ecommunications **Sat**ellite Organization' (1964)

---

[6] See Jackson (2011) for a general overview of the invented vocabularies of Orwell's *1984* and Burgess's *A Clockwork Orange*.

(15) a. *comintern* 'communist international' (USSR, 1919)
 b. *kapstrana* < **kap**italističeskaja + **strana** 'capitalistic country' (USSR)
 c. *filfak* < **fil**ologičeskij + **fak**ultet 'philology faculty' (USSR)
 d. *zavsektorom* < **zav**edujuščij + **sektorom** 'sector director' (USSR)
 e. *gorvoenkom* < **gor**odskoj + **voen**nyj + **kom**itet 'city war committee' (USSR)
 f. *MinCulPop* < *Ministero della Cultura Popolare* 'Ministry of Popular Culture' (Italy, 1937) [Arcodia & Montermini 2012: 104]
 g. *DEFCON* 'defense readiness condition' (USA, 1959)
 h. *mil-spec* 'military specification' [manufacturing/performance standard] (USA, 1950 or earlier)
 i. *comsymp* 'communist sympathiser' (USA/UK?, 1960)
 j. *Stasi* (*Staatssicherheit*, 'state security,' German Democratic Republic era)
 k. *Vopo* (*Volkspolizei*, 'people's police,' German Democratic Republic era)
 l. *Gestapo* (Geheime Staatspolizei, 'secret state police,' Nazi Germany)

(16) a. *Minitrue* 'Ministry of Truth'
 b. *Miniluv* 'Ministry of Love'
 c. *Recdep* 'Records Department'
 d. *Ficdep* 'Fiction Department'
 e. *Pornosec* 'Pornography Sub-Section (of Fiction Department)'
 f. *Ingsoc* 'English Socialism'[7]

(17) *staja* 'state jail' (Burgess, *A Clockwork Orange*)

The Russian clipping-compounding examples (also known as stump compounding, see Molinsky 1973; Billings 1998; Benigni and Masini 2009) appear to be instances of a semi-intentionally created morphological process. Molinsky (1973: 15) claims that these are an innovation in Russian that began to appear as a consequence of the 1917 revolution "i[n] an attempt to 'sovietize' the language." Though the appearance of *MinCulPop* in Italian suggests that perhaps

---
[7] Note also the tendency towards respellings in these forms, e.g., *Miniluv* (vs *Minilove*), *Ingsoc* (vs *Engsoc*) etc. All of the examples in (16) are from Orwell's *1984*.

something about clipped-compounds appeals to totalitarian administrations, whether communist or fascist. Additional examples are found in both Nazi Germany and the German Democratic Republic, although "syllabic acronyms" are (in the German case) not exclusively associated with totalitarian regimes. For example, 'KriPo' *Kriminalpolizei*, 'Criminal Police,' is still used today, and many German business names like Aldi ('Albrecht Discount') have been formed using this process.

We suggest that clipping and compounding may be used in many cases to imply efficiency (in the case of clipping) and precision, progress, or modernity (in the case of compounding). The intersection of these features would certainly appeal to totalitarian regimes, as well as authors seeking to emulate or evoke the language of such regimes. This is, it should be noted, only one motivation among a number of potential others for the use of and preference for such forms in the cyberpunk subculture.

Of course, clipping-compounds exist in English which have no particular connections with technology or oppression/totalitarianism, such as *sitcom* (< *situation comedy*), but a sufficient number of English clipping-compounds, as discussed above, seem to have connections with either technology and/or totalitarianism/dystopia that these connotations may reasonably be assumed to be present and at work in influencing the production and spread of cyberpunk-related neologisms which are formed by clipping and compounding.

While there are cyberpunk neologisms of various morphological types, clipping-compounds appear to be the most characteristic. Respellings are also popular – presumably motivated in part from notions of resistance to norms, but are harder to distinguish from forms found in more general youth- and internet-cultural discussions. There are, however, indications that there may exist a small number of cyberpunk-specific respellings, *cypx* being a particularly notable example. The use of <x> as a multipurpose replacement spelling appears elsewhere only in the jargon of certain specialized domains, the most relevant of these being telecommunications (*Tx/Rx* for 'transmit/receive'), though it perhaps has additional distant connections to technological neologisms ending in *x*, such as *Minix, Unix, Linux*. It is also possible that the <x> in *cypx* is derived from a phonetic respelling of the plural *cyberpunks*, but the progression of its use as a replacement for the singular/adjectival form to a replacement of the plural provides evidence against this.

One aspect of cyberpunk as a subculture which sets it apart from other domains of neologism formation is that *Neuromancer* and its two sequels in particular seem to have served as a cyberpunk primary text, re-seeding the community lexicon over a period of 30 years. Cyberpunk writ large is a subculture revolving around a literary genre, rather than a community in the traditional sense – the interlocutors discussed in this analysis are separated not only by geography but by time, making claims of some sort of monolithic and singular linguistic group of "cyberpunks" impossible. However, shared practices over time, like the diachronic usage of *cyberprep*, hint at continuity. Furthermore, individual sites of communication, like the cyberpunk forum here, do constitute a community wherein the processes of neologism adoption and mediated diffusion can be seen (cf. Spitulnik's 1997 treatment of recycled and recontextualized pieces of radio discourse). In particular, those words which are likely to have originated in the community (e.g., *cyberprep*, and *cypx*) deal with group identity and group membership, further underlining both the centrality of linguistic practice to community-building and the motivation of subcultural engagement in the formation of neologisms. Additional cyberpunk literature and materials like role-playing game *Shadowrun* and videogame *Deus Ex* have internalized these processes to some degree and have continued to influence cyberpunk language as additional primary texts. Cyberpunk remains popular in its own right as a type of media setting – an upcoming PC/console video game from a major publisher, *Cyberpunk 2077*, updates a 90s-era pen and paper roleplaying game.

Future research could compare linguistic innovations in cyberpunk culture with those found in other genres of science fiction, fantasy, or speculative fiction. For example, the "Nadsat" language used in Anthony Burgess' *A Clockwork Orange* uses a number of imagined borrowings and compounds (although it contains few clipped compounds). Additionally, a social network analysis on a community like that of the cyberpunk forums could capture the particulars of mediated diffusion in a more granular fashion.

Numerous questions remain, including distinguishing between neologisms adopted by the online cyberpunk community from primary cyberpunk literature and neologisms created within the community; Table 1 in Section 5.1 includes five examples of forms that appear on both Usenet and the Cyberpunk forums, roughly two decades apart, but which do not appear in any the primary literature we surveyed. This suggests that it is likely that these represent forms that have been coined rather than adopted by the online cyberpunk community and that either these represent internally-coined forms which have survived within the community for over two decades or that these represent forms which have been re-coined by members of the community at different points in time, but presumably reflecting similar internal morphological grammars for forming cyberpunk neologisms. It is interesting to note that three of these forms involve a *cyber-* prefix, and so perhaps reflect a stronger tendency for the online cyberpunk community to form neologisms using this prefix than is exhibited by the creators of cyberpunk literature. Apropos of the frequency of use of this prefix within the online cyberpunk community, an xkcd comic from September 2015 questions the contemporary currency of the prefix *cyber-*:

**Figure 1:** Comic from http://xkcd.com/1573/

The comic suggests that *cyber-* is an outdated prefix; however, discussion of the comic online, including Liberman (2015), suggests that the situation is more nuanced than implied by the comic, and that *cyber-* as a prefix remains current within various subgroups. To what extent the linguistic practices of the online cyberpunk community, such as the use of the prefix *cyber-*, affect the usage of such forms outside of the community is unclear.

It is clear, however, that the engagement of fans with a subculture like cyberpunk in the realm of computer-mediated communication involves the management of identity and group membership through linguistic innovations and reproductions of same; and that this process of linguistic innovation does not exist in a vacuum, but is rather informed by a multiplex system of influences.

# 7 Acknowledgements

We would like to thank the attendees of ICLCE5, who heard an early version of this work, and two anonymous reviewers for their comments and suggestions. We would also like to thank our extremely patient editor, Lauren Squires, for all of her help and suggestions, which have gone a long way toward making this a better chapter. Of course, the responsibility for any remaining errors and infelicities remains ours alone.

# 8 References

Arcodia, Giorgio Francesco & Fabio Montermini. 2012. Are reduced compounds compounds? Morphological and prosodic properties of reduced compounds in Russian and Mandarin Chinese. In Vincent Renner, François Maniez & Pierre J.L. Arnaud (eds.), *Cross-disciplinary perspectives on lexical blending*, 93–113. Berlin: Walter de Gruyter.

Androutsopoulos, Jannis. 2000. Non-standard spellings in media texts: The case of German fanzines. *Journal of Sociolinguistics* 4(4). 514–533.

Atkinson, Kevin. 2014. Spell Checking Oriented Word Lists (SCOWL). http://wordlist.aspell.net/ (accessed 24 March, 2014.)

Bauer, Laurie. 2004. *A glossary of morphology*. Edinburgh: Edinburgh University Press.

Bauer, Laurie & Antoinette Renouf. 2001. A corpus-based study of compounding in English. *Journal of English Linguistics* 29(2). 101–123.

Benigni, Valentina & Francesca Masini. 2009. Compounds in Russian. *Lingue e Linguaggio* 8(2). 171–193.

Bethke, Bruce. 1997. Foreword. *Cyberpunk – A Short Story by Bruce Bethke*. http://www.infinityplus.co.uk/stories/cpunk.htm (accessed 28 September, 2014).

Billings, Loren. 1998. Morphology and syntax: Delimiting stump compounds in Russian. In Geert Booij, Angela Ralli & Sergio Scalise (eds.), *Proceedings of the First Mediterranean Conference of Morphology* (Mytilene, Greece, Sept. 19–21 1997), 99–111. Patras: University of Patras.

Collective Cyberpunk Community. 2013. Collective Cyberpunk Community * Index. http://cyberpunkforums.com (accessed 30 September, 2013).

Cyberpunk Review. 2013. Cyberpunk Review :: View Forum – Virtual Meatspace. http://cyberpunkreview.com/forums/viewforum.php?f=1 (accessed 20 February, 2013).

Evans, Claire L. 2012. What happened to cyberpunk? VICE Motherboard. http://motherboard.vice.com/blog/what-happened-to-cyberpunk-2 (15 November, 2014).

Frank, Erich Schneider, Tim Oerting, & Andy Hawks. 1998. alt.cyberpunk Frequently Asked Questions. http://project.cyberpunk.ru/idb/alt.cyberpunk_faq.html#1 (accessed 30 September, 2013).

Garley, Matt. In Press. Peaze Up! Adaptation, innovation, and variation in German hip-hop discourse. In Cecelia Cutler & Unn Røyneland (eds.), *Multilingual youth practices in computer-mediated communication*. Cambridge: Cambridge University Press.

Gatson, Sarah N. 2011. Self-naming practices on the internet: Identity, authenticity, and community. *Cultural Studies <-> Critical Methodologies* 11(3). 224–235.

Gatson, Sarah N. & Amanda Zweerink. 2004. Ethnography online: 'Natives' practising and inscribing community. *Qualitative Research* 4(2). 179–200.

Hock, Hans Henrich & Brian D. Joseph. 1995/2009 [1st/2nd ed.]. *Language history, language change, and language relationship: An introduction to historical and comparative linguistics.* Berlin: Mouton de Gruyter.

Jackson, Howard. 2011. Invented vocabularies: The cases of Newspeak and Nadsat. In Michael Adams (ed.), *From Elvish to Klingon: Exploring invented languages*, 49–73. Oxford: Oxford University Press.

Liberman, Mark. 2015. Raw "cyber" information. *Language Log*. http://languagelog.ldc.upenn.edu/nll/?p=21224 (accessed 21 September, 2015).

Milroy, James, & Lesley Milroy. 1985. Linguistic change, social network, and speaker innovation. *Journal of Linguistics* 21. 339–384.

Molinsky, Steven J. 1973. *Patterns of ellipsis in Russian compound noun formations*. The Hague/Paris: Mouton.

reddit inc. 2013. "Cyberpunk – High tech, low life!" http://www.reddit.com/r/cyberpunk. (1 March, 2013.)

Spitulnik, Debra. 1997. The social circulation of media discourse and the mediation of communities. *Journal of Linguistic Anthropology* 6(2). 161–187.

Squires, Lauren. 2014. From TV personality to fans and beyond: Indexical bleaching and the diffusion of a media innovation. *Journal of Linguistic Anthropology* 24(1). 42–62.

T, Cyborg, & Mad Maniac. 2004a. Cyberpunk as a subculture. *The Cyberpunk Project*. http://project.cyberpunk.ru/idb/subculture.html (accessed 28 September, 2014).

T, Cyborg, & Mad Maniac. 2004b. Cyberpunk Dictionary *The Cyberpunk Project*. http://project.cyberpunk.ru/idb/dictionary.html (accessed 25 February, 2013).

U.S. Strategic Command. 2015. Factsheet – U.S. Cyber Command. https://www.stratcom.mil/factsheets/2/Cyber_Command/ (accessed 25 March, 2015).

Zwicky, Arnold. 2010. Libfixes. http://arnoldzwicky.org/2010/01/23/libfixes/ (accessed 1 March, 2013).

# Appendix: List of primary sources collected for the novel corpus

## Fiction

Bacigalupi, Paolo. 2005. The Calorie man. *The Magazine of Fantasy & Science Fiction*. October/November 2005.

Bear, Elizabeth. 2005. Two dreams on a train. *Strange Horizons* 2005.

Beukes, Lauren. 2008. *Moxyland*. Nottingham, England: Angry Robot.

Bethke, Bruce. 1980. *cyberpunk!* http://www.infinityplus.co.uk/stories/cpunk.htm

Cadigan, Pat. 1991. *Synners*. New York: Bantam Books.

Cadigan, Pat. 1997. Little Latin Larry. In Stephen McClelland (ed.), *Future histories*. London: Horizon House Publications.

Di Filippo, Paul. 2003. What's Up, Tiger Lily. *The Silver Gryphon* 2003.

Doctorow, Cory. 2006. When sysadmins ruled the earth. http://craphound.com/overclocked/Cory_Doctorow_-_Overclocked_-_When_Sysadmins_Ruled_the_Earth.html
Egan, Greg. 1997. Yeyuka. *Meanjin* 56(1).
Gibson, William. 1982. Burning chrome. *Omni*, July 1982 issue.
Gibson, William. 1984. *Neuromancer*. New York: Ace.
Gibson, William. 1985. *Schismatrix*. New York: Arbor House.
Gibson, William. 1986. *Count zero*. New York: Arbor House.
Gibson, William. 1988. *Mona Lisa overdrive*. New York: Bantam Books.
Gibson, William. 1991. Academy leader. In Michael Benedikt (ed.), *Cyberspace*, 26–29. Cambridge, MA: MIT Press.
Gibson, William. 1996. *Idoru*. New York: Viking.
Gibson, William. 1996. Thirteen views of a cardboard city. *New Worlds* 1996.
Jeter, K.W. 1984. *Dr. Adder*. New York: Bluejay Books.
Jones, Gwyneth. 1996. Red Sonja and Lessingham in Dreamland. In Ellen Datlow (ed.), *Off Limits*. New York: St. Martin's.
Kadrey, Richard. 1988. *Metrophage*. New York: Harper Voyager.
Lethem, Jonathan. 1996. How we got in town and out again. *Isaac Asimov's Science Fiction Magazine* 1996.
Maddox, Tom. 1986. Snake Eyes. *Omni*, April 1986 issue.
Maddox, Tom. 1991. *Halo*. New York: TOR.
Marusek, David. 1999. *The wedding album*. http://poliscifi.pbworks.com/f/Marusek_The+Wedding+Album.pdf
Rosenblum, Mary. 2005. Search engine. *Analog science fiction and fact* 2005.
Rowe, Christopher. 2004. The Voluntary State. *Sci Fiction*.
Rucker, Rudy. 1982. *Software*. New York: Ace Books.
Rucker, Rudy. 1988. *Wetware*. New York: Avon Books.
Rucker, Rudy. 1997. *Freeware*. New York: Avon Books.
Rucker, Rudy. 2000. *Realware*. New York: EOS.
Shirley, John. 1980. *City come a-walkin'*. New York: Dell.
Stephenson, Neal. 1992. *Snow crash*. New York: Bantam Books.
Sterling, Bruce. 1988. *Islands in the Net*. New York: Arbor House.
Sterling, Bruce. 1994. *Heavy weather*. New York: Spectra.
Sterling, Bruce. 1996. The littlest jackal. In Bruce Sterling (ed.), *A good old-fashioned future*. New York: Bantam.
Sterling, Bruce. 1996. Bicycle repairman. In Bruce Sterling (ed.), *A good old-fashioned future*. New York: Bantam.
Stross, Charles. 2001. Lobsters. *Isaac Asimov's Science Fiction Magazine* 2001.
Stross, Charles. 2005. *Accelerando*. London: Orbit.
Swanwick, Michael. 2001. The dog said bow-wow. *Isaac Asimov's Science Fiction Magazine* 2001.
Swanwick, Michael & William Gibson. 1985. Dogfight. *Omni*, July 1985 issue.
Williams, Walter Jon. 1999. *Daddy's world*. Riverdale, NY: Baen Books.

# Non-fiction

Kessel, John and James Patrick Kelly. 2007. Hacking Cyberpunk. In James Patrick Kelly & John Kessel (eds.), *Rewired: The post-Cyberpunk anthology*. San Francisco, CA: Tachyon.

Axel Bohmann
# Language change because Twitter? Factors motivating innovative uses of *because* across the English-speaking Twittersphere

## 1 Introduction

The English lexeme *because* is in the process of expanding its syntactic variability. In addition to finite clauses and prepositional phrases (PP) headed by *of*, previously undocumented complements can now be found to combine with *because* in certain contexts. Some examples of Twitter messages containing such newly emerging uses are given in (1).[1]

(1) a. I miss my daddy. He didn't come home today because work :(. <28342>

   b. Early morning gym because fat <500>

   c. taeyeon is so lucky because goddamnit <7218>

   d. Literally because this *[URL]* <3165>

Structures like these have been the subject of lively discussion in recent years. The first explicit treatments of "the new *because*," to the author's knowledge, occurred in July 2012 (Bailey 2012; Liberman 2012). Commentary among linguists (Carey 2013; McCulloch 2012; Whitman 2013) and laypeople (e.g., Garber 2013; Hartogs 2013; Romano 2013) alike followed suit and culminated in the election of *because* as the *American Dialect Society's* Word of the Year 2013. Several observers (Pullum 2014; Whitman 2014; Zimmer 2014) point out that this choice is remarkable, since it is the first time the title is awarded based on newly developing syntactic options of an established lexical item, rather than honoring neologisms from open-word classes like nouns or verbs.

---

[1] All examples in this paper are taken from the data used in the analysis. The original spelling and punctuation are retained and reference indices from the corpus included in angular brackets. Hyperlinks to users' profiles are replaced by *[URL]* to protect their privacy.

---

**Axel Bohmann,** The University of Texas at Austin

Despite this general level of interest in innovative forms of *because*-complementation, linguistic discussion of such constructions has so far been limited to relatively informal venues of publication (mostly blog entries) and, with the notable exception of Schnoebelen (2014; see 1.2. below), has been largely anecdotal and without a solid empirical basis. The present study addresses this lack of empirical research by examining the "new *because*" in a quantitative, variationist framework, using data from the microblogging service Twitter and tools and concepts developed in corpus linguistic research.

## 1.1 Theoretical background

Corpus linguistics and variationist sociolinguistics share a number of fundamental assumptions, most importantly their insistence on empirical data as their object of study, their attention to contextual influences on language use, and their reliance on quantitative methods of analysis (Baker 2010: 8–9). Yet, for historical and theoretical reasons (c. McEnery and Hardie 2012: 116) there has in the past not been as much cross-fertilization between the two fields as might be expected. A rapprochement is, however, evident in recent publications. Corpora are increasingly built with questions of diachronic and synchronic variation in mind and the corpus-based study of variation and change has been the subject of a number of book-length treatments (Andersen and Bech 2013; Leech et al. 2009; Mair 2006). Conversely, sociolinguists are beginning to collect and annotate data with established corpus-linguistic designs and tools in mind (e.g., Gabrielatos et al. 2010). Combining methods from both fields has led to productive research in the fields of World Englishes (Mair 2009) and discourse analysis (Baker 2006). In a similar spirit, the present paper follows the method of Hinrichs and Szmrecsanyi (2007) and Hinrichs et al. (2015). These studies are variationist in the strict sense of following the principle of accountability (i.e., analyzing all possible variable contexts for the feature of interest and only those contexts; see Labov 1972), but demonstrate the relevance of corpus-based, text-linguistic (Biber 2012) measures as predictors of variation.

Another recent development in both of the above fields is a growing interest in computer-mediated discourse (CMD) as a source of empirical data. While recognizing that in some ways CMD may differ significantly from offline forms of linguistic practice (e.g., Childs, this volume), analyses of language use online have produced insights that can productively be related to other modes, channels, and text types. Tagliamonte and Denis (2008: 25) demonstrate that language in instant messaging displays "the same structured heterogeneity (variation) and the same dynamic, ongoing processes of linguistic change that are currently under way in the [offline] speech community." Key questions from sociolinguistics, like the effect of gender (Herring & Paolillo 2006) or audience (Iorio 2009) on language variation, have been addressed through quantitative analysis of computer-mediated language use.

Corpus linguists' attitudes towards CMD have been characterized by a mixture of excitement and skepticism (e.g., Hundt et al. 2006). While the notion that the Web in its entirety might be used as a corpus has largely been dismissed, there has been an increase in corpora built (partly) from CMD data. In the study of World Englishes, findings from the 1.9 billion word Corpus of Global Web-based English (GloWbE: Davies and Fuchs 2015) closely replicate those from smaller, more carefully compiled corpora of written and spoken English. These results add credence to the reliability of web-based data, although platform- and genre-specific constraints should of course always be taken into account before generalizing from such data. In addition, numerous more specific CMD corpora have been compiled for the study of particular varieties (e.g., Hinrichs & White-Sustaíta 2011; Mair 2011) and communities (Iorio 2012). Apart from providing access to quantities of machine-readable data that might otherwise be difficult to obtain, many CMD platforms include information such as geolocation and network structure that can productively be used to trace language variation within and across different communities.

In particular, Twitter, the platform from which the data in the present paper are taken, has been used extensively in research in linguistics as well as a wide range of other disciplines (see chapters in Weller et al. 2014). The open access to user-generated output that the service provides, the sheer size of that output, and the wealth of structured metadata it contains make it a valuable data source. Much effort has gone into understanding platform-specific language use and communicative practices on Twitter (Gillen and Merchant 2013; Gouws et al. 2011; Honeycutt and Herring 2009; Marwick and boyd 2011; Page 2012; Zappavigna 2012) as well as the place the platform is accorded in the present-day media ecology (Squires and Iorio 2014).

Beyond platform-specific communication, researchers have also turned to Twitter to investigate linguistic variation and change more generally. Squires uses a corpus of tweets to trace processes of "indexical bleaching" (2014) by which an expression acquires increasingly general, less context-specific meanings. Haddican and Johnson (2012) look at particle verb alternation in different English-speaking locales and combine experimental production data with an analysis of tweets. Twitter corpora have further been utilized in the study of gender (Bamman et al. 2014) and regional variation on the level of phonetics (Eisenstein et al. 2012), lexicon (Eisenstein et al. 2010; O'Connor et al. 2010) as well as morpho-syntax (Doyle 2014).

The present chapter adds to this growing body of research by combining a variationist perspective with corpus linguistic tools and concepts, applied to CMD, more precisely Twitter data. The linguistic phenomenon under investigation, innovative strategies for *because*-complementation (see 1.2.), lends itself to this kind of approach for several reasons. As a very recent linguistic development, with the first sporadic attestations in the mid-1990s (Carey 2013), newly emerging complementation strategies for *because* postdate the compilation of many of the reference corpora available to date. But even if this were not the case, the "new *because*" is still a relatively low-frequency feature. Thus, a serious quantitative analysis requires larger amounts of text than most corpora to date contain. Finally, the phenomenon itself is often perceived as originating from the context of CMD. Twitter allows instantaneous access to large quantities of CMD data and consequently is ideally suited for investigations of developments like the one under discussion here. While the synchronic snapshot of data analyzed in the present study and the absence of reliable information about user age on Twitter prevent direct real- or apparent-time conclusions, the study design could be replicated with minimal effort to add a longitudinal, real-time dimension.

## 1.2 Variation in *because*-complementation

The analysis presented here is concerned with a recent innovation in complementation strategies for *because*. According to traditional descriptions, *because* can be followed by a finite clause as in (2a) or combine with *of* to introduce a noun phrase (NP), as in (2b):

(2) a.  Don't even talk to me because I don't care lol #badmood <6271>

  b.  Don't stop just because of a little problem <18925>

Reference grammars differ with regard to their analysis of the constructions above. Both Biber et al. (1999: 75) and Aarts (2011: 78) treat *because* as a subordinating conjunction and *because of* as a separate, "complex preposition." However, Huddleston and Pullum (2002) argue convincingly that such an analysis is difficult to maintain on syntactic grounds (620–22). Instead, the authors treat any occurrence of *because* as a preposition, which according to their analysis can be complemented by a prepositional phrase (PP) headed by *of* as well as by a full clause. In the present paper, I follow this latter analysis, since it is best suited to account for recent developments in *because*-complementation in a variationist framework.

None of the above grammars includes an account of additional forms of *because*-complementation. This is probably owing to the simple reason that constructions like those in (1) seem to have only appeared in the language very recently, with the first reliable attestations dating to the mid-1990s (Carey 2013). As the examples in (1b)–(1d) demonstrate, the new strategies for *because*-complementation are not exhaustively captured by initial descriptions such as "because NOUN" (Liberman 2012; McCulloch 2012) or "because+noun" (Bailey 2012). In addition to nominal complements (1a), one also finds adjectives (1b), interjections (1c), demonstrative pronouns (1d), as well as a number of other constructions (see 2.2. below). I therefore adopt the label "*because X*" introduced by Carey (2013) to refer to all new *because*-complements.

The diversity of material that can occupy the $X$ slot makes a convincing grammatical analysis difficult. Many cases can reasonably be understood as elision of either the *of* in a traditional *because of* construction (e.g., (1a) above) or of parts of the finite clause following *because* ((1b), here with the subject and copula elided). However, in cases like (1c) there seems to be little evidence to indicate an underlying finite clause or PP headed by *of*. Instead, McCulloch (2014) points out that the material in the $X$ slot can typically function on its own as a standalone expression and often has an interjectional character. Similarly, Bailey interprets $X$ as a "root clause (CP) or a propositional/exclamatory non-sentential element" (2014). The question of what grammatical analysis best fits the syntactic variability within $X$ is important and may help explain how the construction arose in the first place. However, the present chapter does not make any strong claims in this regard. Instead, all forms of $X$ occurring in the data are compared against all established forms of *because*-complementation. The question addressed through this procedure is: what characteristics of a tweet make it a likely environment in which to encounter $X$ rather than one of the more traditional complement variants?

Regarding the prototypical context for *because X*, the tenor of most of the available commentary is captured by Garber, who describes the new construction as "exceptionally bloggy and aggressively casual and implicitly ironic" (2013). The first adjective relates to the purportedly media-specific character of *because X*. Indeed, most discussions explicitly link it to CMD and particularly the internet. The majority of examples cited stem from online sources, most prominently Twitter, but notably also political websites like *Wonkette*, *Jezebel* or *Daily Kos* (Garber 2013). In addition, there are a good number of multimodal examples such as memes, T-shirt prints (Garber 2013) or Tumblr posts (Bailey 2012). The extent to which *because X* can be found in offline language use is much less documented. However, Carey (2013) finds examples from other media, mainly TV shows and movies. The only documented instances of *because X* in verbal face-to-face interaction are from children's talk (Whitman 2014). One important question that arises is whether and to what extent the construction is losing its indexical connection to (computer-) mediated forms of discourse over time. Such "indexical bleaching" (Squires 2014) would be both an indicator of and a stimulant for its further spread.

Next among the common characterizations, the "aggressively casual" nature of *because X* is somewhat ambivalent. This phrase might suggest that use of the construction implies a colloquial register on the whole. Yet, as the qualification "aggressively" indicates, most commentators point out that there is a level of conscious deliberation to the casualness. What is meant is perhaps not the carelessness of spontaneous spoken discourse so much as a blatant and possibly strategic violation of formality. One question to be addressed in the present study is whether an overall more colloquial style is a favorable environment for *because X*.

There is least agreement on the assertion that *because X* is "implicitly ironic." Liberman (2012) sees an "implication that the referenced line of reasoning is weak" and cites examples in which users of *because X* clearly employ it to distance themselves from other people's (faulty) logic. Carey agrees that the construction has a "snappy, jocular feel, with a syntactic jolt that allows long explanations to be forgone" (2013). Here, however, there is no necessary distancing effect. On the contrary, use of *because X* may imply a level of shared context that allows much of the causal reasoning to remain implicit. Bailey's (2012) interpretation points in this direction as well. Finally, Whitman sees a "transition from [...] sarcastic usage to [...] sarcasm-free usage by younger speakers" (2013). This observation may indicate a leveling of contextual constraints that *because X* is undergoing in the process of diffusion. Since it is near impossible to model irony or humor quantitatively, the analysis presented here cannot address these aspects systematically. It should be noted, however, that the data analyzed include a large portion of examples which show no explicit signs of ironic or humorous use of innovative complementation strategies.

Adding to these general observations about *because X*, Schnoebelen (2014) subjects a corpus of 28,294 tweets containing the feature to quantitative analysis. He finds that the construction is most prominent in the US and is being adopted most readily by young women, an observation that is in line with the typical pattern found for the spread of prestige innovations (Labov 1990). Tweets that feature *because X* show disproportionate amounts of vocabulary related to popular (especially internet and music) culture, while sports and business vocabulary is dispreferred. Likewise, linguistic features of African American Vernacular English are under-represented in tweets with innovative *because-*complements. Finally, and possibly in support of the construction's characterization as casual/colloquial, *because X* patterns together with direct addressee specification through @-messages, a feature that marks tweets as conversational (Bruns and Moe 2014; Honeycutt and Herring 2009). Schnoebelen also compares different individual expressions and syntactic categories that function as *X*, but since these are not the subject of the present analysis, they are not discussed here.

While Schnoebelen's analysis is empirically supported, it is mainly exploratory and does not test a specific hypothesis as to the development of *because X*. Nor does it consider the construction against established forms of *because*-complementation in a clearly defined variable context. In the study presented here *because*-complementation is treated as a case of linguistic variation, the constraints on which can be analyzed through quantitative, statistical methods. As mentioned above, I follow the grammatical analysis of Huddleston & Pullum (2002). Instead of having to treat the innovative use of *because* as an entirely new lexical item, their analysis provides a unified account of all *because*-complementation strategies as different syntactic options introduced by the same word (see also Pullum 2014). Such an account allows the definition of a clear envelope of variation, which is essential to a variationist study of the construction in question. Any linguistic material complementing an instance of *because* is treated as a case of the variable under investigation, with the variants *clause*, *of*, and *X*, where *X* encompasses all innovative strategies.

The data are taken from the microblogging service Twitter (http://twitter.com). In addition to internal features of the construction itself such as the orthographic representation of *because* and language-external factors such as a user's home country or friend count, I consider text-linguistic (Biber 2012) aspects of each tweet in the data, such as mean word length or ratios between different parts of speech. Such text-linguistic measures are best-suited to identify a text sample's adherence to general trends that have been found to operate in the development of twentieth and twenty-first century (written Standard) English (Leech et al. 2009; see section 1.3. below). Relating linguistic innovations like *because X* to these trends is essential, since any linguistic development is part of the larger trajectory along which the language is progressing.

## 1.3 Determinants of change in Late Modern (written Standard) English

Recent work in corpus linguistics has identified several trends in the development of written Standard English in the latter half of the twentieth century (Leech at al. 2009: chapter 11). Situating individual, short-term changes in morpho-syntax in the context of these larger trends shifts the focus away from treating each case of variation in isolation and towards pervasive underlying tendencies that operate across different linguistic contexts. Such a perspective helps to relate the factors motivating individual changes to an understanding of the drift of the language in general. This has been done successfully for genitive variation in English (Hinrichs and Szmrecsanyi 2007) and for relativizer choice in restrictive relative clauses (Hinrichs et al. 2015).

It must be noted that the trends described below were established through the study of edited written Standard English. Twitter discourse, while existing in a written medium, is often subject to very different norms and constraints, and displays different linguistics features, than more traditional types of edited public writing (Eisenstein 2013). Hence, not all of the developments found in written Standard English are likely to affect language on Twitter to the same extent. The present study contributes towards gaining a better understanding of the relevance of these developments in a CMD text type (see also LaFave, this volume).

First among the most significant trends in the recent history of written English is *densification*, an observed increase in information density affecting all text types but particularly journalistic writing (Biber 2003). Simply put, densification reflects writers' attempts to express the same amount of information with less linguistic material. Established correlatives of densification are higher type-token-ratios (TTR) and increased relative frequencies of nouns (Leech et al. 2009: 211).

Second, the term *colloquialization* refers to the tendency to include more markers of an "involved" and "interactive" style in written Standard English texts (Finegan and Biber 1994). This trend reverses a trajectory of differentiation between spoken and written language that had been ongoing since at least the seventeenth century. Starting in the nineteenth century, some written genres "reversed their direction of change and evolved to become more similar to spoken registers" (Biber 2003: 169), a process that is still in effect in present-day written English. Colloquialization is reflected, for example, in lower frequencies of passive-voice constructions and an increase in personal pronouns (Mair and Hundt 1999).

Third, among changes induced through contact between regional varieties of English, a consistent trend towards *Americanization* is discernible. What is referred to here is the fact that often other varieties follow the lead of US English in adopting new forms (such as quotative *be like*, Buchstaller and D'Arcy 2009) or shifting frequencies in favor of one variant (such as *that* over *which* as restrictive relativizer, Hinrichs et al. 2015). The hyper-central position of Standard American English in the world system of Englishes (Mair 2013) accords it the prevalence and prestige necessary to act as a source of innovations in other varieties.

## 1.4 Research hypotheses

Given what has been written about *because X* and what is known about general trends in Late Modern English morpho-syntax, it is possible to formulate a number of hypotheses about variation in *because*-complementation that can be empirically tested. It seems reasonable to assume that a tendency towards densification would favor X, since it is the most economical strategy for *because*-complementation, requiring fewer characters than either a PP with *of* or a finite clause. Tweets exhibiting other features of densification would consequently be hypothesized to favor occurrences of *because X*. Next, according to the available descriptions, *because X* is a marker of informality. If this were the case, one would hypothesize that tweets that are more colloquial and less formal favor *because X*. Commentary on the construction also frequently mentions online discourse as its prototypical context. A third hypothesis, then, is that *because X* occurs frequently in tweets with high overall ratios of features that are typical of computer-mediated discourse, such as emoticons or hashtags. Finally, Schnoebelen (2014) identifies the US as the geographic center of *because X* use on Twitter. The literature on Americanization suggests a likely process of spread by which other varieties of English follow the American model with some lag. The corresponding hypothesis is that tweets from the US are most likely to contain *because X* over those from elsewhere in the world. It could also be added that countries in a more central position in the world system of Englishes (Mair 2013) are hypothesized to follow the American model more closely than more peripheral ones. The hypotheses, in short, are:

> Hypothesis 1: Tweets displaying higher ratios of features associated with densification favor X.
>
> Hypothesis 2: Tweets displaying higher ratios of features associated with colloquialness favor X.
>
> Hypothesis 3: Tweets displaying higher ratios of features associated with CMD favor X.
>
> Hypothesis 4: Tweets from countries in more central positions in the world system of Englishes favor X.

These four hypotheses do not exhaust all potential dimensions of variation for the outcome variable, but reflect those that can be approximated in a statistical analysis of the data in this particular study. Notably, metalinguistic commentary suggests that there are quite specific social meanings attached to *because X*. One would, for instance, expect to find it used more often among younger people and possibly less among African American Twitter users

(Schnoebelen 2014). However, social variables like age, gender or ethnicity are not available as part of Twitter's user metadata and can therefore not be modeled as predictors in the present study.

## 2 Data

To test all four hypotheses at the same time a large sample of data is required, especially since *because X is* a comparatively low-frequency phenomenon. The analysis below is based on 12,751 instances of *because* occurring in posts ("tweets") from the popular microblogging service Twitter (see Squires 2016). The platform was established in 2006 and allows users to create short messages of up to 140 characters. These messages can be directed at other users but are, in principle, openly available to anyone interested in reading them, unless otherwise specified by the user.

Tweets provide linguistic data that are naturalistic in the sense of being unelicited. However, they should not be equated with Labov's (1984) definition of the vernacular as the style in which the least attention is paid to speech. The 140 character limitation of the format, the asynchronous design of Twitter communication, as well as the potential for different audiences to read a tweet, likely motivate and allow users to be very conscious of what they say and how they say it. Compared to written Standard English as analyzed in many of the corpus linguistics studies cited above, Twitter is also quite messy, as it is much less subject to the norms of standard orthography. This fact can be exploited in sociolinguistic analyses (Jones, this volume) but renders comparisons to other written text types problematic. The necessity to condense messages into 140 characters and users' attempts to render paralinguistic cues by typographic means makes for high frequencies of non-standard spellings, abbreviations, emoticons, and other features not normally found in most written English texts. Conventional part-of-speech (POS) taggers trained on written Standard English do not reach acceptable levels of accuracy with Twitter material, and even taggers especially developed for Twitter need to be critically examined as to their performance (Eisenstein 2013).

Additionally, the Twitter community has developed its own set of specific discourse conventions such as hashtags, @-mentions (Honeycutt and Herring 2009), specific markers for re-tweeted messages (boyd et al. 2010), etc. These fall outside the POS categories covered in other corpus studies, but offer rich information about a tweet's communicative scope and character (Bruns and Moe 2014). Corpus tools applied to Twitter data thus need to be adapted to take these markers into account.

In addition to the text of the post itself, each tweet includes metadata about the user, such as their language setting, the amount of people they follow and are followed by, etc. A particularly useful piece of information for the purposes of the present study is geo-location and place information, which users can optionally include with their messages. All of these levels of metadata are freely available through Twitter. Users are specifically instructed that "[t]he Content you submit, post, or display will be able to be viewed by other users of the Services and through third party services and websites [...]. You should only provide Content that you are comfortable sharing with others under these Terms" (Twitter 2014a). However, individual user names in examples included in the present paper are replaced by the generic <@user> to protect privacy.

## 2.1 Data collection

The data analyzed below were collected through the streaming endpoint of Twitter's application programming interface (API). Unlike the search endpoint, streaming does not access past tweets that are still maintained by Twitter, but establishes an open connection to the service and provides a random sub-sample of all tweets as they are created in real-time (Twitter 2014b). This stream was filtered so as to only include tweets containing the word *because* and a number of abbreviations and alternative spellings (see 2.3. below, henceforth collectively referred to as *because*). Filtering was case-insensitive, i.e., forms like <Because>, <bEcAuSe>, or <BECAUSE> or any other combination of uppercase and lowercase spellings were captured. This method yielded a total of 640,000 tweets containing *because* in roughly one and a half days.

The present study draws on a much smaller subset of the data, namely all those tweets that include geographical metadata, amounting to a total of 12,751 tokens submitted for statistical analysis. This limitation was imposed for three reasons. First, one of the research questions in this study is concerned with the geographical distribution of *because X*, and tweets which do not contain place information have nothing to contribute in this regard. Second, processing and statistical analysis of the full data would have created computational memory overload. And third, while data extraction proceeded automatically for the most part, identification of the dependent variable necessitated some hand-coding, resulting in the need for a more manageable dataset.

In terms of geographical origin of the data, a significant majority of tweets collected came from users in the US. This is not a deliberate choice of the research design but simply reflects the predominance of the platform in that country compared to elsewhere in the world (Sysomos 2014: 14). Other significant locales of origin were the UK as well as countries in Southeast Asia and Central and South America.

## 2.2 Coding for the linguistic variable

The outcome variable, *because*-complement, is defined as the syntactic material following a given instance of *because* or any of its alternative spellings (see the predictor spelling in 2.3. below). It consists of the levels *clause* (a full, finite clause), *of* (a PP headed by *of*), and *X* (any material that does not conform to either of the established complementation strategies described in Aarts (2011), Huddleston and Pullum (2002) and Biber et al. (1999)). Table 1 gives an overview of the overall distribution of the variants. *Clause* is by far the most frequent complementation strategy, an observation that is consistent with the literature. According to Biber et al., "contingency adverbials," among which they include all material introduced by *because*, "are exceptional in that they favor clauses over non-clausal structures" (1999: 788). The *X* variant contributes only just above 6% to the data. However, compared to the long-established variant *of* (7.7%), this is certainly a relevant portion.

**Table 1:** Distribution of different *because*-complements in the data

| | | |
|---|---|---|
| clause | 10,968 | 86% |
| of | 978 | 7.7% |
| X | 805 | 6.3% |
| Total | 12,751 | 100% |

Variation among the linguistic material found within the *X*-slot is not the subject of systematic analysis in the present paper. However, since this is a topic of ongoing discussion for which more empirical evidence is needed, some exploratory observations in this direction are in order. Table 2 gives the distribution of the most frequent kinds of *X* complement in the data. Nouns make up roughly a third of the cases, followed by interjections (20%) and constructions that can best be analyzed as reduced finite clauses (14%), often with a deleted subject. Finally, adjectives also contribute significantly to innovative *because*-complementation strategies, comprising roughly 10% of all cases. Among the less frequent complements are interrogative sentences, hashtags, emoticons, user mentions, adverbs, demonstrative and personal pronouns, hyperlinks, zero complements and a few cases that were unclear without further context. This distribution shows that while "because NOUN" is the prototypical case, there is wide variability in the linguistic material subsumed under the variant *X*. It also bears pointing out that a good portion of the nominal *Xs* include determiners as well as additional pre- or post-modification, as in (3). McCulloch's (2012) description had initially considered complex noun phrases in the *X*-slot ungrammatical and only accepted bare nouns. If such a constraint existed at the time, it now seems to have weakened considerably, which might well be the case with a rapidly diffusing innovation.

**Table 2:** Proportions of different material in the *X*-slot

| Realization of X | Number of cases | Proportion of cases |
|---|---|---|
| Noun/NP | 312 | 38.8% |
| Interjection | 163 | 20.3% |
| Reduced clause | 117 | 14.5% |
| Adjective | 79 | 9.8% |
| Other | 134 | 16.6% |

(3) <@user> like when ball season over..senior year just hurts cause all the work & stuff you gotta do <234>

Table 3 shows the most frequent unique expressions in the *X*-slot. A brief discussion gives some indication of their pragmatic and interactional deployment. All shaded rows in Table 3 contain expressions that can serve as stand-alone utterances. *same* is a conversational, highly condensed form of saying "the same is true for me"; *yolo*, *lol*, *idgaf*, and *ily* are compressed versions of phrases: "you only live once," "laughing out loud," "I don't give a fuck," and "I love you," respectively. These are treated as (semi-)lexicalized, fixed expressions here rather than fully realized finite clauses. This analysis is supported by their comparatively high frequency of occurrence as well as their semantics: saying "yolo" does not have the same meaning as saying "you only live once" and is hence best treated as an independent expression.

The two adjectives in Table 3, *bored* and *tired*, are not conventionalized standalone expressions of themselves, but it is not difficult to imagine situations in which they could function that way. Thus, some credence is given to McCulloch's explanation of *because X* arising from a development allowing interjectional complements. However, the two nouns *work* and *school* seem to contradict such an interpretation. In the appropriate context, both may work as standalone expressions, but they appear in contexts where they clearly aren't, such as in (4).

(4) this week I have work everyday except Thursday bc school and I won't be able to me with Mark and idk if I can handle that ya feel? <57759>

**Table 3:** Most frequent unique expressions in the X-slot.

| Unique X | Raw frequency |
|---|---|
| why not? | 25 |
| bored | 12 |
| work | 11 |
| yolo | 10 |
| same | 9 |
| damn | 7 |
| school | 7 |
| hahaha | 6 |
| lol | 5 |
| tired | 5 |
| fuck you | 4 |
| idgaf | 4 |
| ily | 4 |

Here, interpreting *school* as an interjection seems unwarranted. It rather appears that the user employed strategies to compress the content of his message into as few characters as possible, a reading that is supported by the choice of *bc* for "because" and the compression of "I don't know" into *idk*. It is noteworthy, however, that other common abbreviation strategies (e.g., for *Thursday*) were not used, and that Twitter's character limit would have left just enough space to include *because of*. Textual economy, in this case, should not be seen as a direct effect of length limitations but rather as part of a style that derives from and is legitimized by medium-specific constraints upon message size (see Eisenstein 2013: 361).

## 2.3 Predictor variables

To test the hypotheses laid out in section 1.4, values for a total of 15 predictor variables were retrieved either directly from the metadata included with each tweet or calculated from the text of the tweet itself. Some of these variables are based on relative frequencies of different parts-of-speech. For this purpose, automatic POS-tagging was performed with the openly available ARK Tagger for Twitter (Owoputi et al. 2013). This program has a reported accuracy of 93.2% (Owoputi et al. 2013: 9). However, when tested on a sample of the data in this paper, it performed slightly worse (just below 90%). POS-related variables therefore have to be interpreted with some caution.

The predictors fall into four categories according to which of the hypotheses they relate to, with some relating to more than one category. They are:

Category 1: Predictors related to densification

- **spelling**: The different orthographic variants of representing *because*. All cases that displayed variation in complementation strategies were included in the analysis, namely *because, cause, cos, coz, cus, cuz,* and *bc*. The shorter the variant of *because*, the more information load is carried per character. Hence, shorter variants reflect densification.
- **length**: The length of a tweet in number of characters. Shorter tweets are taken to indicate more compact writing, in which densification plays a heightened role.
- **mean word length**: The average length of a word in the tweet in question, in characters. This is a measure of lexical complexity, contributing to overall textual complexity.
- **noun-verb-ratio**: The ratio of nouns divided against verbs in a given tweet. An overall increase in nouns is one aspect of the trend of densification found in written Standard English (Leech et al. 2009: 211).

Category 2: Predictors related to colloquialization

- **F-measure**: This is an empirically derived measure of the formality (as opposed to contextuality) of a text (Heylighen and Dewaele 2002). Formality here is used in the mathematic sense of relatively context-independent meaning. This is inversely related to colloquialness as less contextual texts are more "interactive" and "involved" (Heylighen and Dewaele 2002: 302). The F-measure is calculated based on POS-frequencies according to the following formula (Heylighen and Dewaele 2002: 309):

$$F = (\text{noun frequency} + \text{adjective freq.} + \text{preposition freq.} + \text{article freq.} - \text{pronoun freq.} - \text{verb freq.} - \text{adverb freq.} - \text{interjection freq.} + 100) / 2$$

While there seems to be a correlation between formality and density, the two dimensions are not the same. For instance, prepositions and articles, which increase the F-measure, are closed-class, grammatical parts of speech that decrease the density of a text (Leech et al. 2009: 249). A text with the same noun-verb-ratio can consequently exhibit different F-measure values, depending on, for instance, whether it predominantly uses synthetic genitive constructions and noun-noun sequences or the of-genitive and prepositional phrases as nominal modification strategies.

- **spelling**: Alternatively to correlating reduced spellings with densification (see above), all variants other than *because* may be interpreted as more colloquial by virtue of their distance from the orthographic standard. *Cause*, *cos*, *coz*, and *cuz* also reflect phonetic reduction typical of casual spoken discourse. However, *bc* does not directly correspond to any spoken form and is therefore more clearly related to densification than to colloquialization.

Category 3: Predictors related to CMD
- **CMD features**: The ARK tagset includes a number of tags for items that are pertinent to CMD and Twitter in particular. These are hashtags, @-mentions, URLs, emoticons, and "indications of continuation across multiple tweets" (Owoputi et al. 2013: 9). The predictor CMD features is the relative frequency of such items (i.e., their proportion of all unigrams) in a given tweet. Higher values indicate a style that is more directly reflective of the Twitter medium compared to tweets with lower values.

    It bears pointing out here that, for operational purposes, features are chosen that are exclusive to CMD and hence maximally distinctive. This should not be taken as an ontological statement about the exceptionality of CMD. It is recognized that CMD is not theoretically reducible to these features and displays characteristics of both spoken and written language in diverse ways. However, for the statistical analysis, a predictor is required that clearly differentiates CMD from other forms of language.
- **experience**: The amount of time the author of a given tweet has been registered on Twitter, in days. This variable is calculated by computing the amount of days between the user's registration and the date the tweet was posted, both of which are part of the metadata provided along with the tweet through the API. More experienced users are expected to be more likely to use features that are allegedly internet-specific, including $X$.
- **activity frequency**: The amount of tweets the author of a given tweet composes per day, calculated by dividing a user's overall output by the number of days they have been registered on Twitter. Like experience, high values for activity frequency indicate users who are more fully fluent in Twitter discourse.
- **friends**: The number of people the author of a given tweet follows. A measure of how extensive a user's Twitter network is. Higher numbers suggest more involved Twitter users.
- **followers**: The number of people that follow the author of a given tweet. A measure of how extensive a user's Twitter network is. Higher numbers suggest more involved Twitter users.

- **mentions**: the inclusion of an <@user> character string to specify the addressee(s) or referent(s) of a tweet. According to Bruns and Moe (2014), tweets that include @-messages constitute the micro-level of interpersonal communication on Twitter. Schnoebelen (2014) finds higher rates of @-mentions for tweets that contain *because X* compared to those that do not.
- **Hashtags:** The use of the <#> character to flag tweets, indicating their relevance to a broader context encapsulated in the hashtag itself. This practice tends to make tweets visible beyond a user's immediate follower network and thus situates them at the macro level of Twitter communication (Bruns and Moe 2014).
- **URL:** The inclusion of hyperlinks that connect the tweet to external web documents.

Category 4: Predictors related to regional variation in English
- **origin:** The home country indicated on a user's profile. Twitter is not used to the same extent in all countries, so the numbers for this predictor are not representative of the whole English-speaking community. The imbalance of the distribution of origins required some further, manual categorization. Only countries that contributed 80+ tokens of *because* in English-language tweets were considered as separate factors. These are, in order of their size in the data set, *USA, UK, New Zealand, Philippines, Malaysia, Canada, Singapore, Ireland, Indonesia, Australia, South Africa,* and *India*. Data points for less heavily represented countries were included in the analysis, but these were conflated into two additional levels according to their position in Kachru's (1992) model of concentric circles of English, adding the levels *outer circle* and *expanding circle*.

Schnoebelen (2014) finds that "folks who use *because X* are mostly in the US (but there are a fair number of Londoners using it)." Considering the hyper-central position American English occupies in the world system of Englishes (Mair 2013), with British English as a close runner-up in terms of centrality, one would expect a trajectory of spread from the center outwards, with *because X* being most frequent in American and British English and all other varieties playing catch-up. Such an expectation is also in line with the trend of Americanization observed in the development of written Standard English in the latter half of the twentieth century (Leech at al. 2009: 252–259).

A number of the above predictors are logically related. For instance, noun-verb-ratio also enters the calculation of the F-measure, and Twitter users with more friends will often (but not always) also have more followers. The collinearity of the present set of predictors, however, does not reach a problematic extent. A test for the condition number κ produced a value of 19.68, which is no more than a moderate, harmless level of collinearity (Baayen 2008: 198).

# 3 Analysis

The way *because*-complementation is conceptualized in the present study is a case of ternary (three-way) variation. As such, a fully accountable statistical analysis requires polytomous modeling, which allows an interpretation of each predictor's influence on each one of the three variants of the response variable. Such a model was fitted to the data, utilizing multinomial logistic regression as implemented in the {mlogit} package[2] (Croissant 2013) for the statistical analysis software R (2014). However, this section reports a simpler, binomial logistic regression model in which the response variable was reinterpreted as a case of binary variation between established (*of* and *clause*) and innovative (*X*) *because*-complementation strategies. There are a number of reasons why this is preferable.

First, binomial models are much more common in the variationist literature and inherently easier to interpret than polytomous ones. Simplifying the outcome variable consequently improves the clarity of presentation while still allowing robust statistical inferences. Second, the phenomenon that is of key interest here can indeed be logically expressed as a binary choice: the selection vs. non-selection of *X* as a complement of *because*. Whatever predictors emerge as significant from such a model can confidently be interpreted as having an impact on this phenomenon. How these predictors exert differential influence on the choice of *clause* and *of* is interesting, but not the central question for the purposes of the present paper.

Finally, a post-hoc comparison of the binomial and the polytomous model reveals that the majority of significant predictors do distinguish *X* from *clause* and *of*, lending empirical support to the choice of a binomial model for the presentation of results. Cases where the multinomial model departs significantly from the one reported are discussed in the Results section.

Table 4 is a summary of the best binomial logistic regression model arrived at by step-up/step-down model comparison in Rbrul (Johnson 2009). This process determines which predictors to retain in the model in order to increase its explanatory power while at the same time avoiding overfitting. The response value of the outcome variable is *X*, compared to *of* and *clause* combined.

---

[2] The {mlogit} package incorporates the {maxLik} package (Henningsen and Toomet 2011).

**Table 4:** Binomial logistic regression model for variation between traditional and innovative *because*-complementation. The response value is *X*-complement (as opposed to *of*- and *clause*-complement)

| Predictor | | Logodds | Centered Factor Weight | p | Related Hypotheses |
|---|---|---|---|---|---|
| length | +1 | −0.018 | | 3.2e-52*** | H1: densification |
| spelling | bc | 0.703 | 0.669 | 1.68e-37*** | H1: densification / |
| | cus | 0.439 | 0.608 | | H2: colloquialization |
| | cuz | 0.228 | 0.557 | | |
| | cos | 0.019 | 0.505 | | |
| | coz | −0.339 | 0.416 | | |
| | cause | −0.473 | 0.384 | | |
| | because | −0.577 | 0.36 | | |
| mean word length | +1 | 0.446 | | 2.4e-30*** | H1: densification |
| variety | Singapore | 0.896 | 0.71 | 1.57e-05*** | H4: Americanization |
| | Indonesia | 0.761 | 0.682 | | |
| | Philippines | 0.261 | 0.565 | | |
| | India | 0.191 | 0.548 | | |
| | Canada | 0.085 | 0.521 | | |
| | Malaysia | 0.072 | 0.518 | | |
| | Australia | 0.016 | 0.504 | | |
| | Ireland | −0.090 | 0.478 | | |
| | Expanding Circle | −0.152 | 0.462 | | |
| | New Zealand | −0.184 | 0.454 | | |
| | USA | −0.324 | 0.42 | | |
| | South Africa | −0.357 | 0.412 | | |
| | Outer Circle | −0.377 | 0.407 | | |
| | UK | −0.386 | 0.405 | | |
| | Nigeria | −0.412 | 0.398 | | |
| mentions | yes | −0.164 | 0.459 | 0.00014*** | H3: CMD |
| | no | 0.164 | 0.541 | | |
| F-measure | +1 | 0.009 | | 0.00135** | H2: colloquialization |
| friends | +1 | 0 | | 0.0138* | H3: CMD |
| hyperlinks | yes | 0.17 | 0.542 | 0.0189* | H3: CMD |
| | no | −0.17 | 0.458 | | |
| Summary statistics | deviance | AIC | df | Fixed R2 | Intercept |
| | 5271.092 | 5325.092 | 27 | 0.202 | −3.217 |

Logodds with a positive sign indicate favoring conditions for the selection of *X*, whereas negative logodds imply the opposite. The *p*-value for each predictor is taken from the best model in step-down model comparison. The predictors in the model – as well as those that did not make it – are interpreted according to the research hypotheses in 1.4.

## 3.1 Predictors related to densification (hypothesis 1)

With the exception of nouniness, all predictors relating to this trend emerge as significant. In fact, the three most significant predictors in the model all relate to densification, and they all exert influence in the direction expected. For tweet length, the logodds decrease with each additional character, meaning that the longer a tweet gets, the less likely we are to encounter *X*. In other words, shorter, more compact tweets favor *X*. The increasing logodds per character in mean word length can be interpreted similarly: as Twitter users construct denser tweets, they get rid of unnecessary material, opting for instance for noun-noun sequences over post-modification with prepositional phrases. The result is that shorter items such as prepositions become less frequent. Such environments, the model suggests, are particularly favorable towards *because X* constructions.

Further confirmation of hypothesis 1 is given by the ordering of the predictor spelling, although a number of interpretations are possible here. With regard to densification, it is striking that the variants of *because* are neatly ordered by the number of their characters, with the shortest one (*bc*) being most favorable to *X* and the full realization *because* least favorable. Thus, the densest variants in terms of information-per-character are most likely to select *X* as their complement compared to others.

In sum, the statistical analysis gives ample support to the hypothesis that *X* is to some extent driven by densification. All the significant predictors related to this trend worked in the expected direction, and only nouniness failed to be included in the model. But this does not mean that densification has to be the only, or even the strongest, factor in promoting *X*.

## 3.2 Predictors related to colloquialization (hypothesis 2)

The next trend to consider is colloquialization. In addition to indicating a densification effect, the highly significant predictor spelling may be read as corroborating hypothesis 2 as well. Since *because* is the only option licensed by standard orthography, and since this variant is the most averse to *X*, there is justification in interpreting *X* as a standard-distant form of *because*-complementation. More, most of the spellings that favor *X* (<cus>, <cuz>, <cos>, <coz>, <cause>) reflect phonetic reduction typical of colloquial spoken discourse. It should be noted as well, however, that *bc*, the most likely spelling to take *X* as a complement, cannot easily be understood as a speech-like form. Instead, it is best explained in terms of textual economy.

F-Measure, the chief predictor designed to model colloquialness directly, enters the model at a moderate level of significance ($p < 0.01$). But the direction of the effect is not what hypothesis 2 predicts. According to Table 4, with increasing formality the likelihood of *X* being selected over the other two complements becomes greater. However, in this case a look at the polytomous model (not reflected in Table 4) provides further insights. Here, the effect of the F-Measure on *X* and *of* is very similar, but sharply different for *clause*, which is clearly favored by less formal texts. Thus, the data do not fully confirm a correlation between *because X* and overall informality or colloquialness.

## 3.3 Predictors related to CMD (hypothesis 3)

With regard to predictors relating to computer-mediated discourse, a number of these are conspicuous by their absence. In particular, in order to confirm hypothesis 3 we would expect CMD features to play a significant role in *because*-complementation. Yet this predictor, as well as others relating more specifically to Twitter such as experience and activity frequency, are absent from the model. The predictors relating to CMD that do reach significance do not uniformly support the notion that *because X* consistently patterns with distinctive features of online discourse. Mentions is highly significant but exerts influence in the opposite direction from what the hypothesis predicts: in direct contradiction to Schnoebelen's (2014) findings, tweets that use the <@user> strategy are comparatively less, not more likely to contain *X*. An increasing number of friends as well as the inclusion of hyperlinks do favor *X*, but they are both only marginally significant ($p < 0.05$). For the data at hand, then, no clear effect of CMD strategies on *because*-complementation could be shown. Note, however, that the limited range of text types in the data might prevent a clearer effect from emerging here. While tweets may incorporate a number of different text types, on the whole Twitter discourse is linguistically relatively coherent when compared to other genres, both of CMD and of offline language (Eisenstein 2013). Expanding the generic range of the present study could help to answer more conclusively the question whether CMD is a particularly favorable environment for *because X*.

## 3.4 Predictors related to Americanization (hypothesis 4)

Finally, the influence of regional variation in the model is worth commenting on. Two observations in particular need to be made. First, both the USA and the UK show lower logodds than most other levels of the factor origin, comparatively disfavoring *X*. The assumption that the two most central varieties in the world system of Englishes might be leading the innovative development in *because*-complementation is not borne out. There is also no discernible ESL effect, at least at the level of granularity the present study provides. Tweets from the expanding circle are situated fairly clearly in the middle of the continuum.

The second thing to note is that at the top of the variety continuum there is a geographically consistent cluster of varieties from South and Southeast Asia (with Canada as the odd one out). It seems that this area is a particularly productive locale for *because X*. Whether there are areal or typological patterns present that help explain this finding is a fruitful avenue for future research. It must be pointed out, however, that the significance of origin is not nearly as pronounced in the full multinomial model. Since not all countries/varieties are represented equally, additional data would be desirable to draw more reliable conclusions.

# 4 Discussion

Of the four hypotheses formulated in 1.4., only hypothesis 1 could be confirmed with the data at hand. *Because X* does seem to be used as a strategy amongst others that helps writers construct more compact, information-dense texts. The 140-character limit is one of Twitter's iconic features and it is evident that it should impose pressure upon users to economize their texts. But densification as a general trend is not as recent as Twitter or even text messaging. It is a force that has been found to operate consistently on written English during the latter half of the twentieth century, although affecting different genres to different degrees (Biber and Finegan 2001). Hence, *because X* is an innovation in line with more general demands on written English in its recent history. While this aspect should increase the chances of the construction to eventually establish itself as a viable option in written English, one should be careful not to extrapolate from the present findings without qualification. Twitter is not only an inherently dense format, it is also much more tolerant towards deviations from the norms of Standard English and conducive to carefully constructed, rhetorical language use (Hinrichs Forthcoming). These characteristics make it an ideal environment for a newly emerging, metalinguistically salient, and economical construction like *because X*. Whether the construction can successfully establish itself in other text types will depend on its social evaluation and the amount of active resistance it faces from gatekeepers of the linguistic standard.

Next, colloquialness or informality, as operationalized by the F-measure, does not have the expected effect direction. While there is a moderately significant F-measure effect, it indicates that more formal texts slightly favor *X* (and also *of*) over *clause*. This is in direct contradiction to commentary on *because X* that equates it with casualness. A possible explanation could be that what is meant here is not the casualness of unmonitored quotidian talk, but a studied, consciously constructed one that is exploited as a poetic device. In other words, *because X* is perhaps not so much an indicator of a generally casual style as a resource that is exploited in the *stylization* of casualness (Coupland 2001). Its effectiveness may then be elevated by juxtaposing the construction with an overall formal style, hence accounting for the effect direction of the F-measure. This interpretation, however, needs further corroboration through qualitative analysis of relevant texts.

Hypothesis 3, that CMD features predict selection of *X*, likewise could not be confirmed. The internal uniformity of the data may be an issue in this regard. The analysis has only considered tweets, which are by definition CMD text types as they are produced and consumed on digital communication devices. The extent to which they display individual features of CMD discourse may simply not be a distinguishing criterion amongst them. It is worth noting, however, that users' experience and propensity to tweet also did not have any notable effect on the outcome variable. The fact that relative newbies and occasional users are just as likely to select *X* as are core Twitter users at least suggests that experience with this particular CMD text type has no influence on *because-*complementation. Data from other CMD platforms such as Facebook or personal blogs, as well as from spoken language, are needed to better understand the sensitivity of *because X* to different modes and media of communication.

The most difficult dimension of variation to account for in the present data is geography. Hypothesis 4, that hyper- and super-central varieties in the world system of Englishes are spearheading the innovation, is not borne out for the data at hand. Origin of a tweet did emerge as a significant factor, but the pattern is complicated. Neither the USA nor the UK are likely to select *X* compared to most other countries. Instead, the most productive locales for the construction seem to be countries in Southeast and South Asia. Since it is unlikely that these outer circle countries act directly as a model for the rest of the English-speaking world, how can this be accounted for? A likely explanation would be that, since *because X* encompasses a large variety of complementation strategies, the concrete shape the construction takes in different varieties differs significantly. One might, for instance, expect transfer or substrate influences in countries where the native language of many speakers is not English. Yet, a cursory comparison between the Asian cluster that favors *X* and all other varieties reveals no clearly distinct pattern. Tweets from these countries use slightly more nouns and slightly less interjections in the *X*-slot, but overall the relative frequencies across different parts of speech are very similar. One would, of course, expect regional differentiation at more detailed levels of the sociolinguistic system, as is always to be expected with globalizing variants (Buchstaller and D'Arcy 2009). Due to the scarcity of reliable demographic information on Twitter, this is an aspect the present study was not able to consider in detail.

# 5 Conclusion

The analysis has shown that innovative forms of *because*-complementation (*X*) have become a viable option in Twitter discourse globally. In the data at hand, such constructions occur with roughly the same frequency as *because of*, which is a long-established form. The data have also revealed considerable variability in what linguistic material can occupy the *X*-slot. Nouns are the prototypical candidates, but a range of parts of speech and constructions occurs. This variability makes it difficult to account for the emergence of *because X*.

The main question addressed in the analysis is what factors motivate the selection of *X*. This was done by collecting text-linguistic and demographic predictors that correspond to the different research hypotheses detailed in 1.4. Here, one trend that has been shown to operate on the development of Late Modern written Standard English, densification, was found to play a decisive role. Shorter, more informationally dense texts draw on *because X* since it is the variant with the most economical information-per-character ratio. Colloquialness and the CMD environment could not be confirmed as factors favoring the innovative form. The former disqualifies perhaps because it equates at least in part to unmonitored, spontaneous language use, whereas commentary suggests that *because X* is drawn upon as a strategic humorous device. Such deliberate, rhetorical functions are in line with work that points out the increased potential for rhetoricity of (asynchronous) CMD (Hinrichs Forthcoming), but are difficult to operationalize in a variationist framework. As regards the lack of significance of CMD linguistic features, two explanations are possible: either *because X* has by now established itself to an extent where it has shed its connections to a specific media environment or, if it is still "exceptionally bloggy"

(Garber 2013), this connotation does not become apparent from looking exclusively at Twitter data. In the latter case, comparisons across text types and modes of communication might still confirm hypothesis 2. Regional variation in *because*-complementation also deserves further attention. While the data display a pattern of geographical distinction, the hypothesis of a US- (and potentially UK-) led change could not be confirmed. Neither does there seem to be a native speaker/non-native speaker distinction. The propensity of tweets from Southeast and South Asian countries to use *because X* points to a regionally systematic pattern, but no convincing explanation of that pattern presents itself at this stage. Further cross-varietal research may reveal to what extent *because X* follows the same trajectory in different varieties and which ones are leading the change.

Methodologically, the study demonstrates that Twitter data can productively be exploited to investigate linguistic variation. In doing so, care must be taken to adequately address the specificity of Twitter discourse. Applying methods developed from corpus-linguistic research on written Standard English to CMD data is not without its problems. Some entities found frequently in CMD and especially Twitter (like hyperlinks or @-mentions) do not usually exist in written English offline. Others that do exist are used in different ways, such as punctuation and conventions of orthography. Multimodality also plays an increasing role in many tweets. Comparison across corpora is consequently difficult. Also, tools like POS taggers need to be adopted to deal with new kinds of structures. On the other hand, the prevalence of Twitter, both in terms of its importance in public discourse as well as the amount of data it creates, should not simply be neglected. In the past, CMD has often been exoticized and treated as maximally different from offline linguistic practice. It would be more productive to recognize the diversity in CMD text types and to see them as just that: text types among others in the textual ecology of a language. Several studies have demonstrated that morpho-syntactic (Doyle 2014) as well as phonetic (O'Connor et al. 2010) linguistic features carry over onto Twitter with their offline constraints fully intact. The present study shows that relating developments in Late Modern written Standard English, notably densification, to data from Twitter can help refine variationist analysis of those data.

This is not to argue, of course, that findings from analyses of Twitter discourse are fully representative of other text types, nor that variationists should rely on this kind of data for all questions at all times. The constraints and characteristics of language on Twitter are different from those found in most written English on a number of counts (e.g., non-standardness, extreme brevity, conversationality, etc.) and, as has been argued above, these differences directly impact the likelihood of occurrence of *because X*. For the question addressed in the present paper, and for others relating to recent, low-frequency and/or nonstandard features, tweets provide an excellent source of empirical data. The extent to which patterns found in such studies can lead to reliable predictions for other text types is a matter of empirical validation.

Will *because X* continue to increase in frequency? Will it soon be found increasingly in traditional, offline text types and spoken language as well? The answer to these questions has a lot to do with the social evaluation of the variant. This is an issue the present study cannot answer directly and that awaits further attention in future research. Acceptability studies could tell us what kinds of *X* are considered grammatical, by whom, and in what context (see Bailey 2014). Further variationist analyses should consider other text types as well as draw longitudinal comparisons with Twitter data from different points in time. The latter would allow not only observations about overall frequency developments but comparisons of how different constraints develop over time. With further spread of the variant, for instance, one would expect a leveling of constraints, enabling *because X* to occur in a wider range of contexts with less specific interactional connotations. Such a development possibly shines through in the present data, in that modified nouns formerly judged to be unacceptable by McCulloch (2012) are now found regularly in the *X*-slot. A fuller understanding of the way *because X* is embedded in different sociolinguistic systems across the world is also needed to understand the globalizing and localizing processes involved. Finally, the question of where the construction originated remains to be answered. The potential of many *X*s to function as interjections (McCulloch 2014) points towards a possible explanation, but more empirical work is needed to corroborate this intuition. The present contribution, then, is meant as a first step towards analyzing a recent morpho-syntactic development in the English language. Future research, both in the context of CMD and other modes of communication, will draw a more complete picture of where *because X* originated, who uses it, and what trajectory of spread (or attrition) the construction is taking.

# 6 References

Aarts, Bas. 2011. *Oxford Modern English grammar*. Oxford & New York: Oxford University Press.
Andersen, Gisle & Kristin Bech (eds.). 2013. *English corpus linguistics: Variation in time, space, and genre (Selected papers from ICAME 32)*. Amsterdam: Rodopi.
Baayen, Harald. 2008. *Analyzing linguistic data: A practical introduction to statistics*. Cambridge: Cambridge University Press.
Bailey, Laura. 2012. Because reasons. *linguistlaura*. http://linguistlaura.blogspot.co.uk/2012/07/because-reasons.html (accessed 14 March 2016).

Bailey, Laura R. 2014. 'Because x': Syntactic restructuring, ellipsis, or internetese? Paper presented at the Annual Meeting of the Linguistics Association of Great Britain. Oxford, 4 September.
Baker, Paul. 2006. *Using corpora in discourse analysis*. London et al.: Continuum.
Baker, Paul. 2010. *Sociolinguistics and corpus linguistics*. Edinburgh: Edinburgh University Press.
Bamman, David, Jacob Eisenstein & Tyler Schnoebelen. 2014. Gender in Twitter: Styles, stances, and social networks. *Journal of Sociolinguistics* 18(2). 135–160.
Biber, Douglas. 2003. Compressed noun-phrase structures in newspaper discourse: The competing demands of popularization vs. economy. In Jean Aitchison & Diana M. Lewis (eds.) *New media language*, 169–81. London & New York: Routledge.
Biber, Douglas. 2012. Register as a predictor of linguistic variation. *Corpus Linguistics and Linguistic Theory* 8(1). 9–37.
Biber, Douglas, and Edward Finegan. 2001. Diachronic relations among speech-based and written registers in English. In Susan Conrad and Douglas Biber (eds.) *Variation in English: Multidimensional studies*, 66–83. London: Longman.
Biber, Douglas, Stig Johansson, Geoffrey Leech, Susan Conrad & Edward Finegan. 1999. *Longman grammar of spoken and written English*. Harlow & New York: Longman.
boyd, danah, Scott Golder & Gilad Lotan. 2010. Tweet, tweet, retweet: Conversational aspects of retweeting on Twitter. Proceedings of the Forty-Third Hawai'i International Conference on System Sciences (HICSS-43). Kauai, HI: IEEE Press.
Bruns, Axel & Hallvard Moe. 2014. Structural layers of communication on Twitter. In Katrin Weller, Axel Bruns, Jean Burgess, Merja Mahrt & Cornelius Puschmann (eds.). *Twitter and society*, 15–28. New York: Peter Lang.
Buchstaller, Isabelle & Alexandra D'Arcy. 2009. Localized globalization: A multi-local, multivariate investigation of quotative *be like*. *Journal of Sociolinguistics* 13(3). 291–331.
Carey, Stan. 2013. 'Because' has become a preposition, because grammar. *Sentence First*. http://stancarey.wordpress.com/2013/11/13/because-has-become-a-preposition-because-grammar/ (accessed 14 March 2016).
Coupland, Nikolas. 2001. Dialect stylization in radio talk. *Language in Society* 30(3). 345–375.
Croissant, Yves. 2013. mlogit: multinomial logit model. R package version 0.2–4. http://CRAN.R-project.org/package=mlogit (accessed 14 March 2016).
Doyle, Gabriel. 2014. Mapping dialectal variation by querying social media. *Proceedings of the 14th Conference of the European Chapter of the Association for Computational Linguistics (EACL)*. http://web.stanford.edu/~gdoyle/papers/doyle-2014-eacl.pdf (accessed 14 March 2016).
Davies, Mark & Robert Fuchs. 2015. Expanding horizons in the study of World Englishes with the 1.9 billion word Global Web-Based English Corpus (GloWbE). *English World-Wide* 36(1). 1–28.
Eisenstein, Jacob. 2013. What to do about bad language on the internet. *Proceedings of the 2013 Conference of the North American Chapter of the Association for Computational Linguistics: Human Language Technologies (NAACL | HLT)*. 359–369. Atlanta, GA: Association for Computational Linguistics.
Eisenstein, Jacob, Brendan O'Connor, Noah Smith & Eric Xing. 2010. A latent variable model for geographic lexical variation. *Proceedings of the 2010 Conference on Empirical Methods in Natural Language Processing*. 1277–1287. Stroudsburg, PA: Association for Computational Linguistics (ACL).

Eisenstein, Jacob, Brendan O'Connor, Noah Smith & Eric Xing. 2012. Mapping the geographical diffusion of new words, NIPS 2012 Workshop on Social Network and Social Media Analysis. http://arxiv.org/abs/1210.5268 (accessed 14 March 2016).

Finegan, Edward & Douglas Biber. 1994. Register and social dialect variation: An integrated approach. In Douglas Biber & Edward Finegan (eds.). *Sociolinguistic perspectives on register*, 315–47. Oxford et al.: Oxford University Press.

Gabrielatos, Costas, Eivind Nessa Torgersen, Sebastian Hoffmann & Susan Fox. 2010. A corpus-based sociolinguistic study of indefinite article forms in London English. *Journal of English Linguistics* 38(4). 297–334.

Garber, Megan. 2013. English has a new preposition, because Internet. *The Atlantic*. http://www.theatlantic.com/technology/archive/2013/11/english-has-a-new-preposition-because-internet/281601/ (accessed 14 March 2016).

Gillen, Julia & Guy Merchant. 2013. Contact calls: Twitter as a dialogic social and linguistic practice. *Language Sciences* 35. 47–58.

Gouws, Stephan, Donald Metzler, Congxing Cai & Eduard Hovy. 2011. Contextual bearing on linguistic variation in social media. *Proceedings of the Workshop on Language in Social Media (LSM 2011)*. 20–29. http://aclweb.org/anthology/W/W11/W11-0704.pdf (accessed 14 March 2016).

Haddican, Bill & Daniel Ezra Johnson. 2012. Effects on the particle verb alternation across English dialects. *University of Pennsylvania Working Papers in Linguistics* 18(2). http://repository.upenn.edu/pwpl/vol18/iss2/5 (accessed 14 March 2016).

Hartogs, Jessica. 2013. English grammar is changing...because Internet. *CBS News*. http://www.cbsnews.com/news/english-grammar-is-changingbecause-internet/ (accessed 14 March 2016).

Henningsen, Arne & Ott Toomet. 2011. maxLik: A package for maximum likelihood estimation in R. *Computational Statistics* 26(3). 443–458.

Herring, Susan C. & John C. Paolillo. 2006. Gender and genre variation in weblogs. *Journal of Sociolinguistics* 10(4). 439–459.

Heylighen, Francis & Jean-Marc Dewaele. 2002. Variation in the contextuality of language: An empirical measure. *Foundations of Science* 7(3). 293–340.

Hinrichs, Lars. Forthcoming. The language of diasporic blogs: A framework for the study of rhetoricity in written online code-switching. In Cecelia Cutler & Unn Røyneland (eds.), *Methods for analyzing youth language in new media and computer-mediated communication*. Cambridge: Cambridge University Press.

Hinrichs, Lars & Benedikt Szmrecsanyi. 2007. Recent changes in the function and frequency of Standard English genitive constructions: A multivariate analysis of tagged corpora. *English Language and Linguistics* 11(03). 437–474.

Hinrichs, Lars & Jessica White-Sustaíta. 2011. Global Englishes and the sociolinguistics of spelling: A study of Jamaican blog and email writing. *English World-Wide* 32(1). 46–73.

Hinrichs, Lars, Benedikt Szmrecsanyi & Axel Bohmann. 2015. *Which*-hunting and the Standard English relative clause. *Language* 91(4). 806–836.

Honeycutt, Courtenay & Susan C. Herring. 2009. Beyond microblogging: Conversation and collaboration via Twitter. *Proceedings of the Forty-Second Hawai'i International Conference on System Sciences (HICSS-42)*. Los Alamitos, CA: IEEE Press.

Huddleston, Rodney & Geoffrey K. Pullum. 2002. *The Cambridge grammar of the English language*. Cambridge: Cambridge University Press.

Hundt, Marianne, Carolin Biewer & Nadja Nesselhauf (eds.). 2006. *Corpus linguistics and the Web*. Amsterdam & New York: Rodopi.

Iorio, Josh. 2009. Effects of audience on orthographic variation. *Studies in the Linguistic Sciences: Illinois Working Papers* 2009. 127–140.

Iorio, Josh. 2012. A variationist approach to text: What role-players can teach us about form and meaning. *Texas Studies in Language and Literature* 53(4). 381–401.

Johnson, Daniel Ezra. 2009. Getting off the GoldVarb standard: Introducing Rbrul for mixed effects variable rule analysis. *Language and Linguistics Compass* 3(1). 359–383.

Kachru, Braj. 1992. World Englishes: Approaches, issues and resources. *Language Teaching* 25. 1–14.

Labov, William. 1972. *Sociolinguistic patterns*. Philadelphia: University of Pennsylvania Press.

Labov, William. 1984. Field methods of the project in linguistic change and variation. In John Baugh & Joel Sherzer (eds.). *Language in use*, 28–53. Englewood: Prentice-Hall.

Labov, William. 1990. The intersection of sex and social class in the course of language change. *Language Variation and Change* 2(2). 205–254.

Leech, Geoffrey, Marianne Hundt, Christian Mair & Nicholas Smith. 2009. *Change in contemporary English: A grammatical study*. Cambridge: Cambridge University Press.

Liberman, Mark. 2012. Because NOUN. *Language Log*. http://languagelog.ldc.upenn.edu/nll/?p=4068 (accessed 14 March 2016).

Mair, Christian. 2006. *Twentieth-century English: History, variation and standardization*. Cambridge: Cambridge University Press.

Mair, Christian. 2009. Corpus linguistics meets sociolinguistics: Studying educated spoken usage in Jamaica on the basis of the *International Corpus of English* (ICE). In Lucia Siebers & Thomas Hoffmann (eds.). *World Englishes: Problems, properties, prospects*, 39–60. Amsterdam: Benjamins.

Mair, Christian. 2011. Corpora and the New Englishes: Using the 'Corpus of Cyber-Jamaican' (CCJ) to explore research perspectives for the future. In Fanny Meunier, Sylvie De Cock, Gaëtanelle Gilquin & Magalie Paquot (eds.). *A taste for corpora: In honour of Sylviane Granger*, 209–236. Amsterdam: John Benjamins.

Mair, Christian. 2013. The world system of Englishes: Accounting for the transnational importance of mobile and mediated vernaculars. *English World-Wide* 34. 253–278.

Mair, Christian & Marianne Hundt. 1999. 'Agile' and 'uptight' genres: The corpus-based approach to language change in progress. *International Journal of Corpus Linguistics* 4(2). 221–242.

Marwick, Alice E. & danah boyd. 2011. I tweet honestly, I tweet passionately: Twitter users, context collapse, and the imagined audience. *New Media & Society* 13(1). 114–133.

McCulloch, Gretchen. 2012. Because reasons. *All Things Linguistic*. http://allthingslinguistic.com/post/26522214342/because-reasons (accessed 14 March 2016).

McCulloch, Gretchen. 2014. Why the new 'because' isn't a preposition (but is actually cooler). *All Things Linguistic*. http://allthingslinguistic.com/post/72252671648/why-the-new-because-isnt-a-preposition-but-is (accessed 14 March 2016).

McEnery, Tony & Andrew Hardie. 2012. *Corpus linguistics: Method, theory and practice*. Cambridge et al.: Cambridge University Press.

O'Connor, Brendan, Jacob Eisenstein, Eric P. Xing & Noah A. Smith. 2010. Discovering demographic language variation. *Proceedings of the NIPS Workshop on Machine Learning for Social Computing*. http://www.cs.cmu.edu/~nasmith/papers/oconnor+eisenstein+xing+smith.nips-ws10.pdf (accessed 14 March 2016).

Owoputi, Olutobi, Brendan O'Connor, Chris Dyer, Kevin Gimpel, Nathan Schneider & Noah A. Smith. 2013. Improved part-of-speech tagging for online conversational text with word clusters. Proceedings of NAACL 2013. http://www.ark.cs.cmu.edu/TweetNLP/owoputi+etal.naacl13.pdf (accessed 14 March 2016).

Page, Ruth. 2012. The linguistics of self-branding and micro-celebrity in Twitter: The role of hashtags. *Discourse & Communication* 6. 181–201.

Pullum, Geoffrey. 2014. Because syntax. *Language Log*. http://languagelog.ldc.upenn.edu/nll/?p=9494 (accessed 14 March 2016).

R Core Team. 2014. R: A language and environment for statistical computing. *R Foundation for Statistical Computing*. Vienna: Austria. http://www.R-project.org/ (accessed 14 March 2016).

Romano, Aja. 2013. We're all using language differently now, because Internet culture. *The Daily Dot*. http://www.dailydot.com/lifestyle/because-preposition-language-internet/ (accessed 14 March 2016).

Schnoebelen, Tyler. 2014. Innovating because innovation. *Idibon*. http://idibon.com/innovating-innovation/ (accessed 14 March 2016).

Squires, Lauren. 2014. From TV personality to fans and beyond: Indexical bleaching and the diffusion of a media innovation. *Journal of Linguistic Anthropology* 24(1). 42–62.

Squires, Lauren. 2016. Twitter: Design, discourse, and the implications of public text. In Alexandra Georgakopoulou & Tereza Spilioti (eds.). *The Routledge handbook of language and digital communication*, 239–255. New York: Routledge.

Squires, Lauren & Josh Iorio. 2014. Tweets in the news: Legitimizing medium, standardizing form. In Jannis Androutsopoulos (ed.). *Mediatization and sociolinguistic change*, 331–360. Berlin: Mouton de Gruyter.

Sysomos. 2014. Inside Twitter: An in-depth look inside the Twitter world. http://sysomos.com/uploads/Inside-Twitter-BySysomos.pdf (accessed 14 March 2016).

Tagliamonte, Sali, & Derek Denis. 2008. Linguistic ruin? Lol! Instant messaging and teen language. *American Speech* 83(1). 3–34.

Twitter. 2014a. Terms of service. https://twitter.com/tos (accessed 14 March 2016).

Twitter. 2014b. The streaming APIs. https://dev.twitter.com/streaming/overview (accessed 14 March 2016).

Weller, Katrin, Axel Bruns, Jean Burgess, Merja Mahrt & Cornelius Puschmann (eds.). 2014. *Twitter and society*. New York et al.: Peter Lang.

Whitman, Neal. 2013. Because as a preposition. *QuickAndDirtyTips.Com*. http://www.quickanddirtytips.com/education/grammar/because-as-a-preposition (accessed 14 March 2016).

Whitman, Neal. 2014. Why is the Word of the Year 'because'? Because... *Visual Thesaurus*. https://www.visualthesaurus.com/cm/dictionary/why-is-the-word-of-the-year-because-because/ (accessed 14 March 2016).

Zappavigna, Michele. 2012. *Discourse of Twitter and social media*. London: Continuum.

Zimmer, Ben. 2014. "Because" wins 2013 Word of the Year vote, because awesome. *Visual Thesaurus*. https://www.visualthesaurus.com/cm/wordroutes/because-wins-2013-word-of-the-year-vote-because-awesome/ (accessed 14 March 2016).

Steven Coats
# Grammatical feature frequencies of English on Twitter in Finland

## 1 Introduction

Technological change affects the parameters of language use, and as internet access has expanded rapidly in recent decades, communicative encounters resulting from online activity have begun to play an increasing role in daily life. Commercial social media platforms such as Twitter, whose content consists of millions of user messages with global extent, represent an important site of online language use. The use of English online has been subject to much attention in public discourse in mass media as well as in academic scholarship, and while research into online language has addressed a wide range of topical considerations, a recurrent typological interpretation of English as it is used in computer–mediated communication (CMC) is that it differs from traditional language varieties in terms of lexis, grammar, and pragmatic features. Crystal (2006: 18) uses the term *Netspeak* to refer to "a type of language displaying features that are unique to the Internet... arising out of its character as a medium which is electronic, global and interactive" (cf. Androutsopoulos 2006).[1]

At the same time, the global status of English as the world's lingua franca continues to evolve, with English now serving not only as the principal language of international communication in academia, business, media and diplomacy (Crystal 2003), but increasingly as an important language for online communication in informal and geographically localized communicative contexts, particularly in the European Union (European Commission 2011).

Despite widespread recognition of the prevalence of English in global CMC, there have been relatively few efforts to systematically investigate variation in the lexis or grammar of English on social media in international contexts.[2] Although studies have investigated the use of particular linguistic features in

---
[1] However, the uniqueness of CMC/Netspeak in this respect has been disputed by e.g., Squires (2010).
[2] Mocanu et al. (2013) provide a survey of language and geography for global Twitter data. Magdy et al. (2014) find that English is the predominant language on Twitter for 41 of 206 countries or territories.

---
**Steven Coats,** University of Oulu

various types of CMC, including Twitter, and the distribution of linguistic features in Twitter language in the United States (e.g., Eisenstein et al. 2014 and Grieve et al. 2015 for lexical innovation and the geographical distribution of lexical items; Bamann, Eisenstein and Schnoebelen 2014 for frequencies of selected lexical and grammatical items), to my knowledge, no corpus-based studies have analyzed Twitter English in non-L1 environments.

The present research characterizes the social media language variety "English on Twitter in Finland" as a Finland-based variety of online English that emerges as distinct when investigated on the basis of aggregate feature frequencies. The approach is not focused on close qualitative analysis of the discourse functionality of individual tweets or the linguistic behavior of individual Twitter users. Rather, it utilizes Exploratory Factor Analysis of aggregate feature frequencies as a means of identifying patterns of co-occurrence and distinguishing underlying functional or situational parameters that may contribute to register, genre or variety difference (Biber 1988, 1995, 2006). Grammatical features with information-marking functions, such as noun phrases, adjectives, complex verb forms, or numerals, tend to co-occur in many types of texts, as do features which may be utilized to negotiate interpersonal interaction, such as first- and second-person pronouns, present-tense verb forms or modal verbs. Factor analysis identifies communicative dimensions of discourse, such as an "Informational versus Involved Production" dimension that contrasts information-marking features with interactive features in some texts (Biber 1988: 107).

This study considers Twitter-specific discourse features (usernames, hashtags, and retweets, i.e., re-broadcastings of tweets by different users) and part-of-speech features, as determined by the output of a probabilistic tagger, in English tweets. In addition, tweet length is examined, as well as two features associated with many types of CMC: emoticons and the non-standard orthographical feature expressive lengthening. The findings are interpreted on the basis of a factor analysis as reflecting underlying communicative dimensions.

The dynamics of English use on social media such as Twitter may differ between traditional L1 English societies and societies in which English is not an official language ("core" and "expanding circle" contexts, in the terminology of Kachru 1990). To that extent, an analysis of English on Twitter in Finland may contribute to our understanding of the ways in which language interacts with the complex forces of globalization. Upon closer examination, the configuration of language feature frequencies most typical of the variety suggests that a characteristic communicative orientation may underlie the interactions of Finland-based users writing in English, who extract meaning-creating potential from new technology at the interface of user functionality and medium constraints (cf. Hutchby 2001; Wikström 2014).[3]

## 2 Background

Twitter has become an important resource for online communication since its launch in 2006. Twitter platform users post public tweets of up to 140 characters and use the service to interact with other users by following or responding to their tweets and providing links to other online information. As of September 2015, the site reported more than 320 million active users monthly, 79% of whom were located outside the Unites States (Twitter 2015). In addition to the text (the "user message" field), the data structure of a tweet can contain additional metadata entities with information about language, location of the author, interaction of the author with other users, or other types of information. While tweets broadcast from desktop or laptop computers typically do not contain location information, a small but nonetheless substantial proportion of messages contain geo-coordinates corresponding to the location of the user (Morstatter et al. 2013 report 1.45–3.17% of tweets are geotagged; Leetaru et al. 2013 report 1.6%).

Twitter users employ platform-specific linguistic resources to interact with other users and situate their own messages within specific contexts of discourse on the platform. One such resource, the utilization of usernames or screen names with an affixed <@> symbol, is often used for direct exchanges between users. Honeycutt and Herring (2009) analyze a corpus of tweets in order to investigate the extent to which Twitter users engage in direct user-to-user exchanges. They find that the presence of <@> in tweet messages correlates with user interactivity, and suggest that microblogging may facilitate collaboration.

Dialogic participation and patterns of user interaction have also been the focus of studies by Ritter, Cherry and Dolan (2010) and Page (2012), who note that a significant proportion of tweets containing the <@> symbol consists of broadcast-style content with no explicit response to the tweet author from other users. Dialogues on Twitter (i.e., multiple-tweet content consisting of a message and at least one response directed to the message's author) tend to be short:

---

[3] An example of meaning creation via unexpected user interaction with technology might be the development of the Short Message Service (mobile telephone texting) from a means for the automatic transmission of emergency broadcasts to an interpersonal communication resource (Hillebrand et al. 2010).

70% of conversations consist of one tweet and one response (Ritter, Cherry and Dolan 2010: 173).

Other features characteristic of Twitter user messages, such as the use of the hashtag (<#>), have been investigated. Zappavigna (2011, 2012) suggests that hashtags, originally employed on the Twitter platform as explicit topic or content markers, have taken on pragmatic functions. Due to the ways in which the Twitter interface allows users to search character strings preceded by the hashtag and interact with users utilizing specific hashtags, the symbol is now frequently used to show evaluative sentiment or broadcast subjective affiliation. Wikström (2014) analyzes several communicative tasks associated with the hashtag on Twitter, noting that in addition to marking topics and conversations, the symbol is used to participate in online communal games, mark metacommentary, or negotiate pragmatic categories such as self-presentation and maintenance of face. To that extent, hashtag use represents an example of how user interaction with communication technology interfaces can prompt the emergence of unexpected communicative behaviors (Wikström 2014: 148–150).[4]

Emoticons are "visual cues formed from ordinary typographical symbols that ... represent feeling or emotions" (Walther and D'Addario 2001, citing Rezabek and Cochenour 1998: 207; see also Dresner and Herring 2010 and Vandergriff 2014a). Non-standard features such as emoticons have not figured as prominently in corpus-based studies of language as have other units such as dictionary words or grammatical types. The relative lack of attention paid to the prevalence and communicative function of emoticons may reflect the somewhat restricted domains of use of these symbols, which are more frequently encountered in CMC text types such as chat, instant messaging, online message boards, or the anonymous imageboards known as "chans," but less frequently in blogs and the online equivalents of print media like news reports or academic writing (Ptaszynski et al. 2011).

Schnoebelen (2012) investigates the expression of affective content on Twitter, particularly through the use of emoticons and their co-occurrence with lexical items. He suggests that emoticons have broader discourse functionality than simply the representation of emotional states, and finds that on Twitter, use of particular emoticon types correlates with word choice.

Non-standard orthography, whether the result of error or used as an expressive resource, is another feature prevalent in CMC genres such as chat or Instant Messenger communication (Herring 2001; Paolillo 2001; Tagliamonte and Denis

---

[4] For a discussion of the discourse features of Twitter, see further Squires (2016), Zappavigna (2011, 2012), and Page (2012).

2008) as well as on Twitter. In the linguistics literature, orthography has traditionally been considered from the perspective of the correspondence between characters and speech sounds, although more recent research has proposed a functional interpretation of orthographic variation (Sebba 2007). For Twitter, Callier (this volume) considers non-standard orthography corresponding to the fortition of dental fricatives in Twitter English as a style marker. Some research has examined *expressive lengthening*: non-standard orthography in which individual characters in a word string are repeated (e.g., *cooooooool, yessssss, dumbbbb*). The feature has been interpreted primarily as an affective discourse marker (Rao et al. 2010; Bamann, Eisenstein and Schnoebelen 2014).

While the varied functionality of Twitter-specific discourse features and the use of non-standard items such as emoticons or expressive lengthening on the platform have been investigated in general, there have been relatively few studies of Twitter English in specific geographical contexts, perhaps due to the relatively small proportion of tweets that are geotagged. Some research has investigated aspects of regional differentiation of Twitter English within the United States. Alis and Lim (2013), for example, analyze the length (in characters) of geo-encoded user messages, and find that overall, tweet length in the US decreased slightly from 2009–2012. They regress tweet length with a number of demographic variables, and find the strongest correlation to be an inverse relationship between tweet length and proportion of African-American inhabitants for US states. Although this demographic parameter may not be relevant for an analysis of English-language Twitter in Finland, correlation of language variation and sociolinguistic identity may shed light on English on Twitter in Finland as well.

Eisenstein et al. (2014) explore the emergence of Twitter dialects, or geographically localized uses of particular word forms in the United States, by using location, population, and demographic identity as parameters in a statistical model of lexical diffusion. Bohmann (this volume) investigates the changing grammatical functions of the lexical item *because* in English-language Twitter data in different geographical contexts. Their findings reinforce a century of dialectological field work in which geographical distance and community size have been shown to be strong correlates of the diffusion of new language forms (Kretzschmar 2009).

Demographic information about Twitter users is limited, as the service, unlike some social media platforms, does not require users to provide real names, gender, or age. Pavalanathan and Eisenstein (2015) use automated methods to extract this information, and find that tweets with geographical coordinates tend to include more non-standard features and are more likely to be authored by young people and females.

Despite such work, research on the use of English on Twitter in non-L1 environments is not extensive. Investigation of individual linguistic behavior has been carried out: multilingual users' language choice on the platform reflects the predominant language of their social networks (Eleta and Golbeck 2014). Corpus-based studies comparing national varieties of English or core, outer circle, and expanding circle varieties (Kachru 1990) in terms of feature frequencies have yet to be conducted, as far as is known, either for standard grammatical classes such as parts-of-speech or for non-standard features such as emoticons or expressive lengthening.

This project looks at feature frequencies in English on Twitter in Finland by means of comparison to a reference corpus of global Twitter English messages with no geographic specification. Although the demographic characteristics of Finland-based users of Twitter can't be determined with any certainty, some inferences about persons writing English-language messages on Twitter in Finland may be made based on previous research into the use of English in Finland.

Taavitsainen and Pahta (2003, 2008), for example, discuss the use of English in Finnish daily life by examining Finnish print media advertisements and public signage that contain English words. They note that English has an "increasing influence" in Finland "in several fields of life" (2003: 12) and suggest that the use of English continues to increase; it may be entering a "new phase" (2008: 37). English lexical items are widely used in Finnish-language advertisements in print and television media (Paakkinen 2008). Leppänen (2007), in a conversation-analytic investigation of the use of English in four short excerpts from spoken and written online language samples by Finnish young people, attests a macro-scale language shift from Finnish to English among Finnish youth in certain contexts (167).

Most considerations of the role of English in Finland have been supported by qualitative analyses of a relatively small number of texts or recordings of spoken language, but there have also been efforts to compile larger-scale data on the use of English in Finland. Leppänen et al. (2011) present the results of a survey about the use of English in Finland administered to a sample of 1,500 Finnish respondents stratified by age, occupation, education, and gender. They find that Finns have good knowledge of English and a positive, pragmatic view towards the value of English skills in a globalized world: "by the 2000s, English had become not only an indispensable vehicular language in international interactions, but also a language used in many domains and settings within Finnish society" (16). The authors note that active users of English in Finland "are more likely to be youthful and involved in youth culture, have an interest in popular culture, use the new media, and be alert to the demands/opportunities of an increasingly global economy" (166).

As English increasingly plays an important role in daily interaction in Finland, including in online communication, a characterization of English on Twitter in Finland in terms of its grammatical frequencies and underlying communicative dimensions contributes to the documentation and characterization of English as it continues to evolve as a global language (or set of global languages).

# 3 Data and methods

Approximately 93,000 tweets were collected from mid-March until early May 2013 via the Twitter Streaming API by selecting geo-tagged tweets originating from within a geographical box with the extent 60–70° N and 21–30° E, circumscribing the borders of Finland. To determine which tweets originated from within the borders of Finland, as well as in which region of Finland they originated, the latitude and longitude coordinates of each tweet were checked with the coordinates of the national and regional borders of Finland as encoded by GIS files publicly available through the Global Administrative Areas database GADM.[5] A comparison corpus, representing a random selection of approximately 305,000 tweets broadcast in late 2008 and early 2009, was downloaded via a commercial service in 2013.[6]

For both corpora, the language of each message was identified using the probabilistic language identification tool langid.py, which assigns language by comparing the frequencies of variable length n-grams (i.e., byte sequences that encode Unicode characters) in the text whose language is to be detected and comparing them with frequencies calculated from corpora in 97 languages, using a Bayesian classification algorithm (Lui and Baldwin 2012). The tool assigns a probabilistic value for the accuracy of the classification between 0 and 1. Because longer messages in a single language contain more byte n-grams that can be compared with the modeling data, they are typically assigned higher values, whereas language mixtures and extremely short user messages are typically assigned low values and sometimes misclassified. For that reason, only user messages determined to be in English with a probability of greater

---

[5] Location disambiguation, factor analysis, and all other calculations were undertaken in *R*.
[6] This data, collected at Texas A&M University, is no longer available for public download: Twitter policy since 2013 has discouraged public availability of Twitter corpora.

than 0.6 were retained in the two final corpora, the *Finland English Corpus* and the *Comparison English Corpus* (Table 1).

**Table 1:** Corpora size

|  | User messages | Tokens |
|---|---|---|
| All Finland tweets | 93,451 | 1,039,865 |
| *Finland English Corpus* | 32,916 | 436,954 |
| All Comparison tweets | 305,310 | 3,361,444 |
| *Comparison English Corpus* | 181,861 | 2,864,798 |

The demographic identity or location of the authors of the messages in the Comparison English Corpus is unknown, but an examination of the messages suggests that a relatively high proportion of the tweets originate from the United States.[7]

Some filtering of tweets sent multiple times (often commercial advertisements generated automatically) was undertaken. Prior research has shown that broadcast-style tweets such as advertisements on Twitter do not figure prominently in conversational discourse (Ritter, Cherry and Dolan 2010). As such, messages are sometimes broadcast multiple times, their lexical and grammatical feature frequencies may be overrepresented in an analysis undertaken without filtering.

Twitter's default Streaming API access for end users is limited to 1% of the volume of traffic on the platform. As Twitter considers its proprietary data to have value to data miners, it provides higher levels of access primarily on a commercial basis. Given the high volume of messages broadcast by the platform, access limitations do not necessarily pose a practical problem for the compilation of a Twitter corpus. However, as noted above, only a small percentage of tweets include geographical coordinates, and data volumes from specific geographical locations are much more limited. Although Twitter is relatively popular in Finland, it is not among the countries with the highest per capita use of the platform (Mocanu et al. 2013). The size of the Finland English Corpus may not permit in-depth study of relatively rare grammatical or lexical phenomena. Nevertheless, large-scale trends in the frequency of grammatical features are evident in the data.

Automatic part-of-speech classification of the user messages in the two corpora was performed using the Carnegie-Mellon University Twitter Tagger

---

[7] 60% of the Comparison tweets are in English. As Twitter had less global penetration in 2008/2009 it is reasonable to assume that a relatively high proportion of the English tweets originate from the US.

(Gimpel et al. 2011; Gimpel et al. 2013; Owoputi et al. 2013). The 37 tags (Table 2) are applied according to a probabilistic model from a selection of tags from the Penn Treebank tagset (Marcus, Santorini, and Marcinkiewicz 1993). In addition to tags from the Penn Treebank set, the tagger applies distinct tags for the Twitter-specific types username, hashtag, and retweet, as well as a tag for URL addresses.

**Table 2:** Part-of-speech tags applied by the CMU tagger and used in the analysis

|  | Tag | Description |  | Tag | Description |
|---|---|---|---|---|---|
| 1. | ' ' | Quotation mark (") | 20. | RB | Adverb |
| 2. | , | Comma | 21. | RBR | Adverb, comparative |
| 3. | . | Period (. ? !) | 22. | RBS | Adverb, superlative |
| 4. | : | Punctuation (: ; ... + − = < > / [ ] ~) | 23. | RP | Particle |
| 5. | CC | Coordinating conjunction | 24. | RT | Retweet |
| 6. | CD | Cardinal number | 25. | TO | *to* |
| 7. | DT | Determiner | 26. | UH | Interjection |
| 8. | EX | Existential *there* | 27. | URL | Universal Resource Locator |
| 9. | HT | Hashtag | 28. | USR | Username (preceded by @) |
| 10. | IN | Preposition or subordinating conjunction | 29. | VB | Verb, base form |
| 11. | JJ | Adjective | 30. | VBD | Verb, past tense |
| 12. | JJR | Adjective, comparative | 31. | VBG | Verb, gerund or present participle |
| 13. | JJS | Adjective, superlative | 32. | VBN | Verb, past participle |
| 14. | MD | Modal | 33. | VBP | Verb, non-3rd person singular present |
| 15. | NN | Noun, singular or mass | 34. | VBZ | Verb, 3rd person singular present |
| 16. | NNP | Proper noun, singular | 35. | WDT | Wh-determiner |
| 17. | NNS | Noun, plural | 36. | WP | Wh-pronoun |
| 18. | PRP | Personal pronoun | 37. | WRB | Wh-adverb |
| 19. | PRP$ | Possessive pronoun |  |  |  |

Emoticons were detected in the corpora by filtering the output of the CMU Twitter Tagger for tokens that had been assigned the interjection tag.[8] Regular expressions were then used to select the subset of those tokens containing the characters that most frequently comprise emoticons, primarily non-letter ASCII characters as well as Unicode symbols. The 449 emoticon types determined in this manner were examined and types whose status as emoticons seemed questionable were removed, leaving a total of 240 emoticons for the ensuing

---

**8** The Penn Treebank model uses the interjection tag for politeness forms, affective particles, and similar word types. The CMU Twitter Tagger, using the Penn Treebank model, applies the tag to emoticons as well.

analysis. Regular expressions were also used to capture expressive lengthenings in the Finland English and Comparison English data. All tokens containing at least three characters repeated in sequence were considered.[9]

Exploratory factor analysis of feature frequencies as determined by the tagger was then undertaken, allowing a preliminary characterization of the communicative and discourse dimensions of English on Twitter. These dimensions are used in the ensuing analysis, which focuses on the differences between English on Twitter in Finland and global Twitter English.

## 3.1 Exploratory factor analysis of feature frequencies

In order to conduct an exploratory factor analysis, mean feature frequencies were calculated from a merged dataset consisting of an equal number of 1000-token chunks from both the Finland English Corpus and the Comparison English Corpus. The frequencies were then used to construct a correlation matrix of the 37 individual features as variables.[10] A scree plot of eigenvalues for the correlation matrices suggested seven factors as optimal for the data. Factor loadings of the resulting factor analysis ≥ 0.3 (calculated using "varimax" rotation) are shown in Table 3.

If we consider the first two factors, shown in Figure 1, a viable interpretation of the communicative functionality of Twitter English features emerges. The first factor has a strongly positive loading on the features personal pronouns and non-3rd-person singular present verb forms (i.e., first- and second-person), while the features adverbs, base or infinitive verb forms, interjections, conjunctions, modal verbs, possessive pronouns, usernames, and Wh-adverbs have moderately positive loadings. There is a strongly negative loading on proper nouns and moderately negative loading on URLs, punctuation, and cardinal determiners (i.e., number words and numerals). This configuration suggests a functional separation between interacting with other users or situating one's own text in relation to discourse and supplying information in the form of specific reference. At one end of this dimension are interactive types and types pertaining to the

---

**9** With three exceptions: tokens containing the sequence <www.> were excluded as URL addresses, and usernames and hashtags were not considered (multiple character sequences in these types are fixed and thus difficult to consider lengthenings in the same way as other lengthening types).

**10** As the Finland English Corpus is shorter, the factor analysis was conducted upon 436 chunks of Finland English data (i.e., all of the tokens in the corpus) and an equivalent number of randomly selected 1000-token chunks from the Comparison English Corpus. See Biber (1988: 61–78, 1995: 85–140) for discussion of the methodology of exploratory factor analysis on textual material.

**Table 3:** Factor loadings for features in both corpora

|  | Factor | | | | | | |
|---|---|---|---|---|---|---|---|
|  | 1 | 2 | 3 | 4 | 5 | 6 | 7 |
| Proper noun, singular | −0.70 |  |  |  | −0.62 |  |  |
| Personal pronoun | 0.89 | −0.32 |  |  |  |  |  |
| Adverb | 0.56 |  |  |  |  |  |  |
| Verb, base form | 0.57 |  |  |  |  |  |  |
| Verb, non-3rd person singular present | 0.78 |  |  |  |  |  |  |
| Determiner |  | 0.74 |  |  |  |  |  |
| Hashtag |  | −0.55 |  |  |  |  | 0.38 |
| Preposition or subordinating conjunction |  | 0.64 |  |  |  |  |  |
| Noun, singular or mass |  | 0.67 |  |  | 0.38 |  |  |
| Interjection | 0.30 | −0.58 | 0.35 |  |  |  |  |
| to |  |  | −0.64 |  |  |  |  |
| Verb, gerund or present participle |  |  | −0.94 |  |  |  |  |
| Period (. ? !) |  |  |  | 0.95 |  |  |  |
| Universal Resource Locator | −0.41 | −0.31 |  |  |  | −0.81 |  |
| Punctuation (: ; ... + − = < > / [ ] ~) | −0.61 |  | −0.33 |  |  |  | −0.68 |
| Quotation mark (") |  |  |  |  |  |  |  |
| Comma |  | 0.36 |  |  |  |  |  |
| Coordinating conjunction | 0.40 |  |  |  |  |  |  |
| Cardinal number | −0.31 |  |  |  |  |  |  |
| Existential *there* |  |  |  |  |  |  |  |
| Adjective |  | 0.43 |  |  | 0.32 |  |  |
| Adjective, comparative |  |  |  |  |  |  |  |
| Adjective, superlative |  |  |  |  |  |  |  |
| Modal | 0.44 |  |  |  |  |  |  |
| Noun, plural |  | 0.46 |  |  |  |  |  |
| Possessive pronoun | 0.31 |  |  |  |  |  |  |
| Adverb, comparative |  |  |  |  |  |  |  |
| Adverb, superlative |  |  |  |  |  |  |  |
| Particle |  | 0.43 |  |  |  |  |  |
| Retweet |  | −0.32 |  |  |  |  |  |
| Username (preceded by @) | 0.41 | −0.43 | 0.34 |  |  |  |  |
| Verb, past tense |  | 0.39 |  |  |  |  |  |
| Verb, past participle |  | 0.44 |  |  |  |  |  |
| Verb, 3rd person singular present |  | 0.32 |  |  |  |  |  |
| Wh-determiner |  |  |  |  |  |  |  |
| Wh-pronoun |  |  |  |  |  |  |  |
| Wh-adverb | 0.39 |  |  |  |  |  |  |

Cum. variance = 0.41, $X^2$ = 3198, deg. fr. = 428, p-value < $10^{-232}$

negotiation of stance expression, epistemic modality, affective orientation and discourse functionality, such as usernames, first- or second-person personal pronouns with present-tense verb forms, possessive pronouns, modal verbs, adverbs, and question words such as *who* or *why*. At the other end are types that specify entities, such as personal or place names, URLs, and numerical values (which have scalar/informational content but rarely organize large units of discourse), along with selected punctuation types.[11]

The second factor has a strong positive loading on determiners, slightly less strong positive loadings on prepositions and singular or mass nouns, and moderate positive loadings on commas, adjectives, plural nouns, prepositional components of phrasal verbs, past tense verb forms, past participles, and 3rd-person singular present verb forms. Moderately strong negative loadings are found on personal pronouns, hashtags, interjections, URLs, retweets, and usernames. This factor separates components of the nominal phrase and verb forms indicating past temporality from the discourse features specific to Twitter and another type used for discourse negotiation, interjections (which include emoticons). This dimension implies functional separation between types employed for reporting on events (nouns, determiners, past tense verb forms, phrasal verb particles) and types used to interact with other users of the Twitter environment and negotiate discourse concerns on the platform.

The interpretation of factors three through seven (not shown in Figure 1) is much more problematic: these factors have loadings with values ≥ 0.3 on only a few features or one feature. Factor three, which contrasts usernames and interjections with present participles/gerunds and *to*, may account for tweets sent by apps that automatically report user activity on a computer or smart device, such as listening to music, in the form: "listening to x,"[12] with no interactive or discourse organization types like emoticons or usernames. Factor five, contrasting singular or mass nouns and adjectives with proper nouns, is difficult to interpret. Factor six simply accounts for tweets with no URLs, and factor seven contrasts what may be alternative methods for the specification of tweet content or topicality: hashtags versus colons.

---

[11] The punctuation types assigned this tag include those used to organize clause- or phrase structure, such as the colon, the semi-colon, and the ellipsis, as well as bracket types used for specification and types used to show relationships between numerals, such as the plus sign. For a discussion of the functions of punctuation types see Jones (1996), Nunberg (1990), and Quirk et al. (1985).

[12] Although effort was made to filter for automated tweets (see above), many remain in the corpora.

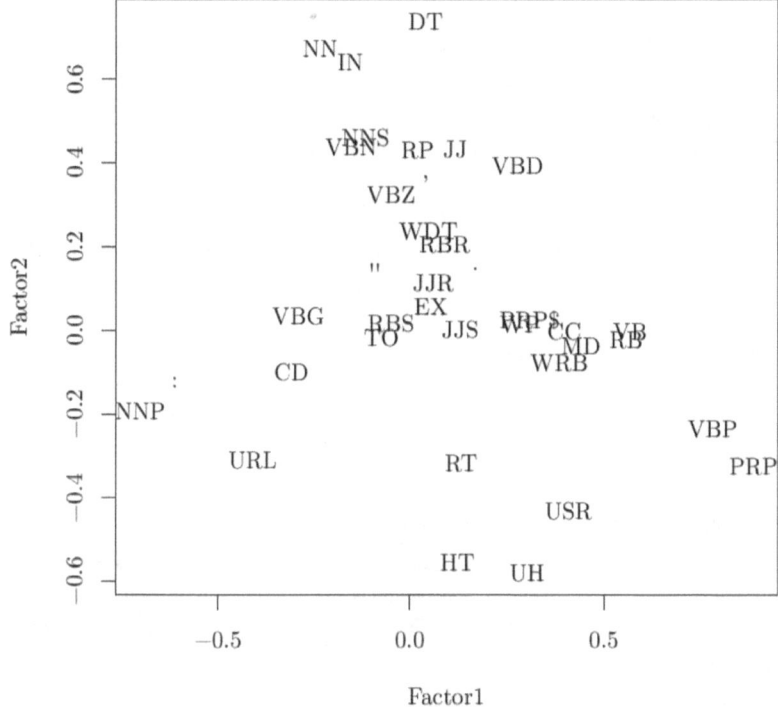

**Figure 1:** Factor loadings for 37 features (Factors 1 and 2 of the combined data)

Exploratory factor analysis suggests that Twitter discourse (in this data) may be interpreted as variable along two main dimensions. The first dimension, *interaction – specification*, contrasts interactive, affective or stance orientation towards discourse-local entities such as the self or other users with reference to entities beyond the immediate discourse of Twitter. A second dimension, *narration – discourse negotiation*, contrasts features such as nominal phrase elements and past-tense verb forms with prominent discourse-organization features such as the Twitter-specific hashtag, username, and retweet as well as the similarly versatile interjection tag (which marks emoticons).[13] When the features (including those with factor loadings less than 0.3) are plotted along

---

[13] These dimensions are analogous to the first two dimensions proposed in Biber's analyses: 'Informational versus involved production' and 'Narrative versus non-narrative concerns' (1988: 115; 1995: 141–155), suggesting that the patterning of grammatical features in Twitter English may be similar to that of other registers and genres.

the first two dimensions (Figure 1), the shared communicative functions of determiners, nouns and prepositions (at the top of the figure); non-3rd-person singular present verb forms and personal pronouns (on the right); hashtags, interjections, retweets and usernames (at the bottom); and proper nouns, punctuation, URLs, and numerals (on the left) become visually apparent by means of proximity.

Returning to differences between the Finland English Corpus and the Comparison English Corpus, relative feature frequencies can be used to situate the varieties along the proposed dimensions. A dimension score is calculated by summing the standardized difference for each unique feature on the first two factors between the individual corpus and the larger, merged dataset used for the factor analysis (Table 4). These aggregate values quantify the differentiation of communicative and functional properties that underlie the discourse of the two corpora.[14]

Table 4: Dimension scores for the Finland English Corpus and Comparison English Corpus

|  | Dimension 1: Interaction – Specification | Dimension 2: Narration – Discourse Negotiation |
|---|---|---|
| Finland English Corpus | 3.27 | −2.04 |
| Comparison English Corpus | −3.19 | 1.77 |

# 4 Results

The data for the Finland English Corpus and the Comparison English Corpus show differences in average message length as well as differences in the frequencies of the features under consideration. Interpretation of the results reinforces the findings of the factor analysis, suggesting that differences in communicative orientation between the two groups of users may underlie the observed patterns.

## 4.1 Tweet and token length

The length of Twitter user messages is limited to 140 characters, but within the range of one to 140 characters, there is wide variation in tweet length. Tweet

---

[14] See Biber (1988: 93–97) for a description of the steps involved.

lengths for the Finland English and Comparison English corpora, as measured by number of characters per tweet, are shown in Figure 2. The spike at n = 140 is due to the automatic shortening of longer tweets by the service; messages longer than 140 characters are automatically shortened to 120 characters and a 20-character url linking to the longer text is added.

Disregarding the spike due to addition of a URL, the most common tweet length for the Finland English data is 28 characters, whereas the mode for the Comparison English data is 58 characters; the corresponding mean values are 71.10 characters for the Finland data and 78.99 characters for the comparison data.

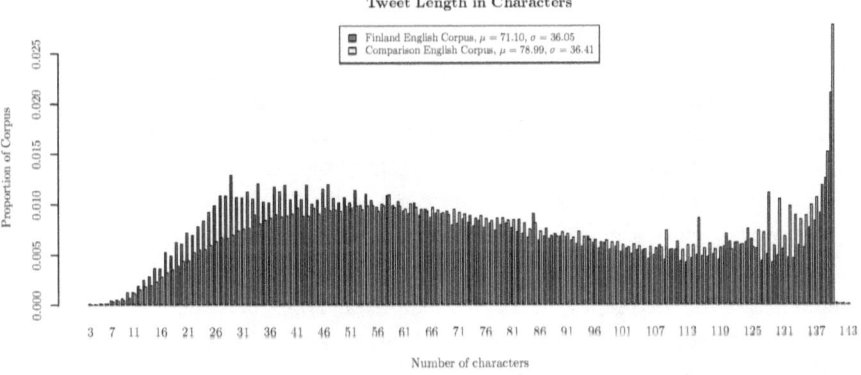

**Figure 2:** Tweet length in characters, Finland English and Comparison English corpora

Previous research has found that mean tweet length has been decreasing since the service was initiated in 2007. Alis and Lim show that mean tweet length for a Twitter user message corpus compiled between 2009 and 2012 decreased by approximately 8 characters, from ~85 to ~75 characters per tweet, values comparable to the mean tweet lengths in in the Finland English and Comparison English Corpora. They also find that for tweets that are geo-encoded, mean user message length for US states may reflect demographic characteristics of their populations (2013: 7).

Average token (word) length also differs between the Finland English and Comparison English corpora. The mean length of the tokens in the Finland English Corpus is 4.54 characters, whereas Comparison English Corpus tokens are on average 4.21 characters long. This is possibly due to much lower rates of article use in the Finland English data. There are no articles in Finnish: Grammatically, the function of providing information on the status of the referent as known or not known in discourse typically falls in Finnish to demonstratives. Unsurprisingly, when L1 Finnish speakers write or speak in English, they tend to use articles less frequently than do L1 English speakers. The Finland English Corpus exhibits much lower frequencies of articles than does the Comparison English Corpus. Indefinite articles are used in the Finland English Corpus at a rate approximately 76% that of the Comparison English Corpus, but the definite article occurs only 64% as frequently.

## 4.2 Emoticons

The data show a large range of variation in the use and distribution of emoticons. In the Finland data, Twitter users who tweet in English are more likely to use emoticon symbols than those who tweet in other languages: 24.9% of English-language tweets from Finland contained at least one emoticon, and 56.1% of the users represented in the Finland English Corpus used at least one emoticon.[15] The prevalence of emoticons in the Comparison English Corpus was much more limited. Only 9.8% of the tweets in the Comparison English Corpus included at least one emoticon, and only 10.2% of the users represented in the Comparison English Corpus utilized at least one emoticon. In terms of regularized frequencies, the frequency of all 240 emoticon types considered is 23.87 per thousand tokens in the Finland English Corpus and 6.79 per thousand tokens in the Comparison English Corpus.[16]

An analysis of emoticon type relative frequencies from Schnoebelen (2012) was replicated in part using the Finland English and Comparison English data; the findings are summarized (along with Schnoebelen's results) in Figure 3. For the most part, the Finland English, Comparison English, and Schnoebelen data show a similar rank/frequency profile for some of the most widely used emoticons. Although Finland-based users employ emoticons far more frequently overall, their proportional use of different emoticon types is similar to that of users elsewhere:

---

[15] Interestingly, the overall rate of emoticon use in the entire Finland corpus (i.e., in all languages) is lower – Finland-based tweeters use more emoticons when writing in English.
[16] It may be the case that this large difference results from an increase in use of emoticons overall on Twitter in 2013 compared to 2008–9: There seems to be no research into the prevalence of emoticon use on Twitter over time.

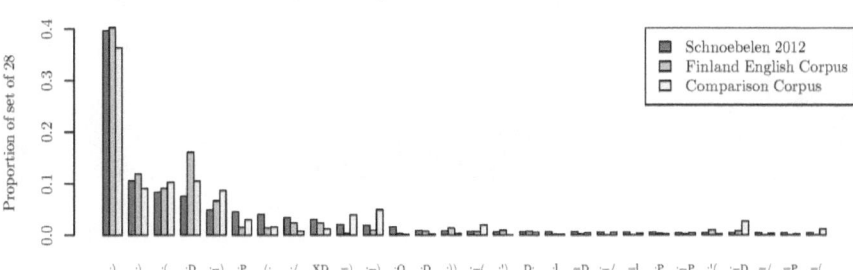

**Figure 3:** Relative frequency of 28 emoticon types in Schnoebelen 2012, Finland English Corpus and Comparison English Corpus

The relative frequencies for this specific set of 28 emoticons are much the same.[17]

## 4.3 Expressive lengthening

Expressive lengthening is also much more prevalent in the Finland English Corpus. The feature occurs at a rate of 5.00 per thousand tokens in the Finland English data and 1.86 per thousand tokens in the Comparison English data. The most frequent lengthened types and their rates of occurrence are shown in Figure 4.

The types *awww, sooo, soooo, ahhh,* and *oooh* are among the most frequent lengthened types in both corpora. The most frequent type in the Finland data is the non-pronounceable non-dictionary word *xxx*, usually interpreted as kiss symbols. Two types among the most frequent Finnish lengthenings, *XDDD* and *:DDD*, can be interpreted as emoticons with multiple mouths. The other most frequent types in the Finnish data consist of lengthened dictionary words (*meee, meeee, sooo, soooo, nooo, noooo, pleaseee, iii, yesss, goood*) and lengthened interjections or pronounceable non-dictionary words (*hmmm, mmm, mmmm, awww, aaawww, ahhh, uuu, aaah*). Eighteen of the twenty most frequent lengthenings consist of three letters in succession; two types (*soooo* and *noooo*) contain 4-character lengthenings.[18]

---

[17] Wilcoxon signed-rank tests show no significant difference between the median ranks of the relative frequencies of the 28 emoticons for the three corpora: For Finnish and Comparison data V = 222, p-value = 0.68; for Finnish and Schnoebelen data V = 161, p-value = 0.35, and for Comparison and Schnoebelen data V = 174, p-value = 0.52.

[18] The distinction between pronounceable and non-pronounceable dictionary and non-dictionary words is from Bamman, Eisenstein and Schnoebelen (2014).

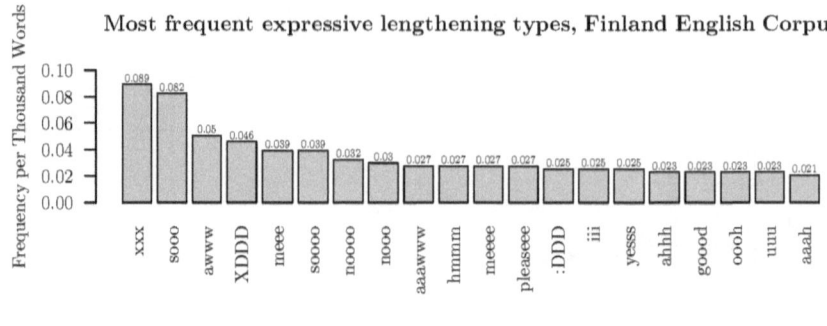

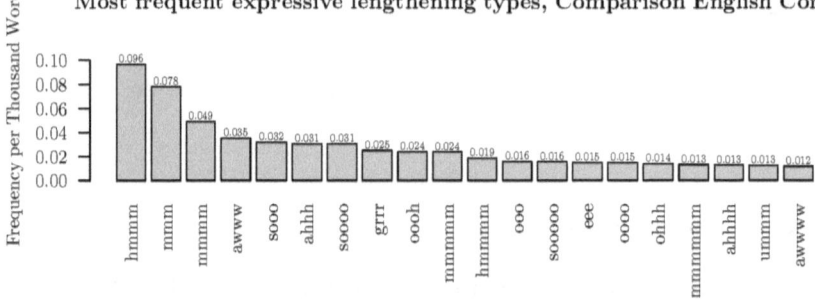

**Figure 4:** Most frequent expressive lengthening types, Finland English and Comparison English corpora

The most frequent types in the Comparison English Corpus are almost all interjections or pronounceable non-dictionary words, most of which correspond to discourse-marking sounds used in spoken conversation (*hmmm, mmm, mmmm, awww, ahhh, grrr, oooh, mmmmm, hmmmm, ooo, eee, oooo, ohhh, mmmmmm, ahhhh, ummm, awwww*). Although lengthenings are much less frequent in the Comparison English Corpus, they are more likely to consist of longer sequences of characters: Thirteen of the twenty most frequent lengthening types contain three-character sequences, four four-character sequences, two five-character sequences, and one a six-character sequence.

An interesting pattern emerges when one considers the proportion of all lengthenings by character in the two corpora (Figure 5). Again, the profiles are similar, but there are some differences.

For the Finland English data, the letter *o* comprises 22% of the lengthenings in the corpus. In general, vowel characters are more subject to lengthening than are consonants, with characters representing open and mid vowels *o*, *e*, and *a* more likely to be lengthened than those that represent close vowels *i* and *u* or

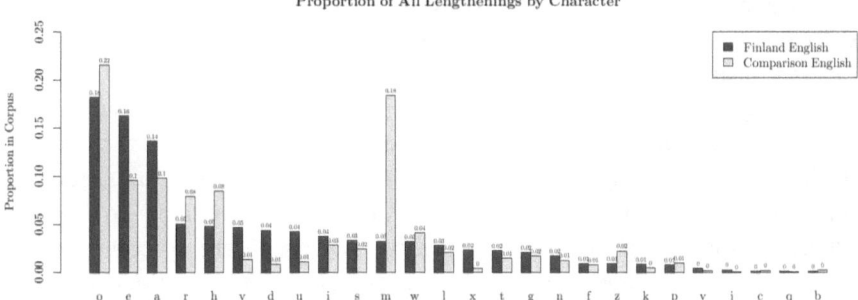

**Figure 5:** Expressive lengthening sequences by character, Finland English and Comparison English corpora

the semi-vowel *y*. Among non-vowel characters, *r* is most subject to lengthening, followed by *h, d, s, m,* and *w*. The characters *l, x, t, g, n,* and *f* are slightly less likely to be subject to lengthening, and the characters *z, k, p, v, j, c, q,* and *b* are the least likely to be lengthened.

The Comparison English Corpus data shows overall lower lengthening frequencies, but also a somewhat different distribution of lengthening types and frequencies. The character most susceptible to lengthening is again *o*. Vowels are also in the Comparison English data somewhat more likely to be lengthened than consonants: Again characters representing open and mid vowels (*o, a, e*) are lengthened more often than characters representing close vowels (*i, u*). The characters *h* and *r* are among the more frequent targets for consonant lengthening. The most striking difference is in the lengthening of *m*, which is proportionately six times more likely to be lengthened in the Comparison English Corpus.[19] The consonants *w, s, z, l, g, t,* and *n* follow in the ranking, with the consonants *p, d, f, k, x, c, b, v, q,* and *j* the least likely to be lengthened in the Comparison English data.

Summarizing the results pertaining to emoticons and expressive lengthening, the two features are far more prevalent in the Finland English Corpus. Although the distribution of emoticon types in the two corpora are similar, the character targets for expressive lengthening differ.

## 4.4 Part-of-speech features

While emoticon and expressive lengthening frequencies were calculated by using regular expressions to retrieve tokens from the corpora, the frequencies

---

**19** Written forms of common disfluency particles or fillers in Finnish include types such as *ööh, siis,* and *niinku,* but not *hmm* or related types.

for other part-of-speech or discourse types were based on tags applied by the CMU Twitter Tagger. The Finland English and Comparison English data exhibit different distributional profiles for the relative frequencies for 37 grammatical feature tags. The relative frequency of each feature is shown in Table 5 as the logarithmic odds ratio θ of frequency in the Finland English Corpus to frequency in the Comparison English Corpus: Features in the left-hand column are overrepresented in the Finland English Corpus; those on the right in the Comparison English Corpus.[20] Differences in frequencies are significant according to the results of a chi-squared test of independence at p < 0.001, except for those features marked with an asterisk.

**Table 5:** Logarithmic odds ratios (Finland English Corpus vs. Comparison English Corpus) for 37 features

| | Feature | θ | | Feature | θ |
|---|---|---|---|---|---|
| 1 | Hashtag | 3.36 | 1 | Phrasal particle | −0.56 |
| 2 | Retweet | 1.68 | 2 | Verb, present participle or gerund | −0.49 |
| 3 | Username (preceded by @) | 0.77 | 3 | Other punctuation | −0.49 |
| 4 | Interjection | 0.75 | 4 | Verb, past participle | −0.39 |
| 5 | Personal pronoun | 0.35 | 5 | Wh-determiner | −0.31 |
| 6 | Wh-adverb | 0.35 | 6 | Proper noun | −0.30 |
| 7 | Verb, non-3rd-person singular present | 0.34 | 7 | to | −0.30 |
| 8 | URL | 0.22 | 8 | Noun, singular or mass | −0.24 |
| 9 | Adjective, superlative | 0.22 | 9 | Determiner | −0.24 |
| 10 | Coordinating conjunction | 0.21 | 10 | Period, question mark, exclamation mark | −0.21 |
| 11 | Adverb | 0.17 | 11 | Verb, 3rd-person singular present | −0.20 |
| 12 | Modal verb | 0.17 | 12 | Comma | −0.17 |
| 13 | Wh-pronoun | 0.16 | 13 | Verb, past tense | −0.16 |
| 14 | Verb, base form | 0.10 | 14 | Noun, plural | −0.15 |
| 15 | Existential *there** | 0.09 | 15 | Adverb, comparative | −0.15 |
| 16 | Adverb, superlative* | 0.08 | 16 | Preposition | −0.10 |
| 17 | Possessive pronoun | 0.07 | 17 | Adjective | −0.08 |
| 18 | Quotation mark* | 0.02 | 18 | Adjective, superlative* | −0.07 |
| | | | 19 | Cardinal number* | −0.02 |

The three features most overrepresented in the Finland English data correspond to the Twitter-specific tags applied by the CMU Twitter tagger. Hashtags are used in the Finland English Corpus at a rate almost 29 times that of the Comparison English Corpus. Retweets, or re-broadcastings of a tweet by a different

---

[20] The statistic is calculated according to the formula log $O_{11}O_{22}/O_{21}O_{12}$, where $O_{11}$ and $O_{21}$ represent the number of occurrences of the feature in the Finland English and Comparison English Corpora, respectively, and $O_{12}$ and $O_{22}$ the corresponding number of tokens that do not represent the feature.

user, are more than five times more common in the Finland English Corpus. Finland-based Twitter users tweeting in English are more than twice as likely as Comparison English users to utilize usernames preceded by <@>.

The frequency of interjections in the Finland English Corpus is more than twice that of the Comparison English Corpus. Tokens assigned the interjection tag include emoticons, non-standard initialisms such as *lol*, non-dictionary pronounceable types such as the hesitation marker *ummm* or the laughter indicator *haha*, as well as lexical items such as profanity and politeness markers. The discrepancy between the corpora reflects the high rate of use of emoticons in the Finnish data: As noted above, emoticons are used approximately 3.5 times more often in the Finland English data.

Personal pronouns and Wh-adverbs are both used in the Finland English Corpus at a rate 1.42 times that of the Comparison English Corpus. Non-3rd-person singular present verb forms are more common in the Finland English Corpus than in the Comparison English Corpus by a factor of 1.4. The final three categories for which the Finland English Corpus has a substantially higher rate of use than does the Comparison English Corpus are URLs, superlative adjectives, and coordinating conjunctions, used in the Finland English Corpus at rates 1.25, 1.24, and 1.23 times that of the Comparison English Corpus.

As can be seen in Table 3, the particle component of phrasal verbs is the most overrepresented part-of-speech in the Comparison English, occurring at a rate 1.75 times that of the Finland English Corpus. Participles, gerunds, and punctuation are approximately 63% more common in the Comparison English data.[21] Types overrepresented by 30%–50% include past participles, the words *what* and *which*, proper nouns, and *to*. Singular or mass nouns, determiners, the punctuation types < . ? ! >, and 3rd-person singular present verb forms are overrepresented by 20%–30%. Past tense verbs, plural nouns, comparative adverbs, and prepositions are more than 10% overrepresented. Adjectives are slightly (8%) overrepresented. Superlative adjectives and numbers are also more common, although the difference is insignificant.

# 5 Analysis and discussion

The findings from the analysis of grammatical features as they are manifest in the two principal corpora help to situate English on Twitter in Finland within the communicative dimensions *Interaction* versus *Specific Reference* and *Narration* versus *Discourse Negotiation*. Specifically, they allow a preliminary assessment of the extent to which Twitter English in Finland differs from global Twitter

---

21 Punctuation marks given this tag are those in the set <: ; ... + – = < > / [ ] ~>.

English and how an emergent Finland-based Twitter English variety could be characterized.

## 5.1 Tweet length

Studies of established corpora have documented average sentence lengths of between 17 and 22 word tokens for sentences from the Brown Corpus, the British National Corpus or the London-Oslo-Bergen Corpus (Ellegård 1978: 23; Fengxiang 2007: 129). As to be expected for a medium with an upper limit on the number of characters per message, Twitter message lengths are much shorter: the mean lengths for the Finland English and Comparison English corpora are 13.27 and 15.75 tokens, respectively. If punctuation characters are not considered tokens (a common approach in corpus-based lexical studies), the mean message lengths are 9.66 and 12.59 tokens, respectively. These values correspond to mean message lengths of 11.9 tokens and 10 tokens found for other corpora compiled from Twitter or from SMS messages (Walkowska 2009: 149; Xu, Ritter and Grishman 2013). They are slightly longer than mean message lengths reported for instant messaging corpora: Baron reports an average IM message length of 5.4 words (2004: 409); Squires calculates an average IM message length from a different IM corpus of 6.18 words (2012: 299).

Finland-based messages in English on Twitter are significantly shorter than non-Finnish English Twitter messages in terms of number of characters per tweet and number of tokens per tweet, and Finland English messages utilize significantly fewer long (≥ 6 characters) words. Zipf noted the inverse relationship between word length and frequency of use, suggesting that a "principle of least effort" optimizes expression length according to communicative efficiency considerations (1949: viii).

Sigurd, Eeg-Olofsson and van Weijer (2004) confirm the inverse relationship between word length in characters or syllables and frequency for English, Swedish and German texts, and observe that sentence length exhibits a similar distributional profile, best approximated mathematically by the Gamma distribution. Agreeing with Zipf, they suggest that communicative economy concerns govern the relationship between length and informational content of words and sentences.

The tweet length findings from the Finland and Comparison English corpora can be interpreted in the context of the communicative economy observations of Zipf and others as indications of the functional–pragmatic dynamics of language use online. Shorter words and shorter tweets generally contain less information than do longer tweets and longer words. In aggregate, Twitter discourse contains less information and is more interactive than the discourse of text types such as news reports, academic writing, or fiction. The shortness of tweets corresponds to communicative functions typical of Twitter, which include self-representation, often in abbreviated form, negotiation of discourse concerns, and interactivity. In this respect, the Finland English Tweets are even less informational and more interactive than the Comparison English Corpus tweets: they are shorter and contain fewer long words. Non-Finland English tweets, although similar to Finland English tweets in many ways, reflect a slightly broader range of communicative functions pertaining to the presentation of information.

These results suggest that language use may differ systematically between Finland-based persons writing on Twitter and other users of English on the platform, and that the difference, at least in part, may reflect language interference phenomena. Shorter words contain less information (Zipf 1949), as do shorter sentences. Tweet length differs between the Finland English and the Comparison English corpora in a way that suggests English on Twitter in Finland may be less information-oriented and more interactive.

## 5.2 Emoticons

Overall, the Finland English Corpus is rich in emoticon usage, and Finland-based Twitter users writing in English are enthusiastic users of emoticons: The Finland English Corpus exhibits much higher rates of use for emoticon types per tweet and per user than does the Comparison English Corpus. For Finland, the relative proportions of all emoticon use comprised by certain specific emoticon types are similar in the Finland English and the Comparison English corpora and comparable to those reported by Schnoebelen (2012), suggesting that whatever the evolution of the communicative or discourse-organization functions of emoticons may be, their type distributions have been somewhat stable across cultural boundaries in English-language Twitter from late 2008–2013.

The interpretation of emoticons as direct reflections of the emotional state of the user or as written equivalents of prosodic features is problematic. In light of a recent study in which emoticons on Twitter are analyzed as discourse markers with various functional roles, it may be the case that emoticons in the Finland data are "interactive in nature, positioning audiences around propositions" (Schnoebelen 2012: 118). The interpretation of emoticons as a linguistic resource whose meaning is contextualized by discourse considerations is reinforced by research into non-L1 use of English on instant messaging, where emoticons may serve as contextualization cues and compensatory gestures for non-native-speaker competence (Vandergriff 2014b).

The idea that emoticons are used for multiple communicative functions is somewhat similar to pragmatic interpretations of hashtag functionality of Zappavigna (2011) or Wikström (2014). According to these analyses, the status of the hashtag, the <@> symbol, or emoticons in online discourse on platforms such as Twitter continues to evolve.

The interpretation of emoticons as symbols with discourse organization functions is strengthened by the results of the factor analysis, which shows a shared communicative space for emoticons and hashtags. Emoticon use in English-language Twitter may correspond to an evolving youth-based communicative functionality pertaining to discourse negotiation strategies which has developed on Twitter and in other social media.

## 5.3 Orthography and expressive lengthening

Widespread orthographical variation in Twitter may represent individuals and groups utilizing non-standard language variants to create social meaning. Non-standard orthography in the form of expressive lengthening is a frequent feature in both the Finland English and the Comparison English Corpus, but the feature is much more extensive in the Finland English Corpus.

Overall, vowel characters are the most likely to be lengthened, but Finland Twitter users writing in English tend to lengthen different somewhat different consonant characters than do non-Finland Twitter users writing in English. This may reflect L1 interference phenomena for the Finland English users: For example, voiced plosives are uncommon in Finnish.

Considering the distributions of lengthening sequences according to character, the phenomenon may reflect phonological and prosodic considerations as well as discourse and pragmatic factors. Phonological and phonetic experiments have shown that longer vowel duration can be perceived by listeners as marked for affect or emotional content (Klatt 1976). Vowels and other characters that correspond to segments in speech with higher sonic prominence, such as the sonorant nasals and approximant laterals, seem more likely to be lengthened than characters corresponding to obstruents such as stops. Morphological considerations such as segment- and word boundaries undoubtedly also play a role in this complex patterning. The extent to which L1 Finnish may play a role in the choice of characters to be lengthened deserves further investigation.

Expressive lengthening was not considered as a variable in the factor analysis used to identify dimensions of functional variation of Twitter language – it is not identified by the CMU Twitter Tagger and may have a status that is not equivalent to that of parts-of-speech or discourse markers (e.g., a string such as *yesss* is both an interjection and an example of expressive lengthening). Nonetheless, as expressive lengthening may mark affective orientation, its prevalence in the Finland English Corpus can be tentatively interpreted as contributing to the interactive nature of English on Twitter in Finland, a variety in which expression of affective stance plays an important role.

## 5.4 Part-of-speech frequencies

Exploratory factor analysis of aggregate part-of-speech frequencies was used to identify two dimensions of functional variation in Twitter English. The examination of feature occurrence ratios between the Finland English and Comparison English data provides further insight into the dynamics of English on Twitter in Finland. Hashtags and retweets, features associated with discourse organization and orientation, are the two most overrepresented features in the Finland English Corpus. Of the four most overrepresented features, three are unique to the Twitter language ecosystem (the hashtag, the retweet, and the username), and one feature, the interjection, is associated with emoticons, another discourse-organization type.

It should be noted that the relative lack of use of hashtags in the Comparison English Corpus may be due in part to the fact that the comparison data was collected in late 2008–2009, prior to the introduction of the "Trending Topics" feature in Twitter which highlighted the most-used hashtags on the homepages of Twitter uses. This interface change by Twitter prompted an increase in the prevalence of hashtags on the service. Still, the extent to which hashtags are overrepresented in the Finland English Corpus (29 times more common than in the Comparison English Corpus) is remarkable.[22] As Wikström (2014) notes, the changing nature of hashtag use on Twitter may represent an example of the ways in which functions originally envisaged for an innovation within the framework of a technological medium are utilized in an unexpected manner by members of a user community and evolve to become emblematic of the medium itself.

Language use online may not differ too dramatically from linguistic behavior under other circumstances, and it would be unwise to consider technological developments to be the sole force driving changes in language use online – what Squires terms "technological determinism" (2010). Nonetheless, it may be

---

[22] A preliminary analysis of smaller but similarly processed data sets collected in 2015 again find a higher rate of use of hashtags in Finland-based English tweets, albeit by a smaller factor than in the data in this study.

the case that the evolving norms of language use on Twitter, as they are manifest in frequency data for Finland, exhibit a technological moment.

# 6 Summary, outlook, and conclusion

English is increasingly used online in societies where it has not traditionally played a large role in daily communication. Factor analysis was used to identify two dimensions of variation in data consisting of a corpus of Finland-based English-language Twitter messages and English-language Twitter messages with no geographical location. The dimensions "Interaction versus Specification" and "Narration versus Discourse Negotiation" best capture the co-occurrence of grammatical and discourse features in the data and clearly distinguish English on Twitter in Finland from global Twitter English: The former is more interactive and its authors make more use of discourse-referential types, whereas the latter is more informational and narrative.

Emoticons are used far more frequently in English on Twitter in Finland compared to global Twitter English, although the proportional use of common emoticon types is comparable. Given previous findings as to the diverse functionality of emoticons in CMC and on Twitter, and in light of the association of emoticons with hashtags, usernames and retweets, according to an exploratory factor analysis, emoticons are best interpreted as types with various functions, including discourse organization, affective stance orientation, and evaluation.

The non-standard feature expressive lengthening is overrepresented in English on Twitter in Finland. Standard word forms and emoticon types are more likely to be lengthened in English from Finland, whereas pronounceable non-dictionary words are more common lengthening targets globally. There is evidence that somewhat different letters are typically lengthened in Finland-based English compared to global English. Expressive lengthening may be a means of imbuing word forms with affective content, but a closer examination of the phenomenon is needed in order to confirm this hypothesis. A consideration of expressive lengthening in different languages and its relationship to the phonological characteristics of those languages would also be informative.

Part-of-speech frequencies for individual features can be interpreted according to the findings of the factor analysis: they suggest that Finland-based users of Twitter writing in English exhibit a more interactive communicative orientation and make particular use of language features on Twitter associated with the organization and negotiation of discourse: hashtags, retweets, usernames, and interjections, many of which are emoticons.

While the present study proposes differences in group communicative behavior based on aggregate feature frequencies, further research is needed to establish the identity of Finland-based persons tweeting in English, especially in light of recent findings that young people in Finland are the most likely to report high levels of fluency in English (Leppänen et al. 2011) and that young female users are overrepresented in tweets that include latitude and longitude metadata (Pavalanathan and Eisenstein 2015). A user base for the Finland tweets skewed towards a younger and more female demographic may account for higher frequencies of some features, such as non-standard orthography and emoticons.

In an era when an increasing proportion of English-language communication is mediated by technology and internet-based services such as Twitter, a survey of the extent of use of English as it continues to evolve globally must take into account local use of English in online contexts. For Finland, English as it is used on Twitter is characterized by shorter message length, high frequencies of non-standard language features such as expressive lengthening and emoticons, as well as a specific configuration of part-of-speech and discourse item frequencies. The study suggests that English on Twitter in Finland emerges as a distinct variety on the basis of the high frequencies of features that are primarily used to interact with others; indicate evaluative, epistemic, or affective stance; and, situate these elements in discourse. In a broader sense, the analysis suggests that users of Twitter utilize non-standard and platform-specific features to construct and negotiate meanings at the interface of online interactivity and technological change.

# 7 References

Alis, Christian & May Lim. 2013. Spatio-temporal variation of conversational utterances on Twitter. *PLoS ONE* 8(10). http://journals.plos.org/plosone/article?id=10.1371/journal.pone.0077793 (accessed 20 March 2016).

Androutsopoulos, Jannis. 2006. Introduction: Sociolinguistics and computer-mediated communication. *Journal of Sociolinguistics* 10(4). 419–438.

Bamman, David, Jacob Eisenstein & Tyler Schnoebelen. 2014. Gender identity and lexical variation in social media. *Journal of Sociolinguistics* 18(2). 135–160.

Baron, Naomi. 2004. See you online: Gender issues in college student use of instant messaging. *Journal of Language and Social Psychology* 23(4). 397–423.

Biber, Douglas. 1988. *Variation across speech and writing*. Cambridge, UK: Cambridge University Press.

Biber, Douglas. 1995. *Dimensions of register variation: A cross-linguistic comparison*. Cambridge, UK: Cambridge University Press.

Biber, Douglas. 2006. *University language: A corpus-based study of spoken and written registers*. Amsterdam: John Benjamins.
Crystal, David. 2003. *English as a global language*. 2nd edn. Cambridge, UK: Cambridge University Press.
Crystal, David. 2006. *Language and the internet*. 2nd edn. Cambridge, UK: Cambridge University Press.
Dresner, Eli & Susan C. Herring. 2010. Functions of the non-verbal in CMC: Emoticons and illocutionary force. *Communication Theory* 20(3). 249–268.
Eisenstein, Jacob, Brendan O'Connor, Noah A. Smith & Eric P. Xing. 2014. Diffusion of lexical change in social media. *PLoS ONE* 9(11). http://journals.plos.org/plosone/article?id=10.1371/journal.pone.0113114 (accessed 20 March 2016).
Eleta, Irene & Jennifer Golbeck. 2014. Multilingual use of Twitter: Social networks at the language frontier. *Computers in Human Behavior* 41. 424–432.
Ellegård, Alvar. 1978. *The syntactic structure of English texts: A computer-based study of four kinds of text in the Brown University Corpus*. Göteborg: Acta Universitatis Gothoburgensis.
European Commission. 2011. *Flash Eurobarometer 313: User language preference online*. http://ec.europa.eu/public_opinion/flash/fl_313_en.pdf (accessed 20 March 2016).
Fengxiang, Fan. 2007. A corpus based quantitative study on the change of TTR, word length and sentence length of the English language. In Peter Grzybek & Reinhard Köhler (eds.), *Exact methods in the study of language and text: Dedicated to Gabriel Altmann on the occasion of his 75th birthday*, 123–130. Berlin & New York: Mouton de Gruyter.
Gimpel, Kevin., Nathan Schneider, Brendan O'Connor, Dipanjan Das, Daniel Mills, Jacob Eisenstein, Michael Heilman, Dani Yogatama, Jeffrey Flanigan & Noah A. Smith. 2011. Part-of-speech tagging for Twitter: Annotation, features, and experiments. Human Language Technologies: North American Chapter of the Association for Computational Linguistics (*NAACL-HLT 2011*) 12. 42–47. Stroudsburg, PA: Association for Computational Linguistics. www.ark.cs.cmu.edu/TweetNLP/gimpel+etal.acl11.pdf (accessed 20 March 2016).
Gimpel, Kevin, Nathan Schneider & Brendan O'Connor. 2013. Annotation guidelines for Twitter part-of-speech tagging version 0.3 (March 2013). Computational Science Department, Carnegie Mellon University, Pittsburgh, PA. http://www.ark.cs.cmu.edu/TweetNLP/annot_guidelines.pdf (accessed 20 March 2016).
Grieve, Jack, Andrea Nini, Diansheng Guo & Alice Kasakoff. 2015. Big data for the analysis of language variation and change. Paper presented at From Data to Evidence: Big Data, Rich Data, Uncharted Data, University of Helsinki, 19–22 October. https://dl.dropboxusercontent.com/u/99161057/D2E_GRIEVEETAL.pdf (accessed 20 March 2016).
Herring, Susan C. 2001. Computer-mediated discourse. In Deborah Schiffrin, Deborah Tannen & Heidi E. Hamilton (eds.), *Handbook of discourse analysis*, 613–634. Oxford: Blackwell.
Hillebrand, Friedhelm (ed.). 2010. *Short message service (SMS): The creation of personal global text messaging*. New York: Wiley.
Honeycutt, Courtenay & Susan Herring. 2009. Beyond microblogging: Conversation and collaboration via Twitter. *System Sciences (HICSS)* 42, 1–10. http://ella.slis.indiana.edu/~herring/honeycutt.herring.2009.pdf (accessed 20 March 2016).
Hutchby, Ian. 2001. *Conversation and technology: From the telephone to the internet*. Cambridge, UK: Polity.
Jones, Bernard. 1996. *What's the point? A (computational) theory of punctuation*. Edinburgh, UK: University of Edinburgh dissertation.

Kachru, Braj. 1990. *The alchemy of English: The spread, functions, and models of nonnative Englishes*. Urbana, IL: University of Illinois Press.

Klatt, Dennis H. 1976. Linguistic uses of segmental duration in English: Acoustic and perceptual evidence. *Journal of the Acoustical Society of America* 59. 1208–1221.

Kretzschmar, William A. 2009. *The linguistics of speech*. Cambridge, UK: Cambridge University Press.

Leetaru, Kalev H., Shaowen Wang, Guofeng Cao, Anand Padmanabhan & Eric Shook. 2013. Mapping the global Twitter heartbeat: The geography of Twitter. *First Monday* 18(5/6). http://firstmonday.org/ojs/index.php/fm/article/view/4366/3654 (accessed 20 March 2016).

Leppänen, Sirpa. 2007. Youth language in media contexts: Insights into the functions of English in Finland. *World Englishes* 26(2). 149–169.

Leppänen, Sirpa, Anne Pitkänen-Huhta, Tarja Nikula, Samu Kytölä, Timo Törmäkangas, Kari Nissinen, Leila Kääntä, Tiina Räisänen, Mikko Laitinen, Heidi Koskela, Salla Lähdesmäki & Henna Jousmäki. 2011. *National survey on the English Language in Finland: Uses, meanings and attitudes* (Studies in Variation, Contacts and Change in English, Volume 5). Helsinki, Finland: Varieng. http://www.helsinki.fi/varieng/series/volumes/05/evarieng-vol5.pdf (accessed 20 March 2016).

Lui, Marco & Timothy Baldwin. 2012. Langid.py: An off-the-shelf language identification tool. *Association for Computational Linguistics* 50, 25–30. http://www.aclweb.org/anthology/P12-3005 (accessed 20 March 2016).

Magdy, Amr, Thanaa M. Ghanem, Mashaal Musleh & Mohamed F. Mokbel. 2014. Exploiting geo-tagged tweets to understand localized language diversity. *Proceedings of Workshop on Managing and Mining Enriched Geo-Spatial Data (GeoRich '14)*, 7–12. New York, NY: Association for Computing Machinery. http://dl.acm.org/citation.cfm?id=2619114&CFID=772834627&CFTOKEN=94166201 (accessed 20 March 2016).

Marcus, Mitchell P., Beatrice Santorini & Mary Ann Marcinkiewicz. 1993. Building a large annotated corpus of English: the Penn treebank. *Computational Linguistics* 19(2). 313–330.

Mocanu, Delia, Andrea Baronchelli, Nicola Perra, Bruno Gonçalves, Qian Zhang & Alessandro Vespignani. 2013. The Twitter of Babel: Mapping world languages through microblogging platforms. *PLoS ONE* 8(4). http://journals.plos.org/plosone/article?id=10.1371/journal.pone.0061981 (accessed 20 March 2016).

Morstatter, Fred, Jürgen Pfeffer, Huan Liu & Kathleen M. Carley. 2013. Is the sample good enough? Comparing data from Twitter's streaming API with Twitter's firehose. *Association for the Advancement of Artificial Intelligence International Conference on Weblogs and Social Media (AAAI-ICWSM 2013)* 7. 400–408. http://www.public.asu.edu/~fmorstat/paperpdfs/icwsm2013.pdf (accessed 20 March 2016).

Nunberg, Geoffrey. 1990. *The linguistics of punctuation*. Palo Alto: CSLI.

Owoputi, Olutobi, Brendan O'Connor, Chris Dyer, Kevin Gimpel, Nathan Schneider & Noah. A. Smith. 2013. Improved part-of-speech tagging for online conversational text with word clusters. *Human Language Technologies: North American Chapter of the Association for Computational Linguistics (NAACL-HLT 2013)* 14. 380–390. http://www.ark.cs.cmu.edu/TweetNLP/owoputi+etal.naacl13.pdf (accessed 20 March 2016).

Page, Ruth. 2012. The linguistics of self-branding and micro-celebrity in Twitter: The role of hashtags. *Discourse & Communication* 6(2). 181–201.

Paakkinen, Terhi. 2008. Coolia englantia suomalaisissa mainoksissa [Cool English in Finnish advertising]. In Sirpa Leppänen, Tarja Nikula & Leila Kääntä (eds.), Kolmas kotimainen: Lähikuvia englannin käytöstä Suomessa [The third domestic language: Close-ups of the use of English in Finland], 299–331. Helsinki, Finland: Suomalaisen Kirjallisuuden Seura.

Paolillo, John. C. 2001. Language variation on Internet Relay Chat: A social network approach. *Journal of Sociolinguistics* 5(2). 180–213.

Pavalanathan, Umashanthi & Jacob Eisenstein. 2015. Confounds and consequences in geotagged Twitter data. arXiv:1506.02275v2 [cs.CL]. http://arxiv.org/pdf/1506.02275v2.pdf (accessed 20 March 2016).

Ptaszynski, Michal, Rafal Rzepka, Kenji Araki & Yoshio Momouchi. 2011. Research on emoticons: Review of the field and proposal of research framework. Association for Natural Language Processing (NLP-2011) 17, 1159–1162. http://arakilab.media.eng.hokudai.ac.jp/~ptaszynski/data/E5-6.pdf (accessed 20 March 2016).

Quirk, Randolph, Sidney Greenbaum, Geoffrey Leech & Jan Svartvik. 1985. *A Comprehensive grammar of the English language.* London: Longman.

Rao, Delip, David Yarowsky, Abhishek Shreevats & Manaswi Gupta. 2010. Classifying latent user attributes in Twitter. Proceedings of the 2nd International Workshop on Search and Mining User-Generated Contents, 37–44. New York, NY: Association for Computing Machinery. http://dl.acm.org/citation.cfm?id=1871993&CFID=772834627&CFTOKEN=94166201 (accessed 20 March 2016).

Rezabek, Landra L. & John J. Cochenour. 1998. Visual cues in computer mediated communication: Supplementing text with emoticons. *Journal of Visual Literacy* 18. 201–215.

Ritter, Alan, Colin Cherry & Bill Dolan. 2010. Unsupervised modeling of Twitter conversations. Human Language Technologies: North American Chapter of the Association for Computational Linguistics (NAACL-HLT 2010) 11. 172–180. http://www.aclweb.org/anthology/N10-1020 (accessed 20 March 2016).

Schnoebelen, Tyler. 2012. Do you smile with your nose? Stylistic variation in Twitter emoticons. University of Pennsylvania Working Papers in Linguistics 18(2). 115–125. http://repository.upenn.edu/cgi/viewcontent.cgi?article=1242&context=pwpl (accessed 20 March 2016).

Sebba, Mark. 2007. Spelling and society: The culture and politics of orthography around the world. Cambridge, UK: Cambridge University Press.

Sigurd, Bengt, Mats Eeg-Olofsson & Joost Van Weijer. 2004. Word length, sentence length and frequency – Zipf revisited. *Studia Linguistica* 58. 37–52.

Squires, Lauren. 2010. Enregistering internet language. *Language in Society* 39. 457–492.

Squires, Lauren. 2012. Whos punctuating what? Sociolinguistic variation in instant messaging. In Alexandra Jaffe, Jannis Androutsopoulos, Mark Sebba & Sally Johnson (eds.), *Orthography as social action: Scripts, spelling, identity and power,* 289–324. Berlin: De Gruyter.

Squires, Lauren. 2016. Twitter: Design, discourse, and the implications of public text. In Alexandra Georgakopoulou & Tereza Spilioti (eds.), The Routledge handbook of language and digital communication, 239–256. London and New York: Routledge.

Taavitsainen, Irma & Päivi Pahta. 2003. English in Finland: Globalisation, language awareness and questions of identity. *English Today* 19(4). 3–15.

Taavitsainen, Irma & Päivi Pahta. 2008. From global language use to local meanings: English in Finnish public discourse. *English Today,* 24(3). 25–38.

Tagliamonte, Sali & Derek Denis. 2008. Linguistic ruin? Lol! Instant messaging and teen language. *American Speech* 83(1). 3–34.

Twitter. 2015. Company facts. https://about.twitter.com/company (accessed 20 March 2016).

Vandergriff, Ilona. 2014a. Emotive communication online: A contextual analysis of computer-mediated communication (CMC) cues. *Journal of Pragmatics* 51. 1–12.

Vandergriff, Ilona. 2014b. A pragmatic investigation of emoticon use in nonnative/native speaker text chat. *Language@Internet* 11(4). http://www.languageatinternet.org/articles/2014/vandergriff (accessed 20 March 2016).

Walkowska, Justyna. 2009. Gathering and analysis of a corpus of Polish SMS dialogues. In M. Alojzy Kłopotek, Adam Przepiórkowski, Sławomir T. Wierzchoń & Krzysztof Trojanowski (eds.), *Recent advances in intelligent information systems*, 145–157. Warsaw: Exit.

Walther, Joseph B. & Kyle P. D'Addario. 2004. The impacts of emoticons on message interpretation in computer mediated communication. *Social Science Computer Review* 19. 324–347.

Wikström, Peter. 2014. #srynotfunny: Communicative functions of hashtags on Twitter. *SKY Journal of Linguistics* 27. 127–152. http://www.linguistics.fi/julkaisut/SKY2014/Wikstrom.pdf (accessed 20 March 2016).

Xu, Wei, Alan Ritter & Ralph Grishman. 2013. Gathering and generating paraphrases from Twitter with application to normalization. *Building and Using Comparable Corpora (BUCC-2013)* 6. 121–128. https://www.cs.nyu.edu/~xuwei/publications/ACL2013_BUCC.pdf (accessed 20 March 2016).

Zappavigna, Michele. 2011. Ambient affiliation: A linguistic perspective on Twitter. *New Media and Society* 13(5). 788–806.

Zappavigna, Michele. 2012. *How we use language to create affiliation on the web*. London: Bloomsbury.

Zipf, George. K. 1949. *Human behavior and the principle of least effort: An Introduction to human ecology*. New York: Hafner.

# III  Style and Identity

Lauren Squires
# Stylistic uniformity and variation online and on-screen: A case study of *The Real Housewives*

## 1 Introduction and background

This chapter presents an exploratory study of English linguistic variation in CMC, examining a group of speakers whose social identities *offline* exhibit salient dimensions of both homogeneity and heterogeneity. The speakers are reality television stars from six American casts of *The Real Housewives*, which portrays middle-aged women living affluent lifestyles in different metropolitan areas. I consider the use of several lexical and orthographic features in the women's Twitter posts as stylistic practice that can be related to their stylistic practice on television and elsewhere. These practices together contribute to the women's overall performance of a public Housewife persona, which is centered uniformly on projecting a gender- and class-based identity, yet shows variability according to region and other social attributes.

The study of linguistic variation in digital media has advanced considerably in the past decade, as evidenced by several chapters in this volume. Studies of regional variation have shown that speakers online represent their spoken dialects via dialect spellings (Androutsopoulos and Ziegler 2004) as well as regionally-specific syntactic patterns (Russ 2012) and lexical items (Eisenstein et al. 2010; O'Connor et al. 2011). Studies have also revealed variation according to gender (Bamman, Eisenstein, and Schnoebelen 2014; Herring and Paolillo 2006; Squires 2012), social networks (Paolillo 2001), age (Tagliamonte and Denis 2008), status and goals within online communities of practice (Iorio 2010), and orientation toward local versus global vernacular norms (Garley 2014; Hinrichs 2012). These studies frequently correlate one linguistic variable with group-level demographic attributes (for instance, men versus women or diasporic versus non-diasporic speakers).

The present study goes beyond the single linguistic variable, looking instead at a cluster of features whose use may be considered part of one's *style* in CMC. This approach aligns with the view of *sociolinguistic style* put forth by Eckert and others (Bucholtz 2015; Eckert 2008, 2012; Moore and Podesva 2009), which posits,

---
**Lauren Squires,** The Ohio State University

"Variables occur only as components of styles" (Eckert 2008: 456). On this view, *styles* are instantiations of practice that delineate the social landscape, constructed from available semiotic resources to express one's identity relative to others as inhabiting a *persona*. To understand the social meaning of individual linguistic features, researchers must look at their use alongside other stylistic markers in the production of *social personae* – socially recognizable types of people (Agha 2003; Eckert 2008).

An approach to linguistic variation grounded in style acknowledges that language is but one symbolic resource available for the production of style. Again quoting Eckert (2008: 456), when interpreting personae, "we connect linguistic styles with other stylistic systems such as clothing and other commoditized signs and with the kinds of ideological constructions that speakers share and interpret and that thereby populate the social imagination" (see also Mendoza-Denton 2008). Such a view is well-suited to the analysis of language in social media, wherein language is both materially rendered through written text and often complemented by a host of multimodal elements in the construction of online personae (see, for instance, the description of *Fakatsa* girls' blogs in Vaisman 2014).

The practices constituting linguistic style in online environments are importantly contextualized within speakers' totality of stylistic practice, including that which occurs offline. This is especially the case when the linguistic features used online are explicit representations of identifiable offline selves, rather than disembodied or anonymous ones (which were often the subject of earlier CMC research; see also Collister, this volume). For the speakers investigated here, material resources – clothing, jewelry, hairstyles, makeup, body adornment/augmentation, commercial tastes, and aesthetics of the home – are salient markers of a shared persona, indexing one's membership in a supposedly "elite" strata of women. The linguistic practices of *The Real Housewives* are therefore interpretable as parts of these women's larger construction of elite and hyper-feminine personae, and these speakers serve as an apt case study for better understanding linguistic style in the online realm as a component of identity work speakers are also undertaking in the offline realm.

The following section provides detailed context about the personae constructed by cast members of *The Real Housewives*. I suggest that these personae are crucially both uniform and variable: there is a certain "type of woman" these women all project, yet there are also meaningful group and individual differences within this primary identity. The central marker of group differences is region, which I discuss below and explore in the analysis that follows. As I will show, there is something of a nested structure in understanding Housewife identity: individuals vary from one another, but come together to form casts;

casts vary from one another, but come together to form *The Real Housewives*. The subsequent linguistic analysis explores the linguistic correlates in CMC of this uniformity and variation.

## 2 Uniformity and variation in the "Housewife" persona

The starting point in *The Real Housewives* phenomenon is *The Real Housewives of Orange County*, a documentary-style reality television show that has aired on the Bravo cable network since 2006, following a group of affluent (or at least aspirational) women in a region south of Los Angeles, California. Since the Orange County show's inception, casts in other American locales have been added to Bravo's programming, each with its own local inflection (international spinoffs have also appeared). *The Real Housewives* (RH) is framed as being about elite lifestyles, following privileged women who present a mainstream femininity that largely takes for granted shared ideals of behavior and beauty. Typically, each cast follows 5–7 women in their late 20s to early 50s, with most in their 40s. The women are predominantly not "housewives" in the ordinary sense: many have been divorced, many have run businesses or had other occupations, and a few have been never-married. Most have had children, however, and the theme of domesticity runs strong through the series, even if the title itself is somewhat tongue-in-cheek. Main topics of on-screen conversation include family, friendships, possessions, childrearing, beauty, and prior talk (Cox and Proffitt 2012; Squires 2014a; Wu and McKernan 2011).

Each RH iteration has portrayed women with particular regional characteristics, with, at the time this chapter was initially written, US casts based in Orange County, California; New York City, New York; Atlanta, Georgia; New Jersey; Washington, D.C.; Beverly Hills, California; and Miami, Florida (international casts have included Athens, Vancouver, Paris, Cheshire, and Melbourne; since earlier drafts of this chapter, US casts had been added in Dallas, Texas and Potomac, Maryland). Yet across all casts, the production cultivates a strong shared "Housewife" persona with both material and behavioral dimensions. Physically, the women tend toward shoulder-length or longer hair, flashy cocktail dresses and put-together casual outfits, heavy makeup, glamorous jewelry, and high-heeled shoes. Many of the women have talked openly about having cosmetic enhancement to attain certain beauty standards (breast augmentation, Botox injections, and so forth), and several Housewives have been married to plastic surgeons. The homes of the Housewives also display similarities: they are often new and custom constructions in sought-after areas, full of carefully-chosen (or professionally-designed) furniture and decorations. These homes are typically accompanied by luxury brand cars, and a good deal of airtime is spent showing such material assets.

In addition to shared material practices/preferences, the Housewife persona centers on shared dispositions that are highly gendered. A typical Housewife is heterosexual, "fun" (she likes to go to parties, go on vacations, and drink wine or cocktails), and while she values the traditional female roles of wife and mother, she also values female empowerment – she pursues her own interests, occupationally or recreationally, and sometimes stresses women's financial independence (given the common reality of divorce). In addition to these behavioral traits, I have elsewhere argued that "classiness" is at the core of shared Housewife identity (Squires 2014a; see also Dunsmore and Haspel 2014). As it manifests on the series, *classiness* can be summarized as encapsulating shared norms of behavior deemed appropriate to an elite social status, including appropriate talk – and ways of talking. On-screen, the women police themselves and each other in their endeavors to present and sustain "classy" personae, and much of the conflict on the show involves perceived violations of the norms of "classy" women. That is, much of the identity work on the show is about negotiating one's position as part of the elite class that the show claims to be representing (on eliteness, see Jaworski and Thurlow 2009).

The perception of a strong Housewife archetype is crystallized in the image in Figure 1, from the celebrity/pop culture webcomic "But You're Like Really Pretty." In this illustration, 45 Housewives are rendered virtually identical from the neck-down, with dresses color-coded according to regional cast. (The image is accompanied by a key that attributes personality characteristics to viewers depending on which Housewife they choose as "favorite.")

This shared Housewife persona draws on and distills a gender- and class-based identity that is recognizable as part of American culture, which goes some way to explain the franchise's initial success and continued popularity (Lee and Moscowitz 2013). The show purports to offer a glimpse into the lifestyles of the rich but through the frame of reality television, which often favors behavior considered "low-class" (Grindstaff 2011). As reality TV, RH offers viewers the opportunity to peek into an elite lifestyle and simultaneously critique that lifestyle and its inhabitants, including their privileged or "out-of-touch" notions of normality, a separation from the values and concerns of "everyday" Americans, money troubles, and interpersonal conflicts (Lee and Moscowitz 2013; Squires 2014a).

Despite strong uniformity among the Housewives, salient social differences are highlighted by the semiotics of the series, and the main goal of my analysis

**Figure 1:** "Who is Your Favorite Real Housewife?" Depiction of 45 Housewives from the six regional casts studied here. Image by Ryan Casey: http://www.butyourelikereallypretty.com/post/47574418840/favorite-real-housewife

here is to explore whether these differentiated identities manifest linguistically in CMC practice. Regional flavor is emphasized through intermittent camera shots displaying the relevant locale (street signs, skylines, highways) and the women's visits to local eateries, shopping locations, and recreational facilities (which often receive promotional consideration). Regional reference points are also commonly made by the women, and mark each cast as representing tokens of the elite in its particular location. One is not just saliently a Housewife, but a Housewife *of* her region. For fans, what begins as a regionally-based identity is recursively applied as a cast-based identity. That is, for example, a Housewife of New Jersey is distinctive not just because she is a *Housewife* who lives in *New Jersey*, but because she is a member of *The Real Housewives of New Jersey* cast.

Cast-based identity further emerges on the series in ways that are orthogonal to region, with varying degrees of subtlety. For instance, most Orange County women have had blond hair. The New Jersey women, by contrast, are mostly dark-haired – they also identify strongly with Italian-American culture. The Atlanta cast has been almost entirely African American, and emphasizes Atlanta's relatively unique Southern and Black elite, including musicians and athletes (see Warner, 2015 for discussion of this series in the context of other reality shows featuring Black women). The Beverly Hills cast is portrayed as the most outrageously wealthy, with ties to the Hollywood entertainment industry, as well as cosmopolitan, with members from outside North America. The Miami cast emphasizes being fashion-forward and the resident Latin culture. The women of New York are less easily grouped by social factors like these (though several of them have the stereotypical "brashness" often associated with New Yorkers). In Figures 2, 3, and 4, screenshots of the series' opening credits from three regional casts give some indication of these cast-based differences. In short, successful Housewives simultaneously construct a central shared identity and identities with greater stylistic specificity; this is what I mean by uniformity and variation in the Housewife persona.

The present study investigates the linguistic practices in CMC that contribute to this uniformity and variation. Given the elite identities enacted by the women on *The Real Housewives*, one might expect their linguistic behavior to be predominantly standard, matching the "neutral" and unmarked American practice that carries mainstream prestige. A full description of the women's televised speech is left to another study, but impressionistically, the women do speak generally in socially unmarked varieties – though with some regional marking. There are a few important exceptions to this. First, the Atlanta cast members' repertoires include features of both African American and Southern American English (see Warner 2015). Second, the Miami cast has included several

**Figure 2:** Opening credits from *The Real Housewives of Orange County* Season 6 (aired 2011). Pictured: Peggy Tanous, Gretchen Rossi, Tamra Barney, Vicki Gunvalson, Alexis Bellino

**Figure 3:** Opening credits from *The Real Housewives of Atlanta* Season 3 (aired 2010–2011). Pictured: Cynthia Bailey, Kim Zolciak, Kandi Burruss, Shereé Whitfield, Phaedra Parks, NeNe Leakes

**Figure 4:** Opening credits from *The Real Housewives of Beverly Hills* Season 1 (aired 2010–2011). Pictured: Taylor Armstrong, Kim Richards, Camille Grammer, Kyle Richards, Lisa Vanderpump, Adrienne Maloof

women who are multilingual in (at least) Spanish and English; phonological features of Latino English are prevalent in their speech, as is code-switching. Third, many women in the New York City and New Jersey casts use features that are regionally marked as part of East Coast dialects. Most notable are post-vocalic /r/-lessness (in both casts) and the second person plural pronoun *yous* (in the New Jersey cast). Finally, the Beverly Hills cast includes women who are not native North American English speakers.

Supplementing the women's on-screen performances, social media has become an increasingly integral part of the identity construction of Housewives in the age of convergent media. On the Bravo website (http://bravotv.com), Housewives maintain personal blogs, where they provide commentary about events on the episodes. The women also have public Facebook pages and Twitter accounts which are linked from Bravo's website. As do other celebrities, Housewives use Twitter to share information, self-promote, and interact with fans (Page 2012). Tweets have increasingly become topics of metadiscursive engagement on the show itself, with the women talking about tweets written by their castmates or by outside parties, and sometimes these have led to conflict. Twitter thus serves as a site of identity management that complements Housewives' televised performances. This study investigates how language online contributes to both shared and distinctive identity performances across Housewives, taking them as a case study for better understanding stylistic variation in CMC.

I am interested in which features in CMC are used by the women to project their personae as simultaneously elite and feminine, while also constructing more specified identities that are variegated across casts or other group-level social factors. Queen (2012) argues that Standard English is indexically linked to both feminine and affluent identities – both in "real life" and, to a lesser extent, in the soap opera language that she studied. That is, nonstandard variants have been found to be more frequent among men as compared to women, and (almost by definition) among lower-class speakers than upper-class speakers. While Queen explored the linguistic resources used to portray gender and class in scripted television dialogue, this study asks what linguistic resources reality television stars use to construct their own "real-life" identities as gendered and classed. Given that the different Housewives casts are represented as distinctive, they provide a useful test case for the construction of styles that are both shared and variable. In English CMC, which linguistic features contribute to representations of social difference within this field of similarity? Which features contribute to the women's portrayal of *different types of the same type of woman*? This study follows others that have investigated the significance of variation and its relation to both gender and class identity work on reality TV, namely Levon and Holmes-Elliott (2014) and Eberhardt and Downs (2013).

The shared Housewife persona, rooted as it is in femininity and elite social standing, might seem to be at odds with many of the trends described as normative in CMC environments. Twitter posts in particular have been characterized by researchers as containing largely nonstandard orthography (Eisenstein 2013; Zappavigna 2012). Institutional public discourse and metadiscourse in the US suggest that nonstandard orthography is ideologized negatively, interpreted as variously a marker of laziness, low status, illiteracy, or youth (Squires 2010; Squires and Iorio 2014; Thurlow 2006). Many CMC features – particularly ones interpreted as performing emotional work, though not only these – are also ideologized as feminine (Jones and Schieffelin 2009; Squires 2010, 2011). Inasmuch as Housewives might use these features, their stylistic practice would break the classic indexical links between *femininity, standardness,* and *affluence* (Queen 2012), instead linking at least one type of *nonstandardness* to *femininity* without (presumably) compromising a link to *affluence*.

As a precursor to my analysis, I provide a sample of tweets from Housewives – one each from each cast – in (1–6). These were chosen semi-randomly from the corpus described below in order to display the diversity of individual text styles in existence among these speakers.

(1) Let the fun begin!! Happy Memorial Day weekend to all my twitter friends!!! XOXO
 – Alexis Bellino, *The Real Housewives of Orange County*

(2) Here i'am again wit @JohnStamos who has been a pleasure 2 work wit! see u when u get 2 the ATL John [URL]
 – NeNe Leakes, *The Real Housewives of Atlanta*

(3) Oklahoma footage is devastating – my thoughts are with all those affected. Stay safe. Xo
 – Caroline Manzo, *The Real Housewives of New Jersey*

(4) Beba narrated our drive while apt hunting. Approaching a woody area she says "heads can b found 2 the right & torsos 2 the left" [emoji] #Bebaisms
 – Ana Quincoces, *The Real Housewives of Miami*

(5) It's 5 am in nyc who else is up?doing some work then back to sleep LOL
 – Ramona Singer, *The Real Housewives of New York City*

(6) This is hanging In Portia's classroom. She put that I'm 20 years old. Haha [URL]
 – Kyle Richards, *The Real Housewives of Beverly Hills*

As seen in these samples, the women's tweets range in the use of features such as spelling, punctuation, and capitalization. Some use completely standard orthography while others include nonstandard orthographic substitutions and other informal features associated with CMC. Clearly, different women have different preferences for using the linguistic resources available on Twitter; the question is which features are in use by which women, and what these correspondences can tell us about the stylistic meanings associated with the features themselves.

While much CMC research has focused on language variation between males and females, *within-gender* differences have not been a major focus. Two important exceptions are Bamman, Eisenstein, and Schnoebelen (2014) and Vaisman (2014). Bamman, Eisenstein, and Schnoebelen (2014) investigated a corpus of tweets from more than 14,000 Twitter users and showed that the gender of authors whose social networks are more strongly same-gendered (more homophilous) include more gender-marked language. Since *The Real Housewives* is mostly homosocial and designed for a female audience, I would expect Housewives' Twitter networks to show a high degree of homophily, and accordingly, their tweets may include a high use of gender-indexing features. On the other hand, if eliteness is being highlighted, we might expect all the women to be relatively conservative in their deployment of any "nonstandard" text features. In a different sort of study, Vaisman (2014) showed how young female bloggers use creative modifications to the Hebrew script to present a particular type of "girlhood" which is trendy and transnational, and which distinguishes the *Fakatsa*-type girl's blog from blogs of other girls as well as boys. Similarly, in this study, I am looking for textual features that may contribute to constructions of difference within the shared Housewife persona.

# 3 Data and method

I created a corpus of Twitter posts from the tweets of each woman who was currently a member of each cast at the time of data collection. This resulted in 40 speakers across 6 casts. Tweets were collected via Twitter's Application Programming Interface using the R package {twitteR}. Tweets were collected on roughly a weekly basis from September 2012 to July 2013.

To process the tweets for analysis, I removed duplicate tweets and tweets prefixed with "RT," which would be retweets (re-broadcasts) of others' tweets. I also removed tweets containing the user's own Twitter handle (@username), which typically indicated that the content was quoted from another user whose tweet was originally directed at the Housewife. This type of quotation was common in the raw data and points to the fact that a large-scale analysis such as this carries no guarantee that the texts I analyze are authored by the women themselves. This guarantee is furthermore elusive because many of the women likely have employees who manage their social media accounts. Though there is no certainty about who authored the tweets analyzed here, I would suggest that two factors recommend this being less of a problem than might be assumed. First, among Housewives, there is a privileging of authenticity and "realness"; Housewives have criticized castmates who they perceive as being fake (see Squires 2014a), and ghostwritten blog posts have been a topic of heated accusation. Second, regardless of original authorship, all of the collected tweets did appear on the women's Twitter accounts, and thus contribute to their overall public performance. That is, the women *animated* this content as part of their identity performance on Twitter, even if they did not themselves *author* it (Goffman 1981; Squires 2011).

The remaining tweets were transferred from .csv to .txt files then analyzed with the program AntConc. The resulting data set is structured as outlined in Table 1. I searched for and tabulated the frequency of 16 lexical/orthographic features, which are listed and exemplified in Table 2. Treating each speaker's tweets as a sub-corpus, I used the raw number of occurrences of each feature to calculate their relative frequencies per 10,000 words (to be realistic to the average number of words in each individual speaker's sub-corpus). I calculated frequencies on a per-words basis (as opposed to a per-tweet basis) in order to align with methods of corpus linguistic research. These by-speaker frequencies were used to establish a quantitative measure of the style of each individual.

**Table 1:** Structure of the corpus of Housewives' tweets

| Cast | Speakers | Approximate Words |
|---|---|---|
| Atlanta | 7 | 178,748 |
| Beverly Hills | 8 | 264,686 |
| Miami | 8 | 188,845 |
| New Jersey | 5 | 155,246 |
| New York City | 6 | 239,935 |
| Orange County | 6 | 127,063 |
| Total | 40 | 1,154,523 |

**Table 2:** The 16 linguistic features analyzed

| Feature | Example search terms |
|---|---|
| Phonetic substitutions | u, r, b, 4 |
| Initialisms | wtf, omg, lmao |
| Abbreviated forms | abt, hav, nite |
| *lol* | lol, lolol, lololol, LOL |
| *haha* | ha, haha, hahahaha, HAHA |
| *hehe* | hehe, hehehehe, HEHE |
| *xx* | x, xx, xxxxx |
| *xo* | xo, xoxoxoxo |
| ASCII emoticons | :-) :-( |
| prosodic lengthening | ooooo, ssss |
| serial punctuation | !!, ???, !? |
| ellipses | ... |
| *wanna* contraction | wanna, gonna, gotta |
| *-in* for (ING) | goin, watchin |
| positive affective words | honey, sweetie, kisses, hugs |
| profanity | shit, damn, hell |

These features were chosen based on my own prior research on English in CMC and that of others; I also chose features that I thought had potential to be used to signal class or gender. Several of the features in Table 2 have previously been shown to associate with gender or other demographic categories. Namely, Rao et al. (2010) report that emoticons, ellipses, expressive lengthening, <OMG>, and serial punctuation were more common among female Twitter users than males. Bamman, Eisenstein, and Schnoebelen (2014) likewise report that prosodic lengthening, initialisms, emoticons, ellipses, serial punctuation, and "emotion terms" were all more common among female authors than male authors. Taboo words, on the other hand, were more common among males. Overall in Bamman et al.'s corpus, men used a higher degree of standard dictionary words – suggesting an interesting inversion from typical gender patterns in traditional sociolinguistic research, and further strengthening the idea that many of these "nonstandard" written features may perform some kind of gendered work in CMC.

All of these features are associated with an informal register. While any of the features on their own might be of interest to a study of linguistic variation in social media, this analysis instead treated the features as potentially co-occurring components of Housewives' total linguistic repertoire. These features exist as resources to be drawn upon in the construction of one's style on Twitter, and I wanted to uncover which variables might be more or less meaningful as markers of identity for these speakers.

To explore this multivariate corpus, I conducted principal components analysis (PCA). PCA identifies underlying structure in a dataset by determining *components* of variance, which are new variables constituted from weighted combinations of observed variables (see Baayen 2008: 127–135). Similar to factor analysis (Coats, this volume), PCA is a data reduction technique, which reveals observed variables that behave similarly; the technique can therefore be used to simplify complex datasets, though that is not my aim here. The analysis computes components based on the correlation matrix of observed variables (or, when all variables have equivalent scale, the covariance matrix). The goal is to identify relatively few new dimensions which are as informative as the original variables together.

Here, I use PCA to explore linguistic style as composed of clusters of multiple features that may pattern according to one or more independent factors. Specifically, I use PCA to identify a) the degree of difference between individual Housewives in the use of features that meaningfully explain variance in the data, b) which clusters of features drives the dimensions of interspeaker and/or intergroup variation in CMC, and c) whether differences between individuals map onto differences between regional RH casts.

I conducted the analysis using the package {FactoMineR} in R (http://factorminer.free.fr), which provides both statistical and graphing functions specifically for PCA. In a two-level approach, the analysis explored the dimensions of similarity/difference between individual speakers, then between casts of speakers. I will first present the individual patterns in terms of degrees of stylistic variation, noting which linguistic features contribute most meaningfully to the variation; then I will discuss the notion of cast-level styles relative to these features.

## 4 Analysis and findings

### 4.1 Style across individual Housewives

The observation matrix submitted to PCA contains the relative frequencies of the linguistic features listed in Table 2, for each of the 40 speakers. That is, each speaker provides 16 observations, one for each feature. The PCA uses this matrix of observations to determine weighted combinations of features that most substantially explain variance in the data; these feature combinations are the *principal components*, visualized as *dimensions* in Figure 5. Figure 5 shows each Housewife positioned according to her component scores on the first two principal components, which together account for 36.86% of the total variance in the data. Scores represent the relation of an individual's observations to the new components: speakers positioned at more extreme distances from the plot's center are more strongly associated with the components. And, speakers positioned more closely together can be interpreted as behaving more similarly with respect to the variables making up the components.

The most striking finding in Figure 5 is that NeNe, from the Atlanta cast, is an extreme outlier as compared to every other speaker. (NeNe is shown as Housewife #34 in the image in Figure 1, and is on the right in Figure 3.) Component 2 is dominated by NeNe's divergence from all other speakers.

In fact, NeNe is an outlier primarily due to her high frequency of just three features contributing to component 2: substitutions, wanna-contractions, and g-dropping. Two of these features, g-dropping and wanna-contraction, are extremely low-frequency overall in the data, with under 1,000 total tokens each (for similar results regarding the rarity of g-dropping, see Dinkin 2014 and Squires 2014b). The only other feature with so few tokens is *hehe*, which is also used disproportionately by one speaker – HeatherT, visible as somewhat outlying in Figure 5.

To eliminate skew from these low-frequency features, I conducted a revised analysis excluding features with fewer than 1,000 tokens in the entire corpus. This left 13 features, and the results of this second PCA are shown in Figure 6. As can be seen, removing these features removes NeNe's distinctiveness, and no other extreme individual outliers remain. In general, the spread of individuals across dimensional space is more even. The variance accounted for by the first two dimensions is marginally higher than in the first analysis (37.02%).

Which linguistic features are most active in the variation underlying the individual differences seen in Figure 6? The features significantly correlated at

## Analysis 1: Individuals

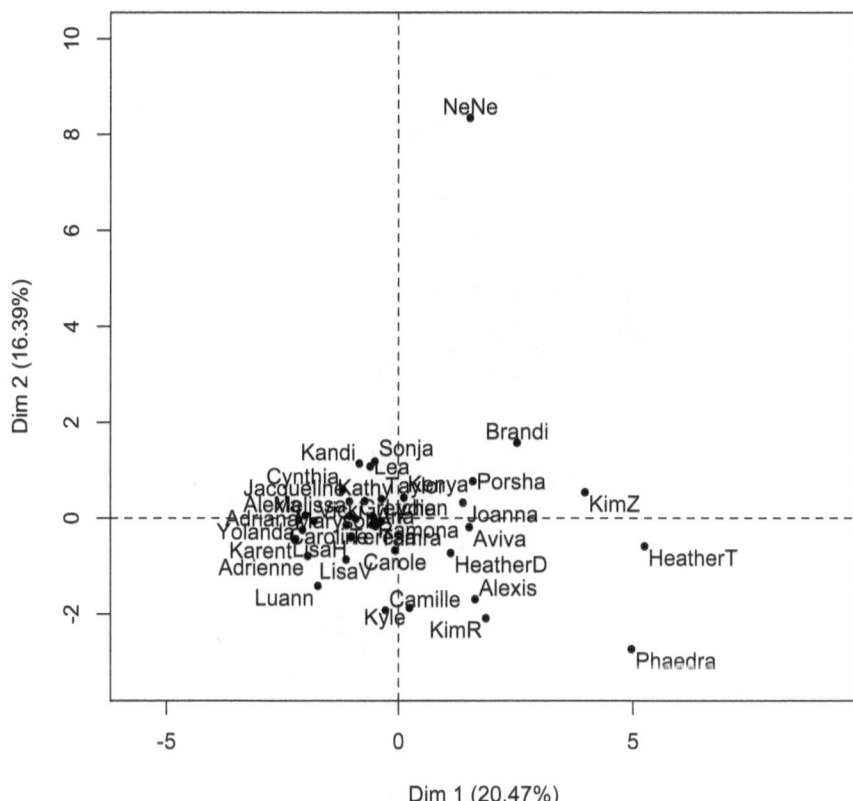

**Figure 5:** Individual Housewives' component scores on first two principal components (component 1: eigenvalue 3.28; component 2: eigenvalue 2.62). Analysis includes 40 speakers and 16 linguistic features (see Table 2)

p < .05 with the two components are listed in Table 3, which gives the correlation coefficients between each variable and component. A positive coefficient indicates that a feature is positively correlated with the component, while a negative coefficient indicates a negative correlation. Thus, in Figure 6, individuals with high scores for component 1 would tend to use more of the features listed for component 1. Individuals with high scores for component 2 would tend to use more of the positive features and fewer of the negative features.

To make this relationship between individuals, components, and features more concrete, consider examples of three different speakers: KimZ, Phaedra, and LisaV. KimZ and Phaedra, both of *The Real Housewives of Atlanta*, have

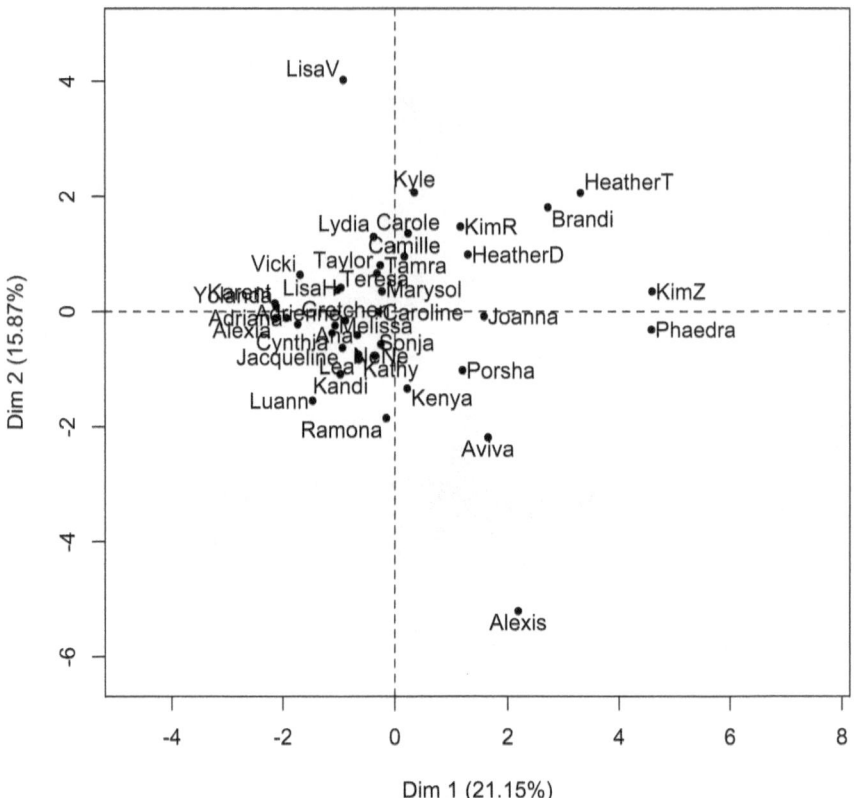

**Figure 6:** Individual Housewives' component scores on first two principal components, second analysis (component 1: eigenvalue 2.75; component 2: eigenvalue 2.06). Analysis includes 40 speakers and 13 features with more than 1,000 tokens

**Table 3:** Features associated with first two components (13 features included in analysis)

| Component 1 (21.15%) | Correlation | Component 2 (15.87%) | Correlation |
| --- | --- | --- | --- |
| +serial punctuation | .8304 | +haha | .4611 |
| +initialism | .7073 | +ellipses | .4510 |
| +lengthening | .6588 | +xx | .4162 |
| +profanity | .569 | +lengthening | .3854 |
| +emoticon | .5417 | -xo | −.4679 |
| +abbreviation | .4013 | -abbreviation | −.5666 |
| +lol | .3665 | -lol | −.7765 |

the highest positive scores for component 1 and share many stylistic attributes. Sample tweets from these two speakers are given in (7) and (8), which include at least one token of every feature in component 1. Out of all 40 speakers, KimZ has the highest frequency of both serial punctuation and lengthening, while Phaedra has the second-highest frequency for serial punctuation and the fourth-highest for lengthening. For initialisms, Phaedra has the highest frequency, while KimZ has the third-highest. And, Phaedra has the sixth-highest frequency of *lol*, while KimZ has the 12th-highest. These features play a more substantial role in these speakers' styles than they do for those speakers who do not associate strongly with component 1. Importantly, it is not the use of just *one* feature that matters, but several features together in weighted combination, which give the tweets in (7) and (8) their stylistic characters.

(7a)  I can't wait to watch @PurveyorsofPop new show "Married To Medicine" Tonight at 9pm on Bravo! It looks sooo goooood!!!

(7b)  @PurveyorsofPop lol alllll becuz of u! Xo

(7c)  This is the 3rd protein box from Starbucks that doesn't have the damn peanut butter in it!! Wtf??!!!
– Kim Zolciak Biermann, *The Real Housewives of Atlanta*

(8a)  @TraceeEvette23 ROTFL!!!!!

(8b)  @TheBillHorn OMG! She is soooo adorable with a face like that who cares if she ever sits on a potty;-) *Just pee where u pls pretty*

(8c)  Since 2008, Latino registered voters r down 5%, African- Ams r down 7% Make ur vote count register by 10/9 #Thursdaytruth
– Phaedra Parks, *The Real Housewives of Atlanta*

In contrast, LisaV of *The Real Housewives of Beverly Hills* provides an example of a different style, as the speaker with the highest positive score on component 2 (and a negative score on component 1). Her tweets, exemplified in (9), read as stylistically quite different from those in (7) and (8), though the feature of lengthening is prominent in all three sets. Among all speakers, LisaV has the highest frequency of ellipses, the second-highest frequency of lengthening, the fifth-highest frequency of *xx*, and the 16th-highest frequency of *haha*. Each of these features is shown at least once in the tweets in (9). Regarding the features with negative coefficients on component 2, LisaV's entire sub-corpus of tweets contains no use of *xo* or *lol*, and she has the fifth-*lowest* frequency of abbreviation out of all speakers.

(9a)  @MossYCFI you know it has been sooo much fun…you guys cheering… it's amazing and I thank you.

(9b) @bobbyciletti @GretchenRossi @tamrabarney...oh darlings I worked till late then I was at Sur...sorry I missed you. X x

(9c) @lttlvixon ha that is Vanderpump vodka!!!! It's mine!
–Lisa Vanderpump, *The Real Housewives of Beverly Hills*

## 4.2 Style across Housewives casts

The foregoing discussion has highlighted stylistic similarities and differences at the level of individuals. The final question examined via PCA is whether the distribution of individuals relative to components reflects cast-based stylistic differences – or other group differences – or whether it is entirely idiolectal. To investigate this, I added *cast* to the PCA as a supplemental categorical variable, allowing for the testing of differences between casts and casts' associations with the components. The first two principal components are again shown in Figure 7, but this time what is plotted is a center for each group, corresponding to where a hypothetical "average" individual for each cast would be located. Figure 3 suggests that Beverly Hills is the most stylistically unique of any cast, separating completely from the others along component 2. Also of note are that Miami and New Jersey are located in the same quadrant and so may be similar, as is the case for Orange County, New York City, and Atlanta.

To get an indication of the strength of these apparent similarities/differences between the casts, Figure 8 again shows the group centers but adds 95% confidence ellipses around them. Overlapping confidence ellipses show no true difference between groups, whereas non-overlapping ellipses represent significant differences. The spread of the confidence intervals also depicts the degree of variance across individuals within the group. Figure 8 therefore lends itself to two primary interpretations: one regarding within-group stylistic differences, and another regarding between-group differences. First, the Beverly Hills, New York City, and Orange County groups appear to have individuals with more diverse styles, indicated by the wider reach of the confidence ellipsis. In contrast, the Miami, New Jersey, and Atlanta groups are composed of individuals with more similar stylistic profiles, since the ellipsis is less dispersed across the dimensional space. Second, the Beverly Hills and Atlanta groups are significantly different from each other, and the Miami and Atlanta casts appear to be different from one another.

The supplementary variable analysis confirmed that component 1 is associated positively with the Atlanta group ($p < .05$), while component 2 is associated positively with the Beverly Hills group ($p < .01$). (Though the Miami cast

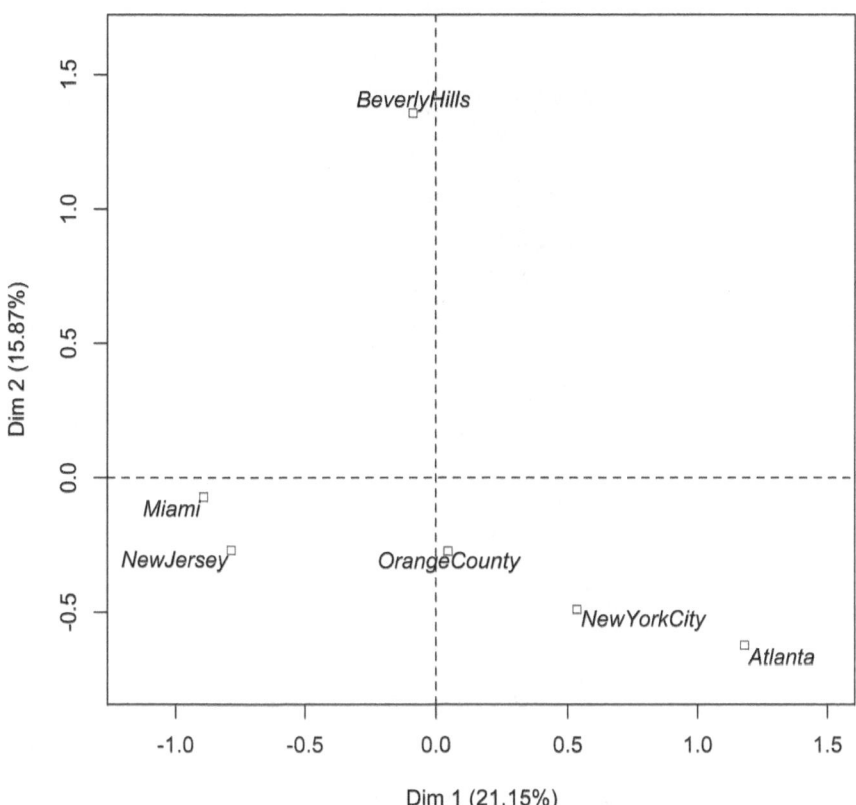

**Figure 7:** For each RH cast, the hypothetical average cast member relative to the first two principal components

also appears distinctive from Atlanta, Miami is not significantly correlated with any component, therefore I will not discuss this difference further.) In general, Atlanta Housewives will use more of the features in component 1, while Beverly Hills Housewives will use more of the positive features and fewer of the negative features in component 2, relative to those in other casts. Though these patterns are inevitably driven by individual behavior at some level, as shown in the tweets in (7–9) above, the analysis offers support for the hypothesis that these individual differences are shared across some cast members in meaningful ways, with their stylistic clusters contributing to the construction of variegated Housewife identities that center on cast as a dimension of social difference.

**Analysis 2: Casts**

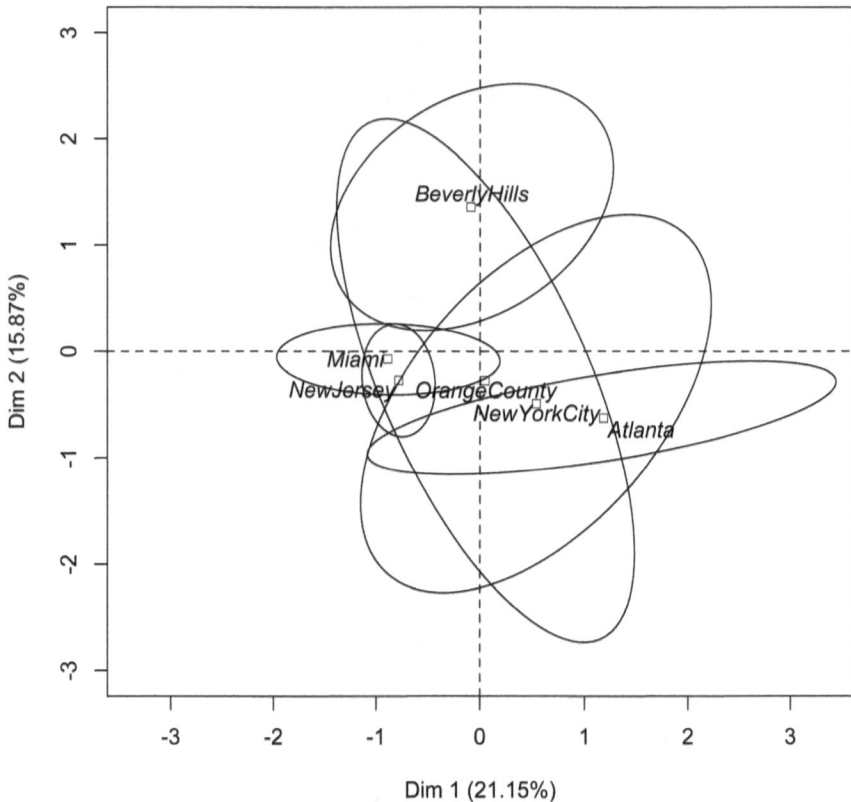

**Figure 8:** 95% confidence ellipses for group differences between individuals in RH casts

# 5 Discussion

The findings of the principal components analysis can be summarized under three topics: individual styles, the styles of individuals within casts, and cast-based styles. I will discuss each in turn, drawing from my knowledge of the women's public personae to contextualize their practices in CMC.

## 5.1 Individual styles

First, individual Housewives varied substantially in their frequency of use of features analyzed. While a few features were used very rarely and by only a few speakers, most features were used by the majority of speakers, but at variable rates: some speakers incorporated these "nonstandard" features more robustly, while others used more "standard" written styles. There were also some speakers who could be considered stylistic outliers, though only one, NeNe, had an overall stylistic profile that was drastically different from that of all other speakers.

The fact that NeNe's style in CMC is distinctive is unsurprising given the personality she has projected across various public platforms – an individualist identity which has earned her material rewards. Among Housewives, she was reportedly the highest-paid by Bravo (*Daily Mail Online* 2014; Leakes has since left the show as a headliner), and she has one of the most successful entertainment industry careers beyond Bravo, appearing on several other primetime TV shows, both scripted and reality/competition-based, and featuring in stage shows in Las Vegas and on Broadway. NeNe was the only original cast member of *The Real Housewives of Atlanta* remaining on the series at the time the data were collected, and she has always projected a strong individual flair (cf. Warner 2015). NeNe's stylistic practice in CMC therefore seems to extend from – and to extend – her broader construction of a distinctive persona.

## 5.2 Individuals within casts

Second, across the six casts, there were varying degrees of stylistic difference between cast members (depicted by the varying spread of confidence ellipses in Figure 8). That is, rather than each cast having its own clear style, casts differed from one another in their degree of internal sociolinguistic diversity. These degrees of uniformity/variation are themselves meaningful attributes of stylistic practice. The specific patterns identified are interpretable in the context of the different casts' characteristics. In particular, the New Jersey and Miami casts had relatively low dispersion amongst individuals when compared to the other groups. Just as NeNe's outlier status makes sense in the context of her stylistic presentation elsewhere, so the stylistic similarities between women in the New Jersey and Miami casts seem anchored by their on-screen performances as socially compact groupings.

Compared to the other casts, the New Jersey women have been the most tight-knit outside the context of the show. The cast members I collected data from are five women from two families of longstanding connection; both families knew each other before the show began. Beyond this familial closeness, Italian-American identity is a recurrent device of self-characterization: the women use it to describe their personalities, family relationships, and values. This gives the women a strong layer of social similarity over and above being Housewives who live in New Jersey.

Similarly, ethnic identity is salient in the Miami cast. Among the eight cast members whose tweets are included here, five identify as Latina, and the predominance of Latin culture in Miami is a common theme on the show. I did not include features specific to CMC in Spanish in my analysis, and it is possible that doing so would create a picture of greater variability among these women (on CMC in Spanish see, e.g., del-Teso-Craviotto 2006). The women's tweets do contain Spanish text, including some lexical items which likely serve as alternatives to the English-language features I tabulated – for instance, the laughter variant *jaja*, which may be equivalent to *haha*, or the affective term *besos* 'kisses,' which may be equivalent to *xx* or *xo*. It is possible that the apparently uniformity of this cast is due to the particular features I analyzed, which were not as applicable to this group of women. This is clearly a limitation of the present study – there are surely additional features that would yield even richer results in understanding CMC practice across Housewives. A challenge for analyses like this is to identify the features that are meaningfully used for a particular group of speakers.

Atlanta is the final cast that appears more uniform, at least on dimension 2, and it is also distinctive along ethnoracial lines: all but one Atlanta Housewife has been African American or multiracial. The markedness of the show's milieu relative to the other casts is revealed through both practice and metacommentary. The women use features of African American English, some with Southern American English features, and there are markers of both African American and Southern culture throughout. Atlanta Housewives also tend to be more diverse physically than the other casts – for instance, they have a broader range of hairstyles that frequently change (as opposed to the stable long-haired styles of the other casts) and they tend to have and ascribe value to fuller-figured bodies, especially butts (as opposed to the ideal of thinness in other casts). Blackness and race are metadiscursive foci within the show, as well as being topics of comment by cast members and outsiders about the show. Warner (2015) has discussed the difficult position the women in this cast are in because of the politics of "black female respectability" (147) – a burden of representation that other RH casts have not faced. (Note that since this chapter was initially drafted, *The Real Housewives of Potomac* [Maryland] had its inaugural season; all cast members were African American or multiracial, and discussions of racial identity constituted a major theme throughout the season.)

So, for these three casts, sociolinguistic similarity between individual cast members in CMC seems to reproduce their similarity on broader planes of self-presentation and social practice. The remaining three casts – New York City, Beverly Hills, and Orange County – have individuals diffused more widely across the dimensional space (Figure 8). The women in these casts are joined by the fundamental attributes of Housewife-ness and their respective regional residences, but there are no additional clear-cut layers of social similarity that run consistently through any of them (other than the fact that they are all White, with Whiteness being the unmarked Housewife ethnic identity; see Dominguez 2015). Thus, the wider stylistic spread of these groups also reproduces a wider social spread between particular types of women within the casts.

## 5.3 Cast-based styles

Two of the casts, Atlanta and Beverly Hills, do seem to represent stylistic poles, each tending toward using a different package of features (as listed in Table 3). For example, Atlanta women have higher frequency of *lol* and abbreviations (component 1), whereas Beverly Hills women have lower frequencies of those same features (component 2). As indicated above, given their general distinctiveness, it is not necessarily surprising that the Atlanta women would be using linguistic resources in CMC differently from those in other casts. Some of the features used here may be more frequent among African American or White speakers in general. For instance, Eisenstein et al. (2011) found that *haha* and its variants were positively associated with White-predominant zip codes and negatively associated with African American-predominant zip codes (using geo-coded Twitter data). My finding that the Atlanta cast scores more highly for a component with *lol* whereas the Beverly Hills cast scores more highly for a component with *haha* might echo this relationship.

Age may also be a factor: for the speakers I collected data from, the Atlanta cast is the youngest, on average, while Beverly Hills is the second-oldest. Tagliamonte and Denis (2008) found that older teens tend to use *haha* while younger teens tend to use *lol*. My finding that Beverly Hills (the older cast) uses *haha* while Atlanta (the younger cast) uses *lol* replicates this distinction. Age is a salient within-group social marker among Housewives – the younger women often make jabs at the age of the older women, and much of the discussion around physical appearance involves discussion of youth and aging. To find age as a driver of different uses of linguistic resources therefore seems reasonable for this group of speakers. I hope that further work can clarify the role of these "traditional" sociolinguistic factors, such as race and age, versus less stable factors without clear-cut categories, in variation in CMC.

Beverly Hills' distinctiveness may additionally come from specific attributes of this cast: it has been positioned by Bravo metadiscourse as the most outrageously wealthy of all of the casts, and its feel is also more "cosmopolitan," with two members from Europe. This may explain their more conservative use of several "nonstandard" features that I investigated, including *lol*, *xo*, and abbreviations. Meanwhile, they use more *haha*, ellipses, and *xx*. I would suggest that these features carry weaker associations with youth and/or stronger associations with international or global CMC (especially *xx*, which seems to be the norm in non-American English CMC, with *xo* being more of an American norm; Thurlow 2003).

In a more general sense, how do these components of style reflect constructions of class- and gender-based identity, which I (and others) have suggested is most central to a shared Housewife persona? Since both social class and gender have strong empirical and indexical links to Standard English, the use of nonstandard features is a natural starting point for understanding this stylistic variability. In that they are not features of Standard Written English, all of the features comprising component 1 could be considered "nonstandard," and the speakers with high scores on component 1 can be considered to use more nonstandard written language in their tweets. Cast-wise, the Atlanta women therefore have more nonstandard stylistic profiles than the other casts. However, if "nonstandardness" were the only indexical meaning of these features, they would not be legible as performances of upper-class identities for *any* of the women. It is certainly not the case that the Housewives' portrayals of eliteness are always successful – in fact, part of the series' appeal is its constant tension between the women's claims to a certain status and their behavior, which often contradicts those claims (see Squires 2014b). Yet the women's stylistic constructions *are* nonetheless oriented to the dimension of class, necessarily so by virtue of their positioning as Housewives.

The women's use of nonstandard written resources suggests that these resources have been (or are being) revalorized as indices of a certain type of gender, youth, and social media savvy. In component 1, many of the features can be classified as emblematic features of CMC cutting across other cultural associations: initialisms, abbreviations, emoticons, and *lol* (see Bohmann, this volume; Heyd, this volume). These may be indexing a kind of youth and social media savviness, orienting more to norms of Twitter than those of other genres/sites of written English. Higher use of these features is associated with the Atlanta cast; examples (7–8) above serve as illustration. Component 2 is a combination of positive associations with *haha*, ellipses, *xx*, and lengthening, and negative associations with *xo*, abbreviations, and *lol*. Other than ellipses and abbreviation, all of these features can be considered to have indexical associations with affect and, indirectly, femininity. In the Beverly Hills cast, *lol* and *xo* are infrequent, whereas *haha* and *xx* are frequent. It is possible that *haha* and *lol* are used as alternatives to one another, while *xx* and *xo* are likewise used mutually exclusively. Individual or group alternation between these forms would make a robust topic for future study.

In terms of the two most-distinctive casts, then, it seems that while the Atlanta women are using more CMC-marked resources to convey style (component 1), the Beverly Hills women are using more gender-marked resources (component 2). These different uses can be linked to projections of differently nuanced femininities. Further, the use or non-use of nonstandard features may index differing stances toward written language itself as a marker of class status or "classiness."

# 6 Conclusion

This chapter contributes to the study of linguistic styles in English CMC, with style conceived as a repertoire of co-occurring linguistic features used to produce a public persona with desired social attributes, achieved through the social meanings of those features. Rather than searching for variation amongst a group of Twitter users about which only rough demographic properties are known (as in most large-scale natural language processing work on social media), my starting point was a group of speakers whose embodied styles are publicly articulated. The ability to triangulate between elements of stylistic practice proved important in interpreting the social meanings of CMC variation within English, particularly as these features are used not in isolation, but as part of a total sociolinguistic package for any given individual.

I explored the idea that the apparent social uniformity and nuanced social variation found within this group of speakers would be reflected in their Twitter practice, focusing on a set of features known to be variable within CMC. I found that these social nuances were evident in some cases in the data, but not in others; I found several instances where what was found in Twitter was clearly interpretable in light of public identity elsewhere. In the process, I identified some features that participate in the construction of styles across individuals and groups of individuals (here, casts). The method I have used is suggestive for future work; it may be especially valuable in pointing out outliers among a group, and pulling out features that perform the most work in explaining variability in CMC.

# 7 References

Agha, Asif. 2003. The social life of cultural value. *Language & Communication* 23(3). 231–273.

Androutsopoulos, Jannis & Evelyn Ziegler. 2004. Exploring language variation on the Internet: Regional speech in a chat community. In Britt-Louise Gunnarsson, Lena Bergström, Gerd Eklund et al. (eds.), *Language variation in Europe* (Papers from iCLaVE 2), 99–111. Uppsala: Uppsala University Press.

Bamman, David, Jacob Eisenstein & Tyler Schnoebelen. 2014. Gender identity and lexical variation in social media. *Journal of Sociolinguistics* 18(2). 135–160.

Baayen, R. Harald. 2008. *Analyzing linguistic data: A practical introduction to statistics using R*. Cambridge: Cambridge University Press.

Bucholtz, Mary. 2015. The elements of style. In Ahmar Mahboob, Dwi Noverini Djenar & Ken Cruickshank (eds.), *Language and identity across modes of communication*, 27–60. Berlin: De Gruyter Mouton.

Cox, Nicole B. & Jennifer M. Proffitt. 2012. The Housewives' guide to better living: Promoting consumption on Bravo's *The Real Housewives*. *Communication, Culture & Critique* 5(2). 295–312.

*Daily Mail Online*. 2014. NeNe Leakes becomes highest-paid reality star with $1.5million per season of RHOA as she suits up for Extra appearance. 8 October 2014. http://www.dailymail.co.uk/tvshowbiz/article-2784186/NeNe-Leakes-highest-paid-reality-star-1-5million-season-RHOA.html. Retrieved 1 December 2014.

del-Teso-Craviotto, Marisol. Language and sexuality in Spanish and English dating chats. *Journal of Sociolinguistics* 10(4). 460–480.

Dinkin, Aaron. 2014. A phonological variable in a textual medium: (ing) in online chat. Paper presented at Change and Variation in Canada. Kingston, Ontario.

Dominguez, Pier. 2015. "I'm very rich, bitch!": The melodramatic money shot and the excess of racialized gendered affect in the *Real Housewives* docusoaps. *Camera Obscura: Feminism, Culture, and Media Studies* 30(1). 155–183.

Draucker, Fawn T. & Lauren B. 2015. Managing participation through modal affordances on Twitter. Open Library of Humanities. 1(1). e8. DOI: http://doi.org/10.16995/olh.21

Dunsmore, Kate & Karen C. Haspel. 2014. Bringing class to light and life: A case study of reality-based television discourse. *Discourse, Context & Media* 6. 45–53.

Eberhardt, Maeve and Corinne Downs. 2013. A department store study for the 21st century: /r/ vocalization on TLC's *Say Yes to the Dress*. *University of Pennsylvania Working Papers in Linguistics* 19(2). Article 7.

Eckert, Penelope. 2008. Variation and the indexical field. *Journal of Sociolinguistics* 12(4). 453–476.

Eckert, Penelope. 2012. Three waves of variation study: the emergence of meaning in the study of sociolinguistic variation. *Annual Review of Anthropology* 41. 87–100.

Eisenstein, Jacob. 2013. What to do about bad language on the internet. *Proceedings of NAACL 2013*. http://citeseerx.ist.psu.edu/viewdoc/summary?doi=10.1.1.378.1048

Eisenstein, Jacob, Brendan O'Connor, Noah A. Smith & Eric P. Xing. 2010. A latent variable model for geographic lexical variation. *Proceedings of the 2010 Conference on Empirical Methods in Natural Language Processing*, 1277–1287.

Garley, Matthew. 2014. Seen and not heard: The relationship of orthography, morphology, and phonology in loanword adaptation in the German hip hop community. *Discourse, Context & Media* 3. 27–36.

Goffman, Erving. 1981. *Forms of talk*. Philadelophia: University of Pennsylvania Press.
Grindstaff, Laura. 2011. From *Jerry Springer* to *Jersey Shore:* The cultural politics of class in/on US reality programming. In Helen Wood & Beverley Skeggs (eds.), *Reality television and class*, 197–209. London: Palgrave MacMillan.
Herring, Susan C. & John C. Paolillo. 2006. Gender and genre variation in weblogs. *Journal of Sociolinguistics* 10(4). 439–459.
Hinrichs, Lars. 2012. How to spell the vernacular: A multivariate study of Jamaican e-mails and blogs. In Alexandra Jaffe, Jannis Androutsopoulos, Mark Sebba & Sally Johnson (eds.), *Orthography as social action: Scripts, spelling, identity and power*, 325–358. Berlin: Mouton de Gruyter.
Jaworski, Adam & Crispin Thurlow. 2009. Taking an elitist stance: Ideology and the discursive production of social distinction. In Alexandra Jaffe (ed.), *Stance: Sociolinguistic perspectives*, 195–226. Oxford: Oxford University Press.
Jones, Graham M. & Bambi B. Schieffelin. 2009. Talking text and talking back: "My BFF Jill" from boob tube to YouTube. *Journal of Computer-Mediated Communication* 14(4). 1050–1079.
Lee, Michael J. & Leigh Moscowitz. 2013. The "Rich Bitch": Class and gender on *The Real Housewives of New York City*. *Feminist Media Studies* 13(1). 64–82.
Levon, Erez & Sophie Holmes-Elliott. 2013. East End Boys and West End Girls: /s/-Fronting in Southeast England. *University of Pennsylvania Working Papers in Linguistics* 19(2). Article 13.
Mendoza-Denton, Norma. 2008. *Homegirls: Language and cultural practice among Latina youth gangs*. Malden, MA: Blackwell.
Moore, Emma & Robert Podesva. 2009. Style, indexicality, and the social meaning of tag questions. *Language in Society* 38(4). 447–485.
O'Connor, Brendan, Jacob Eisenstein, Eric P. Xing & Noah A. Smith. 2011. A mixture model of demographic lexical variation. *Proceedings of NIPS Workshop on Machine Learning in Computational Social Sciences*, vol. 14. http://www.cc.gatech.edu/~jeisenst/papers/nipsws2010.pdf [accessed 12 May, 2016].
Page, Ruth. 2012. The linguistics of self-branding and micro-celebrity in Twitter: The role of hashtags. *Discourse & Communication* 6. 181–201.
Paolillo, John C. 2001. Language variation on Internet Relay Chat: A social network approach. *Journal of Sociolinguistics* 5(2). 180–213.
Queen, Robin. 2012. The days of our lives: Language, gender and affluence on a daytime television drama. *Gender and Language*. 6(1). 153–180.
Rao, Delip, David Yarowsky, Abhishek Shreevats & Manaswi Gupta. 2010. Classifying latent user attributes in Twitter. *Proceedings of the 2nd International Workshop on Search and Mining User-Generated Contents*, 37–44.
Russ, Brice. 2012. Examining large-scale regional variation through online geotagged corpora. Paper presented at the American Dialect Society Annual Meeting. Portland, OR.
Squires, Lauren. 2010. Enregistering internet language. *Language in Society* 39(4). 457–492.
Squires, Lauren. 2011. Voicing "sexy text": Heteroglossia and erasure in TV news broadcast representations of Detroit's text message scandal. In Crispin Thurlow & Kristine Mozcrek (eds.), *Digital discourse: Language in the new media* (Oxford Studies in Sociolinguistics), 3–25. Oxford: Oxford University Press.
Squires, Lauren. 2012. Whos punctuating what? Sociolinguistic variation in instant messaging. In Alexandra Jaffe, Jannis Androutsopoulos, Mark Sebba, & Sally Johnson (eds.), *Orthography as social action: Scripts, spelling, identity and power* (Language and Social Processes), 289–324. Berlin: Walter de Gruyter.

Squires, Lauren. 2014a. Class and productive avoidance in *The Real Housewives* reunions. *Discourse, Context, & Media* 6. 33–44.

Squires, Lauren. 2014b. From TV personality to fans and beyond: Indexical bleaching and the diffusion of a media innovation. *Journal of Linguistic Anthropology* 24(1). 144–172.

Squires, Lauren and Josh Iorio. 2014. Tweets in the news: Legitimizing medium, standardizing form. In Jannis Androutsopoulos (ed.), *Mediatization and sociolinguistic change* (linguae & litterae), 331–360. Berlin: Mouton de Gruyter.

Tagliamonte, Sali A. & Derek Denis. 2008. Linguistic ruin? LOL! Instant messaging and teen language. *American Speech* 83(1). 3–34.

Thurlow, Crispin. 2003. Generation Txt? The sociolinguistics of young people's text-messaging. *Discourse Analysis Online* 1(1). Article 3.

Thurlow, Crispin. 2006. From statistical panic to moral panic: The metadiscursive construction and popular exaggeration of new media language in the print media. *Journal of Computer-Mediated Communication* 11(3). 667–701.

Vaisman, Carmel L. 2014. Beautiful script, cute spelling and glamorous words: Doing girlhood through language playfulness on Israeli blogs. *Language & Communication* 34. 69–80.

Warner, Kristen J. 2015. They gon' think you loud regardless: Ratchetness, reality television, and Black womanhood. *Camera Obscura: Feminism, Culture, and Media Studies* 30(1). 129–153.

Wu, Jingsi C. & Brian McKernan. 2013. Reality check: Real Housewives and fan discourses on parenting and family. In Kathleen M. Ryan & Deborah A. Macey (eds.), *Television and the self: Knowledge, identity, and media representation*, 119–133. Lanham: Lexington Books.

Zappavigna, Michele. 2012. *Discourse of Twitter and social media*. London: Continuum.

Patrick Callier
# Exploring stylistic co-variation on Twitter: The case of DH[1]

## 1 Introduction

This chapter uses Twitter as a resource for answering questions about the composition of style and the structure of stylistic covariation: how do resources widely understood as belonging to particular repertoires – *enregistered*, in Agha's (2007) terminology – covary with other stylistic resources? I use data from Twitter to examine orthographic variability in cases where changes in written form mirror variants from spoken English (cf. Eisenstein 2015). Examining this covariability will shed some light on the potential social meanings of such orthographic variables and possibly their spoken counterparts as well.

The study of linguistic variation has always been concerned with the social functions and indexical meanings of different ways of speaking (Labov 1972a), but the so-called "third wave" of variation studies (Eckert 2012) has placed processes of meaning construction at the forefront. This turn has also forefronted *style*, which has been described (using "styling," a verbal form) as the subjection of socially meaningful linguistic "resources" to active "contextualization" and recontextualization by language users (Coupland 2007a: 105; see also Bauman and Briggs 1990). This work emphasizes how language users cobble together stylistic resources, and how they achieve social effects in doing so. This emphasis acts as a counterbalance to the temptation found in some variationist work to merely catalogue the formal features of speech appearing across certain settings, and helps us ask the question: what are these features doing *here*, together?

Stylistic variation wears many faces, but the approach advocated by the Half Moon Bay Style Collective (2006) looks at style as socially meaningful aggregates of individual features. This view of style bears a resemblance to Agha's conception of register as a set of indexical forms that has been socially accepted

---

[1] Thanks so much to Lauren Squires for inviting me to participate in this volume and offering such insightful feedback on earlier drafts of this chapter. Taylor Jones has been an excellent conversation partner re: style, Twitter and other CMC miscellany. Robert Podesva and Natalie Schilling were a great support over the long arc of the work that went into this project. In this chapter appears the work of many hands, but all faults and errors are of course mine alone.

**Patrick Callier**, Lab41

as belonging to a particular meaningful set – for example, Received Prounciation (RP), Pittsburghese (Johnstone 2009), or "coarse" Javanese (Agha 2007). Recurrent, socially circulating aggregates of covarying forms can be called enregistered styles inasmuch as they have been widely understood by some set of evaluators to make up such meaningful sets of indexical forms. These circulating styles are relatively abstract cultural objects. They have been described as "repertoires" (Coupland 1980) from which language users may select ways of producing or interpreting concrete language in their everyday lives. Varieties of language found on the internet have often been described as repertoires or registers (Squires 2010) and the stylistic distinctiveness of language in computer-mediated communication has remained a salient topic of public discourse since the earliest days of the internet. Some primarily computer-mediated stylistic repertoires even acquire the status of named registers like "LOLSpeak" or "internet language." Of course the internet is also home to stylistic variation that draws on resources available outside computer-mediated contexts. This chapter examines Twitter-mediated uses of forms that can be associated with African American Vernacular English (AAVE), casual and nonstandard registers of spoken English across many dialects, and other spoken and written varieties of English.

But the linguistic performances I report on below are not primarily interesting for the fact of their association with these stylistic repertoires. Besides the idea of repertoire, there is another sense of "style" in the study of linguistic variation. Every concrete linguistic performance offers up a certain stylistic texture depending on which forms of which variables surface together, a combination that Agha calls the "co-occurrence style" (Agha 2007: 186). When a particular co-occurrence style successfully brings together elements from disparate enregistered styles, the result is an act of "bricolage" (Eckert 2012; Hebdige 1984) which Eckert and others have described as central to the process of change in social meaning. Bricolage operates via "text-level indexicality" (Agha 2007): it achieves a creative performative effect via the combination of the individually meaningful features that make it up. For example, Coupland's (2007b) analysis of the dialogic tension between "Valleys" Welsh features and aspects of Received Pronunciation in the speech of Welsh Labor politician Aneurin "Nye" Bevan highlights how Nye's speech animates and enacts social and ideological struggle through the juxtaposition of variants from differently valued registers.

Despite the third-wave variationist focus on meaning construction and its axiomatic position that indexical meanings are mobilized in aggregates of stylistic features, quantitative study of the meaningful covariation of stylistic forms is relatively young. Biber's (1988; Biber and Finegan 1994) quantitative approach to the discovery of registers through factor analysis is an early antecedent to such study.

Biber's approach was innovative in that factor analysis allows stylistic clusters to emerge based on the co-occurrence patterns of formal features themselves. His work is couched, however, in a theoretical approach that sees registers merely as language use appropriate to particular situational contexts. This provides little room to explain how features of registers are mobilized to create context rather than just to conform to it (Silverstein 1976; Hanks 1992). Implicational scaling (Rickford 2002) is another family of techniques examining the interrelationships between different variable features. It establishes whether the presence of one feature in a certain domain unidirectionally implicates the presence of another feature, allowing the reduction of multidimensionality in variation. Similar critiques to those levied against "static" views of register have also been leveled at the ways implicational scaling obscures linguistic creativity. Scales are always violable (Benor 2010), and the creative semiotic consequences of such violation, if there are any, are worthy of investigation.

Recent work in language and sexual identity has been the site of some of the most empirically detailed work on how variable features of language combine for creative stylistic consequences. Podesva, Roberts, and Campbell-Kibler (2001) document how multiple resources combine to create a gay style, and Podesva's subsequent work (2006, 2007, 2011) has paid keen attention to the semiotic contributions of individual variables to the creation of diverse personae, some of which are legible as gay. In experimental work on how the acoustics of /s/ in English interacts with pitch and alveolar (ING), it has been shown that some variables (such as high center of gravity of /s/, also known as "fronted" /s/) have more reliable, context-insensitive impacts on whether male speakers are read as gay or not masculine, compared to others (pitch and (ING) variability), whose semiotic effects have interactions with the presence of other stylistic features (Campbell-Kibler 2011). These interactive relations are culturally and socially specific, as work on Danish (Pharao et al. 2014) shows that /s/ also has ties to masculinity and perceived gayness in male speech in that language, but this relationship is contingent on other factors of the linguistic performance. In a register they caption as "modern Copenhagen speech," fronted /s/ makes male speakers more likely to be rated as homosexual. In "street Danish," a register associated with the nonwhite descendants of immigrants, fronted /s/ makes speakers more likely to be rated as "foreign" or "immigrants."[2]

---

[2] There are likely parallels to this situation in English; Geoff Lindsey (2012) has a fascinating blog post on /s/ fronting in Eminem's songs and American hip-hop more generally, where it does not generally give a gay percept.

Thus, attention must be paid to how semiotic resources interact with one another in production and perception. It cannot be assumed that a particular form stands to offer the same range of possible interpretations in all performances, regardless of co-occurring stylistic elements. This chapter is an initial exploration of one sociolinguistic variant in data from computer-mediated interaction: stopped DH (described below). It pays particular attention to how stopped DH covaries with other meaningful linguistic resources on Twitter. DH-stopping shows two discrete co-occurrence patterns – one with other phonological features of African American Vernacular English, and the other with the use of internet acronyms. This dual patterning provides evidence about the social meaning potentials of DH-stopping in particular, and also shows how it can be drawn into different stylistic contexts with divergent performative effects.

## 2 DH-stopping

DH-stopping is a well-studied variable process whereby voiced interdental fricatives (/ð/) are realized as voiced alveolar stops ([d]) or dental stops ([d̪]) (Labov 2006). It is a feature of multiple varieties of English, including various African American and "white" ethnic varieties of American English (Rose 2006; Dubois and Horvath 1998) and certain nonstandard varieties of British English, as well as some Englishes from other parts of the world, including Yoruba- and Igbo-associated forms of Nigerian English (Olajide and Olaniyi 2014; Gut 2008). It has been called "a fortition [and] ... a hypoarticulation" (Eckert 2008: 471), in reference to its auditory prominence relative to [ð] and its ideologization as a less effortful form.

The use of <d> for the <th> of standard orthography has a history of negative evaluation on the internet. Squires (2010) cites the following stylized example from 2006:

(1)  omfg wtf du care bout dis nubs usin aimspek.. they int gonna be getin da jobs
     i wnt if they continue to speak like this so stfu
     (Squires 2010: 475)

Squires' investigation of evaluations of internet language in general encountered many evaluators who linked the use of internet-specific language forms to young people, women, "idiots," people "from the ghetto," or people who have a "job at McDonald's" (2010: 480). Given enregistered associations between DH-stopping and African American Vernacular English, questions of race are clearly at issue in debates over the form and function of internet language. DH-stopping is also an enregistered feature of the highly restricted online register "LOLspeak" (Gawne and Vaughan 2011), which most often appeared in photos of cats with text in the cat's voice digitally superimposed. LOLspeak often used <da> in the place of <the>. Though Gawne and Vaughan analyze LOLspeak as language play, language play is often inflected by racist language ideologies (Hill 1995), and arguably this is the case in stylized uses of DH-stopping online such as example above, and its use in LOLspeak.

In contrast to work on language ideologies and metapragmatics relative to online discourse, work on black Americans' actual linguistic practices in online venues is somewhat limited (though see Jones, this volume; Childs, this volume). Hobbs (2004) finds that stylistic variation in the online version of an African American women's magazine is testament to the relative "orality" of online contexts compared to traditional print venues. In another study, Twitter is taken as the locus of a number of different African American communicative practices, such as call-and-response and signifying (Long 2012). Speakers of other non-white, non-American varieties of English get even less attention in the formal analysis of online language, though Chiluwa (2008) documents several features of Nigerian English that appear in SMS messaging, including <d> for <th> replacement. More research is needed on the online stylistic and discursive practices of African Americans and speakers of global varieties of English (cf. Heyd, this volume).

I explore the orthographic representation of DH-stopping on Twitter in relation to two other potential co-variables: orthographic representations of /r/-lessness and the use of initialisms or acronyms associated with "internet language." I selected these co-variables to assess two dimensions of DH-stopping's potential stylistic profile. /r/-lessness is a widely reported and highly enregistered feature of African American Vernacular English (Thomas 2001; Labov, Ash, and Boberg 2006), as well as other varieties, and is also relatively easy to represent orthographically (see Childs, this volume). Meanwhile, initialisms capture some of the distinctive affordances available in online venues for doing stylistic work, in particular work related to the construction of affective stance. I find that DH-stopping co-occurs with both of these co-variables at higher-than-expected rates compared to their marginal probabilities of occurrence. In the discussion I offer some suggestions as to what this tells us about the social meanings of DH-stopping in online venues.

## 3 Data and methods

I used a program called "The Archivist" (*The Archivist* [version unknown] 2014[3]) to retrieve publicly available Tweets by keyword search. I searched for tweets containing the keywords <they>, <that> and <this> as well as <dey>, <dat> and <dis>. The nonstandard spellings reflect a stopped realization of an onset which is a fricative in the standard form. I selected these words to be as semantically and pragmatically neutral as possible, so that their contribution to the corpus would be in the realization of <th>~<d> alone.

A certain number of tweets were returned in Dutch, where *dat* is a determiner, and French, where *dis* is the first- and second-person singular indicative present of *dire* 'to say.' I trained letter trigram language models for Dutch, French, and English (Cavar 2004a), with source data from books available on Project Gutenberg. The language models scored each trigram present in the tweet with its frequency in the three candidate languages and classified it as belonging to the highest-scoring candidate language (Cavar 2004b). This was a relatively simple means of weeding out the large number of false positives returned in other languages by the keywords I selected.

I hand-coded the tweets this method identified as being in English. Tweets in foreign languages were excluded, as were tweets whose contents appeared to be English but which I could not understand at a linguistic level. Retweets were not excluded, as (modified) retweeting is a common means of conversing on Twitter, and a very few tweets appeared in the corpus multiple times as a result. The corpus eventually used for analysis contained 1081 tweets, distributed as shown in Table 1.

**Table 1:** Distribution of tweets by search keyword

| Class | Keyword | | | Totals | |
|---|---|---|---|---|---|
| <th> | this | that | they | 433 | 1,081 |
| | 65 | 108 | 260 | | |
| <d> | dis | dat | dey | 648 | |
| | 239 | 292 | 117 | | |

This corpus represents variation in English associated with many varieties. Besides standard English, AAVE has a large presence in this data, as attested

---

[3] Now available in a commercial service, though see Eisenstein (2016) for an example of how to obtain similar data using the Twitter API directly.

by the use of grammatical variants associated with AAVE, such as habitual *be* and copula absence in (2), below.

(2)  @**** lol wats ur name on facebook? I be liking everybody status on fb when I'm BORED . dat ish wack now

Besides tweets written in AAVE or varieties approximating standard English, there are also tweets in vernacular or dialectal varieties that are either clearly not AAVE or whose dialectal provenance is less determinate. Looking at evidence from geographical or cultural references, a number of tweets in the corpus appear to originate in Nigeria (see Heyd, this volume). Especially in the <dey> keyword, references to placenames in Nigeria are common, such as Bowen University in (3), below, or Las Gidi (Lagos).

(3)  Whre gals wud carry foodcooler 2 cafe cz dey wnt 2 save 20box money on pack..smh #bowenuniversity

Since the tweets in this corpus were collected without location information, and most cannot be clearly labeled as belonging to one discrete English variety or another, I did not attempt to exclude tweets based on what variety of English they appeared to belong to. Although the social meanings of DH-stopping likely diverge across such far-flung cultural and linguistic situations, its distribution with regard to other potential co-variables is still an interesting empirical question.

Each tweet was given a binary (yes/no) code for the presence or absence of each of three co-variants:

1. "Other" DH-stopping, that is, DH-stopping not accounted for by the search keyword used to retrieve the tweet. This included further instances of <dis>[4], <dat>, and <dey> above and beyond the first instance of the applicable search keyword, the definite article spelled as <da> or <d>, in addition to <dem>, <dese> and other rarer examples.

   Because the minimum rates at which <dat>, <dey>, <dis>, <that>, <they>, and <this> occurred in the corpus were determined by my search parameters and not their distributions in a larger population of texts, I use "other" DH

---

4 Examples of DH-stopped forms below, as other forms cited from text sources, will be enclosed in angle brackets < > to indicate their status as orthographic forms. I will give a word-form in standard orthography after some such citations as an aid to the understanding of the reader, e.g., <2ma> (*tomorrow*). Such aids are not meant to imply that the orthographic variants in this data, or any phonological variation they may represent, are in any way substandard or incorrect.

below as a proxy for DH-stopping "in the wild." Although the conditional probability of an instance of (DH) given the value of another instance of (DH) is probably affected by constraints different than those affecting the conditional probabilities of the other variables below, the rates of occurrence of "other" DH are much more comparable to those of the other variables in the corpus than the (fixed) frequencies of the search keywords that constituted the corpus.

2. R-lessness. Forms were considered R-less if I recognized their standard orthographic form, the word denoted by the standard orthographic form has a coda /r/, and the form present in the tweet lacked indication of that coda /r/. I will use the terms R-less and R-lessness to refer to the phenomenon of orthographically mediated representations of coda /r/ absence (above and beyond the mere absence of the graph <r>), which I will refer to as /r/-lessness to distinguish it as a phonological phenomenon.

3. Internet initialisms ("OMG"). This feature refers to a set of acronyms commonly associated with internet and SMS communication. After initial exploration of the data, this factor was coded automatically by a regular expression search:
'l[uo]+lz?', 'af', 'tf', 'idk', 'tbh', 'afaik', 'z?omg', 'smh+', 'smdh', 'ham', 'ctfup?', 'stfu', 'lmao+', 'lls', 'wtf', 'atm', 'lmbo+'

Below, I refer occasionally to this feature as "OMG." Though the pragmatic and discourse functions of these forms vary quite widely, I am interested in their capacity to serve as indexes of an "internet language" register (Squires 2010) at a relatively more abstract level (see also Bohmann, this volume).

As an illustration, (4) is one of a few tweets that boasted all three of these features:

(4)  *is there anybdy dat DONT knw wea I wrk at ??? lmao*

Here, <dat> represents a stopped realization of the relative pronoun *that*. In this example, it does not count as "other" DH-stopping, since <dat> is the keyword that brought the tweet into the corpus. <wea> (*where*) appears with a representation of coda /r/ absence, and <lmao> is an initialism widely enregistered as internet language. As a point of contrast, in (5) I reproduce a tweet, collected with the search keyword <that>, that exhibits none of the co-variant features I coded for. As can be seen, it boasts fewer features identifying it as belonging to a particular dialect, but it is hardly formal and its orthography is also not entirely standard. Clearly there are a number of potential covarying features one could extract from Twitter discourse; this study has chosen a few as an exploratory measure.

(5) *That awkward moment when u click the tweet box but you forget what the hell u wanted to tweet..*

The distribution of all the tweets in the corpus is displayed in Table 2.

**Table 2:** Distribution of tweets according to search keyword, "other" DH-presence, R-lessness, and use of internet initialisms (represented by the label OMG in the table, but not limited to <OMG>)

|   |   | Other DH | | | | No other DH | | | |
|---|---|---|---|---|---|---|---|---|---|
|   |   | R-less | | Not R-less | | R-less | | Not R-less | |
|   |   | OMG | no OMG | OMG | no OMG | OMG | no OMG | OMG | no OMG |
| <dh> | dat | 4 | 17 | 17 | 38 | 7 | 20 | 53 | 136 |
|   | dey | 5 | 14 | 7 | 28 | 1 | 12 | 11 | 39 |
|   | dis | 3 | 6 | 5 | 31 | 13 | 26 | 32 | 123 |
| <th> | that |   |   |   |   | 2 | 2 | 13 | 91 |
|   | they |   |   |   | 1 | 3 | 12 | 23 | 221 |
|   | this |   |   |   |   |   | 1 | 10 | 54 |

Orthographic R-lessness was employed by 147 tweets in the entire corpus. Of these, 44 (29.9%) contain R-less forms of "the n-word," which is historically related to the /r/-ful form but may be lexicalized in its /r/-less realization, despite intense ideological struggle over its relationship to the /r/-ful form and its appropriateness in general (Rahman 2012; see also Childs, this volume).

(6) *Dis nigga wear a 17 haha no skates yo size buddy lol*

The particular form of the n-word given in (6) was the most common R-less word-form in the corpus, with 28 instances, followed by a plural form of the same word spelled with <s>, with 15 instances. The next most common R-less forms are <ya> (*your*) with 10 instances and <otha> (*other*), with 5 instances, followed by a long tail of creative R-less spellings such as <wowtta> (*water*) or <2gethaa> (*together*) which occur only once in the corpus.

The relative pervasiveness of forms related to a possibly fossilized /r/-less word raises the question of whether the R-lessness being evaluated in this study is really variable /r/-lessness per se, or rather variable /r/-lessness mixed in with "lexical" /r/-lessness. For the purposes of this study, I count all the tweets with such forms together with other cases of R-lessness, leaving it to future work to determine whether and how the social evaluation of /r/-lessness in that form is related to the evaluation of /r/-lessness in other words.

Below, I use a number of quantitative methods to address the research questions. A common first approximation of covariation has been to produce a correlation matrix of variable rates of occurrence. Choosing the domain such correlations are calculated over has important consequences. Guy (2009) and Squires (this volume) use by-speaker correlations. This means each speaker is represented by a point estimate on each variable of interest – e.g., "speaker A uses stopped DH at 10.3% and R-lessness at 45%." In order to investigate the "co-occurrence style" that surfaces in individual text artifacts, however, it is more appropriate for this study to calculate correlations using the tweet as the domain of possible occurrence (i.e., calculating which realizations go together in a tweet, rather than across all of a person's tweets). I dummy-coded each variable 1 for all "application values" (R-lessness, DH-stopping in both keyword and "other" cases, and OMG), and 0 for the other realizations.

I also employ multiple correspondence analysis (MCA; Venables and Ripley 2002) to give another look at the patterns of co-occurrence in the data. MCA is a method for isolating the dimensions of greatest variability in categorical data, somewhat analogous to Principal Components Analysis in the case of continuous data. The output of MCA is a set of vectors with a score for every possible variant in the data. These vectors are guaranteed to be orthogonal to one another, and the scores therefore allow us to map out variants in a multidimensional space where their proximity to one another is a rough approximation of how likely they are to appear together. I used the {ca} package (Greenacre and Nenadic 2010) in R (R Development Core Team 2015) to perform and plot MCA for this study.

# 4 Analysis

The correlations of all three variables (dummy-coded as 0 or 1 per tweet, as described above) with the independent variable of "keyword" DH are given in Table 3 below.

**Table 3:** Within-tweet correlations of keyword DH-stopping with "other" DH-stopping, use of internet initialisms, and R-lessness. Significance determined by two-way chi-squared tests, performed at a 0.05 alpha level adjusted for 6 multiple comparisons ($\alpha = 0.0167$)

|  | DH (keyword) |
| --- | --- |
| **Other DH** | 0.355* (p < 0.001) |
| **Internet initialisms (OMG)** | 0.156* (p < 0.001) |
| **R-lessness** | 0.216* (p < 0.001) |

Given that the correlations are quantified over Tweets of 140 characters or less, giving a small overall chance for collocates of any sort to surface, the correlations in Table 3 are actually rather high. Two-way chi-squared tests were performed on the categorical data to obtain significance statistics.[5] All correlations are significant at an adjusted $\alpha = 0.05$ level. Numerically, the highest correlation is between keyword DH-stopping – the independent variable – and "other" DH-stopping. Keyword DH-stopping also correlates with OMG and R-lessness.

The multiple correspondence analysis of covariability among stopped DH tweets (described in the methods section above) is represented by the biplot in Figure 1, which shows a summary of the first two dimensions of variability identified by this analysis. Each realization of the covariates is assigned a score along both dimensions that reflects that variant's contribution to the overall variability in the data. The words *dis*, *dat*, and *dey* represent the search keywords, which are by design unable to vary with each other, while descriptive labels are given to the levels of the other included variables.

Dimension 1 distinguishes the difference between the two phonological co-variables: "other" DH-stopping and R-lessness. R-lessness and other DH-stopping pattern especially strongly with <dey>, which is also distinguished from <dat> and <dis> on this axis. Lack of R-lessness, lack of other R-stopping, and lack of initialisms all pattern close to each other.

The second dimension in Figure 1, plotted on the y-axis, mostly captures variability in internet initialisms. The presence of internet initialisms leads to strong loadings on this dimension, with weak loadings in the opposite direction for their absence. Interestingly, this dimension also appears to capture the distinction between tweets retrieved with <dat> and tweets retrieved with <dis>. <dat>-keyed tweets pattern closely with the presence of initialisms.

---

[5] It should be noted that "other" DH-stopping is not strictly independent from keyword DH, so the requirements for chi-squared tests of independence are not satisfied.

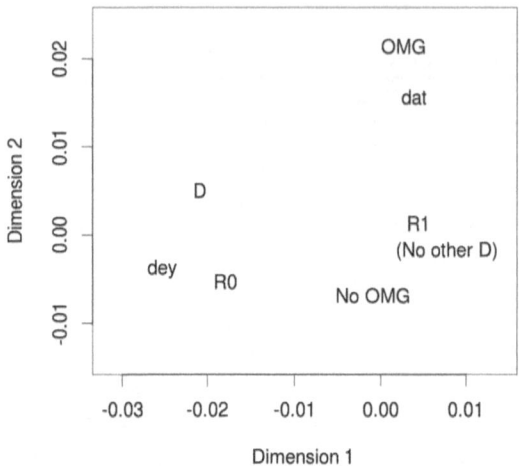

**Figure 1:** Multiple correspondence analysis. R0 = R-lessness, R1 = No R-lessness, D = "other" DH-stopping, No other D = No "other" DH-stopping

## 5 Discussion

While "keyword" DH-stopping is correlated with "other" DH-stopping, R-lessness, and internet initialisms, the correspondence analysis presented above suggests that the probability of initialisms like <lol> and <smh> is independent of the probability of orthographic R-lessness and "other" DH-stopping. This suggests that initialisms are packaged together with DH-stopping via a different process from the one by which R-lessness is associated with DH-stopping.

In mediating phonological processes associated with particular English varieties, orthographic DH-stopping and R-lessness afford the opportunity for a tweet to be legible as being "in" a variety. In addition to the capacity of DH-stopping to cue the use of a particular ethnolinguistic repertoire (Benor 2010) or nationally associated language register (e.g., Nigerian English), this investigation provides evidence that DH-stopping is associated with the use of "internet language" initialisms. There are two aspects of this finding to note. The first of these is that "internet language," as a variety itself undergoing various processes of enregisterment (at multiple sites, with various consequences) is a fairly abstract target. Analogously to the case of ethnic varieties, it is not fruitful to presume that Twitter users have the strategic intention to signal "I'm on the internet." The actual communicative functions of the various initialisms included in this study vary widely (cf. Bohmann, this volume; Squires, this volume).

This caveat, however, leads into the second aspect of note about the association between DH-stopping and initialisms, which is that it indicates a general association between DH-stopping and affective display. Though the initialisms all serve a variety of functions, intensified affective commitment is common to most instances of their use. In the following example, <lol> is used in a position that makes it hard to read it as denoting laughter. Instead it may index a semantically bleached affective emphasis in the question at the end of which it appears:

(7) @betMALCmakeit did u say hoddy was d driver lol? Can't hear dat 1 part

DH-stopping and OMG-style initialisms are not, by this evidence, appearing as components of a single widely-enregistered style. There is no apparently enregistered trope as in the case of LOLspeak's *Lyk dis ok?*, which combines specific orthographic conventions with DH-stopping and certain grammatical features for a recognizable, nameable effect ("LOLCat"; Gawne and Vaughan 2011). Rather, the co-occurrence of DH-stopping and initialisms lends a tweet the productive compositional effect of DH-stopping as an enregistered component of a particular English variety, especially AAVE, and initialisms' heightened affect – again, allowing for the breadth of functionality initialisms may serve.

With regard to the meanings of DH-stopping in general, Eckert (2008) has directly speculated that DH-stopping, in certain communities at least, has indexicalities of emphasis or heightened intensity generated by its status as a strengthened form, intersecting with more complex indexicalities stemming from its being iconized as an imprecise articulation. This latter quality ostensibly goes to DH-stopping's utility for conveying toughness, pragmatism, or uninvolvement in cerebral matters.

An interesting wrinkle is that the different stopped keywords showed highly distinct patterns of co-occurrence, as was revealed in the multiple correspondence analysis. <dey> was much more tightly associated with R-lessness and other DH-stopping than the other two forms; <dat>, meanwhile, was the closest to initialisms, especially on dimension 2 in the MCA, which is where initialisms were the most distinct from the other features under study. This possibly reflects differences in the kinds of communicative situations where forms of *they* are likely to occur versus those where forms of *that* are likely to occur.

Though more investigation is necessary, especially given the small sample size used in this chapter, this account does have interesting resonances with Woolard's (2008) reanimation of pragmatic salience (Errington 1985) to explain some patterns of sound change, wherein deictic forms in particular are privileged sites of ideological activity. Although *dis*, *dat* and *dey* can all function as deictics, it may be that *dat* is somehow a more prototypical site of pointing-like meanings. It is also possible that deictic *dat* is more likely to occur in the vicinity of evaluative talk. Meanwhile, it has been documented that individual words and expressions often accrue outsized amounts of social meaning by virtue of their histories of circulation (Chun 2007), and *dat* has certainly participated in a few such widely circulating key phrases (e.g., *true dat, who dat*).

# 6 Conclusion

In this chapter I have shown how the co-occurrence patterns of a feature like DH-stopping can inform us about its intersecting social meaning potentials. DH-stopping does appear widely in the production of AAVE (among other contexts) on Twitter, as one might expect, and in this respect it also co-occurs with R-lessness. It appears that, despite structural descriptions of AAVE (and many other DH-stopping varieties) including both DH-stopping and /r/-lessness, the social meaning potentials of these two phonological features are somewhat divergent in how their CMC analogues function.

With some limitations, one major contribution of this study has been to bring to light the actual stylistic practices of African Americans on the internet. Given that negative evaluations of African American Vernacular English and anti-black racism more generally have been significant source material for negative attitudes toward "internet language," there is a dearth of work examining African American linguistic practice in online venues. Given that I cannot actually identify any of the tweeters in my corpus as definitely belonging to AAVE-using speech communities or even as African American, a dedicated ethnographic look at African American language online is much needed. Such a study would do even more to elucidate the meanings, cultural dimensions and political implications of African American stylistic practices online (see Jones' and Childs' chapters, this volume, for such explorations in this area). Larger-scale corpus research on tweeters and social media users from AAVE-using communities would complement such work, and this chapter, quite nicely as well.

One issue that goes to the unique nature of CMC data for investigating variables that are more familiar from studies of spoken language is that orthography itself is a somewhat chunky mediating technology, which does not present itself equally for use in representations of R-lessness and DH-stopping. In DH-stopping, a simple <th> to <d> substitution is generally all that is necessary. For R-lessness, however, a number of strategies were used. Simple deletion of <r> is almost never sufficient because of the involvement of the vowel grapheme (though see

<nomoe> for *no more*). <r>-deletion and vowel-to-<a> were fairly common, as in <otha> (*other*) and <fa> (*for*). <uh> was sometimes use for final schwa, or spellings of words homophonous with the R-less form, like <they>. In some cases, higher degrees of orthographic creativity were necessary, as in <wowtta> (*water*) and <wea> (*where*). If R-lessness is harder to represent orthographically than DH-stopping, its meanings when it appears may be more idiosyncratic and context-specific, which could account for its lack of relationship to initialisms as a co-variable.

One potential limitation of the methodology in this chapter is that its approach to phonological variation was not accountable in a Labovian (1972b) sense, as I have not accounted for the environments in which DH-stopping and R-lessness could have occurred but failed to do so. At a certain scale, however, questions of accountability become slightly less important, unless there is reason to suspect that possible environments of occurrence are somehow unequally distributed across the other cells in the design. In addition, accountability is less well-defined for features like internet initialisms, which have very loose coupling with syntactic structure, making it difficult to delineate the structural envelopes in which they are licensed.

Related to the question of the envelope of variation is the inclusion of the non-rhotic "n-word" in the category of R-less realizations. From a semantic or functional perspective, the two realizations of the n-word are not really in variation with each other. At an ideological level, however, the two occupy similar sites, are targets of analogous controversies, and sense is made of each one in terms of the other. In particular, /r/-lessness is highly visible as part of the work that has gone into the reclamation of the non-rhotic form (Rahman 2012). In a larger-scale study, it would be worth seeing how patterns of stylistic co-occurrence change depending on how the non-rhotic n-word is coded.

This study was unable to separate out individual internet initialisms despite the wide variety of communicative functions such forms can serve. In a larger-scale study, each initialism could be entered as a separate feature and broaden the population of internet language features considered. Any replication would also do well to delimit with more certainty the precise variety or set of communities under consideration. Though most of the tweets in the DH-stopped portion of the corpus, and a good swath of the <th> tokens as well, were in AAVE, there were also a number with ties to Nigerian English, which likely has different constraints on both DH-stopping and R-lessness (both in spoken and internet varieties), not to mention social meanings.

At scale, meanwhile, it would also be possible not to take the shortcut I adopted here in collecting tweets by using particular keywords, which, despite attempts to control for semantic and pragmatic content, may have influenced the character of the results. If, instead, a principled sample were taken of the entire feed of tweets (cf. Bamman, Eisenstein, and Schnoebelen 2012), a reliable picture of the relative frequency of DH-stopping, R-lessness, and other features could be constructed. This would also help sort out questions of social meaning, as frequency relates to the predictability of a variant in context and may be a factor in the intensity or content of its social meaning (Podesva 2011; Squires 2014; Callier 2013). In general, the scale of Twitter should allow us to greatly expand the envelope of meaningful features whose co-occurrence patterns we are interested in investigating.

Reseachers should continue investigating the principled ways in which language users piece together meaningful features of language for creative indexical effect. As I have shown, these stylistic complexes are far from un-principled, one-off confabulations (with no disrespect intended to confabulations). Stylistic creativity can have an impact on the co-occurrence patterns of linguistic variation that is quantitatively verifiable in large corpora. Such macro-scale approaches to style are an important counterpart to a fine-grained, hermeneutical approach to style in interaction (e.g., Coupland 2007a), which traces precisely how language users make sense of stylistic resources in particular contexts. Macro-scale work, in fact, may be better equipped, given the right hypotheses, to document the interaction between stylistic practice and language change itself, as quantitative, at-scale forms of linguistic practice are necessary conditions for a phenomenon to count as language change at all. In the meantime, the field of possible questions in covariation is wide open, and sites of investigation like Twitter provide researchers ever easier access to the data needed to answer them.

# 7 References

Agha, Asif. 2007. *Language and social relations*. Studies in the Social and Cultural Foundations of Language. Cambridge, UK: Cambridge University Press.

Bamman, David, Jacob Eisenstein & Tyler Schnoebelen. 2012. Gender in Twitter: Styles, stances, and social networks. *arXiv:1210.4567*, October. http://arxiv.org/abs/1210.4567.

Bauman, R. & C.L. Briggs. 1990. Poetics and performance as critical perspectives on language and social life. *Annual Review of Anthropology* 19. 59–88.

Benor, Sarah Bunin. 2010. Ethnolinguistic repertoire: Shifting the analytic focus in language and ethnicity. *Journal of Sociolinguistics* 14(2). 159–83.

Biber, Douglas. 1988. *Variation across speech and writing*. Cambridge, UK: Cambridge University Press.

Biber, Douglas & Edward Finegan. 1994. *Sociolinguistic perspectives on register*. Oxford University Press.

Callier, Patrick. 2013. *Linguistic context and the social meaning of voice quality variation*. Washington, DC: Georgetown University Ph.D. Dissertation.

Campbell-Kibler, Kathryn. 2011. Intersecting variables and perceived sexual orientation in men. *American Speech* 86(1). 52–68.
Cavar, Damir. 2004a. Lidtrainer.py (version 0.3). LID. http://cavar.me/damir_old/LID/
Cavar, Damir. 2004b. Lid.py (version 0.3). LID. http://cavar.me/damir_old/LID/
Chiluwa, Innocent. 2008. Assessing the Nigerianness of SMS text-messages in English. *English Today* 24(01). 51–56.
Chun, Elaine. 2007. 'Oh My God!': Stereotypical words at the intersection of sound, practice, and social meaning. Paper presented at New Ways of Analyzing Variation 36. Philadelphia, PA.
Coupland, Nikolas. 1980. Style-shifting in a Cardiff work-setting. *Language in Society* 9(1). 1–12.
Coupland, Nikolas. 2007a. *Style: Language variation and identity*. Cambridge, UK: Cambridge University Press.
Coupland, Nikolas. 2007b. Aneurin Bevan, class wars and the styling of political antagonism. In Peter Auer (ed.), *Style and social identities: Alternative spproaches to linguistic heterogeneity*, 213–46. Berlin: Mouton de Gruyter.
Dubois, Sylvie & Barbara M. Horvath. 1998. Let's tink about dat: Interdental fricatives in Cajun English. *Language Variation and Change* 10(3). 245–61.
Eckert, Penelope. 2008. Variation and the indexical field. *Journal of Sociolinguistics* 12(4). 453–76.
Eckert, Penelope. 2012. Three waves of variation study: The emergence of meaning in the study of sociolinguistic variation. *Annual Review of Anthropology* 41. 87–100.
Eisenstein, Jacob. 2015. Systematic patterning in phonologically-motivated orthographic variation. *Journal of Sociolinguistics* 19(2). 161–188.
Eisenstein, Jacob. 2016. Twitter sociolinguistics in the Unix shell. https://github.com/jacobeisenstein/unix-sociolinguistics.
Errington, J. J. 1985. On the nature of the sociolinguistic sign: Describing the Javanese speech levels. In Elizabeth Mertz (ed.), *Semiotic mediation: Sociocultural and psychological Perspectives*, 287–310. Academic Press.
Gawne, Lauren, and Jill Vaughan. 2011. I can haz language play: The construction of language and identity in LOLspeak. In Maïa Ponsonnet, Loan Daov & Margit Bowler (eds.), *Proceedings of the 42nd Australian Linguistics Society Conference*. https://digitalcollections.anu.edu.au/handle/1885/9398.
Greenacre, Michael and Oleg Nenadic. 2010. Package "ca." http://www.carme-n.org/.
Gut, Ulrike B. 2008. Nigerian English: Phonology. In Rajend Mesthrie (ed.), *Varieties of English, Vol. 4: Africa, South and Southeast Asia*, 35–54. New York: De Gruyter Mouton.
Guy, Gregory. 2009. Co-variables: Are sociolects coherent? Paper presented at New Ways of Analyzing Variation 38. Ottawa, ON, Canada.
Half Moon Bay Style Collective. 2006. Elements of Style. Poster presented at New Ways of Analyzing Variation 35. Columbus, OH.
Hanks, William F. 1992. The indexical ground of deictic reference. In Alessandro Duranti & Charles Goodwin (eds.), *Language as an interactive phenomenon*, 43–77. New York: Cambridge University Press.
Hebdige, Dick. 1984. *Subculture: The meaning of style*. New York: Methuen.
Hill, Jane. 1995. Junk Spanish, covert racism, and the (leaky) boundary between public and private spheres. *Pragmatics* 5(2). 197–212.
Hobbs, Pamela. 2004. In their own voices: Codeswitching and code choice in the print and online versions of an African-American women's magazine. *Women and Language* 27(1). 1–12.

Johnstone, Barbara. 2009. Pittsburghese shirts: Commodification and the enregisterment of an urban dialect. *American Speech* 84(2). 157–175.
Labov, William. 1972a. *Sociolinguistic patterns*. Philadelphia: University of Pennsylvania Press.
Labov, William. 1972b. Some principles of linguistic methodology. *Language in Society* 1(1). 97–120.
Labov, William. 2006. *The social stratification of English in New York City*. 2nd edn. Cambridge [UK] and New York: Cambridge University Press.
Labov, William, Sharon Ash & Charles Boberg. 2006. *The atlas of North American English: Phonetics, phonology, and sound change*. New York: Walter de Gruyter.
Lindsey, Geoff. 2012. Eminem and the "gay lisp." *Speech Talk*. February 9. http://englishspeech-services.com/blog/eminems-gay-lisp/.
Long, Tiffani. 2012. As seen on Twitter: African-American rhetorical traditions gone viral. Ypsilanti, MI: Eastern Michigan University MA Thesis.
Olajide, Stephen Billy & Oladimeji Kaseem Olaniyi. 2014. Educated Nigerian English Phonology as Core of a Regional 'RP.' *International Journal and Humanities and Social Science* 3(14). http://ijhssnet.com/journals/Vol_3_No_14_Special_Issue_July_2013/31.pdf.
Pharao, Nicolai, Marie Maegaard, Janus Spindler Møller & Tore Kristiansen. 2014. Indexical meanings of [s+] among copenhagen youth: Social perception of a phonetic variant in different prosodic contexts. *Language in Society* 43(1). 1–31.
Podesva, Robert J. 2006. Phonetic detail in sociolinguistic variation: Its linguistic significance and role in the construction of social meaning. Palo Alto, CA: Stanford University Ph.D. Dissertation.
Podesva, Robert J. 2007. Phonation type as a stylistic variable: The use of falsetto in constructing a persona. *Journal of Sociolinguistics* 11(4). 478–504.
Podesva, Robert J. 2011. Salience and the social meaning of declarative contours. *Journal of English Linguistics* 39(3). 233–264.
Podesva, Robert J., Sarah J. Roberts & Kathryn Campbell-Kibler. 2001. Sharing resources and indexing meanings in the production of gay styles. In Kathryn Campbell-Kibler, Robert J. Podesva, Sarah Roberts & Andrew D. Wong (eds.), *Language and Sexuality: Contesting Meaning in Theory and Practice*, 175–189. Stanford, CA: CSLI Publications.
R Development Core Team (2015). R: A language and environment for statistical computing. R Foundation for Statistical Computing, Vienna, Austria. ISBN 3-900051-07-0. http://www.R-project.org.
Rahman, Jacquelyn. 2012. The N word: Its history and use in the African American community. *Journal of English Linguistics* 40(2). 137–171.
Rickford, John. 2002. Implicational scales. In Jack Chambers, Peter Trudgill & Natalie Schilling-Estes (eds.), *Handbook of language variation and change*, 142–167. Malden, MA: Blackwell Publishers.
Rose, Mary. 2006. *Language, place, and identity in later life*. Stanford, CA: Stanford University Ph.D. Dissertation.
Silverstein, Michael. 1976. Shifters, linguistic categories and cultural description. In Keith H. Basso & Henry A. Selby (eds.), *Meaning in anthropology*, 11–55. (School of American Research Advanced Seminar Series). Santa Fe, NM: University of New Mexico Press.
Squires, Lauren. 2010. Enregistering internet language. *Language in Society* 39(4). 457–492.
Squires, Lauren. 2014. Social differences in the processing of grammatical variation. *University of Pennsylvania Working Papers in Linguistics* 20(2). http://repository.upenn.edu/pwpl/vol20/iss2/20.

*The Archivist* (version unknown). 2014. Tweet Archivist. https://www.tweetarchivist.com/.
Thomas, Erik. 2001. *An acoustic analysis of vowel variation in New World English*. Durham, NC: Duke University Press.
Venables, William N. & Brian D. Ripley. 2002. *Modern applied statistics with S*. New York: Springer-Verlag.
Woolard, Kathryn A. 2008. Why dat now? Linguistic-anthropological contributions to the explanation of sociolinguistic icons and change. *Journal of Sociolinguistics* 12(4). 432–452.

Becky Childs
# Who I am and who I want to be: Variation and representation in a messaging platform

## 1 Introduction

Work on language variation and change has relied on spoken speech as the preferred medium for analysis, and rightly so, since it is the primary form of communication that dominated the 20th century (Labov 1963, 1972, 1994; Milroy 1987; Wolfram 1969). However, with the increased use of technology, specifically online chat platforms, much communication in the 21st century occurs virtually via instant messaging contexts. Within these messaging platforms interlocutors often communicate synchronously in one-to-one conversations (Baron 2004). From early forms of instant messaging such as ICQ to America Online's Instant Messenger to the current Facebook messenger and other messaging and chat plug-ins for social media platforms, a convenient, fast-paced, straightforward messaging interface has been adopted by computer and smartphone users rather readily.

Despite the longevity of these platforms and their significance in the day-to-day communication of many people, popular culture spends a great deal of time debating the merits and pitfalls felt to be associated with the use of a technology-dependent form of communication. While the popular belief among some is that instant messaging can lead to "broken language" or that it is creating a generation of language users who are unable to disambiguate the various linguistic styles that are presupposed by particular conversational situations, instant messaging formats (and for that matter other messaging formats) allow a speaker to manipulate their linguistic resources in ways that may be unavailable to them through their spoken linguistic repertoire (Crystal 2006; Squires 2012; Thurlow 2003, 2006; Thurlow and Poff 2013). From linguistic features (both phonological and morphosyntactic) to linguistic styles and even topics of conversation, online messaging platforms have expanded speaker opportunity for identity creation and challenged linguists to think about the ways in which to characterize, analyze, and consider this language data.

Recent work in language variation and change has moved toward considering the ways that style and identity can affect a speaker's language practices and behaviors (Bucholtz 2003; Coupland 2007; Eckert 2003; Johnstone 1996),

**Becky Childs,** Coastal Carolina University

and language on instant messenger conversations also shows similar tendencies. Speakers in online interactions, because it is collaborative and they are receiving feedback from the other speaker, are constantly adjusting, refining and honing their "online speech" in an effort to communicate in a way that they feel is stylistically appropriate for the conversational situation. Pulling from previous sociolinguistic studies of instant messaging and internet chat data (Paolillo 2001; Squires 2012; Tagliamonte and Denis 2008), this chapter discusses two topics surrounding CMC as related to sociolinguistic research: First, it addresses the significance of messaging data within the framework of studies of language variation and change, offering it as an important source of linguistic data that can show the same type of variability present in spoken speech. Secondly, and most importantly, this chapter examines closely a situation where spoken language data and CMC data from the same speakers do not align; a situation where the frequency of use of a linguistic variable is different in spoken language and online language. It is this area of disconnect where questions arise about the ways in which a speaker can be "authentic" in each situation, using language in different ways and adopting linguistic features for each type of communication.

The chapter begins with a discussion of instant messaging within the framework of computer-mediated communication and within studies of language variation and change, then moves on to a study of instant messenger data. It then considers the ways in which representational choices by young Appalachian African Americans in instant messenger conversations challenge previously collected spoken linguistic data from the same speakers and force researchers to consider the ways in which linguistic choices can either challenge or reinforce their identities. As we will see, often the choices that a speaker makes when engaging in computer-mediated communication are those related to identity and style, personal choices that the speaker makes in representing themselves to their interlocutor/s in each interaction (see Squires, this volume). The chapter ends with a discussion of the perceived divide between spoken and written language data from the same speaker and discusses why areas of little overlap and misalignment in data can actually become crucial points for representational identity work by a speaker. This makes CMC data a hot-bed for linguists interested in the ways in which speakers construct and perform their linguistic identities (Agha 2007).

# 2 Background

The study of language variation looks at the social and linguistic patterns that underlie language use and the change that happens in language across speakers. Historically, the primary data source for this research has been spoken language, not written forms like CMC. With spoken language as the focus, sociolinguists have been able to investigate various speech styles ranging from careful speech, as elicited by reading passages, to more informal and casual speech, like recordings of friends having day-to-day conversations. The wide range of linguistic speech styles that have been elicited have allowed for much research into the ways in which attention to speech (Labov 1972), perceived audience (Coupland 2004), identity (Eckert 2000, 2003), and even feelings about particular linguistic forms (cf. enregistered speech as in Agha 2007) can affect the linguistic choices of a speaker.

Crucial to all of these considerations of variety in language, and a more recent focus of study in sociolinguistic work, is how a speaker belongs to and participates as a member of a particular speech community. That is, the ways in which a speaker through her or his use of particular speech features constructs social meaning and asserts or performs an identity, as a member of a broader group (Bucholtz 2003; Eckert 2000, 2003). To date, most variationist work in this area has been quantitative in nature and has looked specifically at spoken communication. However, given the unique characteristics of online language, specifically instant messenger, it is worthwhile to consider the ways in which the same principles are at hand in this form of CMC. Given the highly social nature of instant messaging platforms and their widespread use, IM is a robust arena for examining not only language variation but also identity creation.

## 2.1 Identity and language variation

Within sociolinguistic work, recent attention has been focused on the ways in which a speaker as social agent constructs local social meaning (for themselves and their communities of practice) through their everyday practices (including language). Researchers are able to examine the local relationship between a linguistic variant and the social identity of those who use it (Johnstone 2004). Further, through studies of this sort, sociolinguistic work has been able to better understand the social significance of language variation. In turn this enables the application of the results of micro-level studies of language to the understanding of macro-level categories (e.g., social class), and challenges sociolinguists to rethink the ways that social classification is typically performed.

The application of this method to current sociolinguistic research has enabled researchers to consider how particular speech features may become enregistered as marking a particular identity (Agha 2007), and further how speakers perform various authentic linguistic identities in their presentation of self. Ultimately this has moved much sociolinguistic research from the idea of a speaker as a monolith to the idea of the linguistic individual (Johnstone 1996), a person who makes purposeful linguistic moves to create a desired and often necessary persona that meets a social function.

## 2.2 IM and CMC

Although now considered by some to be an outdated form of CMC, instant messaging once occupied an important place in the framework of electronic communication, from both popular applications to more private forms (used in universities and within gaming communities, for example). Through it, Web citizens were able to communicate with others removed in space in real-time. With the increased use of IM came accompanying linguistic and communication research, aimed at investigating the ways that new types of language and writing were emerging among users of this medium (Baron and Ling 2007) as well as the ways in which collaborative writing and collaborative social practice were emerging as a result of this technology (Fox Tree et al. 2011). Research that examined the specifics of linguistic representation (Baron and Ling 2007) found that several characteristics of IM stood out as quite different from that of other forms of CMC (specifically text messaging), namely message length, total words, and the use of apostrophes. IM characteristically had fewer words and shorter sentences, but used more apostrophes than that of text messages, demonstrating the complexity of CMC and IM more specifically (Baron and Ling 2007). Thus, IM stands as a form of CMC that while having shorter transmissions than text messages, still maintains standard apostrophe use at a higher rate, making it an interesting area for research as users are constantly negotiating not only language norms (grammar rules), but also the current and emerging social landscape of their online space which may not all value standard language norms in the same ways.

# 3 Data and discussion

## 3.1 The speech community

The data used in this study was collected as part of a larger study examining an African American community located in Appalachia (Childs and Mallinson 2004; Mallinson and Childs 2005). The location of the community, Texana, is within the Appalachian mountain chain, shown in Figure 1. Texana is a community with around 150 residents, the majority of which are African American. The majority of speakers utilize both African American English features and Appalachian English features in their speech.

**Figure 1:** Location of Texana, North Carolina

Being from a rural community, these young people do not have substantive daily contact with urban speech norms and cultural practices. While they do travel to Atlanta a few times a year, most of their time is spent in the local community or in other surrounding (predominantly white, Appalachian) communities. Thus, they look elsewhere for sources of information about a more urban lifestyle and a connection to a broader African American community. These sources include not only popular culture (music and television) but also family members who travel outside of the area more frequently or those who have moved out of the area to more urban centers. From these connections, Texana speakers can learn, "try on," and even test various urban cultural norms, including those of language, dress, and music choices. Still, while they are able to access these norms, they must also negotiate them in the frame of their local community. Thus, it was not uncommon to have a young person state that their favorite music artists were prominent artists at the time in both hip-hop (Nelly) and country music (Kenny Chesney), two genres of music that are often viewed as having fan bases that are mutually exclusive. At this crossroads of identity, this study seeks to explore how variable uses of salient linguistic markers can help a speaker to create an identity that they desire – specifically via instant messenger discourse, and in CMC more broadly.

## 3.2 Data sources

The data used in this study came from both sociolinguistic interviews and from instant messenger conversations with teenage residents of the Texana community (N = 6). The sociolinguistic interviews were collected from 2000–2004 and the instant messenger data was collected during the same time period. The choice to collect and interact both verbally and via CMC was twofold. First, the interactions via IM served as a way for the researcher to stay active with members of the community even when not physically present in the local space. Secondly, language data in both oral and written formats allowed for further investigation of the ways that speakers represent themselves, to the same person, and whether these differed in face-to-face versus more remote interactions. In this way, the data are complementary, functioning as one larger cohesive representation of speakers' broad sociolinguistic identities (oral and written). It should be noted, though, that in all of the interactions (spoken and IM) the participants were interacting with the researcher and not their peer group.

The recordings were done using an ethnographic approach for data collection and the instant messenger data was collected and downloaded as conversations (38) developed between the author and the teenage residents. The instant messaging data was collected from the instant messaging client AOL Instant Messenger (AIM). This is a free client available for download and at the time of data collection most of users of the client used it as a stand-alone interface, meaning that they did not have to have a paid America Online account to utilize this service.

As a result of the popularity of AIM at the time of this data collection, the choice of a messaging platform was the result of critical mass. That is, speakers utilize the platform that gives them the broadest access to their friends, family, and other acquaintances. Since online written discourse is the currency in instant messenger, the online users are looking to communicate with those who share like interests and who they can collaborate with in creating an online dialogue and communicating information; users of messenger platforms tend to coalesce around one particular platform creating a wide social network for online interaction, and at this point in time within the Texana community it was AIM. One of the reasons for the popularity of this platform and some of the stylistic choices that were noted in the data was the availability of "extra" features for this text-based form of communication. These affordances that were employed by the users included changes to text color, the insertion of emoticons (including animated emoticons/.gifs), and the use of away message and status messages, all of which are used in the construction of identity. The latter two, away messages and status messages, can be changed regularly and were also significant sources of data for this study, in addition to the data that was included in the actual instant messenger discourse.

While often conflated into one category, away messages and status messages function in different capacities in CMC. Away messages serve as "a way to establish a continuing social presence" (Baron et al 2005: 293), even in physical absence from a computer. In fact, Nachbaur (2003: 9) notes, "[Away] messages are often quite informative. Imagine calling someone on the telephone and having their answering machine tell you where they are, what they are doing, and when they will return.... Since away messages are highly used, they represent an extensive exchange of personal, pertinent information." This personal information that is made available via away messages serves as a way for an instant message account holder to leave information for all their online contacts to view and can be as descriptive as she or he wishes, but many times will reveal that the user is away from the computer, often promising to get back in touch with a contact if they leave an IM, and potentially revealing when they plan to return to their terminal.

While an away message is used to indicate that a user is indeed not present at the computer terminal, a status message does not necessitate that a user in absent. Rather, a status message serves as a way to let a list of contacts know what a user is doing (including thoughts, activities, or general information about their current state). Often these range from the lyrics to a song or a favorite quotation, to a description of or link to a current activity. There is no doubt that the unsolicited nature of these away messages and status messages, each of which contains content that alerts one to a user's status, helps them to each function as relevant and significant data sources for those investigating language in instant messenger.

## 3.3 Variables

Two linguistic variables are examined in this study. The first variable, a phonological (in speech)/orthographic (in IM) one, is post-vocalic /r/ or <r>. Post-vocalic /r/ as in the words *four* and the second syllable of *brother* has been found to be sensitive to both social and linguistic factors. In spoken language, post-vocalic /r/ has been noted to be absent more frequently in the speech of African American English speakers than in Appalachian English speakers, with Appalachian English being noted as a highly /r/-full dialect (Hall 1942; Kurath and McDavid 1961; Montgomery 1989; Wolfram and Christian 1976). Linguistically, post-vocalic /r/ in an unstressed position (*brother*) is more likely to be absent (*brotha'*) than it is in stressed positions (*four*) (Bailey and Thomas 1998; Labov et al. 1968; Wolfram 1969).

The second set of variables examined, expletives and slang terms, are lexical in nature and are frequently used as stylistic markers. While the use of swear words and slang among adolescents is not itself novel, their use in instant messenger conversations is important when considering stylistic differences that may emerge between spoken and written language practice. Specifically, when we are thinking about the ways that young language users are manipulating linguistic resources that may carry both local and broader cultural currency, stylistic features like expletives and slang become increasingly important as they are "off the shelf" variants that are widely recognizable and can often quickly help to socially position a speaker (de Klerk 2005; Eckert 2003). The use of expletives among adolescents has been noted as "a means to break the rules of convention and (adult) society" (de Klerk 2005:115). Research on expletive use points to higher acceptance of use among males (de Klerk 1991, 1992). However, research notes that expletive use is now increasingly recognized for the overt connection it has to power (Thurlow 2001); for many speakers it is more likely that the use of expletives is tied less closely to gender and more specifically to a sense of self and group identity (de Klerk 2005). That is, expletives are often used by speakers to build cultural capital within a group, showing shared interests and membership. In the CMC medium of text messaging, the use of slang terms has been noted as a way that young speakers can build social capital and can be used as a form of solidarity-building within a friendship group (Thurlow 2003).

# 4 Data analysis

I begin with an analysis of post-vocalic /r/ or <r> as a phonological and orthographic variable and then move on to analysis of the expletives and slang terms and their associated orthographic conventions. In previous work on the Texana community, Christine Mallinson and I (Childs and Mallinson 2004) found that teenagers in the community had overall lower levels of phonological /r/-lessness than their older counterparts in the community (see Table 1 below). This result positioned these younger speakers as more aligned with Appalachian English speech norms than the older residents. While all of the rates of /r/-lessness are quite low in Texana, especially when compared to results found in the speech of other African American communities (Bailey and Thomas 1998; Wolfram 1969), the teenage group had a much more /r/-ful dialect than others in the community.

**Table 1:** Rates of phonological /r/-lessness among speaker groups in Texana

| Speaker Group | Unstressed % r-less | Stressed % r-less |
|---|---|---|
| Texana Residents Overall | 18.3% (85/463) | 3.1% (29/926) |
| Texana Teenagers | 5.9% (5/84) | 2.8% (5/173) |

However, when chatting with these teenagers on instant messenger and observing their away messages, a number of instances of post-vocalic <r> loss emerged. See for example the following excerpts in 1 and 2. In the first example, ABCballa000 omits <r> in his screen name, turning <baller> into <balla>, and within the text of the message, <later> becomes <lata>. Note that all screen names have been changed to allow for anonymity, though relevant orthographic processes have been preserved. <baller> to <balla> is unstressed syllable position <r> loss, the most likely syllabic position for this process to occur within, as noted before. However, if we turn to the second example below from the same speaker, we see inconsistency, even as related to the same word. <r> loss is present on the words <nigga> and <holla>, both of which also serve as stylistic markers and will be discussed later. More importantly, <later> is represented in this exchange in a fully <r>-ful form. In both examples in 1 and 2 below, <later> is functioning in a similar way. This inconsistency in representational choice is of interest, since the patterns of young residents' spoken language appear to be far more /r/-ful than that of the IM data. That is, it is likely that in the speech of these young people the /r/ would be pronounced in each of these words.

(1) [IM CONVERSATION] ABCballa00: well im gonna go so i'll talk to u lata
ABCballa00: 1

(2) [AWAY MESSAGE] ABCballa00: I'm gone out right now but leave a nigga some love and I'll holla at u later if u are still on................

Looking at more instant message data, a somewhat more reliable pattern begins to emerge. In example 3 below, we again find the word <nigga> with an absent orthographic <r>, while the word <under>, which contains a similar unstressed /r/, maintains the <er> ending. It is most likely that <nigga> here is functioning as an in-group-marking lexical item, a stylistic choice of the speaker. However, the retention of the unstressed <er> in <under> is of interest, since it is equally as eligible for deletion but is maintained. Thus, we must consider the ways that speakers may lexicalize particular forms such as <nigga> and utilize them for stylistic reasons, especially in the creation of personae, in this case a more overtly urban and African American identity. Additionally, since <bitch nigga> in this exchange is likely taken from and referencing the Dr. Dre song "Bitch Niggaz," the intertextual nature of the placement of this statement is important, as it signals a particular image to those who recognize it.

Likewise, in example 4, we see the use of <er> in the screen name <baller> but then an absent <er> in the text of the message <nigga>. From the data presented, it appears that the speakers are not actually undergoing a new phonological process when they begin to use instant messenger. That is, they do not have an online phonology and a spoken phonology, but rather, they are utilizing socially salient lexical items to display a particular persona to their audience. That online persona is one that has at its disposal both an <r>-ful and an <r>-less variant of a particular word. Knowing the cultural and social connotations that each variant carries – that an <r>-less word is associated with urban African American norms and an <r>-ful word is associated with Appalachian language norms (Bailey and Thomas 1998; Wolfram and Christian 1976) – these teenagers are able to utilize the form that best meets the needs of their intended audience. In the case of these IM exchanges, this is an audience where their contacts are both within and outside of their local community, with those outside of their community residing in a more urban community than Texana and the audience being people of relatively the same age.

(3) [AWAY MESSAGE] xyzballerpimp22: Theres to kind of peeps in the world a TRU NIGGA OR A BITCH NIGGA which one do i fall under.........

(4) [IM CONVERSATION]  xyzballerpimp22: do u remember andrea
fieldworker: yeah, i do
abcballerpimp00: oh kool
abcballerpimp00: 1 my nigga

These are just a few of the examples of the use of <r>-less forms in IM conversations from the young Texana speakers, who as noted before are highly /r/-full speakers that are moving in contrast to the norms of young, urban African American English speakers (Green 2002; Rickford 1999). All of the <r>-less examples that occurred in the IM data set happened in unstressed syllabic positions and occurred exclusively on the words (*lata, motha, holla, playa, balla, nigga, killa*). A list of these items with an example IM exchange is provided in example 5 below. In each of these instances, the absent <er> was represented orthographically with <a>. With a very circumscribed set of lexical items and their variability, the presence or absence of <er> in these words (i.e., *nigga* vs *under*), it seems that the young residents are using the forms with an absent <er> not based on the phonological composition of a word or segment, but rather on the semantic, pragmatic, and stylistic contexts that govern the use of a particular lexical form over another. Ultimately, they have chosen lexical items that they feel are totemic exemplars of a speech community, namely one that connotes youth and a more urban feel than their local, rural, community. In turn, they employ these "off the shelf" and often intertextually relevant forms as needed for stylistic purposes.

(5) Example /r/-less lexical items from the speakers (N = 6) situated within example context of transmission
 Killaplaya (screen name)
 ABCballa00 (screen name)
 Nigga (1 my nigga)
 Holla (holla at you later)
 Lata (so I'll talk to you lata)
 Motha (MOTHA FUCK IT)

Since these young Texanans are not necessarily representing their oral speech patterns but are utilizing stylistic representations of symbolic lexical items to do social work for them in IM messages, the orthographic conventions are of interest. Strikingly, the speakers never use an apostrophe in their orthographic representations of <r>-less forms. Instead, they choose to write the forms with <a> in place of the missing <er> segment. As can be seen in example 6 below, the speaker chooses to not use an apostrophe in representing <killa>, <playa>, or <holla>. However, the speaker does utilize apostrophes in every contraction that is included in this corpus (as can be seen in example 7). Further, the speaker also does not attach an apostrophe to <chillin>, to represent the omitted <g>. Or as seen in example 4 above, the speaker chooses <kool> for cool replacing the <c> with a <k>, but unlike other forms used in other popular and youth-oriented media (Thurlow 2003), the author does not choose to replace the <oo>

with a <u>, but at the same time he does use <u> for <you>. Thus, it seems that for these speakers the variant that represents a "dialectal" form does not need an apostrophe to note it as dialect or non-standard written form, despite the fact that this is a common process in the writing of dialect (Krapp 1926). The absence of apostrophes and the use of popular online spelling conventions indicate that the young people in Texana are using language practices similar to youth engaged in CMC world wide – regardless of the distance and difference from their spoken language.

(6) [STATUS MESSAGE] killaplaya00: chillin......holla at me.......6

(7) [STATUS MESSAGE] Even if you can't see him, God is always there

Now I will look more closely at the use of expletives and slang as stylistic markers in the instant messages of these young Texana residents. First, we examine the use of expletives in the instant messenger communication of these young people. In the examples below (8, 9, 10), expletives are used to help stress particular aspects of the message and in some cases provide further information and clarification for the speaker to their audience. Looking at example 8 below we focus on the phrase "TRU NIGGA OR A BITCH NIGGA." The use of the word *nigga* twice, first as *tru nigga* and then as *bitch nigga* in this utterance, is used as a way for the speaker to not only elicit opinion about his social status but more importantly to flout the use of the word *nigga*, especially as it references a rap song which was popular at the time. The use of capitalization for the entirety of this phrase within the frame of the whole sentence certainly underscores the desire of the speaker to draw attention to these lexical items. Further, the non-standard spellings of <TRU> for <true> and <to> for <two> are evidence of the speaker positioning himself within the framework of online youth language (Baron 2008).

(8) [AWAY MESSAGE] ABCballa00: Theres to kind of peeps in the world a TRU NIGGA OR A BITCH NIGGA which one do i fall under.........

Looking at example 9 below, this away message from an adolescent female shows a similar pattern to the previous example, in her use of expletives to mark emphasis and to help position herself within a broader framework. The capitalization of "MOTHA FUCK IT," capitalization that extends beyond the first letter and applied to the whole phrase, is done specifically to call attention to the phrase's use. While it is probable that this could be an example of the use of capitalization to signal that a speaker is yelling, as is common in CMC (Danet

1995), the choice to capitalize only one section in the last line of the this away message, not the entire last line, indicates the emphasis on this portion of this message by the speaker.

(9) [AWAY MESSAGE]　Texana is where I have lived my whole life.
　　　　　　　　　　　I love Georgia Bulldogs!!
　　　　　　　　　　　I love Murphy Bulldogs!!
　　　　　　　　　　　tears in a bucket MOTHA FUCK IT!!!

The use of the leave-taking slang items *holla* and *lata* (see examples 6 above, and 10 and 11 below) is also of interest, especially since they frequently occur. Speakers utilize these forms, often included as lines from rap or hip-hop music, in their online discourse to signal the end of a conversation. In some instances these are followed by <1> as seen in example 11. <1> is a common leave-taking marker that comes from "One Love," a term popularized in reggae music. In using this, these speakers ally and situate themselves in broader Black culture.

(10) [IM CONVERSATION]　ABCballa00: gotta go holla

(11) [IM CONVERSATION]　ABCballa00: well im gonna go so i'll talk to u lata
　　　　　　　　　　　　ABCballa00: 1

Example 11 is of further interest as it shows the ways that these young people use multiple stylistic features within one IM exchange. In example 11, we see one instance of the use of an apostrophe in <i'll> but the absence of an apostrophe in <im>. Further we see <gonna> for <going to>, the use <u> for <you>, and <lata> for <later>. The layering of these stylistic features overlays the content with a particular style that helps to create and reinforce the identity that these young people hope to perform.

# 5 Conclusions

To be sure, this study has shown that the linguistic features that are utilized in instant messenger communication do not always wholly reflect the speech features of a speaker or speech community (cf. Jones, this volume). We must be careful to not dismiss online discourse as anomalous language behaviors or a simplified type of performance, but rather consider the ways in which the moves that are made online are a form of identity making for a speaker or members of a speech community. Looking systematically at the use of post-vocalic /r/ in speech and <er> and <a> productions in instant messenger conversations, the misalignment of the data is actually an invitation for a researcher to consider the reasons why language behaviors differ across the two genres and to uncover the potential motivations for why a speaker would choose to differ their language practices across the mediums.

As with /r/-lessness, neither expletives nor slang are abundant in the recorded spoken discourse of this community, so their use in IM reveals even clearer motivations for the use of different linguistic forms in written discourse. The overt capitalization of some of these terms draws attention to these features and creates a persona that is potentially more global and urban than the actual area where these young people are located. In fact, these young people, when asked in ethnographic interviews, commented that they learned many of the terms that were found in their IM language (*holla, 1, lata*) from their relatives who had travelled to Atlanta or Cincinnati. Thus, these lexical items do function as markers of urbanity and broader African American affiliations for these speakers than those currently available in their local community.

For these young people this set of /r/-less lexical items, expletives, and slang items all help them to create an identity that they want to project at a particular moment and that they feel appropriate for a particular audience. Looking closely at not only data from speech (across styles) but also at the different types of messages available in instant messenger applications (conversation vs. away messages vs. status messages), we can begin to appreciate the variation that can occur and more importantly the ways that a speaker can create identity in this medium (cf. Squires, this volume). For example, the data show an away message from ABCballa00 (example 12 below) which contains the lyrics to a popular rap song by T.I. In this away message, the speaker has included apostrophes in all areas where dialectal forms are utilized and has not capitalized any of the expletives that he had in other IM conversations. Indeed, we could argue that the process was a simple one, that the speaker cut and pasted the lyrics from a website which transcribed them with apostrophes and followed standard rules for capitalization. However, the away message is motivated by the speaker's desire to ally himself with urban African American culture. Ultimately, his lack of use of apostrophes in his own representations of /r/-less examples, coupled with the lack of apostrophes in situations where a final <g> is deleted, underscores that he is adapting his persona to meet a goal or set of expectations.

(12) [AWAY MESSAGE]
>You got yo girl with you, better hold her hand, I'm a mack on attack Turn yo head and she bound to get snatched
>Give the dick to her once, get her hooked like crack Takin' cum in the face, yea I like it like that Holdin' on to her waist while I hit it from the back If she come wit *Pussy Popper* she ain't never comin' back Rough sex, talkin' dirty, yea she into all that Gotta movie that'll prove that what I'm sayin' is all fact Bra and panties all black and some real tall stacks Suckin' titties, eatin' cat, shot her off the meat rack

Yet, as this example shows, there are complications when considering authorship in CMC. Researchers must be aware of the possibility of data that is taken from another source. In a smaller corpus like this, where manual extraction was done (as opposed to automated extraction from a large corpus), this type of data stands out from others quite overtly, given not only the difference in conventions but also the difference in the length of the transmission. However to regard this as "throw-away" data would be problematic as this stands as an important representation of the stylistic work that this young man is doing to create and maintain his identity, and therefore is important and valuable data from an identity standpoint (Bucholtz 2003; Eckert 2003; see also Hinrichs, this volume).

It tends to be unusual in studies of contemporary sociolinguistics, with the exception of historical sociolinguistics (e.g., Montgomery 2001; Schneider 1989; Schneider and Montgomery 2001), to include written data as a source of analysis (cf. Jones, this volume). However, with the rise of electronically mediated communication as a significant outlet for communication we must begin to consider the ways that this form of communication can reveal important information about speakers' construction of self within a broader community framework. Data from IM conversations is useful for analyses of speaker construction of identity for a number of reasons. First, one of the goals of interlocutors engaging in IM conversations, as well as many other chat based internet applications, is to mirror spoken speech (Crystal 2001). As many have noted this form of discourse presents researchers with interesting questions where they must consider both spoken and written language forms side-by-side (Tagliamonte and Denis 2008; Jones, this volume). Second, messenger platforms are a common mode of communication among young people, and their discourse in these venues contains items that may never appear in a corpus that has been generated from more codified sources like newspapers and magazines. Finally, these conversations allow for speakers' self-presentation and identity work in non-face-to-face encounters, thus providing data that are rare in typical sociolinguistic studies. The resources allow speakers to be who they are and who they want to be at the same time.

# 6 References

Agha, Asif. 2007. *Language and social relations*. Studies in the Social and Cultural Foundations of Language. Cambridge, UK: Cambridge University Press.
Bailey, Guy & Erik Thomas. 1998. Some aspects of AAVE phonology. In Salikoko Mufwene, John R. Rickford, Guy Bailey & John Baugh (eds.), *The structure of African American English*, 85–109. London: Routledge.
Baron, Naomi. 2004. See you online: Gender issues in college student use of instant messaging. *Journal of Language and Social Psychology* 23. 397–423.
Baron, Naomi, Lauren Squires, Sara Tench & Marshall Thompson. 2005. Tethered or mobile? Use of away messages in instant messaging by American college students. In Rich Ling & P. Pederson (eds.), *Mobile communications: Re-negotiation of the social sphere*, 293–311. London: Springer-Verlag.
Bucholtz, Mary. 2003. Sociolinguistic nostalgia and the authentication of identity. *Journal of Sociolinguistics* 7(3). 398–416.
Childs, Becky & Christine Mallinson. 2004. African American English in Appalachia: Dialect accommodation and substrate influence. *English World Wide* 25(1). 27–50.
Coupland, Nikolas. 2007. *Style: Language variation and identity*. Cambridge: Cambridge University Press.
Crystal, David. 2006. *Language and the Internet*. New York: Cambridge University Press.
Danet, Brenda. 1995. Play and performance in computer-mediated communication. *Journal of Computer-Mediated Communication* 1(2).
de Klerk, Vivian. 2005. Slang and swearing as markers of inclusion and exclusion in adolescence. In Angie Williams & Crispin Thurlow (eds.), *Talking Adolescence*, 111–128. New York: Peter Lang.
de Klerk, Vivian. 1992. How taboo are taboo words for girls? *Language in Society* 20(2). 277–290.
de Klerk, Vivian. 1991. Expletives: Men only? *Communication Monographs* 58. 156–159.
Eckert, Penelope. 2003. Sociolinguistics and authenticity: An elephant in the room. *Journal of Sociolinguistics* 7(3). 392–397.
Eckert, Penelope. 2000. *Linguistic variation as social practice*. Malden, MA: Blackwell.
Green, Lisa. J. 2002. *African American English: A linguistic introduction*. New York: Cambridge University Press.
Hall, John. S. 1942. *The phonetics of Great Smoky Mountain speech*. New York: Columbia University Ph.D. dissertation.
Johnstone, Barbara. 2004. Place, globalization, and linguistic variation. In Carmen Fought (ed), *Sociolinguistic variation: Critical reflections*, 65–83. Oxford/New York: Oxford University Press.
Johnstone, Barbara. 1996. *The linguistic individual: Self-expression in language and linguistics*. New York: Oxford University Press.
Jones, Graham & Bambi Schieffelin. 2009. Enquoting voice, accomplishing talk: Uses of *be + like* in instant messaging. *Language & Communication* 29. 77–113.
Krapp, George. P. 1926. The psychology of dialect writing. *The Bookman* 63. 522–527.
Kurath, Hans & Raven I. McDavid, Jr. 1961. *The pronunciation of English in the Atlantic states*. Ann Arbor: University of Michigan Press.
Labov, William, Paul Cohen, Clarence Robins & John Lewis. 1968. A study of the non-standard English of Negro and Puerto Rican speakers in New York City. *United States Office of Education Final Report, Research Project 3288*.
Labov, William. 1994. *Principles of linguistic change: Internal factors*. Oxford: Blackwell.

Labov, William. 1972. *Language in the inner city: Studies in the Black English Vernacular*. Philadelphia: University of Pennsylvania Press.
Labov, William. 1963. The social motivation of a sound change. *Word* 19. 273–309.
Ling, Rich & Naomi S. Baron. 2007. Text Messaging and IM: Linguistic comparison of American college data. *Journal of Language and Social Psychology* 26(3). 291–298.
Mallinson, Christine & Becky Childs. 2005. Communities of practice in sociolinguistic description: African American Women's Language in Appalachia. *Penn Working Papers in Linguistics* 10(2). 1–14.
Milroy, Lesley. 1987. *Language change and social networks*. 2nd edn. Oxford: Blackwell.
Montgomery, Michael. 1989. Exploring the roots of Appalachian English. *English World-Wide* 10. 227–78.
Nachbaur, Abraham. 2003. College students and instant messaging: An analysis of chatting, flirting, & using away messages. The Mercury Project for Instant Messaging (IM) Studies at Stanford University. http://www.stanford.edu/class/ pwr3-25/group2/main.html (accessed July 2005).
Paolillo, John.C. 2001. Language variation on Internet Relay Chat: A social network approach. *Journal of Sociolinguistics* 5(2). 180–213.
Rickford, John R. 1999. *African American Vernacular English: Features, evolution, educational implications*. Oxford: Blackwell.
Schneider, Edgar. 1989. *American Earlier Black English: Morphological and syntactic variables*. Tuscaloosa: University of Alabama Press.
Schneider, Edgar & Michael. B. Montgomery. 2001. On the trail of early nonstandard grammar: An electronic corpus of Southern U.S. Antebellum overseers' letters. *American Speech* 76. 388–409.
Squires, Lauren. 2012. Whos punctuating what? Sociolinguistic variation in instant messaging. In Alexandra Jaffe, Jannis Androutsopoulos, Mark Sebba, & Sally Johnson (eds.), *Orthography as social action: Scripts, spelling, identity and power*, 289–324. Boston/Berlin: Mouton de Gruyter.
Tagliamonte, Sali & Derek Denis. 2008. Linguistic ruin? LOL! Instant messaging and teen language. *American Speech* 83(1). 3–34.
Thurlow, Crispin. 2001. Naming the outsider within: Homophobic pejoratives and the verbal abuse of lesbian, gay, and bisexual high-school pupils. *Journal of Adolescence* 24. 25–38.
Thurlow, Crispin. 2003. Generation Txt? The sociolinguistics of young people's text-messaging. *Discourse Analysis Online* 1(1).
Thurlow, Crispin. 2006. From statistical panic to moral panic: The meta-discursive construction and popular exaggeration of new media language in the print media. *Journal of Computer-Mediated Communication* 11. 667–701.
Thurlow, Crispin & Michele Poff. 2013. Text messaging. In Susan C. Herring, Dieter Stein & Tuija Virtanen (eds). *Handbook of the Pragmatics of Computer-Mediated Communication*, 163–190. Berlin: De Gruyter Mouton.
Tree, Jean. E., Sarah Mayer & Teresa Betts. 2011. Grounding in instant messaging. *Journal of Educational Computing Research* 45(4). 455–475.
Wolfram, Walt. 1969. *A sociolinguistic description of Detroit Negro speech*. Washington, D.C.: Center for Applied Linguistics.
Wolfram, Walt & Donna Christian. 1976. *Appalachian speech*. Washington, D.C.: Center for Applied Linguistics.

IV **Mode and Medium**

Markus Bieswanger
# Electronically-mediated Englishes: Synchronicity revisited

## 1 Introduction

Overgeneralizations and binary categorizations featured prominently in early "first wave" computer-mediated communication (CMC) research (cf. Androutsopoulos 2006:420). Some scholars, for example, postulated the development of an *electronic English* (e.g., Collot and Belmore 1996) or even some kind of language-independent *Netspeak* (e.g., Crystal 2001 [2006]). Such overgeneralizations have since, for the most part, given way to a more in-depth and differentiated approach, accounting for variation across different CMC technologies or modes and CMC in different languages (cf. e.g., Androutsopoulos 2006; Bieswanger 2007; Herring 2007; for a discussion see Bieswanger 2013: 465–466). One of the most widely known binary distinctions in CMC research (Herring 2001: 614–615), however, the distinction of so-called *synchronous* and *asynchronous* CMC modes, is still commonly used (cf. e.g., Danet and Herring 2007: 25–26; Baron 2008: 15–23; Cho 2010: 2).

While synchronicity without doubt influences language use in electronically-mediated environments (Thurlow and Mroczek 2011: xx), the traditional binary distinction of CMC modes according to their alleged "prototypical" synchronicity is becoming increasingly problematic: The development of an *always-online culture* (cf. e.g., Baron 2008) based on mobile devices and the convergence of CMC modes, as in so-called social media networks, only add to the fact that CMC modes of both "synchronicity-types" have always been employed with varying degrees of synchronicity. Despite this, there is a lack of systematic empirical research on the relationship between synchronicity and language use online. This paper argues for the recognition of degrees of *synchronicity of use* instead of the widely used notion of *synchronicity of mode*. To illustrate this claim, the article presents the results of an empirical analysis of an English-based online discussion forum and links structural differences in the English employed to varying degrees of synchronicity of use. The suggested change from synchronicity of mode to synchronicity of use contributes to the ongoing discussion of factors suitable for a meaningful classification of electronically-mediated Englishes and CMC as a whole.

**Markus Bieswanger,** University of Bayreuth

## 2 Synchronicity in CMC: The state of the art

As early as 1984, in an article on "Social psychological aspects of computer-mediated communication," published in *American Psychologist*, Kiesler, Siegel, and McGuire (1984) distinguished "simultaneous computer conferencing" (Kiesler, Siegel, and McGuire 1984: 1129) from non-simultaneous types such as email which "do not require communication in real time" (Kiesler, Siegel, and McGuire 1984: 1130). They thus distinguished CMC types, or to be more precise CMC technologies, according to the synchronicity of participation of those involved in the communication.

This binary distinction of synchronous and asynchronous CMC types on the basis of the synchronicity of participation was made popular among CMC researchers through Herring's (2001) seminal article on "Computer-mediated discourse" in *The Handbook of Discourse Analysis*. Following Murray (1988: 5), who had used the term *mode* to refer to primarily technologically-defined "specific communication types within" what she calls "[t]he CmC medium," Herring distinguished different *modes* of computer-mediated discourse related to "technologically and culturally determined CMC types" (Herring 2001: 613). These included chat, email and Usenet newsgroups. A mode was defined as "a genre of CMC that combines messaging protocols and the social and cultural practices that have evolved around their use" (Herring 2002: 112; for discussions of the use of the terms *genre* and *register* with reference to CMC, see, e.g., Murray 1988: 5; Giltrow and Stein 2009; Biber and Conrad 2009: 177–211). Synchronicity was identified to be among the most important "medium variables" (Herring 2001: 614) or "medium factors" (Herring 2007: 13) which influence language use in electronically-mediated environments, and the proposed modes were assigned to either the synchronous or the asynchronous category.

The importance of synchronicity was linked to its quality as "a robust predictor of structural complexity, as well as many pragmatic and interactional behaviors, in computer-mediated discourse" (Herring 2007: 14). Herring (2001: 615) provided *chat* and *MUDs* (i.e., Multi-User Dungeons) as examples of synchronous modes and email as well as Usenet newsgroups as examples of asynchronous modes. The latter, Usenet newsgroups, are widely considered to be the precursors of internet-based discussion forums. Similarly to Kiesler, Siegel, and McGuire (1984, see above), Herring (2001) thus took the synchronicity of participation as the basis of her distinction of asynchronous and synchronous CMC types. This becomes even clearer in Herring's (2007: 13) proposed classification scheme, in which she lists *synchronicity* as the first of the "most important *medium* factors that have been observed to condition computer-mediated discourse" and gives the following definition:

> **Asynchronous systems do not require users to be logged on at the same time** in order to send and receive messages; rather, messages are stored at the addressee's site until they can be read. Email is an example of this type. **In synchronous systems, in contrast, sender and addressee(s) must be logged on simultaneously**; various modes of "real-time" chat are the most common forms of synchronous CMC. (Herring 2007: 13–14, my emphasis)

It has become customary in CMC research to use a binary distinction between asynchronous and synchronous modes or types of CMC, usually based on the technology employed and the related prototypical synchronicity of participation. For example, Danet (2001: 14–15) uses the terms *asynchronous modes* and *synchronous modes* to distinguish two fundamentally different "Types of Online Communication" (Danet 2001: 13). Baron (2008: 14) states that "[e]lectronic communication can be divided up along two dimensions. One is synchronicity: Does communication happen in real time (synchronous), or do senders ship off their messages for recipients to open at their convenience (asynchronous)?" Baron (2008: 14) then lists email, texting, newsgroups and blogs as asynchronous types of CMC and instant messaging as well as chat as examples of synchronous types. Thurlow and Mroczek (2011: xx) list three "new media discourse variables" – technological, situational and linguistic variables – and give synchronicity as the first entry in the list of technological variables. This reflects that over the years, a primarily technological definition of CMC modes in CMC has become widespread (Jucker and Dürscheid 2012: 42; cf. also Baym 2009: 438) and many researchers have taken such a binary distinction of synchronicity in CMC as a given. For instance Zyphyris, Ang, and Laghos (2009: 278) say that "[e]mail is an asynchronous mode of communication, [...]"; Cho (2010: 2) states about email and memoranda that "both are *asynchronous*"; Bolander and Locher (2010: 180) claim that "IM [instant messaging] is a synchronous medium"; and Murelli (2011: 377) says that "[l]ike emails, forums are asynchronous forms of communication [...]." Along the same lines, many handbook articles on CMC, such as Lengel (2009) simply list chat and IM as "synchronous forms of CMC" and online discussion forums as "[a]synchronous media" (Lengel 2009: 545).

The reality in CMC, however, has never been so simple and straightforward. Firstly, even the most prototypical examples of synchronous CMC, such as chat and instant messaging, are not fully synchronous, and secondly, the individual modes have always been used in more or less synchronous ways. The absence of real synchronicity in virtually all text-based CMC is pointed out by Baron (2008: 15):

> A word of caution: Although it's common to speak of asynchronous vs. synchronous communication as if the two are polar opposites, in actuality they fall along a continuum. In a sense, the only real synchronous communication is that in which one person can interrupt another – the prototypes being telephone conversations and face-to-face speech. (Baron 2008: 15; see, e.g., also Garcia and Jacobs 1999; Dürscheid 2004; and Jucker and Dürscheid 2012 on *quasi-synchronous CMC*)

As far as electronically-mediated communication is concerned, with rare exceptions such as written Unix "talk," only audio- or video-based communication would thus be truly synchronous, as the interlocutors can interrupt each other and give instant verbal and non-verbal feedback. CMC research, however, has for the most part focused on text-based communication facilitated by networked computers and mobile phones (cf. Herring 2007: 1), which is often claimed to be markedly different from traditional forms of speech and writing. In the context of a lack of real synchronicity, it also has to be noted that traditionally termed synchronous modes such as instant messaging now often provide the possibility to leave a message that will be stored until the addressee logs on again, i.e., they can be used in an asynchronous way.

Email, one of the oldest CMC technologies and an allegedly prototypically asynchronous type of CMC (see above) can serve as an example for the second aspect, i.e., different degrees of synchronicity of use of one mode. Even long before the establishment of an always-online culture in recent years – facilitated by increasingly fast and affordable access to the internet, including mobile devices, in many parts of the world – email messages have been used on a continuum from (near-)synchronous to asynchronous communication: hours, days, weeks, months or even years may pass between a message and the corresponding reply. Alternatively, near-synchronous communication may occur, with both interlocutors accidentally or intentionally present at their respective devices and writing back and forth without much latency, i.e., with a short time gap between individual messages. This was already observed by Danet (2001: 15): "When individuals exchanging email happen to be logged on at the same time, communication feels like chatting, even if technically they are exchanging asynchronous messages." Jucker and Dürscheid (2012: 43) confirm this observation: "Email communication in its typical form [...] is undoubtedly asynchronous since co-presence at the keyboard is not required in any way. But emailing may become quasi-synchronous if by chance the communication partners are both using their mail programs at the same time and sending message [sic] to and fro in short intervals." In other words, even modes widely considered to be prototypical examples of asynchronous CMC, such as email, can be used with different degrees of synchronicity in different situations. Unfortunately, no empirical evidence is provided as to why fast-paced email communication "feels like chatting" (Danet 2001: 15). With the recent advent of the "'always-online' culture in which people expect almost instant responses to email messages" (Cox 2014), there seems to have been a trend towards increasingly synchronous use of traditionally asynchronous CMC modes such as email.

In other modes widely considered to belong to the asynchronous type, such as online discussion forums, a similar trend can be observed. Traditionally, online discussion forums are viewed as an asynchronous type of CMC that allows contributors plenty of time for composition and editing of contributions. This is pointed out as an advantage of the use of discussion forums in e-learning environments by Cole & Foster (2008: 69): "Because forums are asynchronous, students can take their time composing replies. They can draft and rewrite until they are happy with the results instead of feeling under pressure to respond immediately." The described lack of pressure to respond fast, however, does not hold true under all circumstances. In many situations, participants feel the pressure to contribute fast and thus do not have much time to write and edit a message before sending it off, which affects their language use (cf. e.g., Danet 2001: 16–17). Particularly in fast-moving discussions, such as threads dealing with breaking news or ongoing developments, there may be intense pressure to post new information or a reply before somebody else does. (1) gives an example from a corpus of posts on an online discussion forum that was analyzed for the study underlying this paper:

(1) BBC are now saying it went missing at 0600 GMT "off Brazil".

Edit: Not surprisingly in a thread that's going to move pretty fast, someone else beat me to it. My apologies.

The writer of this contribution to a thread dealing with a breaking news situation, in this case the crash of a commercial plane, originally wrote only one sentence, presumably to spread the latest information quickly, but someone else was still faster. The post was then edited to give an explanation for the overlap with a contribution posted slightly earlier and the author describes a situation of time pressure linked to the fast-moving nature of this thread. This seems to confirm that the brevity of the original message was a result of time pressure, attempting to get the information out fast and first. There was definitely no time to "draft and rewrite until they are happy with the results" (Cole and Foster 2008: 69). Contextual pressure determined the necessity to respond fast and to make near-synchronous use of a discussion forum, an allegedly prototypically asynchronous type of CMC. The fact that many more people are now online at any given moment than just a few years ago certainly increases the time pressure to be the first to post a specific piece of information, but there have always been circumstances such as breaking news situations, in which allegedly asynchronous types of CMC have been used in a rather synchronous way.

We have seen that modes traditionally labeled asynchronous, such as email and online discussion forums, have always been used with different degrees of synchronicity. But what does it mean for language use when these allegedly asynchronous modes are used rather synchronically, i.e., which linguistic features can be observed when communication via these modes "feels like chatting" (Danet 2001: 15)? Synchronous online communication is associated with a number of features that are considered to be characteristic of this type. Herring (2002: 112, drawing on Condon and Čech 2010 and Ko 1996) claims that "synchronous CMC (e.g., real-time chat) differs systematically from asynchronous CMC (e.g., email, in which sender and receiver need not be logged on at the same time) in message length, complexity, formality, and interactivity – due, in part, to temporal constraints on message production and processing."

With respect to message length, messages in synchronous CMC such as chat or instant messaging are often said to be on average shorter than in asynchronous CMC (cf. e.g., Baym 2009: 441). This is not surprising, as messages even in so-called synchronous CMC are usually transmitted turn-by-turn and not stroke-by-stroke (cf. Jucker and Dürscheid 2012: 43) and the respective other interlocutor thus has to either wait for a message to be sent and delivered or risk overlap. In chat, for example, short messages and fast response times with little latency between messages are even considered a necessity as "messages are more ephemeral, scrolling up and off participants' computer screens as new messages replace them" (Herring 2001: 615).

Some linguistic features that are characteristic for spoken language are also often claimed to appear frequently in synchronous modes of CMC. Very prominent features of this kind are *syntactic reductions*, i.e., the deletion of syntactic elements (cf. e.g., Wilson 2000 and Quirk et al. 1985: 859–860 on motivation for and constraints of syntactic reduction). As early as 1996, Ko (1996) claimed that syntactic reductions in synchronous CMC are "caused by rapid production under real-time communicative constraints." In a similar vein, Hård af Segerstad (2002: 245) found missing subject pronouns to be characteristic of instant messaging, a prototypically synchronous mode in traditional terminology. With the exception of written CMC and very informal pieces of writing, such as fridge-door notes, this kind of ellipsis of the subject is "restricted to familiar (generally spoken) English" (Quirk et al. 1985: 896) and "very common in everyday speech" (Wilson 2000: 62), again linking features of spoken language with synchronous CMC. Correspondingly, Biber and Conrad (2009: 194) report that they found "some ellipsis, particularly skipping subject pronouns" in CMC and that "[s]uch ellipsis is more typical of conversation than writing, and corresponds to the quick interactive nature of these postings." As syntactic reductions reduce message length and complexity, and are particularly frequent in informal spoken or other highly interactive language, they are related to all four of Herring's (2002: 112) measurements of synchronicity: message length, complexity, formality, and interactivity.

Syntactic reductions, however, are not the only type of reductions that are characteristic of synchronous modes of CMC. Another frequent linguistic feature of synchronous CMC – also found in other types of CMC, particularly frequently in character-restricted kinds such as text messages – are reductions of words or phrases that Hård af Segerstad (2002: 57) refers to as "lexical reductions," Bieswanger (2007) terms "shortenings," Baron (2008: 154) addresses as "lexical shortenings" and Herring and Zelenkauskaite (2008: 79) call "deletions." Whatever the term used, there is general agreement that all "lexical forms that are made up by fewer characters than the full form of a word or a combination of words" (Bieswanger 2007) are considered to be reductions of this kind. Hård af Segerstad (2002: 201) claims that lexical reductions are used "to reduce time, effort and keystrokes." Other researchers explicitly emphasize their importance in synchronous CMC; for example, Herring (2002: 136) found "that chat exhibits abbreviation to a greater extent than email (or speech)" and Baron (2003: 70) assumes that "saving time and energy is often a motivation [to use lexical reduction such as abbreviations and acronyms] when writing chat, IM, or SMS messages." As "speed is all-important" (Danet 2001: 16) in chat, instant messaging and other synchronous CMC modes, lexical shortenings are widely considered to be characteristic features of synchronous CMC.

This short review of the use of the concept of synchronicity in CMC research and the examples discussed above show that it is somewhat problematic to categorize language use in CMC according to a binary distinction of primarily technologically defined CMC modes, which are defined on the basis of the synchronicity of participation required by the respective systems employed for communication. We have seen that many researchers suggest, albeit without providing empirical evidence, that the individual CMC modes can be used with varying degrees of synchronicity. As a result, the language use in one mode should exhibit more or less of the linguistic features associated with synchronous or asynchronous CMC respectively. An empirical investigation of this issue is the focus of the following sections.

## 3 Research questions

The main concern of this paper is the role of the concept of synchronicity in the description and explanation of certain features of English, and also other languages, in CMC. Based on previous claims of variability of language use related to variable synchronicity within individual modes in the available literature on language use in electronically mediated contexts, outlined in Section 2, and my own observations during more than a decade of CMC research, two connected research questions are relevant:

> (1) Do patterns of language use in a particular CMC mode vary with variable synchronicity of use in the mode?
>
> (2) If patterns of language in a particular CMC mode vary with variable synchronicity of use in the mode, can we really use the binary distinction of synchronous vs. asynchronous CMC modes to label patterns, or is there another way to use the concept of synchronicity as a meaningful category in CMC research?

The second of the two research questions only has to be answered if the answer to the first research question is positive, i.e., if the investigation shows that the patterns of language use in one CMC mode vary with variable synchronicity of use in the mode. The research questions will be addressed empirically in the following sections.

## 4 Data and methodology

In order to answer the research questions underlying this paper, an empirical study of language use in an English-based online discussion forum, a prototypically asynchronous CMC mode according to previous accounts, was conducted. The small-scale study presented is based on a comparison of a fast-moving and a slow-moving section of the same thread of an aviation-related discussion forum.

### 4.1 Data

The decision to use data from an online discussion forum was made for a number of reasons. In traditional and still widespread terminology, email and online discussion forums are among the best known of the so-called asynchronous CMC modes. To address the research questions, communication in an allegedly asynchronous mode had to be analyzed for features of synchronicity. Unlike email communication, much of the language material on online discussion forums is publicly accessible (cf. Murelli 2011: 377). Additionally, while many types of CMC come and go, online discussion forums have been very popular for many years and continue to be so today. They have reached a certain level of technological maturity and have been relatively stable in terms of technology and followership for a long time. Online discussion forums are thus much more suitable for studying the use of English in CMC than immature and potentially temporarily hyped technologies in a state of flux (cf. also Heyd's study, this volume).

Two parallel project-related subcorpora of raw data were compiled for comparison (cf. Beißwenger and Storrer 2008 for corpus types frequently used in CMC research and challenges faced by the researchers). In order to get material that is as comparable as possible, only differing by synchronicity in terms of time gap between the contributions, two portions of the same thread addressing a breaking news situation, in this case the crash of a commercial airliner, were selected. The thread was taken from one of the longest-running and largest discussion forums on aviation on the internet, with close to one million distinct users every month. Threads based on breaking-news situations tend to be very fast-moving at the beginning – creating pressure on the contributors to the discussion forum to produce and send off messages quickly – and then to slow down after a while. Such threads also have the advantage that they tend to continue and can be analyzed for weeks or even months.

Subcorpus one (S1) consists of the first 100 replies following the original post that created the new topic, and subcorpus two (S2) is made up of 100 replies of which the first was made exactly one week after the thread was started. The subcorpora are thus created from the same thread addressing the same topic on the same discussion forum, i.e., there are no differences concerning topic, technology or pool of potential users. This means that we are also not concerned with two subtypes of the same mode, as would be the case in comparisons such as email to friends vs. business email (cf. e.g., Biber and Conrad 2009: 185–190) or public multi-party chat vs. private two-party chat, which makes this approach different from many other studies.

To ensure that S1 was actually a considerably faster-moving section of the thread than S2, the average time gap (or latency) between contributions was calculated. The 100 replies that make up data set S1 were posted within one hour, four minutes and 56 seconds of the original post, i.e., the average time gap between contributions was 39 seconds. The 100 replies of data set S2 were posted in 6 hours, 50 minutes and 27 seconds, i.e., the average time gap between the individual contributions was 4 minutes and 6 seconds (Figure 1). A *Welch-test* confirms that the two data sets "S1 (fast-moving)" and "S2 (slow-moving)" are statistically different with regard to the average time gap between the individual contributions ($t(103.22) = 7.13$, $p < .001$, Cohen's $d = 1.01$); according to Cohen's (1988) guidelines, the effect size of mean differences is large.

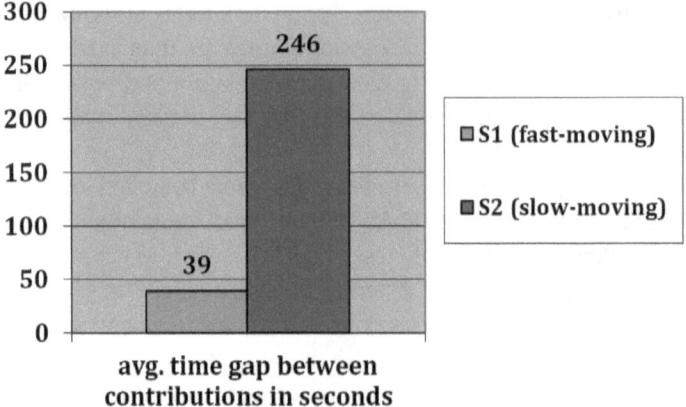

**Figure 1:** Average time gap between contributions in seconds

The pace of contributions in data set S1 is more than 6 times higher than in S2, resulting in a much higher pressure to write and post contributions fast. The situation in S1 is thus not unlike the prototypical environment that Herring (2001: 615) describes for synchronous CMC, where users are under pressure to be quick, as messages are "scrolling up and off participants' computer screens," despite the fact that S1 is taken from the same allegedly asynchronous online discussion forum as S2.

## 4.2 Methodology

With reference to the research questions formulated above, the data sets S1 and S2 were compared for three different parameters that are frequently linked to the synchronicity of CMC modes: message length, frequency of syntactic reductions, and frequency of lexical shortenings (see Section 2).

As mentioned above, relatively short messages are considered to be a characteristic feature of synchronous CMC modes. To be able to compare the two data sets, all language material other than the actual contributions to the forum were removed from the corpus, such as quotations from previous posts and computer-generated standardized information about the user as well as the date and time when the post was sent. Then an electronic word count tool was used to count the number of words for each contribution, yielding the number of so-called orthographic words defined by Plag (2003: 4) as "an uninterrupted string of letters which is preceded by a blank space and followed either by a blank space or a punctuation mark." Finally, the average number of words per contribution was calculated for each data set (cf. Biber and Conrad 2009: 193–194).

Additionally, syntactic reductions, as mentioned in Section 2, are said to be characteristic of synchronous CMC modes. One of the syntactic reductions most frequently identified in previous research is the ellipsis of the subject in declarative sentences. Quirk et al. (1985: 895) argue that reductions of this kind belong to the type "situational ellipsis," as they do not depend "on the linguistic context for their interpretation" but "on knowledge of a precise extralinguistic context." Along the same lines, Wilson (2000: 62) claims for situational ellipsis that "the situational context supports or resolves meaning." Quirk et al. (1985: 895–898) list two main types of situational ellipsis, which tend to be "initial, especially taking on the form of omission of subject and/or operator" (Quirk et al. 1985: 896). Type one is described as "[e]llipsis of subject alone," as in *Told you so* (Quirk at al. 1985: 896), and type two as "[e]llipsis of subject plus operator," as in *Good to see you* (Quirk at al. 1985: 898). Both types can be illustrated with examples from the corpus:

(2) ellipsis of the subject alone (with recovered subject in square brackets)
    (a) [I] Hope it's only radar failure on board this Airbus... [S1-D14]
    (b) [It] Took off from GIG at 08.00 (Paris time) [S1-D13]

(3) ellipsis of subject plus operator (with recovered subject in square brackets)
    (a) [I am] Not sure if France is one of them. [S1-D210]
    (b) [It is] hopefully intact and everyone alive [S1-D111]

According to Quirk et al. (1985: 884), verbatim recoverability of the missing word or words is a key characteristic of ellipsis and an important criterion for distinguishing ellipsis from other kinds of omission. In the environment of online discussion forums, the missing subject can be recovered precisely in most sentences. In the examples above, the omitted subject is either the first person singular personal pronoun *I*, since the sentence is written from the perspective of the writer, or *it*, meaning 'the aircraft.' To determine whether the two data sets differ with respect to the frequency of subject deletion, each data set was analyzed for the frequency of subject omissions per 100 main clauses in declarative sentences.

Finally, the material was analyzed for lexical shortenings, which are also considered to be characteristic features of synchronous CMC modes and additionally of character-restricted modes such as texting (cf. Section 2). Both data sets were searched for six different types of lexical shortenings which I proposed in an earlier study contrasting shortened lexical forms in English and German texting (Bieswanger 2007, which also gives exact definitions of individual types of lexical shortenings) and have been used in several other studies (cf., e.g., Herring and Zelenkauskaite 2008; Bieswanger 2011; Bieswanger and Intemann 2011), as they seem to cover most of the abbreviated lexical forms used in CMC. The total number of lexical shortenings per 100 orthographic words was calculated for each data set to find out whether the frequency differs noticeably between the fast-moving first section of the thread and the slower-moving second section.

In sum, the two data sets "S1 (fast-moving)" and "S2 (slow-moving)" from an allegedly asynchronous discussion forum were analyzed for reportedly characteristic features of synchronous CMC modes. As outlined in this section, short messages as well as high frequency of syntactic reductions and lexical shortenings are claimed to be characteristic of synchronous modes and would thus be expected to be more prominent in the fast-moving part of the thread, i.e., data set S1.

# 5 Results and discussion

The results of the comparison of the features identified in Section 4 should help to answer the question whether the patterns of language use in a fast-moving and a slow-moving section of the same thread on an online discussion forum differ noticeably with respect to features of synchronicity.

## 5.1 Message length

The average length of the messages, i.e., the average number of orthographic words per message, in the two subcorpora is strikingly different. The contributions in data set S1, the fast-moving section of the thread, are on average significantly shorter than in the second data set. Data set S1 consists of a total of 3,173 words, and as each of the data sets consists of 100 contributions, the average message length in S1 is thus under 32 words per message. Data set S2 consists of a total of 8,341 words, i.e., the average length is more than 83 words per message. Figure 2 illustrates that the average message in data set S2 consists of almost 3 times as many words as in S1. Concerning the average length of contributions in the data sets "S1 (fast-moving)" and "S2 (slow-moving)," a *Welch*-test confirms that the two samples are statistically distinct ($t(118.04) = 5.63$, $p < .001$, Cohen's $d = .80$); the effect size of mean differences is large.[1]

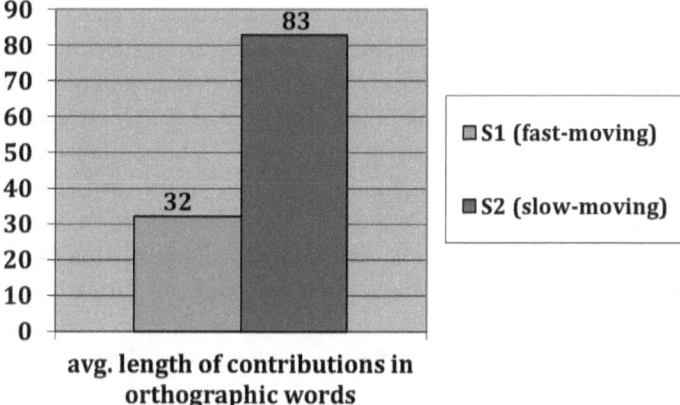

**Figure 2:** Average length of contributions in orthographic words

Additionally, it should be noted for S1 that only 3 of the contributions are more than 100 words in length, and the longest message is 191 words long, whereas 26 of the 100 messages in S2 are more than 100 words in length, with the longest contribution consisting of 563 words.

The significantly shorter messages in the fast-moving section S1 are an indicator that the forum is used in a much more synchronous way in S1 than in the slow-moving section S2, as short messages are considered to be a characteristic feature of synchronous CMC. The relative brevity of the messages in S1 is in line with the much shorter time gap between individual messages. Language use thus reflects the more synchronous use of the allegedly prototypically asynchronous technology of online discussion forums.

---

[1] Statistical tests of reduced data sets "S1red" and "S2red," consisting of only the first contribution of each individual contributor, which were carried out for "average length of contributions in orthographic words" and "lexical shortenings per 100 words" (cf. 5.3), yielded very similar results. This procedure check was meant to address the potential problem that multiple contributions of the same author (with a particular way of writing) might influence the general characteristics of the sample; the tests showed that this is not the case. Since equal variances across samples could not be assumed for any of the variables analyzed, a setup that would violate the assumption of the independence of observations for the widely used independent-samples *t*-tests, the results of *Welch*-tests rather than *t*-tests will be reported.

As the data sets S1 and S2 are sections of the same thread of an online discussion forum, technological differences and differences in the potential pool of users cannot be responsible for the empirically established and clear difference in message length. Consequently, the difference must be due to the extra-technological situation rather than the technology used (cf. Herring 2007: 10 on "medium (technological)" vs. "situation"). Comparisons of material from different modes would be much more problematic, not only because the technology, among other things, influences language use, but also because it is impossible to create identical situations. For example, Biber and Conrad (2009) compared "a mini-corpus of [e-mail] messages sent to one of the authors" (Biber and Conrad 2009: 181) with a "mini-corpus of [e-forum] postings" (Biber and Conrad 2009: 193) and then draw the conclusion that the number of words "is far higher for e-mail" (Biber and Conrad 2009: 193), although the situation underlying their mini-corpora was not similar at all. Such a conclusion can certainly not be generalized.

There are a number of possible reasons for the much more synchronous-like message length in data set S1, which probably work in combination here. In a breaking news situation, such as a plane crash, the immediately available information tends to be limited and sketchy. Additionally, contributors to the forum generally want to inform other members of the community as fast as possible. To get the information out first and avoid overlap with messages from other users, there is simply no time to write and edit long messages. This near-synchronous use of a mode traditionally classified as asynchronous leads to a pattern of language use usually linked to synchronous CMC modes. The relative brevity of the messages in data set S1 is thus due to the situation, the relatively higher degree of synchronicity of use in S1 than in S2. Synchronicity seems to be more of a situational than a technological variable (cf. Thurlow and Mroczek 2011: xx), at least in cases such as the one in the investigated thread.

## 5.2 Syntactic reductions

The frequency of ellipses of the subject in main clauses of declarative sentences also differs markedly between the data sets S1 and S2. There are a total of 76 instances of ellipsis of the subject in 253 such clauses in data set S1, i.e., the subject is omitted in approximately 30 per cent of these clauses. In contrast to that finding, the subject is omitted in just over 10 per cent of the clauses of this kind in data set S2, where there are 49 instances of subject ellipsis in 463 main clauses of declarative sentences. This means that this type of syntactic reduction, which is characteristic of spoken language and prototypically synchronous

CMC, is about 3 times more frequent in the fast-moving section of the thread than in the slow-moving section (Figure 3).

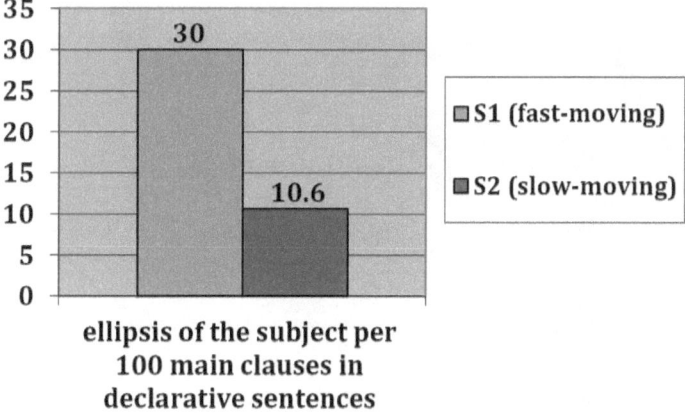

**Figure 3:** Ellipsis of the subject per 100 main clauses in declarative sentences

With respect to the explanation of the difference in frequency of syntactic reductions, the situation is similar to message length (cf. section 5.1.). Most likely, time pressure and the need for speed are key factors in the fast-moving first part of the thread and the subject is thus omitted much more frequently there, creating the "speech-like" impression that is often attributed to synchronous CMC. The slow-moving second part, in contrast, is characterized by much more "writing-like use of language" (Danet 2001: 16), in which ellipses of this kind seem to be much rarer. This confirms the findings on message length (see section 5.1) that the perceived synchronicity seems to be influenced more by the situation than by the technologically defined mode.

## 5.3 Lexical shortenings

Lexical shortenings occur in both data sets. Initialisms such as *btw* for 'by the way,' contractions such as *it's* for 'it is' and clippings such as *approx* for 'approximately' are the most frequent types of abbreviated lexical forms in the corpus. Comparing the overall frequency of lexical shortenings in both data sets, however, yields a much higher frequency in data set S1. This data set from the fast-moving beginning of the thread contains almost exactly 5 lexical shortenings per 100 words, whereas data set S2 contains only about 3.2 abbreviated lexical forms per 100 words (cf. Figure 4). A *Welch*-test confirms that the data sets "S1 (fast moving)" and "S2 (slow moving)" differ statistically concerning the number of lexical shortenings per 100 words ($t(145.12) = 2.37$, $p = .019$, Cohen's $d = .34$); the effect size of mean differences is small.

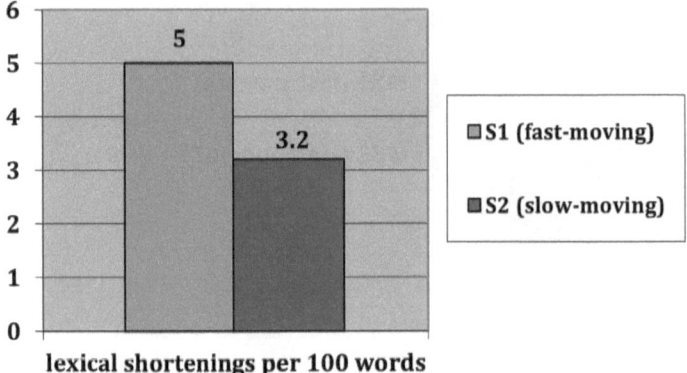

**Figure 4:** Lexical shortenings per 100 words

Abbreviated lexical forms have been found to be particularly characteristic of synchronous CMC modes as well as of modes with limited length of individual messages, such as texting (as discussed above). As forum contributions are generally not character-restricted, the fairly high frequency of lexical shortenings in data set S1 is an indicator of a considerably higher degree of synchronicity than in S2 and likely due to the fast pace of this section of the thread and the ensuing time pressure to produce and send off messages quickly. Again, the frequent use of a feature associated with synchronous CMC on an allegedly asynchronous online discussion forum shows that the synchronicity of use of the same CMC technology can influence language use fundamentally.

# 6 Conclusion

The concept of *synchronicity* has played a prominent role in CMC research ever since Kiesler, Siegel, and McGuire (1984) distinguished CMC technologies by the synchronicity of participation of those involved in the communication (cf. Section 2). Based on the empirical analysis of two subcorpora compiled from the same thread on an online discussion forum, i.e., a mode that is traditionally labeled as asynchronous in CMC research, the study presented here found that linguistic features regarded as characteristic of synchronous CMC modes are by no means restricted to the latter type. The first data set "S1 (fast-moving)," from an early and fast-moving section of the thread, is characterized by short average message length and a high frequency of syntactic reductions as well as lexical shortenings. All of these features are said to be characteristic of synchronous CMC and thus indicate a high degree of synchronicity of use, most likely related to the time pressure to get the message out as fast as possible. In contrast, the individual contributions in data set "S2 (slow-moving)," from a later and slower-moving section of the thread, contain a significantly higher average number of words and a considerably lower frequency of both syntactic reductions and abbreviated lexical forms. In line with the longer time gap between individual contributions in data set S2, this finding indicates a much lower degree of synchronicity of language use than in data set S1. Obviously, allegedly asynchronous modes can be used synchronously (or quasi-synchronously) as well.

As the two data sets were taken from different sections of the same thread of an online discussion forum to ensure maximum comparability and eliminate the so-called medium factor, the fundamental difference in language use between the two data sets cannot be caused by the mode. In response to the research questions, the findings of the analysis indicate that there can be considerable variation in language use within the same mode, which is related to differences in synchronicity of use of this mode. This study of an online discussion forum thus shows that a mode may be heterogeneous and gives empirical support to claims such as Baron's (2008: 16), who said about another mode, in this case email, that "[t]rying to characterize email style with a 'one size fits all' definition is about as meaningless as describing an 'average' American meal." Claims in the literature, such as Baron's (cf. also Section 2), and the findings of the present study seem to suggest that the binary distinction of *synchronous* and *asynchronous* CMC modes is conceptually problematic and not necessarily closely linked to actual patterns of language use.

There is, however, a need for categories that facilitate the systematic description and explanation of language use in electronically-mediated contexts, and Herring (2007: 14) is probably right when she says that "[s]ynchronicity is [...] a robust predictor of structural complexity, as well as many pragmatic and interactional behaviors, in computer-mediated discourse." Since electronically-mediated communication is different from traditional speech and writing – speech in face-to-face and mediated contexts such as telephone or video calls is, as a rule, synchronous and traditional writing is generally, with very few exceptions, asynchronous – in that synchronicity is variable within individual modes, this CMC-specific variability has to be accounted for in research on electronically-mediated communication.

The findings of the study presented here confirm, at least with regard to the analyzed thread from an English-based discussion forum, that synchronicity is indeed a factor that influences language use online, but also show that patterns of language use linked to synchronicity may be more closely connected to the situation than to the technology. Contrary to the terminology of Thurlow and Mroczek (2011: xx), synchronicity would thus be a situational factor rather than a technological factor (cf. also Herring 2007: 10). Just as situations are arranged on a continuum between extremes, synchronicity as a situational factor in text-based CMC should also be interpreted as a continuum with asynchronous and synchronous (or quasi-synchronous) communication as opposite poles. As a result, I would suggest that we should rather speak of different degrees of *synchronicity of use* in CMC research than binarily of synchronicity of mode, despite the fact that the traditional "either-or category" is certainly easier to operationalize. In the shape of the concept of synchronicity of use, synchronicity could thus continue to serve as a meaningful factor in the description of CMC, while at the same time reflecting the reality of the electronically-mediated environment of language use more accurately.

More systematic empirical research on different kinds of electronically-mediated communication and different situations is necessary before we can draw more far-reaching conclusions. However, the study presented here, albeit limited to the analysis of data from one English-based discussion forum, seems to contribute empirical evidence to support the claims in the literature (cf. Section 2) which suggest that the binary distinction of synchronous and asynchronous CMC modes has always been, at least to a certain extent, a convenient fiction, essentially ignoring the fact that particularly so-called asynchronous modes have always been used in more or less synchronous ways. The suggested change from synchronicity of mode to synchronicity of use addresses just one aspect of the need to rethink many of the established categories in CMC research to better reflect the ever-changing environment of language use in electronically-mediated contexts. This is particularly necessary now, because binary distinctions such as the (a-)synchronicity of CMC modes are becoming increasingly blurred and problematic due to the convergence of CMC modes and the spread of an always-online culture.

# 7 References

Androutsopoulos, Jannis. 2006. Introduction: Sociolinguistics and computer-mediated communication. *Journal of Sociolinguistics* 10(4). 419–438.
Baron, Naomi S. 2003. Language of the Internet. In Ali Farghaly (ed.), *Handbook for language engineers*, 59–127. Stanford: CSLI Publications.

Baron, Naomi S. 2008. *Always on: Language in an online and mobile world.* Oxford et al.: Oxford University Press.

Baym, Nancy. 2009. Language in computer-mediated communication. In Jacob L. Mey (ed.), *Concise encyclopedia of pragmatics*, 438–444. 2nd edn. Amsterdam: Elsevier.

Beißwenger, Michael & Angelika Storrer. 2008. Corpora of computer-mediated communication. In Anke Lüdeling & Merya Kytö (eds.), *Corpus linguistics: An international handbook* (Vol. 2), 292–309. Berlin & New York: Mouton de Gruyter.

Biber, Douglas & Susan Conrad. 2009. *Register, genre and style.* Cambridge: Cambridge University Press.

Bieswanger, Markus. 2007. 2 abbrevi8 or not 2 abbrevi8: A contrastive analysis of different space- and time-saving strategies in English and German text messages. In Floyd, Simeon, Taryne Hallet, Sae Oshima & Aaron Shield (eds.), *Texas Linguistic Forum, Volume 50*, n.p. Austin: Texas Linguistic Forum.

Bieswanger, Markus. 2011. The sociolinguistics of texting: Methodological considerations and empirical results. *Sprache und Datenverarbeitung: International Journal for Language Data Processing* 35(1). 7–24.

Bieswanger, Markus. 2013. Micro-linguistic structural features of computer-mediated communication. In Herring, Susan C., Dieter Stein & Tuija Virtanen (eds.), *Pragmatics of computer-mediated communication (Handbooks of pragmatics,* Vol. 9), 463–482. Berlin & New York: Mouton de Gruyter.

Bieswanger, Markus & Frauke Intemann. 2011. Patterns and variation in the language use in English-based online discussion forums. In Martin Luginbühl & Daniel Perrin (eds.), *Muster und Variation in den Medien* (Reihe Sprache und Kommunikation in den Medien), 157–187. Bern: Lang.

Bolander, Brook & Miriam Locher. 2010. Constructing identity on facebook: Report on a pilot study. In Karen Junod & Didier Maillat (eds.), *Performing the self*, 165–187. Tübingen: Narr.

Cho, Thomas. 2010. Linguistic features of electronic mail in the workplace. *Language@Internet* 7, article 3: 1–28. http://www.languageatinternet.org/articles/2010/2728/cho.pdf (accessed February 16, 2013).

Cohen, Jacob. 1988. *Statistical power analysis for the behavioral sciences.* 2nd edn. New York: Lawrence Erlbaum Associates.

Cole, Jason & Helen Foster. 2008. *Using Moodle.* 2nd edn. Sebastopol: O'Reilly.

Collot, Milena & Nancy Belmore. 1996. Electronic language: A new variety of English. In Susan C. Herring (ed.), *Computer-mediated communication: Linguistic, social and cross-cultural perspectives*, 13–28. Amsterdam & Philadelphia: Benjamins.

Condon Sherri L. & Claude G. Čech. 2010. Discourse management in three modalities. *Language@Internet*, article 6. http://www.languageatinternet.org/articles/2010/2770 (accessed April 25, 2015).

Cox, Anna L. 2014. Digital epiphanies. http://www.digitalepiphanies.org/ (accessed December 22, 2014).

Crystal, David. 2001, 2006. *Language and the Internet.* 2nd edn. Cambridge et al.: Cambridge University Press.

Danet, Brenda. 2001. *Cyberpl@y: Communicating online.* Oxford & New York: Berg.

Danet, Brenda & Susan C. Herring. 2007. Introduction. In Brenda Danet & Susan C. Herring (eds.), *The multilingual Internet: Language, culture and communication online*, 1–39. New York et al.: Oxford University Press.

Dürscheid, Christa. 2004. Netzsprache – ein neuer Mythos. In Michael Beißwenger, Ludger Hoffmann & Angelika Storrer (eds.), *Internetbasierte Kommunikation* (Special Issue of *Osnabrücker Beiträge zur Sprachtheorie 68*), 141–157. Osnabrück: Gilles & Francke.

Garcia, Angel Cora & Jennifer Baker Jacobs. 1999. Eyes of the beholder. Understanding the turn-taking system in quasi-synchronous computer-mediated communication. *Research on Language and Social Interaction* 32(4). 337–369.

Giltrow Janet & Dieter Stein. 2009. Genres in the Internet: Innovation, evolution, and genre theory. In Giltrow Janet & Dieter Stein (eds.), *Genres in the Internet*, 1–25. Amsterdam & Philadelphia: Benjamins.

Hård af Segerstad, Ylva. 2002. *Use and adaptation of written language to the conditions of computer-mediated communication* (Gothenburg Monographs in Linguistics). Gothenburg: Gothenburg University Press.

Herring, Susan C. 2001. Computer-mediated discourse. In Deborah Schiffrin, Deborah Tannen & Heidi Hamilton (eds.), *The handbook of discourse analysis*, 612–634. Oxford: Blackwell.

Herring, Susan C. 2002. Computer-mediated communication on the Internet. *Annual Review of Information Science and Technology* 36. 109–168.

Herring, Susan C. 2007. A faceted classification scheme for computer-mediated discourse. *Language@Internet* 4, article 1. http://www.languageatinternet.org/articles/2007/761 (accessed April 25, 2015).

Herring, Susan C. & Asta Zelenkauskaite. 2008. Gendered typography: Abbreviation and insertion in Italian iTV SMS. In Jason F. Siegel, Traci C. Nagle, Amandine Lorente-Lapole and Julie Auger (eds.), *IUWPL7: Gender in language: Classic questions, new contexts*, 73–92. Bloomington, IN: IULC Publications.

Jucker, Andreas H. & Christa Dürscheid. 2012. The linguistics of keyboard-to-screen communication. A new terminological framework. *Linguistik Online* 56(6). 39–64.

Kiesler, Sara, Jane Siegel & Timothy W. McGuire. 1984. Social psychological aspects of computer-mediated communication. *American Psychologist* 39(10): 1123–1134.

Ko, Kwang-Kyu. 1996. Structural characteristics of computer-mediated language: A comparative analysis of InterChange discourse. *The Electronic Journal of Communication* 6(3). http://www.cios.org/www/ejc/v6n396.htm (accessed August 20, 2013).

Lengel, Lara. 2009. Computer-mediated communication. In William F. Eadie (ed.), *21st century communication: A reference handbook*, 543–549. Thousand Oaks: Sage.

Murelli, Adriano. 2011. *Relative constructions in European non-standard varieties*. Berlin & Boston: de Gruyter.

Murray, Denise E. 1988. Computer-mediated communication: Implications for ESP. *English for Specific Purposes* 7. 3–18.

Plag, Ingo. 2003. *Word-formation in English* (Cambridge textbooks in linguistics). Cambridge: Cambridge University Press.

Quirk, Randolph, Sidney Greenbaum, Geoffrey Leech & Jan Svartvik. 1985. *A comprehensive grammar of the English language*. London: Longman.

Thurlow, Crispin & Kristine Mroczek. 2011. Introduction: Fresh perspectives on new media sociolinguistics. In Crispin Thurlow & Kristine Mroczek (eds.), *Digital discourse: Language in the new media*, xix–xliv. Oxford: Oxford University Press.

Wilson, Peter. 2000. *Mind the gap: Ellipsis and stylistic variation in spoken and written English*. Harlow: Pearson.

Zaphyris, Panayiotis, Chee Siang Ang & Andrew Laghos. 2009. Online communities. In Andrew Sears & Julie A. Sacko (eds.), *Human-computer interaction*, 275–292. Boca Raton: CRC Press.

Nathan LaFave[1]
# Social factors and lexical frequency influencing English adjective gradation in speech and CMC

## 1 Introduction and background

It has now been more than 20 years since the first publication of the *Journal of Computer-Mediated Communication*. In this period of time, studies of computer-mediated communication (CMC) have become increasingly popular, just as the types of digital media that fall under the umbrella of CMC research have become more numerous and more diverse. Often, inquiries into CMC as a communicative medium have focused on the various "limitations and facilitations" (Crystal 2006: 26) that characterize its language use, specifically with respect to whether the properties of various genres of the digital medium situate it more closely to spoken or written language. Baron (2000) viewed CMC as a composite of speech and writing, though one which was entirely its own species. Crystal (2006: 51) went a step further, suggesting an additional component of "electronically mediated properties," which are distinct from properties found in either speech or writing. Researchers have often foregrounded these distinctive features (emoticons, novel abbreviations, and other non-traditional orthography, to name only a few) in their work on CMC – in particular, when investigating communication via Internet Relay Chat (IRC) and instant messaging (IM) (see for instance Baron 2004 and Ling and Baron 2007). This focus was justified, as it is these seemingly unusual properties which have captured the attention of linguists and non-linguists alike. However, many linguists have also argued for the importance of investigating CMC for features, particularly grammatical phenomena, which are not restricted to CMC, but instead exist across communicative modalities. One study which exemplifies both research paradigms is the work of Tagliamonte and Denis (2008).

---

[1] A version of these analyses originally appeared as a paper at NWAV 40 with Gregory Guy, to whom I am indebted for his contributions to that project and this one. I would also like to thank John Singler, Bambi Schieffelin, and members of the NYU Sociolinguistics Lab for their sage advice on various stages of this research. Lastly, I would like to thank Matthew Adams for providing me with his dissertation.

---

**Nathan LaFave,** New York University

The present research seeks to contribute to the literature addressing grammatical phenomena in multiple communicative modalities, with Tagliamonte and Denis (2008) as a primary point of departure. Specifically, I provide statistical analysis of a feature, adjective gradation, which compares a population of both teen and adult IM users to several speech corpora of American English: the Santa Barbara Corpus of Spoken American English (SBCSAE; Du Bois et al. 2000–2005) and the Linguistic Data Consortium Switchboard Corpus (henceforth, Switchboard; Godfrey and Holliman 1993). In addition, the present study investigates social factors as predictors of variation in adjective gradation, a previously untested avenue of inquiry.

Adjective gradation refers to the process by which comparative and superlative adjectives are derived from their root, ungraded forms. The encoding of expressions for making comparisons of degree (and, relatedly, quantities) appears to be a universal property of language, although individual languages can differ in how this is done (Syrett 2014). In English the process of adjective gradation usually occurs in one of two ways. The synthetic (i.e., morphological or inflected) form involves adding *-er* or *-est* to the root adjective to produce the comparative (e.g., *bolder*) and superlative (*boldest*). The analytic (or periphrastic) graded adjective is generated by preceding the adjectival stem with *more* or *most* (*more beautiful, most beautiful*). Some adjectives seem to exclusively take one of the two forms, while many exhibit variation. Internal factors influencing this variation will be introduced in Section 2.

A substantial difference between the present work and that of Tagliamonte and Denis (2008) is the statistical analysis that is brought to bear in examining adjective gradation across multiple modalities (cf. Yates 1996). In their analysis, Tagliamonte and Denis (2008) utilize a large corpus of IM messages collected from Canadian teenagers, as well as speech data from these same individuals. The authors target "well-known IM features" (Tagliamonte and Denis 2008: 3), along with five grammatical features in order to characterize the IM-speech affiliation. The set of grammatical features investigated by Tagliamonte and Denis is comprised of personal pronouns, intensifiers (e.g., *really, so*), quotatives (*be like, said*), future temporal reference (*gonna, will*), and modals of necessity (*have to, gotta*). The authors present evidence that IM has a greater similarity to speech in terms of content of the discourse, based on the similarity in distribution of first-, second-, and third-person pronouns in their speech and IM datasets (i.e., both showed higher rates of first-person pronouns).

Tagliamonte and Denis (2008) contrast these distributions with the distribution of personal pronouns in written data analyzed by Yates (1996) which displayed higher rates of third-person pronouns – a pattern that Yates has also noted in his comparison of spoken and written language to computer conferencing data. The findings of the grammatical feature analysis, however, were not uniform in situating IM alongside spoken language on a written-spoken modality continuum. The authors conclude that speech both "has a more innovative profile" and is "more vernacular" than IM, as the former shows higher rates of incoming forms such as quotative *be like* and the intensifier *so* (Tagliamonte and Denis 2008: 23). Furthermore, IM language consistently exhibits "a wider range of variants than speech and, in particular, contain[s] a higher proportion of standard forms than speech" (Tagliamonte and Denis 2008: 23). Whereas Tagliamonte and Denis (2008) focused on IM data from teens, other researchers on IM have relied on data solely from undergraduate students (Baron 2004; Ling and Baron 2007). The present study includes data from teen and adult populations.

Motivation for including social factors in this study will be presented at the end of the following Section 2, which includes more detailed research background on adjective gradation, as well as the impetus for studying this phenomenon across modalities. Additional information on the speech and IM corpora that comprise the data sources for this research, along with descriptions of social information available for contributors to these corpora, is presented in Section 3. Section 4 details the methods utilized to code and otherwise prepare the data for analysis. Section 5 presents the analysis itself, with Section 6 providing further discussion and concluding thoughts.

# 2 Adjective gradation

Adjective gradation has been a significant topic of linguistic inquiry, not only as an object of study itself, but also as evidence for certain theoretical and cognitive processes. As an example of the latter, comparatives have served as one of the main focal points in debates on the existence of competition-based models of "blocking" at or above the word level (Poser 1992; Kiparsky 2005; Embick 2007; Boyd 2007; LaFave 2014). Poser (1992) argued that "the acceptability of the periphrastic [analytic] forms is inversely related to that of the lexical [synthetic] forms" and concluded that "the only plausible explanation" is that the existence of a grammatically acceptable synthetic form of graded adjective (e.g., *faster*) blocks the use of an analytic form of the same root (*more fast*). However, experimental research which elicited acceptability ratings from speakers of American English for analytic and synthetic forms of comparatives and superlatives showed that while this inverse relationship did obtain for acceptability of high frequency root adjectives, it did not hold for low frequency stems (LaFave,

2015). This finding poses a complication for blocking models since they are not selectively applied to word roots based on criteria related to lexical frequency. Further discussion of the effect of frequency on adjective gradation is included in Section 2.1.

Additional investigations involving adjective gradation include Boyd's (2007) use of a judgment task of analytic and synthetic graded forms as a way of assessing off-line and on-line processing. Syrett (2014) has looked to young children's elicited production of graded adjectives to determine how they make comparisons and track quantities – both fundamental components of human cognition. Finally, and of the greatest relevance to the present work, a number of corpus linguistics investigations into the nature of the phenomenon itself have sought to assess which internal factors influence the variation that occurs between graded forms. These are introduced in the following section.

## 2.1 Linguistic factors

There already exist several excellent accounts of the history of adjective gradation and corpus linguistics investigations into adjective gradation: chief among the latter are Hilpert (2008) and Mondorf (2009). I refer the reader to these texts for a more thorough background on this phenomenon. Here I briefly summarize a few of the many linguistic variables that researchers have considered, as well as the findings that are relevant to the present investigation.

The number of syllables in the word root has been identified as the primary determinant of which form an adjective takes when undergoing gradation (Quirk et al. 1985; Hilpert 2008), though the picture is substantially more complicated than the earliest of these investigations presumed. Quirk et al. stated that "monosyllabic adjectives normally form their comparison by inflection" and "trisyllabic or longer adjectives can only take periphrastic forms" (1985: 461). Leech and Culpeper (1997) report that approximately 99% of monosyllables extracted from the British National Corpus (BNC) (BNC Consortium 2007, see also Leech 1992) and Lancaster-Oslo-Bergen Corpus (LOB) (Johansson, Leech and Goodluck 1978) are produced with synthetic form. Although Quirk et al. (1985) allude to possible variation in monosyllabic adjectives, disyllabic adjectives are seen as the main locus for variation: all disyllabic adjectives have the analytic form available to them, but many can also take the synthetic form. However, the list of disyllabic adjectives that most readily accept the synthetic form is narrowly encompassed by the subset that ends in an unstressed vowel /o/ or /i/ (as distinct from /li/), /l̩/, or /ɚ/ (Quirk et al. 1985: 462). Thus, *blatant* will likely become *more blatant*, whereas *happy* could become either *more happy* or *happier*. As Hilpert (2008: 399) notes, the disyllables in the BNC and LOB corpora show much more variation in form than the monosyllables in these corpora: disyllables in the BNC are 51.3% synthetic and disyllables in the LOB are 42.1% synthetic (cf. Kytö and Romaine 1997).

Lexical frequency, as measured in a number of different ways, has been shown to have a significant effect on the form of graded adjectives in many investigations of the phenomenon. Hilpert's (2008) statistical analysis of comparatives from the BNC included two measures of lexical frequency, the first adopted from Quirk et al. (1985) and the second from Mondorf (2003). Quirk et al. pointed to the raw frequency of the root as a determinant in whether an adjective favored synthetic or analytic form, such that "many of the occurrences of *-er/-est* adjectives [in their dataset] represent a small number of relatively frequent adjectives" (1985: 463). That is, the authors observed a tendency for higher frequency word roots to prefer synthetic form. Hilpert (2008: 396, 402) elaborated on the effect of raw frequency when he suggested that this variable underlies the difference between adjectives like *easy*, which is highly frequent (N = 14,760 in the BNC) and strongly prefers the synthetic form (*easier*), and *choosy*, which has the same morphophonological properties but is less frequent (N = 49) and does not show this tendency. In addition to raw frequency, Hilpert tested a measure which involves a ratio of the occurrence within the corpus of the adjective in its graded form (*prettier, more pretty*) compared to the occurrence of the root adjective (*pretty*) (cf. Mondorf 2003). This frequency ratio is an attempt to provide a measurement for how readily the root adjective lends itself to gradation. More recently, experimental work eliciting participant judgments on graded adjectives found support for the significance of the within-corpus, raw root frequency measurement (LaFave 2015) which is employed in the present study.

## 2.2 Previously unanalyzed factors

Several gaps still exist within the study of adjective gradation. For example, superlatives have largely been ignored in the corpus literature, which has focused on comparatives. Notable exceptions include the work of Kytö and Romaine (1997) and Leech and Culpeper (1997), which included both comparatives and superlatives. However, these studies did not analyze statistically whether synthetic or analytic realizations were conditioned by comparative versus superlative gradation. As mentioned briefly in the introduction, another absence in the research on adjective gradation is consideration of social factors. Their effect was hypothesized at least as far back as Kytö and Romaine (1997), but the research to test the hypotheses was not carried out. The present work seeks to address both of these gaps in the corpus linguistics literature, investigating comparative and superlative forms and potential social conditioning facts.

In addition to the desire to fully delineate the full spectrum of variation for this phenomenon, the inclusion of still more factors (beyond those outlined in Section 2.1) in a quantitative analysis of adjective gradation is motivated by the following fact. Diachronic studies of adjective gradation show an increase in rates of the synthetic form and a corresponding decrease in rates of the analytic form between Late Middle and Early Modern English and Modern English (Kytö and Romaine 1997). It remains to be seen whether this tendency towards synthetic forms obtains within a time period of Modern English and, if it does, whether the change is characterized by differences between, for instance, men and women or among speakers with varying levels of education.

Furthermore, there are a number of reasons to situate adjective gradation as a point of comparison for IM and spoken American English. Whereas many grammatical phenomena, including those investigated by Tagliamonte and Denis (2008), have three or more different variants available for speakers to choose from, adjective gradation in English has only two options: the synthetic (*happier*) and analytic (*more happy*) forms.[2] Thus, a binary dependent variable such as adjective gradation should facilitate comparison of IM with spoken and written modalities, as the envelope of potential patterns of graded form distribution is limited. That is, with this binary variable, a given modality can display either higher rates of synthetic forms, higher rates of analytic forms, or comparable rates of synthetic and analytic forms.

However, previous studies of adjective gradation have strongly privileged traditional (non-CMC) written sources. Almost all of the corpus investigations have involved corpora of Modern British English, or else Late Middle English (Kytö 1996), and these data have typically come from formal, written sources. For instance, two corpora that figure prominently in the adjective gradation research are the aforementioned BNC and LOB. The LOB is comprised entirely of written texts, the majority of which are academic works or newspaper articles and hence assumed to be quite formal in nature. The BNC contains both traditional written and speech data; however, the data sources are 90% traditional

---

2 Though see González-Díaz (2007) for discussion of a third – albeit very rare – option, double comparisons, which combine both the analytic and synthetic forms (*most excellentest*). This construction is so exceedingly infrequent as to necessitate being set aside in essentially all accounts of adjective gradation. For instance, Kytö and Romaine (1997) uncovered 10 examples in their analysis of the spoken portion of the BNC that contains approximately 10 million words. Two instances occur in the speech data collected for this study: *more stricter* and *more healthier*.

written and 10% spoken. One of the only corpus studies of American English adjective gradation is Adams (2014) (though see also Lindquist 1998, 2000), which includes a large dataset of comparatives extracted from the Corpus of Contemporary American English (COCA). These data were analyzed primarily to determine the effects of several syntactic factors on adjective gradation. However, COCA also heavily favors traditional written sources with approximately 368 million words of text data (79% of the total corpus, from highly formal academic journals and newspapers, and – in comparison to speech and CMC – relatively formal magazines and fiction sources), as opposed to 95 million words of speech data (21%).

A notable exception to the focus on formal written texts when investigating adjective gradation is Kytö and Romaine (1997), which looked at a subset of spoken British English data from the BNC. A footnote in Leech and Culpeper (1997: 372–373) points out differences in overall comparative form distribution between written BNC data and spoken BNC data analyzed by Kytö and Romaine (1997). That is, the speech data showed 84% synthetic forms and 16% analytic forms, while the written data displayed 74.7% synthetic and 25.3% analytic forms. Leech and Culpeper suggest that "the different distribution is perhaps not surprising, given that in speech adjectives tend to be relatively simple in structure and thus predisposed towards inflectional [synthetic] comparison, whereas in writing adjectives tend to relatively complex... and [are] thus predisposed towards periphrastic [analytic] comparison" (1997: 373). The authors call for further investigation into the extent to which the medium influences choice of graded form, which they considered "an important area of investigation" (1997: 371). Thus, adjective gradation remains ripe for corpus inquiry that specifically takes into consideration the communicative medium itself – particularly for English in CMC. This study explores whether users of IM tend toward synthetic gradation (perhaps because they employ simple adjectives such as those in spoken language) or show a predisposition toward analytic comparison (as a result of utilizing complex adjectives like those in written language).

An additional benefit of utilizing CMC (and modern speech corpora) as a source for investigating grammatical variation, beyond the ability to examine modality itself as a predictor of variation, is that CMC also represents an excellent locus for the analysis of social factors, which have yet to be considered at all in corpus research on adjective gradation. Thus, the present work is the first research on this grammatical feature to examine social factors, including age, sex, education level, and American English dialect region.

## 3 Data collection

### 3.1 Instant messaging corpus

The IM data come from a corpus made available to me by a professor at a large university on the East Coast who collected IM examples from students. The corpus comprises two collections of self-reported copies of IM conversations between friends or acquaintances within different social networks. These social networks center around ten separate students who collected and reported these data. Therefore, these collections may be understood as interactions occurring in ten different social networks which included a total of 65 speakers who produced graded adjectives. One collection contained IM from speakers, almost all of whom were undergraduate students between the ages of 18–22, from nine friendship networks. A second collection contained IM conversations from a single social network of high school speakers between the ages of 14–18. Information is provided on the speakers' sex, age, and education level. The speakers' geographic region was provided for only some of the speakers in this corpus.

Every instance of adjective gradation was extracted from the IM corpus. As adjective gradation is a fairly infrequent phenomenon, the two IM collections yielded a total of 460 graded adjective tokens. Both IM collections were predominantly conversations involving two participants. If enough tokens had been extracted from both of the IM collections in the corpus, then in addition to comparing the IM data to the spoken data (described in Section 3.2), a further analysis would have allowed for a comparison of age and/or education level effect (on a reduced scale) between the two IM collections. However, only 38 tokens were produced in the high school dataset, so all of the IM tokens were coded as being in the Young age category (with the exception of one middle-aged speaker, who was coded as such). The corpus is therefore not ideal in terms of disentangling the potential effects of age and modality. Future work will more systematically collect IM data from users across age groups in order to test any age-related hypotheses.

### 3.2 Spoken corpora

As mentioned above, the spoken data come from two sources which were accessed online: Switchboard and SBCSAE. The SBCSAE is predominantly made up of face-to-face conversations which range from informal social settings (e.g., talk among family members during home meals) to comparatively more formal situations (e.g., classroom lectures and town hall meetings). The Switchboard corpus contains conversations between pairs of participants speaking to each other over the telephone. The participants do not know one another prior to the interaction. Thus, these data represent a single speech style (Labov 1972) – one that likely falls somewhere on the formality continuum between the two extremes demonstrated by the SBCSAE data. Speech in both corpora is transcribed and information is available on the speakers' sex, age, education level, and geographic region (though gaps in this information do exist for some speakers).

In order to obtain an amount of speech data comparable to the total number of graded adjectives collected from the IM corpora, as well as to have comparable numbers of speakers among the corpora, I chose speakers at random from the SBCSAE and Switchboard corpus and exhaustively extracted the graded adjectives from their speech. 60 speakers from the SBCSAE yielded 257 graded adjectives, with an additional 65 speakers from the Switchboard corpus contributing 252 graded adjectives.

## 4 Methods

The description of the speech and IM data in the previous section included the observation that social factors were noted for many of the speakers in those corpora (including age group, sex, education level, and dialect region), but that for a number of speakers (over half), one or more of these factor groups was unknown. For this reason, the collected data lend themselves well to variable rule statistical modeling with a program such as Goldvarb (Sankoff, Tagliamonte and Smith 2005): Goldvarb permits tokens with unknown values in certain factor groups to be removed from the stepwise logistic regression involving those factor groups, while including that token for consideration elsewhere. As adjective gradation is fairly infrequent in both speech and IM, having to set aside a majority of tokens because they are missing information for one or more of the numerous social factors investigated in this study would be prohibitive.

A preliminary survey of the data (total N = 969) revealed that a substantial number of the collected adjectives were the word *good* (N = 185), which was the most frequent adjective in the dataset. The adjective *good* in these data was found to take the synthetic form (*better, best*) in every single case. There are two characteristics of *good* that likely contribute to its categorical use of the synthetic form. The first is that this word is far and away the most frequent graded adjective, not only among the collected data for this study but in other, significantly larger corpora as well. A search of the spoken data in the Corpus of Contemporary American English (COCA), a corpus subset with approximately 95 million words, revealed *good, better,* and *best* were the most frequent examples of root, comparative, and superlative forms of adjectives, respectively (Davies 2008–). Table 1 shows the raw counts of each form among the spoken portion of COCA.

**Table 1:** Frequency of three most numerous root, comparative, and superlative adjective forms in spoken subset of COCA

| Rank | Root | | Comparative | | Superlative | |
|---|---|---|---|---|---|---|
| | Adjective | N | Adjective | N | Adjective | N |
| 1 | *good* | 138,537 | *better* | 20,567 | *best* | 28,325 |
| 2 | *new* | 86,673 | *higher* | 7,413 | *latest* | 11,347 |
| 3 | *great* | 64,282 | *worse* | 7,329 | *biggest* | 9,931 |

The other characteristic which makes *good* exceptional among the adjectives in this study is the fact that its synthetic forms are suppletive: the comparative (*better*) and superlative (*best*) forms have a stem that is not the same as the root form, *good*. There is a very small class of adjectives with suppletive graded forms in English – *good* (*better, best*), *bad* (*worse, worst*), one of the variants for *far* (*further, furthest* [also *farther, farthest*]) and a limited use of *old* (*elder, eldest*), as when referring to siblings (Bobaljik 2011). While two tokens of graded *bad* were also collected, none of the other suppletive adjectives appear in the dataset. The two tokens of *bad* were not removed from the analysis due to the fact that, surprisingly, one appeared with analytic gradation (*most bad*) in the IM corpus.

Since *good* did not exhibit any variation with respect to graded form, all of these tokens were set aside prior to the analyses in the following section; *good* is the only individual word root that was excluded in this way. The remaining dataset contained 784 tokens. All remaining collected data were coded for three internal factors: number of root syllables, degree of comparison, and lexical frequency. Each of these factors will be addressed in turn. The number of root syllables variable ranged from monosyllables to roots with five syllables. However, Goldvarb revealed a knockout for roots with three or more syllables, such that they took analytic form in every case (e.g., *more romantic, most credible, more applicable, most enthusiastic, more unsanitary*). Thus, only monosyllables (N = 404) and disyllables (N = 186) among these data are considered for the number of root syllables variable. All graded adjectives were coded for their degree of comparison, whether comparative (N = 562) or superlative (N = 222).

The final internal factor group is lexical frequency. The relatively small range of raw, within-corpus lexical frequencies (especially compared to much larger studies such as Hilpert 2008 and LaFave 2015) was coded as a binned factor group with four levels determined by how many instances of each adjective occurred in the collected dataset: Very Low (1–5 tokens; N = 360), Low (6–9 tokens; N = 78), High (10–20; N = 154), Very High (≥21; N = 192). Similar to the knockout in the number of root syllables factor group, the factor level with the greatest lexical frequency (Very High) appeared with only one graded form. In this case, the highest frequency words only took synthetic form (*bigger, easiest*). This strong preference for synthetic form among the highest frequency roots is in keeping with previous findings (Hilpert 2008). Very High frequency tokens were therefore omitted, with the result that lexical frequency was analyzed as a ternary variable (with possible values Very Low, Low, and High).

In addition to these three internal factor groups, five external factors were considered for the variable rule analysis. The first of these external factors is the communicative modality in which the token was uttered. Tokens were coded as being produced by either speech or instant messaging, depending on whether they were extracted from the SBCSAE and Switchboard corpora (N = 431) or the IM corpus (N = 353). The other four external factors[3] are social attributes of the speakers who produced the tokens: the speaker's age, sex, dialect region, and education level. Speakers' ages[4] were analyzed as a ternary variable – Young (speakers under 30; N = 438), Middle (ages 31–59; N = 292), and Older (ages 60 and above; N = 45). Sex was a binary variable with factor levels female (N = 439) and male (N = 345). Dialect region was coded very broadly into five different geographic areas: Northeast, Mid-Atlantic and New York City (N = 77), North and South Midlands (N = 216), Inland North (N = 44), South (N = 64), and West (N = 86).

The final social factor that was coded for speakers' tokens was their education level. Originally this factor group had four categories that consisted of speakers with Less than High School education (N = 5), High School (N = 68), Undergraduate (N = 503), and Graduate (N = 110) education levels. However, due to the paucity of tokens from speakers who had less than a high school education level, the first two groups were subsequently combined as High School or Less (N = 73). It is important to note that there is a degree of correlation between the age group and education level factor groups. These two variables are not completely collinear, because there are speakers in each age group who represent each of the different levels of education. However, to some degree these factors are measuring the same thing, since some of the youngest speakers in the Young

---

[3] Since information on each social factor is not provided for every speaker, Ns will not necessarily show the same total in each case.
[4] Recall that age and modality for the IM corpora are synonymous or, at minimum, covarying.

(under 30) age group would not have had the opportunity to attain either an undergraduate or a graduate level education. This relationship is in fact true for any categorical analysis of education level and age that includes American speakers under the age of 23 as contributors to its dataset.

Many more internal factor groups exist which could have been included – for example, a number of phrase-level prosodic and syntactic properties which have been shown to significantly influence variation in graded form (Mondorf 2003; Hilpert 200; Adams 2014), not to mention phonological variables (Kytö and Romaine 1997; Leech and Culpeper 1997; Lindquist 1998; Mondorf 2003; Hilpert 2008). However, these additional variables were not examined in the present study in order to focus the analysis on communicative modality and the speakers' social characteristics.

# 5 Results and analysis

Variable rule analysis was performed on all data (excluding the tokens of the adjective *good*, as previously mentioned) using Goldvarb. Table 2 shows all factor groups selected as significant by Goldvarb, as well as their factor weights (in bold) and the quantity of tokens for each factor level. Factor weights indicate the degree to which the factor favors synthetic gradation over analytic gradation, with possible values ranging between 1 and 0. Factor weights greater than 0.5 indicate a preference for synthetic form, while those less than 0.5 indicate a preference for analytic form. Factor weights of exactly 0.5 show no preference. The further a factor weight is from 0.5 (i.e., the closer it is to 1 or 0), the greater the preference for one variant over the other. The input ($P_0$) indicates the average tendency for synthetic gradation in the dataset.

Two linguistic and two social factor groups were selected as significant contributors to variation in the graded form of the adjectives in this study: number of syllables, lexical frequency, education level, and sex (Table 2). The number of syllables factor group replicates the findings of previous research: monosyllables (*older*) prefer synthetic form (94.1% synthetic, 5.9% analytic), whereas, compared to the input level ($P_0$) of 84.6% synthetic, disyllables (*more famous*) prefer analytic form (53.8% synthetic, 46.2% analytic). Low frequency roots (e.g., *more fun*; 69.2% synthetic, 20.8% analytic) and especially Very Low frequency roots (*more bitchy*; 26.7% synthetic, 83.3% analytic) favored analytic form more than adjectives with High frequency roots (*longer*; 89.6% synthetic, 10.4% analytic), though only Very Low frequency roots actually exhibited higher rates of analytic form than synthetic form. This pattern has also been observed by others, but only with continuous measures of frequency (Mondorf 2003; Hilpert 2008). Thus, these results suggest that analyzing lexical frequency using binned measures of within-corpus frequency can yield comparable results to other measures of lexical frequency, such as those outlined in Section 2.1.

Speakers with lower levels of education were more likely to use synthetic forms, such that individuals with a High School (or Less) level of education strongly preferred synthetic gradation and individuals with a Graduate level education strongly preferred analytic gradation. Finally, women in these corpora show greater use of synthetic forms, while men favored analytic forms.

**Table 2:** Significant factor groups in Goldvarb analysis for synthetic (vs. analytic) adjective gradation (factor weights in bold)

| | | | |
|---|---|---|---|
| Number of Syllables | One<br>N = 404<br>**0.666** | Two<br>N = 186<br>**0.182** | |
| Lexical frequency | High<br>N = 154<br>**0.508** | Low<br>N = 78<br>**0.365** | Very Low<br>N = 360<br>**0.290** |
| Education level | High School (or less)<br>N = 73<br>**0.659** | Undergraduate<br>N = 503<br>**0.514** | Graduate<br>N = 110<br>**0.333** |
| Sex | Female<br>N = 439<br>**0.547** | Male<br>N = 345<br>**0.440** | |

Non-significant factor groups: modality, degree of comparison, age group, dialect region input ($P_0$) = 0.846, log likelihood = −144.343, $p < 0.01$

The relative effect strength for each factor group can be determined by subtracting the factor weight with the lowest value from the factor weight with the highest value. The higher the relative effect strength, the more that particular factor group influences the variation in graded form. As may be seen in Table 3, the number of syllables factor group shows the largest effect size, followed by education level, lexical frequency, and speaker sex. These data suggest that the social factor education level, which has not been included in previous corpus research, has a larger effect size than even lexical frequency, a factor which Hilpert (2008), among others, has shown to be a substantive predictor of graded form.

Table 3: Ranking of significant factor groups in model by relative effect strength

| Variable | Number of syllables | > | Education level | > | Lexical frequency | > | Sex |
|---|---|---|---|---|---|---|---|
| Relative effect strength | 484 | | 326 | | 218 | | 107 |

The two social factor groups determined to be significant by the statistical analysis will be addressed further in subsections 5.2–5.3, following a more detailed look at communicative modality and the distribution of graded forms in the spoken and IM corpora. In the evaluation of these external factor groups, it will often be instructive to break down the dataset along the lines of number of root syllables and lexical frequency, in order to determine how proportions of monosyllables vs. disyllables and High vs. Low vs. Very Low frequency roots are modulated by the external variables (and vice versa).

## 5.1 Communicative modality

The distribution of graded forms in each medium is such that speech showed a higher rate of synthetic gradation in monosyllables and disyllables (87.4% synthetic, 12.6% analytic) than IM (73.9% synthetic, 26.1% analytic). This trend does not make sense from a perspective of economy, such that IM users might have a greater desire to use the shorter, synthetic form. However, the modality of a token (speech vs. IM) was not selected as a significant predictor of the adjective's form. That is, adjective gradation in the IM data is statistically similar to that of spontaneous speech. The fact that the roughly 14% difference in rates of synthetic and analytic gradation is not significant illustrates the importance of using statistical methods in analyses such as these: without statistical testing, these differences might have been taken at face value. Instead, this finding suggests that some other factor may be accounting for the variation exhibited by the IM and speech data.

As indicated in Section 3, stylistic differences exist in the type of speech that was collected for the SBCSAE and Switchboard corpora. In order to determine whether the adjective gradation in these two corpora might in fact be different, which could then change the relationship between the two speech corpora and the IM corpus as well, a parallel stepwise logistic regression analysis was performed in Goldvarb nearly identical to the one described in Section 4, with the only difference being that the modality factor group was replaced with a corpus factor group with factor levels IM, Switchboard, and SBCSAE. The Switchboard corpus showed slightly lower rates of synthetic gradation (85.6%

synthetic, 14.4% analytic) than the SBCSAE (88.1% synthetic, 11.9% analytic). The results of the statistical analysis for this parallel run were identical to those put forth in Table 2. The corpus factor group, like the original modality factor group, was not found to be statistically significant in determining the form of adjective gradation.

Despite the fact that no statistically significant effect of modality was found, it can nonetheless be informative to compare the distribution of graded forms in the corpora analyzed in this research with proportions available from prior studies. Although an additional variable rule analysis cannot be performed in order to compare the speech and IM data with written and speech data from previous investigations of British English, a preliminary comparison (Table 4) can be made using frequency counts that Leech and Culpeper (1997) and Kytö and Romaine (1997) provide for their data from the BNC and LOB. The BNC "core" written corpus is a representative subsample that Leech and Culpeper (1997) extracted from the much larger BNC corpus of written data. The counts reflect monosyllables and disyllables only, as each corpus had at most one token of analytic gradation in adjectives with three or more root syllables.

**Table 4:** Raw frequency counts for graded form in American English speech/IM (present study) and British English speech (Kytö and Romaine 1997) and text (Leech and Culpeper 1997) corpora

| Corpora (by Modality) | Synthetic form | Analytic form |
|---|---|---|
| **Text** | | |
| BNC "core" written (Leech & Culpeper 1997) | 1,374 | 229 |
| LOB (Leech & Culpeper 1997) | 1,731 | 233 |
| **Speech** | | |
| SBCSAE | 148 | 18 |
| Switchboard | 137 | 23 |
| BNC speech (Kyto & Romaine 1997) | 1,888 | 182 |
| **Instant Messaging** | | |
| IM corpus | 195 | 69 |

The proportion of synthetic to analytic form for each dataset (calculated from the values in Table 4) is presented in Figure 1, from least to most synthetic. What is perhaps most interesting about the pattern displayed in Figure 1 is that it does not display a simple continuum with speech data concentrated on one end and written data on the other, with IM situated either in the middle or nearer to one terminus. Instead, the rate of synthetic gradation in the IM data is much lower than in any corpus containing speech or written data, which are much less clearly delineated from one another.

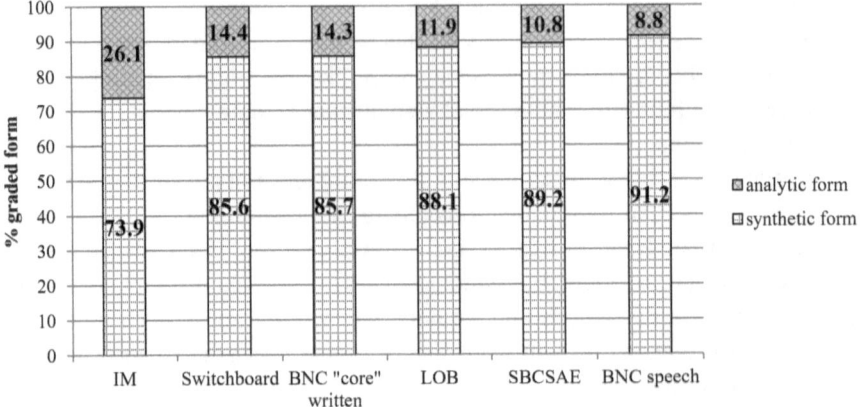

**Figure 1:** Percent synthetic and analytic form of graded adjectives by corpus

A Pearson's chi-squared test reveals a significant difference between the frequency of synthetic and analytic forms in the six corpora containing written, speech, and IM data ($\chi^2 = 78.478$, $df = 5$, $p < 0.001$). This finding indicates that the form that a graded adjective takes and the corpus in which it was aggregated are not independent. What, then, should be made of the fact that both written corpora fall in the middle of the spectrum and are bookended by speech corpora? It is not the case that the inclusion of the count data from the IM corpus forces a significant result; when the IM frequencies are removed from the chi-squared contingency table, the test still achieves significance ($\chi^2 = 28.786$, $df = 4$, $p < 0.001$). One might argue that a simple explanation for the pattern observed in Figure 1 could be that there is a non-random distribution of adjectives with properties shown to influence graded form. Recall that Leech and Culpeper (1997) suggested that spoken language uses structurally less complex adjectives than written language, which would suggest a higher proportion of monosyllabic adjectives[5] in corpora with data from this medium. An increasingly larger amount of monosyllables, which favor the synthetic form, in the corpora ordered from IM to BNC speech (as on the x-axis in Figure 1), could account for the difference in proportions of synthetic form. The same would be true for a non-random distribution of high frequency tokens among different corpora. It is possible to examine the distribution of monosyllables and disyllables

---

5 Leech and Culpeper (1997) might also have included morphologically simple (i.e., monomorphemic) disyllabic adjectives (*acute*, *bizarre*) in this characterization. However, monomorphemic roots only account for 22% of the disyllables collected from the IM and speech corpora in this study.

in all six corpora, but it is not possible to examine the frequency of adjectives in the three corpora analyzed by Kytö and Romaine (1997) and Leech and Culpeper (1997).

Table 5 below shows the distribution of monosyllables and disyllables across the six corpora. If the pattern observed in Figure 1 was a result of a data collection artifact influencing the proportion of monosyllables in the corpora, one would expect to see the proportion of monosyllables in the bottom row of Table 5 increasing from left to right. It is true that the IM corpus has a substantially lower proportion of monosyllables than the other corpora; consequently, this distribution may be a factor in the lower rates of synthetic form for the IM data. However, the BNC speech corpus does not show the highest proportion of monosyllables, nor does the distribution of monosyllables and disyllables in the other four corpora match the pattern shown in Figure 1.

**Table 5:** Percent synthetic gradation for monosyllables and disyllables in speech, IM and text corpora

|  | IM | Switchboard | BNC "core" written | LOB | SBCSAE | BNC speech |
|---|---|---|---|---|---|---|
| Monosyllables | 150 | 126 | 1,221 | 1,518 | 128 | 1,622 |
| Disyllables | 114 | 34 | 382 | 446 | 38 | 448 |
| % Monosyllables | 56.8% | 78.8% | 76.2% | 77.3% | 77.1% | 78.4% |

Furthermore, although the number of syllables in an adjective's root is a substantial determinant in the form that it will take as a comparative or superlative, the rates of synthetic form for the monosyllables, and especially the disyllables, contained in these corpora do not correlate with the proportion of monosyllables to disyllables (Figure 2). Neither is the behavior of the disyllables with respect to graded form in a corpus dependent on the rate of synthetic gradation of the monosyllables from the same medium.

Just as it is useful to break down the corpora in terms of number of root syllables, it is likewise illuminating to separate the corpora according to the other statistically significant internal factor, lexical frequency. The distribution of adjectives in the IM and speech corpora that are analyzed in this study is illustrated by Figure 3, which shows the proportion of High, Low, and Very Low frequency roots in each corpus. The increase in High frequency adjectives and decrease in Very Low frequency adjectives across the corpora in Figure 3 (i.e, IM, Switchboard, SBCSAE) suggest a possible explanation for the corresponding increase in synthetic gradation shown in Figure 1. By extension, it is possible that the differences seen between the IM and speech data which failed to

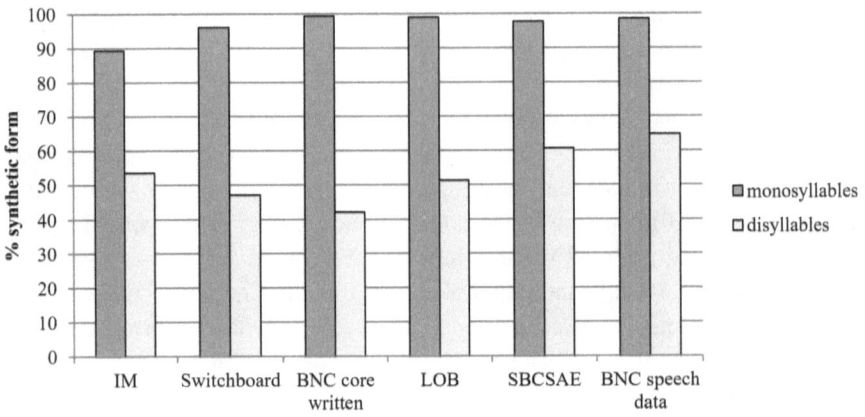

**Figure 2:** Percent synthetic form for graded monosyllables and disyllables by corpus

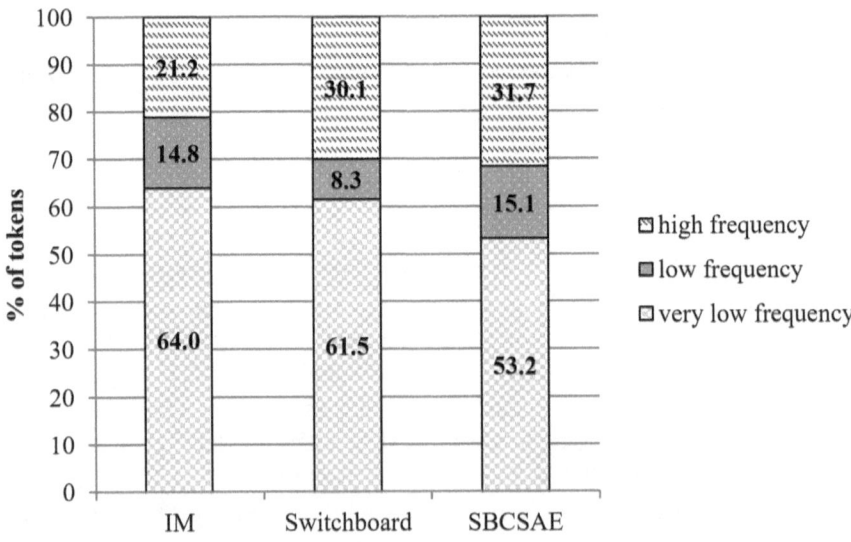

**Figure 3:** Percent of High, Low, and Very Low frequency tokens per corpus

achieve significance are being accounted for in the variation of the dataset by the significant effect of lexical frequency. Without having some measure of lexical frequency from the work carried out by Leech and Culpeper (1997) and Kytö and Romaine (1997), it is impossible to know whether this explanation extends to the corpora they analyzed. Lexical frequency as a point of comparison across communicative modalities is explored further in Section 6.

## 5.2 Education level

The education level of the speaker producing the graded adjective was one of the two social factors which were found to have a statistically significant effect on the form that the gradation took. As education level increases from High School (or less) (factor weight 0.659; 68.5% synthetic) to Undergraduate (0.514; 62.8%) and Graduate (0.333; 59.1%), the rate of synthetic forms decreases. In other words, people with higher levels of education produced a greater proportion of analytic comparatives and superlatives as compared to those with lower levels of education.

One might assume that speakers with a higher education level use infrequent adjectives to a greater extent (for instance, due to their presumably having a larger vocabulary), and this could account for an apparent effect of education level. However, the opposite tendency obtains, as illustrated in Figure 4. Speakers with a high school education level (or lower) exhibit the highest usage of Low and Very Low frequency graded adjectives, as well as the lowest use of high frequency forms. An alternative explanation for why individuals with higher levels of education show higher rates of analytic gradation will be explored in Section 6.

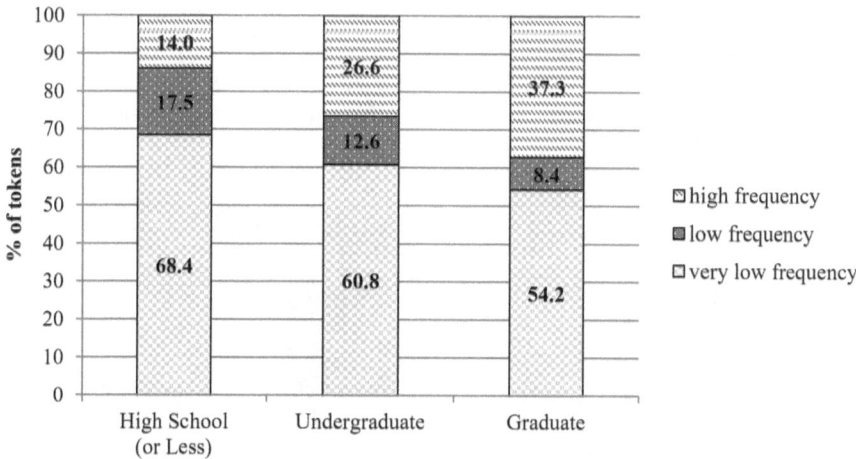

**Figure 4:** Percent of High, Low, and Very Low frequency tokens by education level

As indicated at the end of Section 4, additional analysis is required to separate the education level and age group social factors, owing to the fact that speakers in these corpora who are 18 could not have achieved a graduate level education. Therefore, the significant effect of education level determined by the analysis above could in fact be related to an effect of age. However, when the logistic regression analysis is run with the education level factor group removed, age group is not selected as a significant predictor of variation. This suggests that, while the factor groups are clearly related to some degree, the education level factor group is not masking an effect of age group that would otherwise achieve significance.

## 5.3 Sex

The final factor group in the multivariate analysis that was selected as significant was the speaker's sex. Female speakers produced higher rates of synthetic comparatives and superlatives (64.5% synthetic, 35.5% analytic) than male speakers produced (57.1% synthetic, 42.9% analytic). Unlike with education level, there is no reason to assume that women and men might differ in the extent to which they employ frequent and infrequent graded adjectives. At any rate, a cursory examination of the data reveals women (92%) and men (86%) used comparable, proportions of high frequency roots (a Pearson's chi-squared test indicated no significant difference). Breaking down the analysis of the sex variable along the lines of the number of root syllables proves useful for understanding where the differences between men and women's use of gradation is truly occurring among the collected data. Figure 5 reveals the disyllables as the primary point of differentiation. Female speakers produced much higher rates of synthetic disyllables (62.7%) than male speakers (40.8%), though both groups

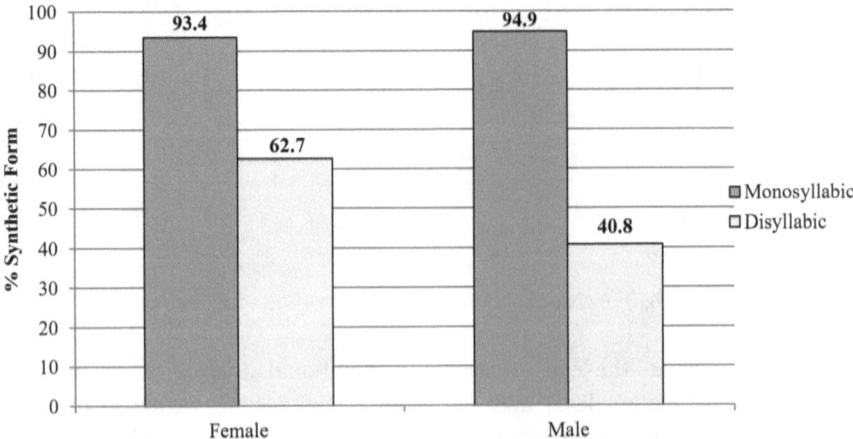

**Figure 5:** Percent synthetic form of graded adjectives by sex and number of root syllables

showed comparable rates of synthetic monosyllables (93.4% and 94.9%, respectively). In the following section, a theory will be presented which attempts to account for this difference.

## 6 Discussion and conclusion

The analysis in the previous section revealed several contributions to our knowledge of the relationship of IM to speech and formal written data with respect to adjective gradation. It also revealed how adjective gradation patterns in language use by different groups of speakers. The key findings are summarized below.
- Adjective gradation did not show a statistically significant difference between instant messaging and speech alone.
    - However, graded form was found to be dependent on the corpus when examining six corpora that represent multiple registers and styles of three different modalities – IM, speech, and formal written language.
- Speaker sex and education level were found to significantly predict choice of graded form:
    - Speakers with higher levels of education made more use of the analytic form.
    - Female speakers showed greater use of the synthetic form, particularly in graded disyllabic adjectives.

In Section 5, evidence was presented that ruled out the effects of speaker sex and education level as stemming from the distribution of lexically frequent roots among speaker groups. An alternative interpretation of these findings is related to the grammatical ideology which holds that more explicit morphosyntactic variants are perceived to be prescriptively "better" by speakers. For instance, complementizer *that* is prescriptively preferred to the null complementizer (Kroch and Small 1978). On this view, the analytic form would be perceived as preferable (more grammatical) because the addition of *more* or *most* to the root is more explicit than the inflected *-er/-est* suffix of the synthetic form. The fact that speakers with higher levels of education produced the greatest number of analytic forms could be taken to suggest that these speakers are more susceptible to, or perhaps are more invested in, this prescriptive ideology.

Turning now to the consideration of speaker sex, it remains to be addressed why female speakers would use more synthetic gradation with their disyllabic adjectives than male speakers. A common pattern in linguistic change from below is that women use higher frequencies of innovative forms than men (Trudgill 1972; Labov 2001). With rates of synthetic form approaching ceiling for monosyllables in nearly all datasets (Kytö and Romaine 1997; Leech and Culpeper 1997) and roots with three or more syllables categorically taking analytic form, disyllables remain the primary locus of variation. Kytö and Romaine indicate that a change toward greater use of the synthetic form (which has been underway since the introduction of the historically newer analytic form of English gradation) may still be ongoing. Thus, women may be leading this change through higher rates of the innovative variants, synthetic graded disyllables (e.g., *lovingest*, attested in the Switchboard corpus), than men. Further investigation into the existence of such a change in progress is required, particularly with a corpus that includes more robust quantities of tokens from speakers and IM users in the Older age group.

This research represents a continuation of analyses on CMC utilizing grammatical features, as well as a comparison of these data with investigations into multiple formal written and speech corpora. The chi-squared tests suggest a less-than-straightforward distribution of written and speech corpora with respect to adjective gradation. However, they also present compelling evidence that IM is not merely an aggregate of grammatical properties from written and spoken media (cf. Baron 2000; Crystal 2006) – IM clearly shows lower rates of synthetic gradation than either speech or written language. Interpreting the corpus distribution in terms of formality of interaction (i.e., academic publications and newspapers are more formal than personal letters, speech at town hall meetings is more formal than family dinners; cf. Labov 1972) does not quite work. Certainly the SBCSAE and BNC spoken data represent a range of social interactions, many of which are much more informal than the telephone conversations in the Switchboard corpus between strangers. Hence, it may be the case that the Switchboard data are stylistically more similar to written language in terms of formality. However, extending this interpretation to the IM data would mean that the IM conversations between friends in their social networks would be the most formal of all the interactions captured by the corpus data, which seems implausible.

It is much more likely that the producers of gradation in the various corpora are making use of different types of adjectives, particularly with respect to lexical frequency. The IM corpus shows the highest percentage of Very Low frequency graded adjectives, which also means that IM users display the greatest variety of adjectives that are attested with gradation (i.e., in terms of *type* versus *token*, IM users produced more types). It is possible that there are fewer restrictions in a visual medium on what adjectives are permitted in comparisons – that is, there is a lower risk associated with making a graded comparison in IM using an adjective that could "sound funny" than if it were actually to be spoken aloud to another person (perhaps because it violates some phonological or semantic rule). This greater freedom of expression does not extend to formal written language, particularly as this modality is rife with "language police" (e.g., teachers, editors) that would discourage non-standard language (Tagliamonte and Denis 2008: 27). Thus, the attestation of many Very Low frequency adjectives among the IM data may be the result of language play among members of a social group, in the same way that Tagliamonte and Denis (2008) discovered teenagers were more likely to mix and match colloquial and formal variants in their IM communications with one another than in their speech, which was more mono-stylistic. The interpretation of these graded adjectives as language play in IM is especially likely in instances where other unconventional language use is involved, for example the attested graded forms *more college-y* and *most non-vampirical*.

It is clear that there is more work to be done in this area: greater numbers of graded adjectives from IM sources would be preferable in order to more thoroughly assess the comparison between communicative modalities that is being made in Section 5.1. If the pattern of synthetic gradation that the corpora display in Figure 1 is indeed a consequence of, in part or total, the distribution of lexically frequent and infrequent forms, it explains why the lexical frequency factor group, but not modality or corpus, was found to be statistically significant in the regression model. However, in order to carry out additional research on this topic and other grammatical features, linguists must continue to not only compile large-scale CMC corpora, but also to make them available for analysis in the same manner as the many excellent, freely available corpora of speech and formal written language.

# 7 References

Adams, Matthew E. 2014. *The comparative grammaticality of the English comparative*. Stanford, CA: Stanford University dissertation.

Baron, Naomi S. 2000. *Alphabet to email: How written language evolved and where it's heading*. London: Routledge.

Baron, Naomi S. 2004. See you online: Gender issues in college student use of instant messaging. *Journal of Language and Social Psychology* 23. 397–423.

BNC Consortium. 2007. *The British National Corpus*. Oxford: Oxford University Computing, version 3, BNC XML edition.

Bobaljik, Jonathan D. 2011. *Universals in comparative morphology: Suppletion, superlatives, and the structure of words*. Cambridge, MA: MIT Press.

Boyd, Jeremy K. 2007. *Comparatively speaking: A psycholinguistic study of optionality in grammar*. San Diego, CA: University of California San Diego dissertation.
Crystal, David. 2006. *Language and the Internet*. New York: Cambridge University Press.
Davies, Mark. 2008–. *The Corpus of Contemporary American English: 425 million words, 1990–present*. http://corpus.byu.edu/coca/ (accessed 12 October 2012).
Du Bois, John W., Wallace L. Chafe, Charles Meyer, Sandra A. Thompson, Robert Englebretson & Nii Martey. 2000–2005. *Santa Barbara Corpus of Spoken American English, Parts 1–4*. Philadelphia: Linguistic Data Consortium.
Godfrey, John & Edward Holliman. 1993. *Switchboard-1 Release 2 LDC97S62*. DVD. Philadelphia: Linguistic Data Consortium.
González-Díaz, Victorina. 2007. On the nature and distribution of English double periphrastic comparison. *The Review of English Studies* 57(232). 623–664.
Hilpert, Martin. 2008. The English comparative – language structure and language use. *English Language and Linguistics* 12(3). 395–417.
Kiparsky, Paul. 2005. Blocking and periphrasis in inflectional paradigms. In Geert Booij & Jaap van Marle (eds.), *Yearbook of morphology*, 113–135. Dordrecht: Springer.
Kroch, Anthony & Cathy Small. 1978. Grammatical ideology and its effect on speech. In David Sankoff (ed.), *Linguistic variation: Models and methods*, 45–55. New York: Academic.
Kytö, Merja. 1996. 'The best and most excellentest way': The rivalling forms of adjective comparison in Late Middle and Early Modern English. In Jan Svartvik (ed.), *Words. Proceedings of an International Symposium, Lund, 25–26 August 1995* (Konferenser, 26), 123–144. Stockholm: Kungl. Vitterhets Historie och Antikvitets Akademien.
Kytö, Merja & Suzanne Romaine. 1997. Competing forms of adjective comparison in Modern English: What could be more quicker and easier and more effective? In Terttu Nevalainen & Leena Kahlas-Tarkka (eds.), *To explain the present: Studies in the changing English language in honour of Matti Rissanen*, 329–52. Helsinki: Memoires de la Société Néophilologique de Helsinki.
Labov, William. 2001. *Principles of linguistic change, Vol. 2: Social factors*. Malden: Blackwell Publishers Inc.
Labov, William. 1972. *Sociolinguistic patterns*. Philadelphia: University of Pennsylvania Press.
LaFave, Nathan. 2015. The most apt experimental investigation of English comparative and superlative formation. *University of Pennsylvania Working Papers in Linguistics* 21(1). Article 16. http://repository.upenn.edu/pwpl/vol21/iss1/16 (accessed 15 May 2015).
LaFave, Nathan. 2014. The *most apt* experimental investigation of English comparative and superlative formation. Poster presented at 38th Penn Linguistics Conference, University of Pennsylvania, 28–30 March.
Leech, Geoffrey N. 1992. 100 million words of English: The British National Corpus. *Language Research* 28(1). 1–13.
Leech, Geoffrey N. & Jonathan Culpeper. 1997. The comparison of adjectives in recent British English. In Terttu Nevalainen & Leena Kahlas-Tarkka (eds.), *To explain the present: Studies in the changing English language in honour of Matti Rissanen*, 353–74. Helsinki: Memoires de la Société Néophilologique de Helsinki.
Lindquist, Hans. 1998. The comparison of English disyllabic adjectives in *-y* and *-ly* in Present-day British and American English. In Hans Lindquist, Staffan Klintborg, Magnus Levin & Maria Estling (eds.), *The major varieties of English: Papers from MAVEN 97*, 205–12. Växjö: Acta Wexionensia.

Lindquist, Hans. 2000. *Livelier* or *more lively?* Syntactic and contextual factors influencing the comparison of disyllabic adjectives. In J. M. Kirk (ed.), *Corpora galore: Analyses and techniques in describing English*, 125–32. Amsterdam: Rodopi.

Ling, Rich & Naomi S. Baron. 2007. Text Messaging and IM: Linguistic Comparison of American College Data. *Journal of Language and Social Psychology* 26. 291–98.

Mondorf, Britta. 2003. Support for *more*-support. In Günter Rohdenburg & Britta Mondorf (eds.), *Determinants of grammatical variation in English*, 251–304. Berlin: Mouton de Gruyter.

Mondorf, Britta. 2009. *More support for* more-*support. The role of processing constraints on the choice between synthetic and analytic comparative forms.* Amsterdam & Philadelphia: John Benjamins.

Poser, William J. 1992. Blocking of phrasal constructions by lexical items. In Ivan Sag & Anna Szabolcsi (eds.), *Lexical matters*, 111–130. Stanford: CSLI Publications.

Quirk, Randolph, Sidney Greenbaum, Geoffrey Leech & Jan Svartvik. 1985. A comprehensive grammar of the English language. New York: Longman.

Sankoff, David, Sali Tagliamonte & Eric Smith. 2005. *Goldvarb X: A variable rule application for Macintosh and Windows.* Toronto: University of Toronto Department of Linguistics.

Syrett, Kristen. 2014. Comparatively speaking: Accounting for children's unexpected interpretations of comparative constructions. Paper presented at Princeton University, Princeton, NJ.

Trudgill, Peter. 1972. Sex, covert prestige and linguistic change in the urban British English of Norwich. *Language in Society* 1(2). 179–195.

Yates, Simeon J. 1996. Oral and written linguistic aspects of computer conferencing: A corpus based study. In Susan C. Herring (ed.), *Computer-mediated communication: Linguistic, social and cross-cultural perspectives*, 29–46. Amsterdam: Benjamins.

Josh Iorio
# Implications of attitudes about non-standard English on interactional structure in the computer-mediated workplace: A story of two modes

## 1 Introduction

Contemporary spoken and written Englishes contain a variety of non-standard phonological, morphological and grammatical features. When attitudes or judgments about non-standard language surface, they can polarize communities. For instance, in the US context, the Oakland Ebonics debate in the 1990s focused on the role of African American Vernacular English (AAVE) in educational institutions, i.e., whether it should be used as the language variety of instruction for students who speak AAVE. Central to the debate were conflicting attitudes and ideologies by the public, politicians and language professionals about the legitimacy of AAVE as a language variety (Wolfram 1998) versus "slang, mutant, lazy, defective, ungrammatical or broken English" (LSA 1997). Although these types of language attitudes were made socially explicit during the Ebonics debate, they exist often silently in the everyday contexts in which speakers interact (Fairclough 2015).

Speakers develop language attitudes about varieties of English and a variety's non-standard features often carry social meaning. A large and still growing body of research on the social meanings associated with features of non-standardness dates back to the late 1960s and has explored social meanings within and between different groups of speakers, e.g., local residents and tourists (Labov 1972), Southern and African American English Speakers (Wolfram 1974), high school students (Eckert 1989), and gay men (Podesva 2007). By the late 1990s, the study of language variation also explored non-standard writing (Androutsopoulos 2000; Jaffe and Walton 2000), particularly in computer-mediated contexts (e.g., Eisenstein 2015; Hinrichs 2012; Squires 2010) such as instant messenger communities (Paolillo 1999; Tagliamonte and Denis 2008), online games (Iorio 2009, 2010), and social networking sites (Squires and Iorio 2014; Thurlow and Mroczek 2011).

---

**Josh Iorio**, Virginia Tech

While all of this work has led to new knowledge about the social meanings of non-standard language, very few studies have examined how language attitudes impact the ways that individuals interact with each other. Research on the impact of language attitudes has typically been limited to: 1) classroom contexts (Jessmer and Anderson 2001) particularly concerning the case of curricular reform (e.g., Tollefson 2012), and 2) national language policy (e.g., Korth 2005; Marley 2004). Although this research has confirmed that language attitudes can shape institutional practice, it does not provide any insight into the role of attitudes in shaping interaction between individuals on an interpersonal level, e.g., in the school, on the bus or at the workplace.

The goal of the research described in this chapter is to explore attitudes about non-standard English and their impact on interaction between professionals collaborating in a computer-mediated workplace. Since these types of workplaces often support interaction through a variety of media and modes, they are uniquely suited to study the interface between attitudes about speech and attitudes about writing. Unlike in other types of interactional settings where participation is voluntary (e.g., on a social networking site), virtual workplaces are sites where interaction is *required*. Conflicting language attitudes are unavoidably brought into contact because interaction between individuals is required in workplace settings.

## 2 Non-standard English in Global Virtual Project Networks

Computer-mediated or virtual workplaces are becoming more common, as a variety of industries such as construction (Colella et al. 2012), software development (Barr and Tessler 1996), and engineering (Vest 2008) are globalizing. In these types of industries, geographically distributed workers from a variety of language backgrounds interact to execute complex projects through technological mediation (Maznevski and Chudoba 2000). *Complex projects* require workers to execute tasks that are both independent and interdependent in nature and thus interaction between workers is a key driver of productivity. For instance, in the construction industry, construction of an airport requires that an architecture team integrate their independent design with the independent construction plan developed by an engineering team. In turn, the design and plan must be executed on-site by a team of contractors. Because the knowledge required to execute complex projects is specialized and specialists are often geographically distributed (Messner 2007), these types of projects are typically executed in

*Global Virtual Project Networks* (GVPNs). GVPNs are "teams of teams" that interact primarily through technology. Because the teams are globally distributed, GVPNs are characterized by their cultural (Shachaf 2008) and linguistic diversity (Henderson 2005) and by their interdisciplinarity (Bletzinger and Lahr 2005).

A variety of challenges to effective collaboration often results from this diversity. For instance, GVPNs are associated with higher instances of conflict (Hinds and Mortensen 2005) and have greater difficulty in establishing trust between teams and team members (Jarvenpaa and Leidner 1999) compared to co-located teams. Their characteristic diversity also requires that GVPNs develop new communication norms and new strategies for work coordination (Nayak and Taylor 2009). Taken together, these interactional challenges result in lower performance of GVPNs when compared to traditional teams across a variety of metrics (Adler and Gunderson 2007; Massey et al. 2001; Shachaf 2008), although performance can be improved over time (Comu et al. 2010). Global industries are particularly keen to develop a better understanding of these challenges in order to leverage the positive aspects of diversity, such as creative problem solving (Lattimer 1998).

Because of its status, English is typically adopted as the language of work interactions (Dubé and Paré 2001) within GVPNs. However, because the workers come from a variety of native language backgrounds with different historical relationships to English, potential exists for the development of cultural "faultlines" (Polzer et al. 2006). Evidence for these faultlines exists in the form of attitudes about different language varieties of spoken and written English. For both speech and writing, language attitudes often focus on linguistic features that deviate from a real or imagined standard variety. Speech may vary from the standard based on a speaker's nationality (Bamgbose 1998), gender (Eckert and McConnell-Ginet 2003), sexuality (Podesva 2007), income (Labov 1972), age (Eckert 1997) or ethnicity (Rickford 1992). Variability in writing involves linguistic choices to use standard or non-standard orthographic forms (Sebba 2003). For instance, Androutsopoulos (2000, p. 528) describes how, for a German punk community, the choice to use non-standard orthography can be viewed as "transgressive," which aligns with the group's positioning outside of German mainstream cultural practice. In such cases, use of non-standard orthography contributes to the development of language attitudes because of the link between orthography and its social meaning to different groups.

Although previous research has served as a foundation for our understanding of how speaking and writing carry social meaning as part of everyday life, surprisingly, very little work has been conducted in professional contexts (cf. Darics 2010 for work on politeness). Because interaction is required for collaborative professional tasks, computer-mediated workplaces are excellent sites in which to study the impact of attitudes on interaction. Additionally, these settings provide a common context in which to compare the impact of attitudes about spoken and written language. Given the mixed-modal character of the computer-mediated workplace, it is surprising that more research has not been conducted in these settings to explore the links between attitudes about speech and writing (cf. Murray 1988).

Because the use of organizational structures like GVPNs is increasing, research aimed at developing a better understanding of how language attitudes about speech and writing can impact the interactional dynamics of geographically distributed work teams must be expanded to keep pace with professional practice. To this end, the following research questions focus on: 1) identifying language attitudes about non-standard English in the discourse of a GVPN, and 2) assessing the impact of these attitudes on interaction between members of the GVPN.

> RQ1: Are language attitudes about non-standard features of English salient in GPVNs?
> RQ2: If so, how do the attitudes impact interactional structure?
> RQ3: Does the impact differ for speech and writing?

## 3 Research design and methodology

In order to explore these questions, an experiment was conducted in Spring 2013 that was designed to approximate the interactional dynamics of a global virtual construction design and planning project. This small-sample, comparative experiment was based on a novel methodological approach. Thus, the goal of this exploratory study is not to forward claims about different language groups or GVPNs as organizational structures, but rather to identify potentially significant relationships between language attitudes and interaction as a "proof of concept" for further research on larger populations in more varied computer-mediated contexts.

The experiment was based on two GVPNs composed of graduate students from universities in the US, the Netherlands and India. Each of the two GVPNs contained two students from each country. In total, twelve students participated in the study with six students per GVPN. Each national team within the two GVPNs was responsible for a different independent component of a complex project. In turn, each component was interdependent with the other components, as the teams were evaluated based on an optimized design that required each component to be effectively integrated.

The Indian teams were responsible for creating the architectural design of the construction project, the Dutch teams were responsible for estimating the cost of construction, and the US teams were responsible for scheduling the construction. To ensure that the teams were interdependent (and thus interaction was required), they were not cross-trained on the tasks assigned to the other teams. For instance, the Indian team had not learned the software used by the Dutch team to conduct the cost estimate. The teams entered the GVPN interactions having already developed their individual project components (i.e., the design, cost estimate, and schedule) and the experimental period began when the teams were required to integrate these components. Changes to one component triggered changes to the other components. For instance, any change in the architectural design of the construction project (e.g., adding or removing windows) warranted a change in both the schedule and cost estimate. Because the three components were tightly integrated, collaboration was required throughout the process in order to create an optimized design.

The experiment was designed to ensure comparable levels of exposure to and competence with English as a non-native language. All US participants were native speakers of American English. Dutch participants were native speakers of Dutch and learned English as part of a compulsory curricular component of their secondary education. All of their graduate courses were taught in English. Participants from India spoke Telugu and started learning English during primary school. As in the Netherlands, English in India is the language of "education, administration, the mass media, science and technology" (Sahgal 1991: 299) and is often associated with an increase in social mobility. In sum, all non-native English speaking participants used English as the language of instruction for four or more years of university education. The common frequency of opportunity for the participants to use English in an academic or technical setting over their undergraduate studies helped to ensure that any non-standard features of speech or orthographic forms were not the result of a lack of proficiency in English but were rather stylistic choices (for writing) and dialect features (for speech).

The GVPNs met for two hours each week totaling approximately 16 hours of interaction. The GVPNs were limited to using either text or voice over for two weeks at a time. GVPN1 worked only through email and instant messenger for the first two-week period and then transitioned to working only through Voice over Internet Protocol (VoIP) for the second two week period. The pattern was reversed for GVPN2 in order to determine whether ordering of access to the two modes impacted the results. From these sessions, the following data were collected: 1) interactions in the three experimental labs were video recorded locally to capture offline conversations, 2) participants submitted text logs from the instant messenger client to the research coordinator after each session, 3) participants carbon copied the research coordinator on any email interactions, and 4) audio recordings were automatically exported from the VoIP client. Each of these data sources were time stamped for synchronization in ELAN (Brugman and Russel 2004), a multi-media annotation software package, and audio/video data were transcribed.

The methodological framework (Figure 1) is based on a mixed-method, grounded-theory approach (Glaser and Strauss 2009) in which observation was used to determine whether language attitudes were salient in the experimental context and then statistical techniques were used to identify significant patterns between the experimental groups in terms of language use and the identified attitudes. Based on the types of attitudes identified through the observations, a survey was developed that asked participants to rate their fellow participants based on the emergent categories. The survey responses were used as the basis for specifying and quantifying any of the emergent language attitudes.

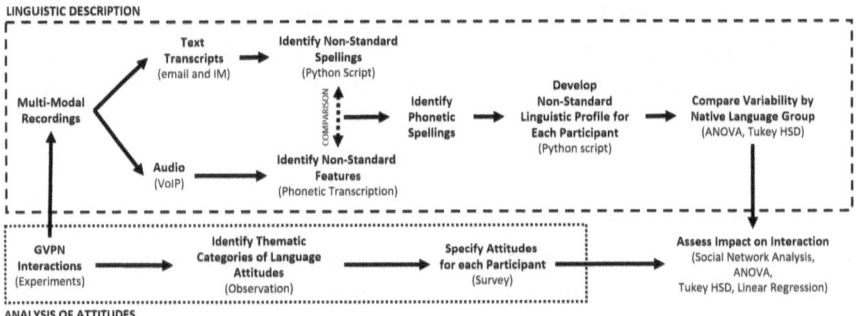

**Figure 1:** Methodological framework

This data was then organized into two subsets for each of the two GVPNs, one representing the interactions through the text-based mode and another for the audio-based mode. The audio-based mode included (phonetic) transcriptions of the VoIP recordings combined with audio extracted from the video recordings that captured face-to-face interaction within teams in the experimental labs. The text-based subset included the email and instant messenger transcripts.

During real-time observation of the co-located teams in the experimental labs and the geographically distributed networks in the virtual workplace, salient examples of language attitudes were identified and grouped into themes. The instant messenger and email transcripts were then reviewed to identify any additional attitudes. Many of the attitudes emerged in private or semi-private discourse within co-located teams or between one team and another. Very few cases emerged during the work interactions when all teams were co-present in the interactional space.

The text transcripts were then analyzed using a Python script to identify the presence of non-standard orthographic forms. Non-standard forms present in the text transcripts were cross-referenced with targeted phonetic transcriptions of each participant's speech to identify any phonetic spellings (Androutsopoulos 2000), i.e., those spellings that reflect non-standard pronunciation. Then, each participant's non-standard linguistic profile (Squires and Iorio 2014) was calculated based on the ratio of standard spellings to phonetic spellings. By limiting the dataset to only phonetic spellings that corresponded with the participants' pronunciation, a comparison between language attitudes focused on specific features/forms was possible. Analyses of variance (ANOVA) combined with Tukey post-hoc tests were used to determine whether there was a significantly distinct relationship between: 1) the native language groups and their use of phonetic spellings, and 2) attitudes about the use of phonetic spellings.

Based on the analytical method described in Iorio and Taylor (2014), the transcriptions were annotated with a focus on identifying interactional patterns between the participants, i.e., who was communicating with whom and how frequently these communications occurred in order to conduct a Social Network Analysis (SNA) (Paolillo 2001). The SNA was conducted based on the *degree centrality* (i.e., presence of an interaction between one network member and another) and *tie strength* (i.e., total number of interactions between each member of the network) as indicators of each participant's position in the network. Finally, a linear regression model was developed to determine whether the language attitudes could be used to predict the interactional patterns uncovered through the SNA.

# 4 Results

The first step in the analysis is to determine whether participants represent non-standard spoken features in their writing and whether the use of these phonetic spellings is distinct for the three native language groups. The sample transcript in Example 1 demonstrates that phonetic spellings are attested in the text transcripts, in addition to other types of spellings such as those enregistered as emblematic of CMC (Squires 2010). Because all of the participants used orthography associated with CMC (including emoticons and abbreviations), the study focused specifically on phonetic spellings as a potential marker of distinction between the groups.

(1) Sample Transcript of GVPN Interactions (Phonetic spellings noted in bold. Dut = Native Dutch Speaker, Tel = Native Telugu Speaker, Eng = Native English Speaker)

01. Dut1: yeah well basically you should get it like to line up with the column and grid
02. Tel1: u mean on **de fort** floor
03. Dut1: which floor? what is a fort floor?
04. Tel1: we have **werkt** the top floor as per the screen shot u have sent through drop box.
05. Eng1: I think they're referring to the 4th (top) floor?
06. Tel1: ya
07. Eng1: On the 4th floor, the wall that is parallel with the balcony railings
08. Tel1: the wall **pass de** structural columns?
09. Eng2: you need to move the wall back so it's flush with the existing columns
10. Eng2: Does that make sense?
11. Tel2: **ve** understand **dat**.
12. Tel1: **vll** create a opening (door) **der**
13. Tel1: **n vll** send **de** revised file in couple of mins

A Python script was used to identify each case of a non-standard spelling by comparing all words in the email and instant messenger transcript to the 12dicts wordlist (Beale 2007). Of the non-standard spellings returned, potential phonetic spellings were manually identified and then exemplars of speech for these potentials were phonetically transcribed for a sample of the audio recordings for the associated speaker. While there were cases of phonetic spellings for the Dutch speakers (e.g., devoicing of final stops in [cart] vs. /card/) there were no examples of phonetic spellings for the English speakers. There were examples of representation of word initial stops for fricatives in the Dutch and Indian writing (e.g., [dat] vs. /that/ in Line 11), which corresponded to the features of both groups' speech. For the Dutch, the phonetic spelling based on this speech feature was not consistent across participants nor was it systematically represented in their writing. In contrast, the Indians used phonetic spellings systematically, particularly in the case of word-initial replacement of labiovelar glides with labiodental fricatives (e.g., [ve] vs. /we/ in Line 11).

The results indicate that 21% of all words in the email and instant messenger transcripts by the Telugu speakers are phonetic spellings, compared to 9% for the Dutch. Again, there were no examples of phonetic spellings for the English speakers. A one-way between subjects ANOVA (Table 1) was conducted to compare use of phonetic spellings by the English, Dutch and Telugu speaking groups. There was a significant effect on use of phonetic spellings at the $p < 0.001$ level for the three groups [$F(2,4) = 45.93$, $p < 0.001$]. Post hoc comparisons using the Tukey HSD test indicated that the mean use of phonetic spellings for the English speakers ($M = 0$, $SD = 0$) was significantly different than for the Dutch ($M = 0.9$, $SD = 0.02$) and Telugu speakers ($M = 0.21$, $SD = 0.05$). In other words, all three groups exhibited statistically distinct use of phonetic spellings.

**Table 1:** Comparison of non-standard profiles

| Descriptive Statistics | | | |
|---|---|---|---|
| Native Language | M | | SD |
| Tel | 0.21 | | 0.05 |
| Dut | 0.09 | | 0.02 |
| Eng | 0.00 | | 0.00 |
| **Tukey HSD** | | | |
| Comp | Diff | 95% CI | p |
| Tel-Dut | −0.12 | −0.18 to −0.06 | 0.001 |
| Tel-Eng | −0.21 | −0.27 to −0.15 | <0.001 |
| Dut-Eng | −0.09 | −0.15 to −0.03 | 0.007 |
| **ANOVA** | | | |
| SS | df | $\sigma^2$ | F | p |
| 0.09 | 2 | 0.04 | 45.93 | <0.001 |

Having determined that phonetic spellings are present in the transcripts, the next step in the analysis is to determine whether language attitudes are salient within the two GVPNs. Not surprisingly, much of the metalinguistic commentary that explicitly expressed attitudes occurred through private emails between two teams and during offline conversations in the experimental labs within teams. Examples of metalinguistic commentaries that clearly express language attitudes are presented in Table 2 and organized by theme.

These examples demonstrate that not only were language attitudes present, they were wholly negative, were always covert, and in each case, were directed at the Telugu-speaking team. From a thematic standpoint, the participants indicated that the writing style of the native Telugu participants: 1) was difficult to comprehend, 2) did not inspire trust, 3) was related to poor quality work, and 4) and suggested a lack of education. These findings are in line with similar studies

Table 2: Examples of language evaluations by theme

| Theme | Count | Example | Context |
|---|---|---|---|
| Comprehension | 23 | "I think I understand about one out of every five words they write." | Dutch to English speaker via private message about the Telugu team |
| Trust | 9 | "I don't trust that they understand what we asked them to do." | Offline conversation in the lab between two English speakers about Telugu team |
| Quality | 7 | "It's not ok if they type like that in their section of the report." | Dutch speaker to English team via email about the Telugu team |
| Education | 3 | "Do you have to pass a writing test to get into university there?" | Offline conversation in the lab between two English speakers about the Telugu team |

on non-standard speech (e.g., Cargile and Giles 1997; Labov 1972) and with findings linking evaluations of non-native language fluency with expected quality of work output (Kankanhalli et al. 2007). Because the metalinguistic commentary focused extensively on attitudes about comprehensibility, a survey was designed to quantitatively explore the relationship between comprehensibility and the non-standard spelling practices of individual participants.

The 10-question survey was designed to assess the comprehensibility of each participant by asking respondents to rate their collaborators based on a 5-point Likert Scale. The survey contained 3 focus questions and 7 distractors. The focus questions included:

1. How difficult was it to understand Person X? (1 = very difficult, 5 = very easy)
2. How hard did you have to work to understand Person X? (1 = not hard at all, 5 = very hard)
3. How often did you have to ask Person X to repeat themselves? (1 = all the time, 5 = not often)

All three focus questions assessed comprehensibility but did so from different angles, which reinforced the internal validity of the survey. Distractors were also included, which focused on evaluation of the task outputs (e.g., How well did Person X execute Task Y?), and questions about the role of the technology (e.g., How well did Technology X support Task Y?). The direction of the Likert scales was alternated to help ensure reliability. Participants responded to the survey for each of the other participants in their GVPN. The survey was administered twice: once after the GVPNs switched communicative modes (i.e., when

GVPN1 switched from text to audio and GVPN2 switched from audio to text) and then again at the conclusion of the experimental period. In sum, participants were asked to rate the comprehensibility of the speech and writing of their collaborators through responses to ten surveys each.

**Table 3:** Comparison of comprehensibility ratings for text

| Descriptive Statistics | | | |
| --- | --- | --- | --- |
| Native Language | M | | SD |
| Tel | 1.92 | | 0.27 |
| Dut | 4.84 | | 0.22 |
| Eng | 4.82 | | 0.27 |
| **Tukey HSD** | | | |
| Comp | Diff | 95% CI | p |
| Tel-Dut | 2.91 | 2.41 to 3.41 | <0.001 |
| Tel-Eng | 2.90 | 2.40 to 3.40 | <0.001 |
| Dut-Eng | −0.02 | −0.52 to 0.38 | 0.995 |
| **ANOVA** | | | |
| SS | df | $\sigma^2$ | F | p |
| 22.51 | 2 | 11.26 | 175.46 | <0.001 |

Results for the ratings of written comprehensibility (Table 3) indicate that the Telugu speakers were rated as significantly less comprehensible compared to the Dutch and English speakers. Moreover, the comprehensibility ratings for the Dutch ($p < 0.001$) and English speakers ($p < 0.001$) were statistically indistinct ($p = 0.995$). On a scale of 1–5 with 5 indicating highly comprehensible, the average rating for the Telugu speakers was 1.9, while it was 4.8 for both the Dutch and the English speakers.

However, the in-group comprehensibility rating for the Telugu speakers in the text-based mode was significantly higher compared to the ratings of the Telugu speakers by the English and Dutch speakers at the $p < 0.001$ level (Table 4). Post hoc comparisons using the Tukey HSD test indicated that the mean Telugu in-group ratings ($M = 4.75$, $SD = 0.50$) were significantly different from the ratings of the Telugu by the Dutch ($M = 2.13$, $SD = 0.64$) and English speaking groups ($M = 1.75$, $SD = 0.71$). This result supports Sahgal's (1991) observation that Indian English speakers, in general, preferred a more local style of English compared to the more formal style associated with Standard British English.

**Table 4:** In-group vs. out-group comparison of text comprehensibility ratings for Telugu speakers

| Descriptive Statistics | | |
|---|---|---|
| Native Language | M | SD |
| Tel | 4.75 | 0.50 |
| Dut | 2.13 | 0.64 |
| Eng | 1.75 | 0.71 |

| Tukey HSD | | | |
|---|---|---|---|
| Comp | Diff | 95% CI | p |
| Tel-Dut | −2.62 | −3.64 to −1.60 | <0.001 |
| Tel-Eng | −3.00 | −4.02 to −1.98 | <0.001 |
| Dut-Eng | −0.38 | −1.21 to 0.45 | 0.485 |

| ANOVA | | | | |
|---|---|---|---|---|
| SS | df | $\sigma^2$ | F | p |
| 25.85 | 2 | 12.92 | 30.74 | <0.001 |

For speech, a different pattern emerged (Table 5). The Tukey HSD post hoc test indicates that the Telugu and Dutch speakers were statistically indistinct (p = 0.700) in terms of their comprehensibility rating. Nonetheless, the Native English Speakers were rated as significantly more comprehensible than both the Telugu (p < 0.001) and the Dutch speakers (p = 0.003). This result is not surprising because the language of interaction for the GVPNs aligns with the native language of the Americans. Although the Telugu and Dutch speakers were rated as significantly less comprehensible compared to the native English speakers, they were nonetheless rated highly, scoring 4.6 and 4.7 respectively compared to the 4.9 rating for the native English speakers.

The results thus far have demonstrated that: 1) the three groups are distinct in terms of their use of phonetic spellings, 2) language attitudes focused on comprehensibility are present in the metalinguistic commentary of the GVPNs, 3) the Indians are rated as less comprehensible than the other two groups when writing, and 4) the Dutch and Telugu speakers are rated as less comprehensible than the native English speakers when speaking, but the effect is rather small. Crucially, the writing of the Telugu speakers was downgraded, whereas the speech of the Telugu speakers is by comparison well-regarded. However, it is not clear what impact, if any, these language attitudes and differences have on how team members interact with one another.

To explore the interactional patterns between teams, sociograms were extracted from the interactional matrices for both GVPNs based on who communicated

**Table 5:** Comparison of comprehensibility ratings for speech

| Descriptive Statistics | | |
|---|---|---|
| Native Language | M | SD |
| Tel | 4.59 | 0.11 |
| Dut | 4.64 | 0.09 |
| Eng | 4.93 | 0.04 |
| **Tukey HSD** | | | | |
| Comp | Diff | 95% CI | | p |
| Tel-Dut | 0.05 | −0.12 to 0.22 | | 0.700 |
| Tel-Eng | 0.34 | 0.17 to 0.51 | | <0.001 |
| Dut-Eng | 0.23 | 0.12 to 0.46 | | 0.003 |
| **ANOVA** | | | | |
| SS | df | $\sigma^2$ | F | p |

with whom for both the audio- and text-based segments of the experiment. The result of the network analysis is represented in Figures 2 and 3. In these figures, each participant is represented by one of the nodes in the network. The comprehensibility rating for each participant is represented as a node attribute with larger nodes indicating higher comprehensibility ratings. The number of interactions between two participants is represented as the thickness of the lines connecting each node. The direction of the interaction (e.g., who initiated the interaction to whom) is represented with arrows. Native language group membership (as well as technical task in the project) is reflected in the color of the node. For each member of the network, the sociograms summarize who is talking to whom, how often, and his or her comprehensibility for speech and text.

When GVPN1 is interacting through voice, the GVPN is characterized by having a high degree of connectedness (Figure 2). The Telugu and English speakers are all connected to 4 of 5 other individuals, whereas the Dutch speakers are connected to every other individual in the network. The number of interactions between network members is robust, with repeated and reciprocal interaction occurring most often between Dut3 – Eng4 and Tel 4 – Dut4. However, when the GVPN shifts their interactions to text, a subgroup consisting of the English and Dutch speakers forms, with the Telugu speakers pushed to the periphery. In fact, Tel3 loses all contact with English and Dutch speakers and contact between Tel4 and the rest of the network is infrequent. When compared to the sociogram for voice, the network interactions between the Dutch and English

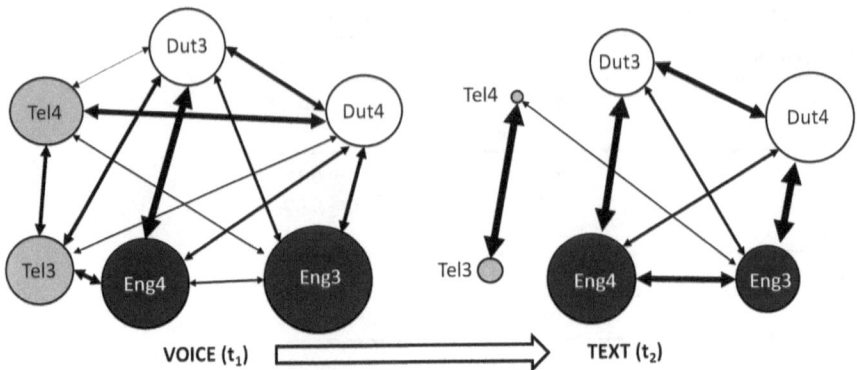

**Figure 2:** Interactional structure for GVPN1

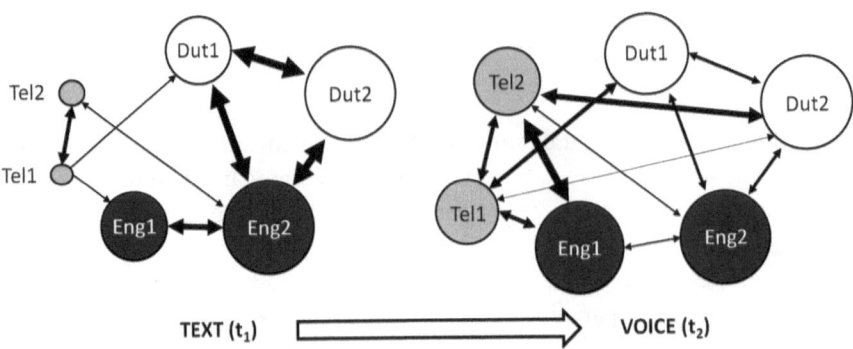

**Figure 3:** Interactional structure for GVPN2

speakers is stronger, with more frequent interaction. Once GVPN1 shifts to text, the native Telugu speakers become marginalized.

The pattern observed for GVPN1 may be due to the order in which the GVPNs interacted through the two modalities. For instance, the individuals may have established a familiarity with the non-standard features in each other's speech, which helped them to "translate" the phonetic spellings. To test this impact, GVPN2 first interacted through text and then shifted to voice (Figure 3). Results show that regardless of whether the GVPNs interacted through voice or text first, the same interactional pattern emerged, i.e., that the network was less cohesive when interactions were written. To illustrate, when interacting through text, Tel2 only has reciprocal ties to the network through Eng2 (Figure 3). Although Tel1 has a higher degree of centrality with three connections to the network, only one connection is reciprocal. These non-reciprocal connections indicate that Tel1 was communicating with the network (e.g., by asking a question), but the network was not communicating with Tel1 (e.g., by providing a response). Note also that the tie strength or number of interactions by Tel1 and Tel2 with the network (as indicated by line weight) is also much lower compared to the interactions between the other members of the network. As the GVPN shifts to communicating through speech, all ties to the Telugu speakers are reciprocal, each of their degree centralities increases to 4, and tie strength increases dramatically.

While the visualization of the interactional dynamics for the two GVPNs in Figures 2 and 3 suggest that the native Telugu speakers are less central to the networks and participate less when they are communicating through writing, a statistical test is required to confirm whether this observation is significant. The results of this analysis are presented in Tables 6–9. Tables 6 and 8 represent a comparison of the mean values for the degree centrality of each network for text and voice respectively. Tables 7 and 9 represent a comparison of the mean values for the tie strength of each network for text and voice respectively. In general, the results confirm that the Telugu speakers have significantly lower degree centralities and tie strengths compared to both the English and Dutch speakers for text, but not for voice.

**Table 6:** Comparison of degree centrality for text

| Descriptive Statistics | | | |
|---|---|---|---|
| Native Language | | M | SD |
| Tel | | 1.5 | 0.58 |
| Dut | | 3.25 | 0.50 |
| Eng | | 3.50 | 0.58 |
| **Tukey HSD** | | | |
| Comp | Diff | 95% CI | p |
| Tel-Dut | 1.75 | 0.65 to 2.84 | 0.004 |
| Tel-Eng | 2.00 | 0.91 to 3.09 | 0.002 |
| Dut-Eng | 0.25 | −0.84 to 1.34 | 0.803 |
| **ANOVA** | | | |
| SS | df | $\sigma^2$ | F | p |
| 9.5 | 2 | 4.65 | 15.56 | 0.001 |

**Table 7:** Comparison of tie strength for text

### Descriptive Statistics

| Native Language | M | SD |
|---|---|---|
| Tel | 60.75 | 35.72 |
| Dut | 159.3 | 43.89 |
| Eng | 191.0 | 39.47 |

### Tukey HSD

| Comp | Diff | 95% CI | p |
|---|---|---|---|
| Tel-Dut | 98.55 | 19.9 to 177.2 | 0.017 |
| Tel-Eng | 130.25 | 51.6 to 208.9 | 0.003 |
| Dut-Eng | 31.70 | −46.9 to 110.3 | 0.523 |

### ANOVA

| SS | df | $\sigma^2$ | F | p |
|---|---|---|---|---|
| 36909 | 2 | 18454 | 11.63 | 0.036 |

**Table 8:** Comparison of degree centrality for voice

### Descriptive Statistics

| Native Language | M | SD |
|---|---|---|
| Tel | 4.00 | 0.00 |
| Dut | 4.25 | 0.96 |
| Eng | 3.75 | 0.25 |

### Tukey HSD

| Comp | Diff | 95% CI | p |
|---|---|---|---|
| Tel-Dut | 0.25 | −0.88 to 1.38 | 0.815 |
| Tel-Eng | −0.25 | −1.38 to 0.88 | 0.815 |
| Dut-Eng | −0.50 | −1.63 to 0.63 | 0.398 |

### ANOVA

| SS | df | $\sigma^2$ | F | p |
|---|---|---|---|---|
| 0.5 | 2 | 0.25 | 0.76 | 0.495 |

**Table 9:** Comparison of tie strength for voice

| Descriptive Statistics | | | |
|---|---|---|---|
| Native Language | M | | SD |
| Tel | 263.0 | | 40.31 |
| Dut | 224.8 | | 22.38 |
| Eng | 219.3 | | 11.88 |
| **Tukey HSD** | | | |
| Comp | Diff | 95% CI | p |
| Tel-Dut | −38.2 | −92.47 to 16.07 | 0.177 |
| Tel-Eng | −43.7 | −97.97 to 10.57 | 0.116 |
| Dut-Eng | −5.50 | −59.77 to 48.77 | 0.957 |
| **ANOVA** | | | |
| SS | df | $\sigma^2$ | F | p |
| 4532.2 | 2 | 2266.1 | 2.99 | 0.100 |

The final step in the analysis is to determine whether the comprehensibility ratings by the participants can be used to predict both the degree centrality and the tie strength, i.e., the indicators of interaction. Results of a linear regression analysis demonstrate that comprehensibility rating is significantly and positively associated with an increase in tie strength ($\beta$ = 34.67, p = 0.002) and with an increase in degree centrality ($\beta$ = 0.87, p = 0.035) for text. In more concrete terms, for an increase in comprehensibility rating by 1, the network members are predicted to interact approximately 35 more times and with approximately one additional network member. Not surprisingly, there was no statistically significant relationships observed between comprehensibility ratings and tie strength (p = 0.978) or degree centrality (p = 0.887) when the interactions occurred through speech. These summative findings demonstrate the powerful role that language attitudes about the comprehensibility of text can have on interaction in computer-mediated environments (RQs 2–3).

# 5 Discussion

In both of the GVPNs that were examined, language attitudes about non-standard speech and writing impacted interaction differently. This finding aligns with Biber (1991) who demonstrated that social meanings associated with speech differed from those associated with writing. Negative attitudes about the comprehensibility of non-standard writing negatively impacted network cohesion in terms of degree centrality and tie strength, but no such pattern was found for attitudes about comprehensibility of non-standard speech. For the Dutch and English speakers, the results suggest that there was a shared understanding about the appropriateness of using more standard spellings in a professional context. This understanding was not shared by the Telugu speakers, who aligned their linguistic practices more closely with norms for the technological context of text messaging (Thurlow and Brown 2003) and with the norms of Indian English from their local communities (Sahgal 1991).

The results also suggest that participants who used more phonetic spellings had lower tie strength and degree centrality compared to participants who used more standard spellings, indicating that the use of phonetic spellings resulted in less central positioning of participants within the interactional networks. As prior research suggests, when the culture of one team within a network is dominant, collaboration is made more challenging (Lee-Kelley and Sankey 2008). Had the experimental context been focused on non-professional interactions between participants, this finding would not be surprising because we would expect that participants who did not align their linguistic practices with the team norms would be shifted to the interactional periphery. Over time, we would expect them to be pushed out of the network. However, the results are surprising because the teams were required to work together, with no option to exclude members based on norm misalignment. In this experimental context, the lack of collaboration with the Telugu speakers during the text-based interactions in GVPN1 (voice to text) was resolved by the Dutch speakers learning design software and executing much of the final modeling work that was assigned to the Telugu speaking team. In GVPN2 (text to voice), the network had difficulty with the initial integration phase, and made up for the resulting lag by working more efficiently when interactions were audio-based. In an authentic professional context, this resolution strategy of GVPN1 may not be feasible and the professionals may be required to make explicit the perceived lack of comprehensibility while simultaneously fostering the "tolerance and empathy [that] are necessary to encourage participation in [a GVPN] context" (Dubé and Paré 2001: 72).

Although this research demonstrates that strong and negative attitudes about the use of phonetic spellings by the Telugu speakers existed in the two GVPNs, at no time did any of the English or Dutch speakers suggest (either directly or indirectly) that the Telugu speakers adopt a more standard – and in their view, comprehensible – linguistic style. However, participants may be aware that a direct confrontation may lead to the types of conflicts that characterize GVPNs

(Hinds and Mortensen 2005) and thus, through avoidance of a direct confrontation, believed that they were maintaining the interactional integrity of the network. The Telugu speakers were certainly capable of adopting a more standard orthographic style, but in doing so, would also be adopting the meaning(s) ascribed to non-standard writing by their Dutch and English speaking teammates. In other words, it is not the case that the native Telugu speakers were unable to write more formally. They learned to write standard (Indian) English throughout their primary and secondary studies and yet *chose* a linguistic style that reflected their own meaning, one that more closely aligned to the linguistic norms of their local community. Because the Telugu speakers rated themselves as significantly more comprehensible compared to the ratings by the Dutch and English speakers (Table 5), this reinforces the shared meaning that the phonetic spellings had for the Telugu speaking in-group.

This meaning is similar to that of British Creole for Jamaicans (Sebba 1998) and Gulf Arabic (Palfreyman and Khalil 2003) for some Pan-Arabic message board communities. For both British Creole and Gulf Arabic, non-standard spellings can be used as a tool for communities to take an oppositional stance (Maybin 2007) to the dominant language. For many communities in India, English is viewed as the language of the colonizer. The substitution of <der> for *there* and <ve> for *we* (Example 1, Lines 11–12) (see Heyd, this volume) is a way that Indian speakers of English can differentiate themselves from the written language of their colonial past by drawing on the sounds from spoken Indian English that distinguish it from spoken British English (Kachru 1965). For the Dutch participants who exhibited the same alternations in their speech and writing, English is perceived as the language of work and of education and thus the standardness of their writing follows naturally from the contexts in which it is used (Lakoff 1972). There is no colonial relationship between the Dutch participants and the English language, and thus, the Dutch may view English as a pragmatic communication tool required for participation in a globalized industry that uses English as a lingua franca. English is also pragmatic for the Indians, but a historically-based ideology underlies the pragmatism.

The results underscore the importance of improving the vernacular literacy of the next cohort of professionals who will enter the workforce in industries that have undergone or that are undergoing globalization (Iorio 2016). Because the participants made significantly different evaluations of comprehensibility based on non-standard features in speech compared to writing, the results suggest that, in general, the participants were able to listen to and comprehend non-standard spoken features, but did not understand (or chose not to try to understand) the non-standard orthographic forms. Because the Dutch participants learned English non-natively, they may have had an intuitive understanding of how difficult it can be to shape the non-standard features of speech (e.g., to modify one's accent). The American participants are enrolled in an international graduate degree program, and have extensive experience speaking and working with other students from different language backgrounds. Thus, for the Dutch and American participants, accepting the Indians' non-standard speech may have been seen as "accepting them for who they are." For writing, all participants had some level of exposure to non-standard orthography enregistered as emblematic of CMC (Squires 2010). So, the participants had experience with both non-standard speech and with non-standard orthography. The results suggest that they were not prepared to work in a context where some groups incorporated non-standard orthographic forms in their writing, in part, because they may have viewed writing as a practice that was intentional and could be changed rather than as natural or unintentional as was their interpretation of speech.

# 6 Limitations, future research, and conclusion

The central limitation to this research is that a variety of factors could have shaped the language attitudes of the participants in addition to non-standard speech and writing that were core to the analysis. For example, the Dutch and American teams were in engineering roles within the network while the Indians were in architectural or design roles. Within the construction industry, these two roles are often in opposition as a focus on form versus function can create antagonistic identities for architects and engineers. Additionally, the analysis did not consider the role that racial stereotyping may have played in impacting the results, e.g., due to closer cultural alignment between the Dutch and Americans compared to the Indians. However, the comprehensibility ratings of the Indians differed for speech and writing, which suggests that the Dutch and Americans were not entirely negative in their attitudes about language use by the Indians. Given the small sample size for each native language group and the limited number of GVPNs examined, the impact of additional factors such as these could be significant.

Regardless, future research must focus on exploring additional factors that can explain the relationship of language attitudes and interactional patterns within these professional settings. One benefit to the study methodology is that it can be replicated across a variety of contexts and modified to reflect the emergent attitudes held by networks composed of workers from a variety of national, cultural and linguistic backgrounds. The methodological framework described in Figure 1 scales both up (e.g., to examine larger networks) and out (e.g., to examine more diverse networks), thus improving the generalizability of the findings.

Taken together, the results demonstrate that global virtual workplaces are sites where attitudes about non-standard English can negatively impact professional interactions. The results also demonstrate that these attitudes may not be consistent for different communication modes as individuals displayed higher levels of tolerance for non-standard speech compared to writing. As organizations and industries continue to globalize, it becomes increasingly important to understand how and why language attitudes impact professional contexts, particularly as these contexts increasingly support interaction through a variety of communication modes. By improving this understanding, society will be better suited to develop strategies for addressing the challenges that emerge when diverse teams are geographically distributed and interact through CMC.

# 7 Acknowledgements

This material is based in part upon work supported by the National Science Foundation under Grant No. IIS-0943069 and an Alfred P. Sloan Foundation Industry Studies Fellowship grant. Any opinions, findings, and conclusions or recommendations expressed in this material are those of the authors and do not necessarily reflect the views of the National Science Foundation or the Alfred P. Sloan Foundation. I would also like to thank the Myers-Lawson School of Construction at Virginia Tech for additional project funding as well as the other CyberGRID collaborators; Ashwin Mahalingam at the Indian Institute of Technology Madras, Timo Hartmann at the University of Twente, Carrie Sturts Dossick at the University of Washington – Seattle, and John Taylor at Virginia Tech. Earlier versions of this paper were presented at the 2014 Engineering Project Organization Conference in Winter Park, CO and at the 2013 International Conference on the Linguistics of Contemporary English in Austin, TX as part of a panel on Orthography and the Sociolinguistics of CMC. The chapter has been substantially improved based on comments from the audience at both of these venues as well as two anonymous reviewers.

# 8 References

Adler, Nancy J. & Allison Gundersen. 2007. *International dimensions of organizational behavior*. Mason, OH: Cengage Learning.

Androutsopoulos, Jannis K. 2000. Non-standard spellings in media texts: The case of German fanzines. *Journal of Sociolinguistics* 4(4). 514–533.

Androutsopoulos, Jannis. 2008. Potentials and limitations of discourse-centered online ethnography. *Language@Internet* 5. Article 8. http://www.languageatinternet.org/articles/2008/1610.

Bamgbose, Ayo. 1998. Torn between the norms: Innovations in World Englishes. *World Englishes* 17(1). 1–14.

Barr, Avron & Shirley Tessler. 1996. The globalization of software R&D: The search for talent. *Council on Foreign Relations' Study Group on the Globalization of Industrial R&D*. http://web.stanford.edu/group/scip/avsgt/cfr1296.pdf (accessed 25 September 2015).

Beale, Alan. 2007. *12dicts Wordlists*. http://wordlist.sourceforge.net/12dicts-readme-r5.html (accessed 13 May 2015).

Biber, Douglas. 1991. *Variation across speech and writing*. Chicago: Cambridge University Press.

Bletzinger, Kai-Uwe & André Lähr. 2006. Prediction of interdisciplinary consequences for decisions in AEC design processes. *Journal of Information Technology in Construction* 11(1). 529–545.

Brugman, Hennie & Albert Russel. 2004. Annotating multimedia/multi-modal resources with ELAN. Paper presented at the Fourth International Conference on Language Resources and Evaluation, Lisbon.

Cargile, Aaron C. & Howard Giles. 1997. Understanding language attitudes: Exploring listener affect and identity. *Language & Communication* 17(3). 195–217.

Colella, S., J. Roca, J. Brun & G. Christophne. 2012. Achieving high performance in the construction industry. *Accenture Construction Industry Report 2012*.

Comu, Semra, Hakan I. Unsal & John E. Taylor. 2010. Dual impact of cultural and linguistic diversity on project network performance. *Journal of Management in Engineering* 27(3). 179–187.

Darics, Erika. 2010. Politeness in computer-mediated discourse of a virtual team. *Journal of Politeness Research* 6(1). 129–150.

Dubé, Line & Guy Paré. 2001. Global virtual teams. *Communications of the ACM* 44(12). 71–73.

Eckert, Penelope. 1997. Age as a sociolinguistic variable. In Florian Coulmas (ed.), *The handbook of sociolinguistics*, 245–267. Oxford: Basil Blackwell.

Eckert, Penelope. 1989. *Jocks and burnouts: Social categories and identity in the high school*. New York: Teachers College Press.

Eckert, Penelope & Sally McConnell-Ginet. 2003. *Language and gender*. Cambridge: Cambridge University Press.

Eisenstein, Jacob. 2015. Systematic patterning in phonologically-motivated orthographic variation. *Journal of Sociolinguistics* 19(2). 161–188.

Fairclough, Norman. 2015. *Language and power*. 3rd edn. New York: Routledge.

Glaser, Barney G. & Anselm L. Strauss. 2009. *The discovery of grounded theory: Strategies for qualitative research*. Chicago: Transaction Publishers.

Henderson, Jane K. 2005. Language diversity in international management teams. *International Studies of Management and Organization* 35(1). 66–82.

Hinds, Pamela J. & Mark Mortensen. 2005. Understanding conflict in geographically distributed teams: The moderating effects of shared identity, shared context, and spontaneous communication. *Organization Science* 16(3). 290–307.

Hinrichs, Lars. 2012. How to spell the vernacular: A multivariate study of Jamaican e-mails and blogs. In Alexandra Jaffe, Jannis Androutsopoulos, Mark Sebba & Sally Johnson (eds.), *Orthography as social action: scripts, spelling, identity and power*, 325–358. Berlin: De Gruyter.

Iorio, Josh. 2016. Vernacular literacies. In Alexandra Georgakopoulou & Tereza Spilioti (eds.), *The Routledge handbook of language and digital communication*, 166–179. New York: Routledge.

Iorio, Josh. 2010. *Explaining orthographic variation in a virtual community: Linguistic, social, and contextual factors*. Austin, TX: University of Texas at Austin Ph.D. dissertation.

Iorio, Josh. 2009. Effects of audience on orthographic variation. *Studies in the Linguistic Sciences: Illinois Working Papers* 2(1). 127–140.

Iorio, Josh & John E. Taylor. 2014. Boundary object efficacy: The mediating role of boundary objects on task conflict in global virtual project networks. *International Journal of Project Management* 32(1). 7–17.

Jaffe, Alexandra & Shana Walton. 2000. The voices people read: Orthography and the representation of non-standard speech. *Journal of Sociolinguistics* 4(4). 561–587.

Jarvenpaa, Sirkka L. & Dorothy E. Leidner. 1999. Communication and trust in global virtual teams. *Organization Science* 10(6). 791–815.

Jessmer, Sherri L. & David Anderson. 2001. The effect of politeness and grammar on user perceptions of electronic mail. *North American Journal of Psychology* 3(2). 331–346.

Kankanhalli, Atreyi, Bernard C.Y. Tan & Kwok-Kee Wei. 2007. Conflict and performance in global virtual teams. *Journal of Management Information Systems* 23(3). 237–274.

Korth, Britta. 2005. *Language attitudes towards Kyrgyz and Russian: Discourse, education and policy in post-Soviet Kyrgyzstan*. New York: Peter Lang.

Kachru, Braj B. 1965. The Indianness in Indian English. *Word* 21(3). 391–410.

Labov, William. 1972. *Sociolinguistic patterns*. Philadelphia: University of Pennsylvania Press.

Lakoff, Robin. 1972. Language in context. *Language* 48(4). 907–927.

Lattimer, Robert L. 1998. The case for diversity in global business, and the impact of diversity on team performance. *Competitiveness Review* 8(2). 3–17.

Lee-Kelley, Liz & Tim Sankey. 2008. Global virtual teams for value creation and project success: A case study. *International Journal of Project Management* 26(1). 51–62.

Marley, Dawn. 2004. Language attitudes in Morocco following recent changes in language policy. *Language Policy* 3(1). 25–46.

Massey, Anne P., Yu-Ting C. Hung, Mitzi Montoya-Weiss & Venkataraman Ramesh. 2001. When culture and style aren't about clothes: perceptions of task-technology fit in global virtual teams. Paper presented at the *International ACM SIGGROUP Conference on Supporting Group Work*. Boulder, CO.

Maznevski, Martha L. & Katherine M. Chudoba. 2000. Bridging space over time: Global virtual team dynamics and effectiveness. *Organization Science* 11(4). 473–492.

Messner, John, C. Chen & G. Joseph. 2007. Effective use of the global engineering workforce. *The Construction Industry Institute*, Research Report, No. 211-11.

Murray, Denise E. 1988. The context of oral and written language: A framework for mode and medium switching. *Language in Society* 17(3). 351–373.

Nayak, Nilesh V. & John E. Taylor. 2009. Offshore outsourcing in global design networks. *Journal of Management in Engineering* 25(4). 177–184.

Palfreyman, David & Muhamed al Khalil. 2003. A funky language for teenzz to use: Representing Gulf Arabic in instant messaging. *Journal of Computer-Mediated Communication* 9(1).

Paolillo, John C. 2001. Language variation on Internet Relay Chat: A social network approach. *Journal of Sociolinguistics* 5(2). 180–213.

Paolillo, John. 1999. The virtual speech community: Social network and language variation on IRC. *Journal of Computer-Mediated Communication* 4(4).

Polzer, Jeffrey T., C. Brad Crisp, Sirkka L. Jarvenpaa & Jerry W. Kim. 2006. Extending the fault-line model to geographically dispersed teams: How colocated subgroups can impair group functioning. *Academy of Management Journal* 49(4). 679–692.

Podesva, Robert J. 2007. Phonation type as a stylistic variable: The use of falsetto in constructing a personal. *Journal of Sociolinguistics* 11(4). 478–504.

Rickford, John R. 1992. Grammatical variation and divergence in Vernacular Black English. In Marinel Gerritsen & Dieter Stein (eds.), *Internal and external factors in syntactic change*, 175–200. New York: DeGruyter.

Sahgal, Anju. 1991. Patterns of language use in a bilingual setting in India. In Jenny Cheshire (ed.), *English around the world: Sociolinguistic perspectives*, 299–307. Cambridge: Cambridge University Press.

Sebba, Mark. 2003. Spelling rebellion. In Jannis K. Androutsopoulos and Alexandra Georgakopoulou (eds.), *Discourse constructions of youth identities*, 151–172. Amsterdam: John Benjamins.

Sebba, Mark. 1998. Phonology meets ideology: the meaning of orthographic practices in British Creole. *Language Problems and Language Planning* 22(1). 19–47.

Squires, Lauren & Josh Iorio. 2014. Tweets in the news: Legitimizing medium, standardizing form. In Jannis Androutsopoulos (ed.), *Mediatization and sociolinguistic change*, 331–360. Berlin: De Gruyter.

Squires, Lauren. 2010. Enregistering internet language. *Language in Society* 39(4). 457–492.

Shachaf, Pnina. 2008. Cultural diversity and information and communication technology impacts on global virtual teams: An exploratory study. *Information & Management* 45(2). 131–142.

Tagliamonte, Sali A. & Derek Denis. 2008. Linguistic ruin? LOL! Instant messaging and teen language. *American Speech* 83(1). 3–34.

Thurlow, Crispin & Alex Brown. 2003. Generation Txt? The sociolinguistics of young people's text-messaging. *Discourse Analysis Online* 1(1). 1–30.

Thurlow, Crispin & Kristine Mroczek (eds.). 2011. *Digital discourse: Language in the new media*. Oxford: Oxford University Press.

Tollefson, James W. (ed.). 2012. *Language policies in education: Critical issues*. New York: Routledge.

Vest, Charles. 2008. Context and challenge for twenty-first century engineering education. *Journal of Engineering Education* 97(3). 235–236.

Wolfram, Walt. 1974. The relationship of White Southern speech to vernacular Black English. *Language* 50(3). 498–527.

Wolfram, Walt. 1998. Language ideology and dialect. *Journal of English Linguistics* 26(2). 108–121.

Lauren B. Collister
# "At least I'm not Chinese, gay, or female": Marginalized voices in *World of Warcraft*

## 1 Introduction

*World of Warcraft*, the world's most popular massively multiplayer online role-playing game (MMORPG), is a virtual world set in a fantasy-style environment where millions of players from around the world can interact with each other through avatars and in the game's multiple text chat channels. The game has existed since 2004 with multiple game expansions and additions to the story and world, which has created an ongoing gaming experience for the players. Because of its relatively long history and international player base, *World of Warcraft* provides an interesting site for analysis of player interaction and identity; by acting through an avatar and text chat, players can remain relatively anonymous, which can provide an element of identity leveling and play (Paasonen 2005).

However, the setting of *World of Warcraft* is not immersive due to one particular aspect of player interaction, which is the widespread adoption of voice chat to facilitate communication. Because much of the control of the avatar is done with the keyboard in addition to using the same keyboard for typing in text chat, players have adopted voice chat using various voice-over-IP software programs to facilitate communication while playing the game. This use of communication technology intersects with a widespread stereotype of the identity of the average player of online games. The use of the voice adds additional information to the communication context and removes part of the anonymity of communication in the game, leading to identity-based repercussions for players who do not fit the stereotype of the average player. This chapter investigates how communicative mode – the use of text versus voice chat – interacts with certain stigmatized identities in *World of Warcraft* and how players develop strategies of communication to mitigate the negative repercussions of revealing their identities. Furthermore, this work explores the implications of silencing the marked voices and identities in the game.

To illustrate how communication type and identity interact, I will first provide an example in the form of a narrative of an event from my ethnographic study of *World of Warcraft*. Following this narrative, I will explain the methodology used to collect such narratives and experiences from players of the game, and

---

**Lauren B. Collister,** University of Pittsburgh

then provide some background information about the research on language use in virtual worlds that informed this study. The subsequent analysis section first presents background and observations about two groups of players who do not fit the stereotype of a WoW player: players who are not male and/or not heterosexual, and players who are not American or not American-sounding. To conclude the analysis section, the strategies employed by these two groups when communicating in *World of Warcraft* are presented. The chapter ends with discussions of implications of these strategies on perceptions of the voice and identity of the player base.

## 1.1 Ethnographic introduction

You are an average player of the online game *World of Warcraft*, and you log in one night to play and find an invitation appearing on your in-game chat box. It's from another player, one named Stragos, who you met a few nights ago while you were both trying to kill a particularly annoying creature that was roaming the virtual countryside. Stragos has invited you to a raid, which is a large co-operative event involving many players who work together to defeat a series of resilient enemies called *bosses*. You accept his invitation.

The next thing that appears on your screen is a flood of orange and red colored text chat, full of unfamiliar names in the middle of a familiar discussion – the roles of the players in the raid – but then conversation turns to you and your character.

> [Raid] Stragos: This guy is a hunter I met a couple of days ago and can fill our last DPS spot.
>
> [Raid] Minky: k, we need a hunter for CC on the trash
>
> [Raid] Andersonz: ok as long as ur not a huntard too bad
>
> [Raid] Xternal: Hey hunter, nice pet, is that the wolf from Blades Edge?

Stragos has vouched for you, Minky appreciates your character's relevant skills, and Xternal has demonstrated a friendly interest in your character choices, but this is all accompanied by the insult "huntard." This term is a common derogatory name for hunter-type characters in the game, made from a blend of "hunter" and "retard" and intended to disparage the playing ability of people who play those types of characters. Before you can type anything in reply, Stragos moves things along.

> [Raid] Stragos: VENT INFO ALL ON VENT NOW

Vent, short for *Ventrilo*, is a voice chat platform used by many *World of Warcraft* groups to coordinate raids. Since raid events are fast-paced and require players to make extensive use of their keyboards to control their characters, another method of communication outside of the text chat box is often preferred. Voice chat in the form of Ventrilo is the preferred mode of communication for this group. You already have this software installed on your computer from previous raids and you have a headset that helps you hear and talk to the other raid members, and you quickly load the program and type in the access information.

You listen for a few moments to the chat room where the other members of your raid are talking. Stragos (indicated by his name on the Ventrilo screen) and several other voices (all male and American-sounding) are discussing the finer points of positioning of the group during the first fight.

"Hey new guy," says another American male voice that you don't recognize, "have you done this fight before?" You look at your Ventrilo information and see that it is Andersonz, the player who called you a "huntard" just moments ago.

Now you must make a decision.

You have a microphone right by your mouth. Do you speak your answer?

The response depends on your experience in *World of Warcraft* and your own identity. Are you an American male like the rest of the people talking in the chat channel? If you are, like many of the men I interviewed for my ethnography of *World of Warcraft*, then you are likely to engage your microphone and speak your response without worry. If you are not like the American males in the channel, other considerations come into play surrounding whether you will speak your reply or not.

My in-game friend, Mork, would often say that he preferred to type his responses as opposed to speaking them into voice chat because it was loud where he was and people could never hear him due to background noise. The actual reason, as he explained to me long after we became friends, was because other players claimed to have a hard time understanding his non-native English.

Donnal, a member of the group that I studied, never talked on voice chat outside of our guild, because, as he explained, he often felt "like a zoo animal on display," even sometimes "uncomfortably sexualized by the way people reacted" to his Scottish English variety (see Cutler's chapter in this volume for more discussion of the Scottish English variety).

Theon, a gay American man, confided that he had no problem speaking in voice chat, but he would avoid talking at length with people that he did not know very well because he was afraid that his gay-sounding speech would slip into the conversation.

In this particular situation, I responded like this:

```
[Raid] Parnopaeus: Sorry, my mic isn't working for some reason.
I have done this fight several times and I always stand way back
against the wall.
```

My microphone was working fine, but I did not want to speak to this group of men – one of whom had already insulted me by calling my character a "huntard." The reason was that I did not want this group of men to hear my female-sounding voice and deduce, correctly, that I am a woman. In my limited experience in the game at the time that this happened, I already knew that to use my voice to speak over Ventrilo was to invite, at best, disbelieving comments about my gender ("whoa girls actually play *WoW*?" was a common reaction to my voice) or, at worst, months of unwanted advances and in-game sexual harassment.

Players who are not American males, meaning that they are female or Chinese or Scottish or even speak a non-standard variety of American English, are far more likely to avoid using voice chat because of these potential repercussions. This chapter is an ethnographic account of this phenomenon: the voluntary self-exclusion of *World of Warcraft* players from a prominent form of communication (voice chat) because of their way of speaking and the marked identities indexed by those voices. Although this exclusionary practice arises out of pragmatic concerns from the players affected, it contributes to the perceived homogeneity of the *World of Warcraft* player base and the erasure of minority identities. The player base of *WoW* is often stereotyped as young adult, white, male, heterosexual Americans, even though the majority of players do not fit into this category (Williams, Yee, and Caplan 2008). Approximately one-third of the *WoW* population is female[1] and most game servers are located outside of the United States, yet these populations are frequently erased or overlooked because many members of these groups of players do not want to admit to their identities for fear of identity-based repercussions. This silencing is part of a historic trend in gaming culture that occurs in many different forms; for example, Anastasia Salter and Bridget Blodgett's (2012) analysis of the silencing of female voices in gaming blogs and forums shows the vitriolic and multimodal quashing of protests from women about the casual use of the word "rape" in game culture.

---

1 No reliable demographic numbers exist for *World of Warcraft*. A 2010 study by Schiano et al. found that 34% of players on American servers were female, which is the basis for this statement.

## 1.2 Method

The source for this paper is a five-year participant-observation ethnography conducted from June 2007 until May 2012 (modeled after ethnographies of virtual worlds such as Boellstorff (2008) in *Second Life*). I spent approximately twenty hours per week playing *World of Warcraft* as a player and member of a guild called <Ragnarok>. A *guild* is a game-sanctioned social structure, organized and run by individual players as a team. Guilds can be groups of friends, people with similar playing styles and goals, or random assortments of players. <Ragnarok> was a guild that was created near the beginning of my ethnography by an in-game friend of mine, and the guild was focused on providing a safe space for female and LGBT-identifying players while also participating in advanced gaming activities such as raids. The guild was the site for the ethnography and my observations include how members interacted within the guild and with the wider *WoW* population. This chapter represents one portion of the ethnographic study; other outcomes of the ethnography include investigation of surveillance tactics (Collister 2014), multimodal communication (Collister 2013), symbol use and semantic shift (Collister 2012, 2011), and discourse structure (Collister 2008).

All of my public and semi-public interactions in text chat were recorded to a text file on my computer using the chat logging function built in to the *WoW* interface. Members of <Ragnarok> were made aware of the research project via posts on the guild's forums and in-game announcements, and all players were given the opportunity to decline to have their text chat included in the study. When possible,[2] players whose text chat is quoted extensively were contacted directly for permission and given another opportunity to opt out. All names included in this chapter are pseudonyms for the names of the characters.

Select voice interactions were recorded with permission from all parties using an audio recorder in the software Ventrilo. Additionally, twenty in-depth participant interviews were conducted with members of the guild, which were transcribed and form the bulk of the data used in this chapter. Finally, I also supply my personal experience and observations as both a regular player and an ethnographer to supplement the insights given by participants.

## 2 Background: Identity, interaction, and the internet

Early research paints a picture of the internet as a place where identity is fluid and malleable and where all identities are welcomed. Because physical cues are

---

[2] Some players disappeared from the guild or the game and did not leave any follow-up contact information, so they were not able to be contacted for this secondary form of permission.

filtered out in online contexts (Kiesler, Siegel, and McGuire 1984), scholars like Danet (1998) theorize that communicators are easily able to perform any identity that they choose. Filiciak (2004) suggests that the player's experience in a game like *World of Warcraft* is "an idealized image of the situation of the postmodern human creature, in which a user can freely shape his own 'self'" (90). Similarly, Bessiere, Seay, and Kiesler (2007: 534) suggest that the character in the game is a representation of the "ideal" physical self, that "anonymity and fantasy frees players from the yoke of their real-life history and social situation, allowing them to be more like the person they wish they were." Assertions that the "real self" can be best expressed online insinuate a separation between one's physical identity and one's online identity (e.g., McKenna, Green, and Gleason 2002; Paasonen 2005); the extreme version of this position is that online personas are independent from their physical animators (Stone 1995).

In response to these separate constructions of self, Nancy Baym questions: "...how do we know where, exactly, true selves reside? Furthermore, what if the selves enacted through digital media don't line up with those we present face to face, or if they contradict one another? [...] Is there such a thing as a true self anymore? Was there ever?" (2010: 3). O'Brien (1999) has theorized that the self online and the self offline are not separate, but rather that the self exists in fragments, some that are anchored in the physical world and others anchored in the virtual world. To O'Brien, this multiplicity of identity is licensed because of the expectations associated with online communication – that is, we are taught to expect a fluid or fragmented identity in online spaces, and so we feel comfortable presenting ourselves this way and interacting with others who do the same. These expectations help participants in online communities understand the limits and possibilities in their medium of communication; this understanding constitutes what Ilana Gershon (2010) and others call "media ideologies" about the material forms of communication and the contexts that come along with them. Gatson (2011: 224) has shown an example of these expectations and ideologies in her work on online fandom spaces, concluding that presentation of self in online communities happens in both online and offline spaces but that "a rendition of the online persona as inherently less truthful – or at least less dense/rich/full – than offline presentations is problematic at best." In fact, following Gatson's logic, online presentations of identity may be *more* authentic because there exist safe spaces online with different rules from the offline world (and the rest of the online world), where people are able to reveal aspects of their identities that they might feel they need to hide offline for fear of harmful repercussions.

In virtual worlds and online games especially, scholars describe the separation of online and offline identity and rules through the concept of the *magic circle*, or the idea that playing a game is "a stepping out of 'real' life into a temporary sphere of activity with a disposition all of its own" (Huizinga 1955: 8). The magic circle is often taken to mean that the temporary sphere of activity, e.g., an online game, exists independently of the rules of "real life," which has resulted in numerous criticisms of the magic circle. Consalvo (2009) asserts that "real life" rules *do* apply to game worlds in addition to the rules of the game, that they are not separate because we can never fully remove ourselves from the society that we are embedded in. Bainbridge (2010: 13) recast the magic circle as a "membrane" or a more porous boundary where the virtual and the physical influence each other. There may be significant "bleed" between the multiple fragments of the self across the lines of the magic circle, in which aspects of a player's physical identity may affect the choices they make inside of the game world (Waern 2010). However problematic the particulars of the concept may be, the idea of the magic circle is important to retain because participants in virtual worlds are aware of the boundary between the virtual and the physical, and those boundaries may be reinforced by interaction with the same people in online and offline spaces (Boellstorff 2010; Cherny 1999).

Although it is important to remember that the magic circle is a problematic construct, I reference the magic circle because it exists as an important emic construct in the *World of Warcraft* community. In general, when I refer to the magic circle, I mean the fluid and porous boundary between offline and online contexts. Dmitri Williams's *mapping principle* (2010) helps to understand how the context of the virtual world affects player behaviors in important ways. Williams's example is the concept of death. In the physical world, death is a permanent state and carries with it weighty emotions and implications; however, in virtual worlds, death is often temporary. The temporary nature of virtual death leads to players intentionally killing each other as practical jokes, purposefully infecting others with virtual diseases, or laughing off a friend's death – all behaviors that would never be appropriate offline. Understanding the context of the virtual world is key to understanding the way players behave inside the magic circle and outside of it. The characteristics of the magic circle may change in different interactions and may shift throughout time, but the circle is always salient to participants in some capacity because it provides a boundary for the contexts that influence and guide their behavior.

Another behavior that is affected by the magic circle is the act of making connections between players. As players interact more with each other inside of the game's magic circle and eventually form relationships, they will inevitably come into contact with multiple fragments of identity in multiple contexts and begin to construct a larger picture of their interlocutors' identities. When a player is interacting only briefly with another in a game environment, the physical identity of the other player is not as important as their abilities in the game and their play style. If these interactions continue into stable game relationships, whether as part of a regular raid team, questing and adventuring partners, or friends in a guild, players seek to know about the identity of their comrades beyond the virtual space. Once a player begins to engage with other players in ways that reference identity outside of purely in-game features, they interact with broader aspects of their interlocutors' identities. They begin to understand that not only is their friend a Night Elf hunter in the game, but they learn that their friend is a female linguist in "real life" who enjoys science fiction novels and jazz music.

However, in learning more about the offline selves that belong to a player's online friends, a tension arises between online and offline identities in which people struggle with what to reveal about their "real-life" selves, what to keep hidden, and how to do so (Li, Jackson, and Trees 2008). Language is one oft-used resource for showing membership in certain demographic categories through the use of enregistered linguistic variables such as (ING)/(IN) variation, shifted vowels, or lexical choices (Agha 2006; Campbell-Kibler 2011). Some language features that index identity features cannot be changed or hidden easily if they are connected to an identity that a speaker does not want to reveal – for example, the pitch of one's voice and the amount of politeness are indicators of gender (Herring and Matinson 2004) and different sets of pronunciations index a speaker's location, ethnicity, or native language. Age is another identity that can be problematic in gaming performances, such as children or young adults with young-sounding voices who are playing adult characters in online games (Wadley and Gibbs 2010). If a player decides to use their voice to communicate with their fellow players, there are some identity traits that they could hide and others that will be easily conveyed by the sound of their voice or their manner of speaking. WoW players are aware of this; furthermore, they become aware of the consequences for possessing particular types of easily-conveyed identities through interaction with the broad community of players.

When I was interviewing participants during my ethnography, a young man called Pollux described the various ways that he perceived that he had been treated poorly due to being much younger than the average *World of Warcraft* player. He described how he had been denied leadership positions, constantly referred to with demeaning and diminutive names, and even had his voice made fun of in public forums. After he listed the ways that he felt marginalized, he said a phrase that stuck with me: "It could have been worse. At least I'm not Chinese, gay, or female. They have it really bad." In the following section, I will explore those marked identities that were problematized by the *World of Warcraft* player population during my ethnography, and the resulting impact on the players and their use of language and communicative mode.

## 3 Marked identities in *World of Warcraft*

The dominant, unmarked identity in *World of Warcraft* is a white, heterosexual, American male; for those who do not fit into this classification, how does the dominant identity shape their experience? In this work, I will focus on two particular sets of marked identities: non-male/non-heterosexual, and non-white/non-American. While each of these four identities have different experiences (and there are many other identities that are not the focus of this paper), they are grouped into two sets because each set has similar experiences. Those who are non-male and/or non-heterosexual face exclusion from events and general harassment based on their status as a threat to the dominant identity in the game; those who are non-American and/or non-white are linguistically profiled based on their language, both negatively and positively.

In the following sections, I will discuss the cultural environment in *World of Warcraft* for players with marked identities, beginning with gender and sexuality and followed by ethnicity, highlighting the role of language variety in the communication and identity landscape. These sections will include examples from broad gaming culture as well as examples from my ethnography. In subsequent sections, I will describe the communication methods (including the choice of which mode of communication to use) that players used to avoid identification with marked identities. Finally, I will discuss the impact on players themselves as well as the game environment resulting from avoidance of these identities.

### 3.1 Gender and sexuality

Hegemonic masculinity is a useful concept for understanding behavior in *World of Warcraft*. Kiesling (1998: 71) explains it as an "ideology based on a hierarchy of dominant alignment roles, especially men over women, but also men over other men." Hegemonic masculinity accepts and, in fact, *relies* on the existence of multiple forms of masculinity that exist in any culture, and can therefore only be understood in relation to other forms of identity that exist around it (Coates 2001: 3). In the *World of Warcraft* community of my ethnography, the dominant form of masculinity was the white, American, young adult, heterosexual male; other male identities were more or less accepted (older men, native English speakers from non-American countries), while some were explicitly marked (gay men, non-native English speakers).

Nardi (2010) devotes a chapter of her ethnography of *World of Warcraft* to dealing with the hegemonic masculinity that exists in the game community. Nardi (2010: 152) characterizes the space inside of the *WoW* magic circle as "the boys' tree house," with women existing as a minority that must be subsumed in the tree house or overtly excluded. In Nardi's account, "male discourse" (she labels it this way because it was primarily males who engaged in it) was the norm rather than the exception, and women were expected to conform to the discourse around them (including homophobic and sexist language) and accept the overt sexualization of women for the enjoyment of the male players. Women or gay men may intrude upon the tree house and threaten the status of heterosexual men as the dominant identity and target audience for the game. To avoid this, many heterosexual male players often engage in masculinist discourse during advanced gaming activities (such as raiding), and this discourse is considered effective if it offends or excludes female and gay male players (162).

The masculinist discourse and the assumed maleness of players creates an environment where women and LGBT individuals have to "come out" and publicly display their identity in contrast to their assumed heterosexual maleness, and where they assume risks for doing so. In such an environment, many players in these populations either hid their identities or conformed to the discourse around them. In Nardi's study, she described that those who did conform to the discourse generally avoided "hardcore masculinist rhetoric" themselves; however, part of conforming to the discourse is being silent about others' use of these terms (Nardi 2010: 156). Taylor (2003) has described how women in online games are not subjected to the same risks as they are in the physical world (another application of Williams's (2010) mapping principle), which gives some a sense of empowerment that allows them to confront those who use such rhetoric; in fact, some female players called out others on their uses of such terms, but overall, the masculinist rhetoric went largely unchallenged.

Some women in Nardi's study as well as in Gray's (2012) study of players of games on the Xbox Live network avoided the masculinist discourse by building their own networks of people they enjoyed playing with. The guild that served as the home for my ethnographic study is an example of this kind of network; known as a "safe space" guild, <Ragnarok> was a guild where women as well as lesbian, gay, bisexual, and transgender players were welcome to play while not being forced to hide their identities. It was not the only guild of its type on the server, and was one of hundreds of safe space guilds in the *World of Warcraft* community. To ensure the safety of its players, guild leadership enacted rules against derogatory language and harassment and relied on participatory surveillance tactics to enforce the rules (see Collister 2014 for an in-depth discussion of the guild's surveillance culture).

These tactics kept guild members safe while interacting with members of the guild itself and at guild-sponsored game events, but players still had to worry about the rest of the *World of Warcraft* culture outside of the guild. Players often encounter others from different guilds who play by different rules when it comes to identity-based harassment. To this end, while many women and LGBT individuals felt safe within the *World of Warcraft* space occupied by their guild <Ragnarok>, they had to adjust their expectations and behavior when interacting outside of the scope of the guild. Like Gatson's (2011) study of fandom communities as safe spaces for identity expression online, <Ragnarok> and guilds like it essentially created another magic circle for themselves inside of the magic circle of the *World of Warcraft* game. There was movement across the boundaries, but rules applied differently inside of the guild than outside of it, and players were highly conscious of the boundaries and the rules outside of the guild.

## 3.2 Non-nativeness, linguistic profiling, and linguistic adoration

Another stereotype of the *World of Warcraft* player is that it is dominated by American English speakers. "Nativeness" and accent when speaking are thus another source of scrutiny, and the perceived level of nativeness leads to practices of *linguistic profiling*, or the act of assigning identities and stereotypes based on the language variety used by the speaker (Baugh 2003; Moyer 2013). The protections in the <Ragnarok> guild against gender- and sexuality-based harassment did not extend to linguistic profiling. While the guild's bylaws included prohibitions of racist language, it was not a focus of the guild's mission and therefore did not receive the type of surveillance and scrutiny that gender- and sexuality-based harassment did. Players who spoke non-American or non-native forms of English received scrutiny and sometimes identity-based harassment both inside the guild and outside of it.

In *World of Warcraft* specifically, the Chinese identity is problematic due to the racialization of cheating and gold farming, practices which are propagated by player-made videos such as *Ni Hao* by Nyhm[3] that generalize all Chinese-speaking players as cheaters (Dibbell 2007). The Chinese players in Nardi's (2010) study of gaming cafes in China did not judge each other so harshly (176), but when Chinese players come into contact with other players, especially from English-speaking countries, they are often linguistically profiled based on their level of nativeness in speaking English. Any speaker who is judged to be not a native speaker is assumed to be using questionable methods to achieve in-game success (Nakamura 2009). Nick Yee (2006) writes, "it is not the behavior

---

[3] "Ni Hao" by Nyhm can be viewed here: https://www.youtube.com/watch?v=0dkkf5NEIo0

per se that is the damning piece of evidence as to whether a player is a gold farmer, but rather, whether they are fluent in the English language" (6). Yee supports this assertion with a number of stories from his large-scale survey project, but the most striking is the following story from a French-Canadian player:

```
I'm French Canadian and it happen to me to answer in French to
get rid of moron.
So there is this guy: "can I get gold, I will send it back to you
by mail, I want to buy an epic"
Me: "pardon je ne parle pas anglais!"
Him: "WTF hey do you have GOLD"
Me: "Vraiment desole, je ne comprends pas!"
Him: "I'll report you, f*** farmer, china FARMER are the suckx!"
(Yee 2006: 2)
```

In this example, simply not speaking English at all resulted in another player assigning a "china FARMER" identity to a French-speaking Canadian. For many, the diversity in non-English speakers is erased, and non-English speakers are leveled into one stigmatized identity group: Chinese Gold Farmer.

Players in Yee's and Nakamura's studies report repeatedly harassing players who were suspected to be gold farmers because of their level of English fluency. Simply not speaking English renders a player automatically cast as "Chinese" and therefore a target for racist discourse and harassment. This has led to a conflation between the Chinese ethnicity and a style of play referred to as "Chinese," similar to that which was observed by Steinkuehler (2006) in the game *Lineage II* and which contributed to animosity between Asian and American players in that game (209). This conflation of ethnicity and play style was problematic for Chinese players in *World of Warcraft*, many of whom resented being reduced to the status of "gold farmer" because of their ethnicity. Because of this, some Chinese players choose to remain on Chinese language servers, because they are less likely to encounter these stereotypes. They do this despite the fact that Chinese servers are less populated and game content is often changed in China due to government regulations (Nardi 2010: 185).

It is not only the Chinese population of *World of Warcraft* that is viewed this way, but like Yee's (2006) study, any non-English speaking population may be subjected to xenophobic treatment from members of the dominant identity group. Due to changes to the *World of Warcraft* server structure beginning in late 2013, participants in my ethnography have identified xenophobia on their server centered around an influx of Portuguese speakers. The American server that players from my ethnography inhabit is often paired up with a Portuguese-speaking Brazilian server for events, resulting in a mixing of the populations.

The American residents of the server have expressed a xenophobic attitude towards Portuguese speakers, categorizing the Brazilians as less skilled than their American counterparts, and resulting in the exclusion of players on Brazilian servers from American-led groups. This behavior results from the English-speaking population assigning the communicative burden – or the responsibility to ensure a successful conversation – to the non-native English speaking players. Lippi-Green (2011: 70) suggests that when speakers hear a foreign accent, they have to decide whether to accept a role in accommodation of that accent or disfluency in speech. Furthermore, she writes, "members of the dominant language group feel perfectly empowered to reject their responsibility, and to demand that a person with an accent carry the majority of the burden in the communicative act."

I did not observe the interaction between Portuguese speakers and English speakers in *World of Warcraft* because the server structure change did not happen until after my ethnography was over; however, a participant in my ethnography, Hohenheim, wrote to me in an e-mail to inform me of this phenomenon:

> Hohenheim: There have definitely been groups where people have been kicked [out] for being from Brazilian servers [...] there have been nights where people are like "Nobody from Brazil" or such. I've seen people complain about groups started by someone on a Brazilian server not speaking English. There seems to be a tendency of those folks to use all caps- like, it doesn't seem to be shouting to them, it's just kind of like whatever, caps lock on away we go, which leads to friction with the English speaking players who view that as rude and shouting. I haven't noticed any sort of quality of player correlation- like, you get good, bad, and mediocre out of both groups at roughly equal distributions, I think. But they're definitely perceived as lesser players more often than is fair, in terms of getting kicked [out] more quickly. I think condescending speech could be either actually condescending or just a stereotypical American not really knowing how to communicate with someone whose command of English is not perfect.
> (Hohenheim, personal communication, September 2014)

Hohenheim singled out some common observations, including the conflict between languages in the media ideology surrounding typing in all capital letters; the necessity of speaking English; and, the associated perception that these players are not as skilled as American, English-speaking counterparts. To further illustrate the point, Hohenheim shared the screenshots in Figure 1 with me. These screenshots (with speaker names obscured) show text chat during a raid. In Figure 1a, the speaker lists off the Brazilian servers and indicates that the "#1 rule of WoW" is to never invite anyone from these Brazilian servers to a group. The second screenshot, in Figure 1b, shows players excluding another player from participation in a raid event due to not speaking English.

**Figure 1a:** Screenshot provided by Hohenheim of a player excluding members of Brazilian servers from groups

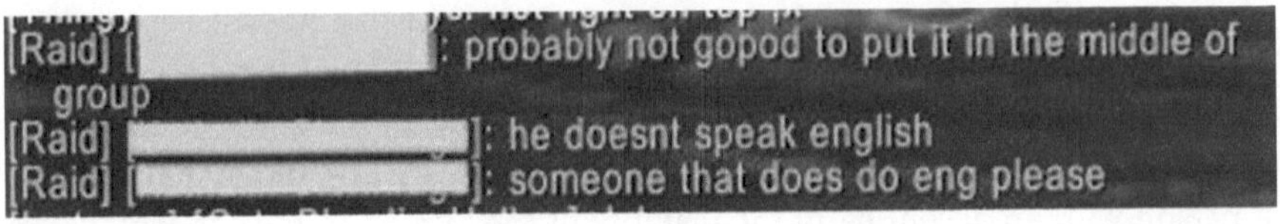

**Figure 1b:** Screenshot provided by Hohenheim of players excluding a non-native speaker from a raiding activity

Hohenheim's report is reminiscent of the treatment of Chinese players, although without the correlation to gold farming. Brazilians are perceived as rude, and get kicked out of (or excluded entirely from) groups for being from a Brazilian server due to a perception of being less skilled at playing the game; the perception of their skill comes only from the perception of their language abilities and the English-speaking Americans' belief that they do not know how to communicate with the Brazilian players. The communicative burden, or the responsibility of mutual comprehension to ensure successful communication, is placed on the non-native English speakers to accommodate to the American population that is presumed to be the dominant population. The linguistic profiling of players from the Brazilian servers illustrates that exclusion from gaming activities based on language variety is not limited to Chinese players.

At the other end of the spectrum from linguistic profiling, *linguistic adoration* refers to the assignment of positive values (sometimes uncomfortably so) to a speaker of a prestigious variety (Baugh 2003). Baugh refers to linguistic adoration by American English speakers for speakers of what he calls "British English" as well as speakers of French. Baugh pointed out that only some varieties of British English receive such adoration; conversely, Lippi-Green's (2011: 101-129) analysis of voice acting in animated films revealed an overwhelming use of British English varieties for villains in these films (see also Cutler, this volume). In *World of Warcraft*, players from Australia and the United Kingdom often chose to play on American servers and encountered linguistic adoration while doing so. Elisa, a young woman from Australia who was a member of <Ragnarok>, worked overnight in a busy hospital and liked to play *WoW* to relax after her shift ended at 5:00 AM. This time happened to coincide with the time when most players on our American server were starting nightly gaming activities, giving Elisa an active group of friends across the world who happened to be gaming at the same time she was. On more than one occasion, Elisa reported that she felt like some people took her along on raids or other gaming activities not just for her playing abilities, but because they liked her Australian accent and found her voice to be sexy. This was not an unfounded assumption: when Elisa went offline after a raid one night in August of 2009, I observed the following conversation in text chat between two participants still online:

```
[Raid] Dakster: so sad she went offline
[Raid] Dakster: pretty voice is gone =(
[Raid] Terna: yeah I'm so glad when shes here
[Raid] Terna: shes an ok player but nothin like that aussie accent to keep you up on a long raid nite
[Raid] Dakster: if u kno what I mean ha ha ha
```

The two (American male) players Dakster and Terna made an overt connection between Elisa's Australian accent and positive evaluations ("pretty voice," "so glad when shes here"); however, Dakstser's response "if you kno what I mean" makes an explicitly sexual connotation out of Terna's phrase about the accent "keep(ing) you up." The implication here is that Elisa is valued in the raid more for her voice and the sexual response it elicits in these male players than for her playing ability ("shes an ok player").

The language variety itself – whether it was one that elicited linguistic profiling or linguistic adoration – is not explicitly addressed in any policies in the guild; only harassment using derogatory language toward another individual was addressed. A player's way of speaking could still elicit these negative responses even when protective policies were in place. To avoid these negative responses, players developed strategies for their communication and use of different communicative modes to avoid negative repercussions for the sound of their voice.

## 4 Interactional strategy: Avoiding voice chat

I have illustrated how when a player's identity does not fit into the dominant identity of the culture, there are repercussions for revealing that identity including sexual-based harassment for women and gay men (Nardi, 2010), animosity based on racial identity constructs (Steinkuehler 2006), or the linguistic adoration of non-American (particularly United Kingdom) "accents" of English (Baugh

2003). While there were protections written into <Ragnarok>'s charter prohibiting harassment of any guild member based on gender, sexuality, or race, these protections did not extend outside of the guild and, in the case of ethnicity and race, were problematic even inside of the guild. When players stepped outside of <Ragnarok>'s own "magic circle," they were aware of the rules at play in the larger community and had strategies for dealing with other players who operated under that rule set.

In general, the players that I interviewed from the guild did not express reservations about talking to unknown players using text chat – in contrast to attitudes about voice chat. Even aggressive players who used forms of speech prohibited in the guild seem more distant and, consequently, less threatening in the text chat (see Iorio's chapter in this volume for another discussion of the impact of communicative mode on the interpretation of language use). Reasons for this include the ability to use the built-in /ignore function (which blocks all communication from the ignored player), as well as the lack of physical cues present in text chat which would otherwise reveal marked identity traits. Furthermore, text chat was policed by protective Game Masters (GMs), and if a player reported harassing behavior it was likely to be investigated by the GMs (even if players did not always see results of this protective measure – see Collister (2014) for a more thorough discussion).

Players expressed the majority of their concerns and fears about interacting with unknown, non-guild players when the modality they would be using would be voice chat. The situation in which players most often found themselves interacting with unknown others is during *pick-up-groups* (PUGs), or collections of otherwise unrelated players which most often formed for the purpose of raiding. Voice chat was almost universally required in these groups; however, if there was not a guild hosting the event, many times no set rules were in place for conduct beyond the most basic gaming norms (being a competent player, not stealing loot, etc.). Beyond these minimal *World of Warcraft*-wide norms, conduct can vary widely; players could abide by similar rules that <Ragnarok> had in place (often resulting in that player being asked to fill-in for guild raids) or they could be aggressive and unpleasant. Furthermore, voice chat platforms were not policed by GMs or any other authorities besides these unknown players, and offered little protection for users against harassment or unwanted behavior.

Fears about potential conflict with other players based on voice chat were alleviated in two ways: carefully attending to one's way of speaking or not speaking at all. Some players could hide their identities by carefully attending to the way they spoke. One member of <Ragnarok>, Theon, was often identified as gay by his use of features of gay-sounding speech; in an interview during the ethnography, he described the ways that he would not lie about his identity, but be careful about overt markers in his speech when around players he did not know.

> Theon: I guess when people talk to somebody that they know is gay online they automatically assume that they're going to have the stereotypical voice, you know, like they expect me to talk like Sacha Baron Cohen's Bruno [a film character with a stereotypical flamboyant gay style] or something, and I don't, so I guess that, that, that's a surprise for some people. And then for actual ticks in the voice I suppose that there is a little bit of a lisp there but it's not completely in-your-face. [...] I do try to be careful about it. Although I make no effort to hide it, I will not outwardly say it, or say anything about it unless I'm in a situation that I deem where I'm able to do something like that. Like, say for example, I'm meeting somebody for the first time, I usually will gauge their openmindedness a little bit before I say anything at length.

Speakers like Theon, who used a variety of gay-sounding speech and were aware of it, often style-shifted when using Ventrilo to avoid having to deal with potential harassment from unknown players. When I listened to Theon speak in a raiding context with a guild other than <Ragnarok>, he spoke with much shorter sentences and a clipped tone than when it was just friendly guild members. This style-shifting is reminiscent of the observations by Podesva (2008) on gay males and style shifts from a professional workplace and a casual gathering of friends. Theon's speaking style in a mixed-member raid situation might align with a professional setting, while his style in casual guild-only settings may be similar to those observed in casual offline settings by Podesva.

Not all speakers are able to hide the identifying features in their voices. Because voice chat and raiding are so closely linked, many women with female-sounding voices feel great discomfort when (and often exclusion from) participating in raids (Nardi 2010: 163). For these reasons, women often reported being afraid to speak on Ventrilo for fear of being "discovered" as a woman and subjected to unwanted treatment or exclusion. The women in <Ragnarok> encountered unwanted treatment outside of the guild, such as one guild member, Haley, who expressed in her interview that she was uncomfortable talking on Ventrilo outside of the guild because of "creepy guys":

> LBC: Has there ever been a circumstance for you in which you were reluctant to use voice chat?
>
> Haley: I don't think I have so far. Um, I think there's been a few times where I've been in a random PUG and it was a joke–not a bad joke or anything but I was just joked about like "Oh, it's a girl!" or something like that, you know, but it was never a way that made me uncomfortable, I think. I don't really have too much of a qualm too, I know some people don't wanna be known as a girl because they don't wanna be looked down on as far as ability. I don't really care about that 'cause if

>they, you know, if they're gonna be a stickler about it I'd rather not play with them anyway. [laughing] But I probably wouldn't willingly talk on voice with people outside of our guild, either, unless, say, I knew them and they were friends or something like that.

LBC: Why not, do you think? Why wouldn't you be willing to talk to strangers?

Haley: I think it depends on the situation, I think for me as a girl there's definitely the factor of there's some creepy guys out there. [laugh] And I don't wanna deal with that at all, or even be put in that situation, and so it'd be easier just to chat first on text with them for a while.

Haley describes a multimodal strategy for deciding whether another person outside of the guild is safe to talk to on Ventrilo – by chatting with them in the text chat mode first. Her strategy suggests that she presumes that text chat can effectively conceal one's identity; indeed, this is a long-standing observation in the research literature, that online text-based contexts lend anonymity to the users and allow them to experiment with identity (see, e.g., Danet 1998). Haley does note that this strategy is in place only for those "outside of our guild" – reinforcing the existence of the magic circle created by <Ragnarok> inside of the guild itself.

Eversoul, an officer of <Ragnarok> with far-reaching connections on the server, expressed a similar sentiment to Haley. She describes her first interactions on Ventrilo and how she was shy to talk at first because she did not know anyone in the raid group, but also that she felt that the others were surprised that she was a female. During her interview, I asked her if she felt awkward in her previous guild being the only woman on Ventrilo with a group of men.

Eversoul: Yeah, it was a little weird being the only girl, but it somehow didn't surprise me. I don't think that was why I didn't talk, I think it was just because I didn't really know anybody else just yet.

LBC: How did they react to you being a female? Was it just like no big deal, or did they make a big deal out of it or comment on it in any way?

Eversoul: They didn't really make a big deal out of it. I guess when I first started going on runs with <Apathy> [another guild] and being in their chat program, some of them were surprised that I was a girl.

LBC: Like in that they thought – they had thought previously that you were a guy or that they were just surprised that there was a girl in general?

Eversoul: Probably both, because I don't think they – I think they have one female player and she never speaks in Vent. [laugh] And other than that they don't really run into too many female players, I guess.

LBC: So how did they react when you talked on Vent?

Eversoul: It was just general surprise and the standard line that "girls don't play *WoW*."

Eversoul's experience echoes Haley's and Theon's – she was reluctant to use voice chat with unknown others because she did not know the quality of the people she was interacting with, but felt more comfortable after she had interacted with the group more regularly and had gotten to know them.

Women were not the only ones who used these avoidance strategies to allow them more time to assess the people around them before talking on Ventrilo. A player named Donnal participated in a few of <Ragnarok>'s raids to fill in for missing guild members, and after several times filling in, he decided to join the guild formally. Only after he joined the guild and had time to read the guild's charter and talk in text chat with other members did he speak on Ventrilo, and it was then that we heard his Scottish-sounding English for the first time. I took down the following conversation between Donnal and Mindy, a veteran female <Ragnarok> member, from a casual conversation on Ventrilo in my ethnographic notebook:

Mindy: Your accent is so cool.

Donnal: Oh, are you going to tell me I'm sexy now?

Mindy: Not really, it's just nice to hear a new voice. I like hearing people from different places.

[silence]

Donnal: In my last guild, there was this woman who would not leave me be because of my accent. She even asked me to marry her and told me way more than I wanted to know about her reaction to my voice. I'm pretty sure she didn't know anything about me besides the fact that my accent turned her on. I never wanted to talk when she was around, and that's why I wanted to leave.

In this interaction, there are two expressions of linguistic adoration: the discomfort that Donnal felt when another player sexualized his way of speaking, and Mindy's judgment that his accent was "so cool." Donnal described how he avoided talking on Ventrilo in order to distance himself from the unwanted attention from his guildmate, and that being uncomfortable about talking on Ventrilo made him want to leave the group. Being uncomfortable about voice chat leads to feelings of distance from the rest of the group and can weaken ties between community members.

A similar discomfort about talking on Ventrilo as a non-American English speaker also occurs for non-native English speakers but with a much more derogatory connotation. An example of this from my ethnography is the experience of <Ragnarok> member Mork, a native Mandarin Chinese speaker. Mork was from China and was living in the United States while going to a university.

Mork's non-native English was quite evident when speaking on Ventrilo, sometimes to the extent that I could not understand the message that he was trying to convey. The particular variety of non-native English that Mork spoke was easily identifiable as Chinese, especially since Mork was proud of his heritage and often mentioned going "home" to China to visit his family during breaks from school.

Mork experienced linguistic profiling often, and vehemently voiced protestations against members of the guild who shared the *Ni Hao* video that mocked Chinese players as being gold farmers. Even though the guild had prohibitions against racist language, a lot of players did not understand how the *Ni Hao* video was racist and hurtful towards Chinese players. Mork told me once in November of 2008:

> Mork whispers: its not funny !! i don't even want to talk anymore
>
> Mork whispers: everytime someone talks to me on vent, they say, oh your Chinese?
>
> Mork whispers: and i say yes...
>
> Mork whispers: and they say "you hear about that ni hao song" and ask me a question about like how to make money
>
> Mork whispers: like they think i'm some gold farmer... so annoying !!

Mork's experience shows how the stereotypes about Chinese players in online games come up in everyday conversations. The association between his language variety and gold farming was so problematic for Mork that he refrained from speaking on Ventrilo to anyone except those that he had carefully vetted. While he was certainly forthcoming with his identity in casual speech, most often the first clue to players about Mork's Chinese identity was the variety of language he spoke. The association with gold farming was problematic for Mork, and it started with something he could not change – the way he spoke in voice chat. Because he avoided Ventrilo to avoid gold farming comments from other players, he missed much of the social interaction that happened in voice chat, causing him to feel left out of the guild's community. Eventually, through loneliness, he quit the guild and moved on to play on a different *World of Warcraft* server based in China. Mork's story is similar to Donnal's story, even though they experienced very different reactions to their language varieties from the community. The pressure to use Ventrilo in the community thus interacts with stereotypes about identity to create an unwelcoming environment for both Mork and Donnal, leading to their exclusion from part of the gaming community.

## 5 Discussion

The hegemonic masculinity of *World of Warcraft* and the full identity associated with it – white, heterosexual, American – leads to behavior that discriminates against those who do not conform to those identities. This behavior manifests in linguistic adoration of non-American English speakers, xenophobia and discrimination towards non-native speakers, and harassment of women and gay men. To play the game and participate with the larger *WoW* culture, players are expected to conform to and accept the discourse that surrounds them. This is why guilds like <Ragnarok> exist – to create a safe space inside of the magic circle where different rules apply.

The alternative – that is, objecting to masculinist and racist discourse and/or freely performing an identity outside of the safe space – has problematic consequences. Those women who objected to the masculinist discourse were often forced into more casual guilds because of the threat of female sexuality in *WoW* culture. Nardi describes two examples of this happening during her ethnography: women were unwillingly silenced on Ventrilo because their voices were said to disturb the men, and women were refused membership to very hardcore guilds like the top European guild <Nihilum> (163). This is not isolated to *World of Warcraft*; in studies of other virtual worlds, women in *Second Life* reported being sexually harassed after revealing their gender by talking on voice chat, and women playing *Dungeons and Dragons Online* reported feeling "weird and uncomfortable" when speaking on voice chat (Wadley and Gibbs 2010: 193). Tucker (2011) describes the widespread practice of *griefing*, or extensive harassment of a single player, as a means of policing the assumed masculinity and heterosexuality of populations of online game players. In Tucker's work, griefers often focused on those players who expressed a non-male or non-heterosexual identity that threatened the hegemonic masculinity of the gaming culture. Griefers like this have often extended their behavior to those outside of the game that they play with consequences that affect the lives of the people they target.

During my ethnography, a player named Laira was targeted by a group of male players with threats against her person, and in the broader gaming culture there have been repeated attacks on feminist commentator Anita Sarkeesian for her critiques of tropes in video games (for a summary, see Kocurek (2014) and Backe (2014)). It is not just the rules of the physical world that transcend the boundaries of the game's magic circle, but in these cases the social rules from the game world have moved outside of the boundaries of the game and impacted the lives of the players. To avoid such consequences, some players choose to avoid expressing their offline identities inside the magic circle of the game, including never using their speaking voice, as it would reveal their way of speaking, consequently making them vulnerable.

This exclusion of other identities leads to a perceived leveling of the culture through erasure of identities outside of the stereotype. The dominant discourse around online gaming suggests that the average player is a young adult, white, heterosexual, American male (Yee 2005), even though several studies have shown that games like *World of Warcraft* in particular have a quite varied demographic base (Williams, Yee, and Caplan 2008). In parodies of *World of Warcraft* such as the South Park episode *Make Love, Not Warcraft*, the stereotypical identity portrayed is that of a young, white, American male. Where does this come from and why does it persist? The answer lies in the dominant voices that shape the perception of the culture and the small actions like commenting about Chinese gold farmers or claiming that women are bought to events solely for their voice or their accent. Each one of these small actions contributes to the larger silencing of a substantial portion of the game-playing population.

In practice and in participation in the game, the population is much more diverse than what can be seen in the leveling of voices. In this work, I have described how the hegemonic masculinity of *World of Warcraft* culture silences the voices of those who do not fit into its identity. This includes women and gay men, whose presence threatens the dominant gender and sexual identities; as well as non-American and non-native English speakers, whose presence suggests that gaming is a global cultural phenomenon. This leads to pockets of safe spaces in gaming communities which often must police themselves with little or no help from the developers of games or the most powerful figures in the industry or community. However, the examples described in this work also show that these identities are present and participating in the culture, and they are accessible to those who look beyond the surface of the game and study the contexts that shape gaming behaviors. Safe spaces like <Ragnarok> have grown in number as more players of different types flock to the game; news around the harassment of women and allied individuals in the gaming industry has gained mainstream attention;[4] even the player-staffed Tribunal in the game *League of Legends* (Riot Games 2011) exists as an attempt to punish harassing behavior in

---

4 e.g., The 2014 "gamergate" coverage in the *Washington Post* (http://www.washingtonpost.com/news/morning-mix/wp/2014/09/12/with-gamergate-the-video-game-industrys-growing-pains-go-viral/), *Forbes* Magazine (http://www.forbes.com/sites/erikkain/2014/09/04/gamergate-a-closer-look-at-the-controversy-sweeping-video-games/), Al Jazeera (http://stream.aljazeera.com/story/201409032102-0024126), and the BBC (http://www.bbc.co.uk/news/technology-29028236), to name a few.

online games. The makeup of the community has begun to change as players become aware of the culture around them and the tools they have to work with.

The ethnographic observations presented in this chapter serve as examples of the cultural constructs in the *World of Warcraft* community. The lived experiences of players show the intersection of the norms of an online society with the language ideology of the offline world, as well as how the context and rules of the gaming environment change the behavior of players. The use of voice is a bridge across the boundary of the magic circle that brings those ideologies into play in the gaming space. To avoid changing the dynamics of their gaming space and their gaming identity, many players choose to not use their voice and never build that bridge. These players and their voices do exist, however, and they are an important part of gaming communities that may not be readily visible to outsiders. Using an in-depth approach like ethnography to study the people who play the games and their everyday experiences, including those that silence them, brings these voices out for researchers. These voices demonstrate how diverse the community is and how its members struggle with offline language ideologies even in an online world. The existence of safe spaces like <Ragnarok> and groups like it, while not perfect, provide a site for players with marked identities and marginalized voices to make themselves heard, allowing for the intersection of cultures that can be enriching for those involved. I will close on a hopeful note with another excerpt from my interview with Pollux, the young man who told me "at least I'm not Chinese, gay, or female":

> Pollux: Although I would have never met all these people if I hadn't played WoW, and probably not if I hadn't been in <Ragnarok>, you know. Now I can say I have friends, all kinds of friends. [...] I would have never known them growing up where I did. And now I have all these people I can ask, like, any question at all, and get real life advice. And I'm going to college now, and I've started my own business, and I think I'm better because I played the game and found this group.

# 6 References

Agha, Asif. 2006. *Language and social relations*. Cambridge: Cambridge University Press.
Backe, Emma Louise. 2014. Violence and victimization: Misogyny in geek culture (and everywhere else). http://thegeekanthropologist.com/2014/09/09/violence-and-victimization-misogyny-in-geek-culture-and-everywhere-else/ (accessed 9 September, 2014).
Bainbridge, William S. 2010. Introduction. In William S. Bainbridge (ed.), *Online worlds: Convergence of the real and virtual*, 1–6. London: Springer.
Baugh, John. 2003. Linguistic profiling. In Sinfree Makoni, Geneva Smitherman, Arnetha F. Ball & Arthur K. Spears (eds.), *Black linguistics: Language, society, and politics in Africa and the Americas*, 155–168. London: Routledge.

Baym, Nancy. 2010. *Personal connections in the digital age.* Malden, MA: Polity.

Bessière, Katherine, A. Fleming Seay & Sara Kiesler. 2007. The ideal elf: Identity exploration in World of Warcraft. *CyberPsychology & Behavior* 10(4). doi: 10.1089/cpb.2007.9994 (accessed 30 September 2014).

Boellstorff, Tom. 2008. *Coming of age in Second Life: An anthropologist explores the virtually human.* Princeton: Princeton University Press.

Boellstorff, Tom. 2010. A typology of ethnographic scales for virtual worlds. In William S. Bainbridge (ed.), *Online worlds: Convergence of the real and virtual*, 123–133. London: Springer.

Campbell-Kibler, Kathryn. 2011. The sociolinguistic variant as a carrier of social meaning. *Language Variation and Change* 22(3). doi: 10.1017/S0954394510000177 (accessed 30 September 2014).

Cherny, Lynn. 1999. *Conversation and community: Chat in a virtual world.* Stanford: CSLI Publications.

Coates, Jennifer. 2001. Pushing at the boundaries: The expression of alternative masculinities. In Janet Cotterill & Anne Ife (eds.), *Language across boundaries* (Selected Papers from the Annual Meeting of the British Association for Applied Linguistics Held at Anglia Polytechnic University, Cambridge, September 2000), 1–24. London: British Association for Applied Linguistics/Continuum.

Collister, Lauren B. 2008. *Virtual discourse structure: An analysis of conversation in World of Warcraft.* Pittsburgh, PA: University of Pittsburgh MA thesis. http://d-scholarship.pitt.edu/7992/ (accessed 29 April 2015).

Collister, Lauren B. 2011. *-repair in online discourse. *Journal of Pragmatics* 43(3). doi: 10.1016/j.pragma.2010.09.025 (accessed 27 April 2015).

Collister, Lauren B. 2012. The discourse deictics ^ and <– in a World of Warcraft community. *Discourse, Context and Media* 1(1). doi: 10.1016/j.dcm.2012.05.002 (accessed 27 April 2015).

Collister, Lauren B. 2013. *Multimodality as a sociolinguistic resource.* Pittsburgh, PA: University of Pittsburgh Ph.D. dissertation. http://d-scholarship.pitt.edu/18514/ (accessed 29 April 2015).

Collister, Lauren B. 2014. Surveillance and community: Language policing and empowerment in a World of Warcraft guild. *Surveillance & Society* 12(3). http://library.queensu.ca/ojs/index.php/surveillance-and-society/article/view/warcraft (accessed 30 September 2014).

Consalvo, Mia. 2009. There is no magic circle. *Games and Culture* 4(4). doi: 10.1177/1555412009343575 (accessed 30 September 2014).

Danet, Brenda. 1998. Text as mask: Gender, play, and performance on the Internet. In Steven G. Jones (ed.), *Cybersociety 2.0*, 129–158. Thousand Oaks, CA: Sage.

Dibbell, Julian. 2007. The life of the Chinese gold farmer. *The New York Times Magazine*, 36–41. June 17. http://www.nytimes.com/2007/06/17/magazine/17lootfarmers-t.html?pagewanted=all (accessed 30 September 2014).

Filiciak, Miroslaw. 2004. Hyperidentities: Postmodern identity patterns in massively multiplayer online role-playing games. In Mark J. P. Wolf & Bernard Perron (eds.), *The video game theory reader*, 87–102. New York: Routledge.

Gatson, Sarah N. 2011. Self-naming practices on the Internet: Identity, authenticity, and community. *Cultural Studies <–> Critical Methodologies* 11(3). doi: 10.1177/1532708611409531 (accessed 30 September 2014).

Gershon, Ilana. 2010. Media ideologies: An introduction. *Journal of Linguistic Anthropology* 20 (2). doi: 10.1111/j.1548-1395.2010.01070.x (accessed 27 April 2015).

Gray, Kishonna L. 2012. Intersecting oppressions and online communities: Examining the experiences of women of color in Xbox Live. *Information, Communication & Society* 15(3). doi: 10.1080/1369118X.2011.642401#.VCrjlGcVp8E (accessed 30 September 2014).
Herring, Susan C. & Anna Martinson. 2004. Assessing gender authenticity in computer-mediated language use: Evidence from an identity game. *Journal of Language and Social Psychology* 23(4). doi: 10.1177/0261927X04269586 (accessed 30 September 2014).
Huizinga, Johan. 1955. *Homo ludens: A study of the play-element in culture*. Boston: Beacon Press.
Kiesler, Sara, Jane Siegel & Timothy W. McGuire. 1984. Social psychological aspects of computer-mediated communication. *American Psychologist* 39(10). doi: 10.1037//0003-066X.39.10.1123 (accessed 30 September 2014).
Kiesling, Scott Fabius. 1998. Men's identities and sociolinguistic variation: The case of fraternity men. *Journal of Sociolinguistics* 2(1). 69–99.
Kocurek, Carly A. 2014. Gamers vs. Tropes vs. Women in Video Games. *Journal of Digital and Media Literacy* 2(2). http://www.jodml.org/2014/12/15/gamers-vs-tropes-vs-women-in-video-games/ (accessed 29 April 2015).
Li, Nan, Michele H. Jackson & April R. Trees. 2008. Relating online: Managing dialectical contradictions in massively multiplayer online role-playing game relationships. *Games and Culture* 3(1). doi: 10.1177/1555412007309529 (accessed 30 September 2014).
Lippi-Green, Rosina. 2011. *English with an accent: Language, ideology, and discrimination in the United States*. London: Routledge.
McKenna, Katelyn Y. A., Amie S. Green & Marci E. J. Gleason. 2002. Relationship formation on the Internet: What's the big attraction? *Journal of Social Issues* 58(1). 9–31.
Moyer, Alene. 2013. *Foreign accent: The phenomenon of non-native speech*. Cambridge: Cambridge University Press.
Nakamura, Lisa. 2009. Don't hate the player, hate the game: The racialization of labor in World of Warcraft. *Critical Studies in Media Communication* 26(2). doi: 10.1080/15295030902860252 (accessed 30 September 2014).
Nardi, Bonnie. 2010. *My life as a night elf priest: An anthropological account of World of Warcraft*. Ann Arbor: University of Michigan Press.
O'Brien, Jodi. 1999. Writing in the body: Gender (re)production in online interaction. In Marc Smith & Peter Kollock (eds), *Communities in cyberspace*, 76–104. New York: Routledge.
Paasonen, Susanna. 2005. *Figures of fantasy: Internet, women, and cyberdiscourse*. New York: Peter Lang Publishing.
Podesva, Robert J. 2008. Three sources of stylistic meaning. Paper presented at the Symposium About Language and Society at Austin (SALSA) 15, Austin, Texas. http://studentorgs.utexas.edu/salsa/proceedings/2007/Podesva.pdf (accessed 18 April 2016).
Riot Games Inc. 2011. Policy and procedure for 'The Tribunal'. http://beta.na.leagueoflegends.com/legal/tribunal/ (accessed 12 April 2011).
Salter, Anastasia & Bridget Blodgett. 2012. Hypermasculinity & dickwolves: The contentious role of women in the new gaming public. *Journal of Broadcasting & Electronic Media* 56(3). doi: 10.1080/08838151.2012.705199 (accessed 4 August 2015).
Schiano, Diane J., Bonnie Nardi, Thomas Debeauvais, Nicolas Ducheneaut & Nick Yee. 2011. A new look at World of Warcraft's social landscape. Paper presented at the 6th International Conference on the Foundations of Digital Games (FDG 2011),Bordeaux, France, 28 June–1 July. http://www.nickyee.com/pubs/FDG%20-%20Social%20Landscape%20(2011).pdf (accessed 30 September 2014).

Steinkuehler, Constance. 2006. The mangle of play. *Games and Culture* 1(3). doi: 10.1177/1555412006290440 (accessed 30 September 2014).

Stone, Allucquère Rosanne. 1995. *The war of desire and technology at the close of the mechanical age*. Cambridge, MA: MIT Press.

Taylor, T. L. 2003. Multiple pleasures: Women and online gaming. *Convergence: The International Journal of Research into New Media Technologies* 9(1). doi: 10.1177/135485650300900103 (accessed 30 September 2014).

Tucker, Staci. 2011. *Griefing: Policing masculinity in online games*. Eugene, OR: University of Oregon MA Thesis.

Wadley, Greg & Gibbs, M. R. 2010. Speaking in character: Voice communication in virtual worlds. In William S. Bainbridge (ed.), *Online worlds: Convergence of the real and virtual*, 187–200. London: Springer.

Waern, Annika. 2010. "I'm in love with someone that doesn't exist!!": Bleed in the context of a computer game. Paper presented at the 2010 Nordic DiGRA conference, Stockholm, Sweden, 16–17 August. http://www.digra.org/wp-content/uploads/digital-library/10343.00215.pdf (accessed 30 September 2014).

Williams, Dmitri. 2010. The mapping principle, and a research framework for virtual worlds. *Communication Theory* 20(4). doi: 10.1111/j.1468-2885.2010.01371.x (accessed 30 September 2014).

Williams, Dmitri, Nick Yee & Scott E. Caplan. 2008. Who plays, how much, and why? Debunking the stereotypical gamer profile. *Journal of Computer-Mediated Communication* 13(4). doi: 10.1111/j.1083-6101.2008.00428.x (accessed 30 September 2014).

Yee, Nick. 2005. *WoW* gender–bending. http://www.nickyee.com/daedalus/archives/001369.php (accessed 18 April, 2016).

Yee, Nick. 2006. Yi-Shan-Guan. http://www.nickyee.com/daedalus/archives/001493.php (accessed 18 April 2016).

# Index

abbreviation 135, 158–162, 228–229, 235–236, 287, 333
 – see shortening, lexical
accent
 – Australian 364–365
 – British 118–119
 – non-American 365, 369
 – nonnative 361–372
 – Scottish 69–92, 353, 369
adjective 136, 153, 160–163, 180, 187–190, 198–199
 – gradation 301–325
adolescence 23, 34–38, 86, 268, 272
adulthood 23, 38
affixation 131–138
African American (Vernacular) English 7, 43–48, 104, 154, 157, 242–245, 254, 268, 271, 274
 – see identity, African American
Appalachian English 264–270
audience 22–29, 33–39, 158, 222, 270–274, 360
audience design theory 22
authenticity 71–72, 75, 92, 107–108, 111, 116–118, 125, 223, 262–263, 356

blending 124, 129–132, 139

change
 – language 101, 150, 155–159, 256, 321
 – sociolinguistic 9
chat
 – text 275, 282–287, 351, 355
 – voice 351, 353–354, 365–371
code-switching 18, 34, 36–37, 220
complementation 151–173
compounding 123–124, 129–133, 137–138, 140–143
communicative mode
 – see mode of communication
community 75, 104–108, 116–120, 124–126, 139, 142–144, 270–271, 345, 370
 – speech 103, 120, 126, 254, 263–264, 271–274

corpus 46, 107–110, 112, 120, 127–129, 181–182, 184–186, 188–203, 223–224, 246–248, 254, 275, 289–290, 302, 308–309, 321–323
corpus linguistics 150–152, 155, 158, 304–307
cyberpunk 123–144

DH-stopping 7, 111, 116, 244–256
diaspora 102–111, 117–121
discourse 8, 9, 17–18, 20, 22, 34–35, 37, 107, 109, 117, 119, 137, 157, 158, 169, 173, 180–182, 186, 188, 190–192, 199–205, 248–249, 273–275, 332, 360, 362, 371–372
 – public 8, 9, 179, 208, 221, 242
 – see metadiscourse
discourse marker 86, 109, 183, 196, 201, 202
discussion forum 104–108, 124–143, 282–298

emoticons 80, 84, 87–88, 91, 164, 182, 187, 191, 194–197, 199, 201–202, 204–205, 224–225, 228, 267
English as a lingua franca 25–26, 37–39, 105–106, 179, 345
enregisterment 3, 57, 62, 74–75, 79, 88, 91, 92, 114, 119, 131, 241–245, 248, 252–253, 263, 358
ethnicity 5, 6, 19, 45, 85–86, 92, 104–105, 107, 234–235, 242, 244, 252, 358–359, 362, 366
ethnography 17, 22, 266, 352–359, 362–363, 371–373

Facebook 17–39, 48, 52, 220
femininity 214–215, 221, 236–237
fiction 123–126, 140–143, 201, 307
Finland 179–205
forum
 – see discussion forum
frequency 107, 120, 124, 128, 152, 158, 161–164, 172–174, 186, 194, 198, 200, 223, 226, 229, 246, 256, 262, 290–292, 294–297, 303–305, 310–320, 322

game
- role-playing 133, 351–373
- video 123, 130, 137, 143
gender 5, 9, 23, 74, 89, 108, 151, 184, 213, 216, 221–222, 224–225, 236–239, 268, 354, 358, 359–361, 366, 371–372
- grammatical 110
Global Englishes 102, 204
- see World Englishes
globalization 17–20, 39, 180, 345
- sociolinguistics of 101–102, 105, 107, 120–122
grammatical features 180, 186–187, 189, 191, 199–201, 253, 302–303, 323

identity 2, 4, 5, 6, 9, 23, 38, 44, 49, 55, 57, 61, 62, 74–75, 87, 104, 107, 108, 111, 117–119, 143–144, 183, 213–223, 233–237, 243, 261–266, 268, 273–275, 351–362, 365–366, 368, 370, 371–373
- African American 218, 234–235, 262–274
indexicality 6, 20–21, 37, 55, 57, 74–76, 86, 111, 117, 134, 151, 154, 221–222, 236–237, 241–242, 253, 256, 358
innovation
- lexical 9, 124, 126, 180, 322
- linguistic 18–19, 101, 143–144, 150, 152–155, 161, 170–174
- orthographic 43
- see neologism
instant messaging 201, 261–274, 283–284, 286–287, 301, 308–323, 331–334
intertextuality 8, 29–32, 35, 36, 38, 270–271

language
- attitudes 4, 8–9, 71–72, 74–76, 106, 327–333, 335–338, 343–347
- choice 17–18, 20–21, 22, 24–27, 32–36, 39, 184
- ideology 7–10, 74, 245, 373
Latin 49–56, 60, 63
lengthening
- expressive 180, 18–184, 188, 195–197, 202–205, 224
- prosodic 224–225, 228–229, 236
- vowel 73, 78, 84

lexical
- frequency
  - see frequency, lexical
- shortening
  - see shortening, lexical
linguistic profiling 6, 361, 364–365, 370

magic circle 356–359, 361, 366, 368, 371–373
mapping principle 357, 360
masculinity 92, 243, 359, 371–372
medium 4–6, 52, 156, 162, 164, 179, 181, 200, 203, 264, 274, 282–283, 294, 297, 301, 307, 314, 316–317, 322, 356
metadiscourse 78, 220–221, 234–235
metalinguistic
- commentary 10, 56, 69, 75–76, 78, 85–87, 90–92, 111, 117–119, 157, 171
- highlighting 133, 135, 137
metapragmatics 20, 69–70, 76, 85, 91–92, 245
migration 20, 101–102, 106
modality
- see mode of communication
- see multimodality
mode of communication 5–6, 270, 275, 281–289, 294–298, 303, 307–308, 311–315, 323, 332–337, 351, 353, 358–359, 366
morphology 50, 73, 124, 129–144, 202, 302, 316
multidimensional analysis 243, 225–232, 250
multilingualism 3, 7, 18–20, 27, 34–39, 102–105, 184, 220
multimodality 8, 153, 173, 214, 354–355, 368
multiple correspondence analysis 250–253
multivariate analysis 225, 320

nationality 26, 117, 184–185, 252, 329–330, 346, 351
neologism 123–124, 126–132, 139–143, 149
Nigerian Pidgin 6, 101–121
nonnative English 173, 201, 331, 336, 353, 359, 361–364, 369–372

nonstandard
– language 6, 43, 102–104, 107–111, 119–120, 221, 233, 236–237, 244, 327–330, 340, 343–347, 354
– orthography 43–44, 47–49, 65–83, 88, 92, 112–116, 158, 180, 182–184, 199, 202, 204–205, 221–222, 246, 268, 272, 333–336

orthography
– see nonstandard, orthography
– see variation, orthographic
– see spelling

performance 35–37, 104, 117, 213, 220–221, 223, 236, 242–244, 273, 358
– dialect 69–70, 79–85, 91–92
phonology 7, 43, 47–63, 72, 116, 202, 244, 247–252, 255, 268–271, 305, 312
play
– language 32, 34–35, 38, 91–92, 245, 323
– speech 75, 85
principal components analysis 225–232, 250

reduction
– syntactic 286–287, 290–292, 294–295, 297
register 9, 154, 180, 225, 241–245, 248, 282
regression
– linear 333, 343
– logistic 166–167, 309, 314, 320, 323
repertoire 17–39, 103–108, 120, 225, 237, 241–242, 252, 261
r-lessness 7, 54, 220, 245, 248–250, 254–255, 269–271, 274

Scottish 63, 69–92, 353–354, 369
semantics 131, 132, 161, 246, 253, 255, 323
– see variation, semantic
shortening
– lexical 53, 112, 125, 287, 290, 292, 295–297
situational factor 180, 261–262, 283, 285–286, 289–291, 294–295, 298

SMS
– see text messaging
social meaning 6, 8–10, 56, 70–72, 74–76, 79, 85, 90–92, 102–103, 106–108, 116–119, 157, 214, 237, 241–242, 245, 247, 254–256, 263, 327–239
social media 22, 39, 43–45, 48–49, 179–180, 183, 214, 220, 225, 236, 254
social network 17, 21–22, 36, 143, 222, 267, 308, 333, 339–341, 344–347, 360
sociolinguistics 4, 5, 9, 18–20, 22, 34, 62–63, 92, 103, 106, 116, 126, 150–151, 225, 235, 262–264, 275
speech style 263, 309
spelling 43–63, 80, 82–84, 91, 109–121, 124, 129–132, 134–136, 142, 159–160, 163–164, 168–169, 246, 249, 255, 272, 333–336, 338, 340, 344–346
– see nonstandard, orthography
stance 31, 74, 80, 81, 83–85, 88, 90–92, 117–119, 190–191, 204–205, 237, 245, 345
style 2–4, 22, 38, 74, 91, 156, 158, 162, 164, 171, 183, 213–214, 221, 224–237, 241–243, 256, 261–263, 273–274, 335–337, 344–345, 367
– see speech style
stylization 56, 61, 70, 106, 134, 171, 244–245, 256
subculture 75, 123–129, 132–144
substitution 222, 224, 226, 254, 345
synchronicity 10, 261, 281–298
– of use 281, 284, 288, 294, 296–298
syntax 5, 73, 109, 115, 149–174, 286–287, 307, 321

text messaging 45, 53, 170, 200, 245, 248, 264, 287, 344
Twitter 43–49, 52–58, 61–63, 149–174, 179–205, 220–225, 236–237, 241–256

variation
– accent 86
– co-variation 241–256
– language 5–6, 49, 72, 90, 101, 116, 151, 155, 173, 213–214, 222, 225, 241, 261–263, 183, 302

– orthographic 104–113, 116–120, 183, 163–164, 268
  – *see* nonstandard, orthography
  – *see* spelling
– semantic 104–111, 113–120
varieties of English 4, 6–8, 17–18, 71, 116, 73, 102, 108, 156–157, 173, 184, 244–247, 327, 353, 364
voice 23, 29, 38, 88, 331–346, 351–373
– *see* chat, voice
– *see* mode of communication

word formation
– *see* lexical innovation
– *see* neologism

workplace
– virtual 327–347
World Englishes 17, 150, 151
– *see* Global Englishes
writing 17, 27, 37, 52, 80, 115–116, 156, 264, 284, 286–287, 295, 297, 301–330, 333–347
– *see* mode of communication

YouTube 8, 46, 56, 57, 69–92

www.ingramcontent.com/pod-product-compliance
Lightning Source LLC
Chambersburg PA
CBHW030431300426
44112CB00009B/943